Portfolio Risk Analysis

Portfolio Risk Analysis

Gregory Connor

Lisa R. Goldberg

Robert A. Korajczyk

Princeton University Press
Princeton and Oxford

Published by Princeton University Press,
41 William Street, Princeton, New Jersey 08540

In the United Kingdom: Princeton University Press,
6 Oxford Street, Woodstock, Oxfordshire OX20 1TW

Library of Congress Cataloging-in-Publication Data

Connor, Gregory.
Portfolio risk analysis / Gregory Connor, Lisa R. Goldberg, Robert A. Korajczyk.
p. cm.
Includes bibliographical references and index.
ISBN 978-0-691-12828-3 (alk. paper)
1. Portfolio management. 2. Risk management. I. Goldberg, Lisa R. II. Korajczyk, Robert A., 1954– III. Title.

HG4529.5.C657 2010
332.6–dc22 2009050913

British Library Cataloging-in-Publication Data is available

This book has been composed in LucidaBright using TEX
Typeset and copyedited by T&T Productions Ltd, London

Printed on acid-free paper. ∞

press.princeton.edu

Printed in the United States of America

10 9 8 7 6 5 4 3 2

To our families

Contents

Acknowledgments

Our thanks to Patrick Braun, Aaron Brown, David Buckle, Scott Cogswell, Christopher Culp, Dan Dibartolomeow, Stuart Doole, Janice Eberly, Ed Fishwick, Kay Giesecke, Rupert Goodwin, Michael Hayes, Ely Klepfish, Jason MacQueen, Charles Cederfeldt-Malinas, David Miles, Guy Miller, Brian O'Kelly, Andrew Patton, Riccardo Rebonato, Ronnie Sadka, Bernd Scherer, Alan Scowcroft, James Sefton, Peter Shepard, David Tang, Michela Verardo, and Tim Wilding for helpful comments on the manuscript, and to Jonathan Brogaard, Pooja Kesavan, Anu Kulkarni, Sharad Prakash, Zhigang Qiu, Terence Teo, Yi Yu, and Alminas Zaldokas for excellent research assistance and for their infectious enthusiasm for financial research. Lisa Goldberg is grateful to her colleagues at MSCI Barra for their insights and invaluable contributions to this book.

We thank Richard Baggaley of Princeton University Press, our editor, for constant support and feedback on this project. We also thank Sam Clark, at T&T Productions Ltd, for converting our disparate TEX code into a finished product. We also thank Laden Gehring and Stephanie Winters, of MSCI Barra, for assistance with graphics.

We would like to thank MSCI Barra for its generous support of this project through a donation to the Financial Markets Group at London School of Economics. We also thank Northfield Information Services and UBS Inc., who sponsored and helped organize a Portfolio Risk Forecasting Workshop at the Financial Markets Group (in spring 2006) on the topic of this book. Gregory Connor wishes to acknowledge support from the Science Foundation of Ireland under grant 08/SRC/FM1389. Robert Korajczyk wishes to acknowledge the research support of the Zell Center for Risk Research and the Jerome Kenney Fund.

Introduction

This book provides a quantitative, technical treatment of portfolio risk analysis with a focus on real-world applications. It is intended for both academic and practitioner audiences, and it draws its inspiration and ideas from both the academic and practitioner research literature. Quantitative modeling for portfolio risk management is an active research field. Virtually all institutional investment management firms use quantitative models as an integral part of their portfolio risk-management procedures. Research and development on these models takes place at investment management firms, brokerage houses, investment consultants, and risk-management software providers. Academic researchers have explored the econometric foundations of portfolio risk analysis models, the relative performance of the various types of models, the implications of the various models for the understanding of capital market behavior, and the models' implications for asset pricing equilibrium. This book attempts to synthesize the academic and practitioner research in this field. We argue that portfolio risk analysis requires a balanced, multidisciplinary perspective combining statistical modeling, finance theory, microeconomics, macroeconomics, and a behavioral–institutional understanding of modern capital markets.

Who Should Read This Book?

Among practitioners, an ideal reader of this book would be someone with a good background in finance and statistics working in the risk-management office of an institutional fund manager. He or she[1] may be relying entirely on vendor software for portfolio risk analysis, or entirely on routines developed in-house, or on a combination of in-house and vendor products. The book is not a how-to manual for building a portfolio risk analysis model, but it gives the reader a solid understanding about the many difficult issues and choices in model design and estimation and about current research frontiers in estimating and evaluating these models. Practitioners working in related functions, including

[1] To avoid unnecessary verbal clutter, in the remainder of the book we use the male pronoun for gender-neutral third-person singular.

portfolio managers, investment consultants, and risk analysis software providers, are also part of our target audience. As an important caveat, those working in the central risk-management offices of investment banks, with responsibility for a full range of trading desks, will find that this book is not comprehensive, since we do not cover risk analysis for financial engineering.

Among academics, an ideal reader of this book would be a graduate student or faculty member interested in portfolio-risk-related research. Many of the best new ideas in academic finance come from the interface with business practice. The book might be suitable as a main or secondary text in an advanced master's level course on portfolio management or financial risk management.

Topics Covered

In this section we discuss some broad topics that are included or excluded from the book and then briefly describe the content of each chapter.

Managerial, Accounting, and Regulatory Issues

The main objective of the modeling techniques described in this book is to provide accurate, reliable portfolio risk analysis and forecasts. Portfolio risk analysis serves as a crucial input into a range of managerial and regulatory decisions, but we do not address, except peripherally, the broader policy problems of financial risk management and regulation. We also do not address accounting and disclosure issues.

Portfolio Risk Analysis versus Portfolio Management

The book is addressed to the problems of portfolio risk analysis rather than the broader problems of portfolio management. There are two main reasons for this. First, the methods and techniques for portfolio risk analysis are distinct from those for portfolio management. Second, almost all institutional managers separate the portfolio management function from the risk analysis function; there are very strong business and regulatory reasons for this separation. Many of the worst scandals in the investment management industry occurred when this functional separation was breached or inadequately monitored. We touch upon portfolio management issues outside the risk analysis domain, such as asset valuation, security selection, and trading strategies, whenever it is illuminating for our main focus.

Portfolio versus Asset Risk Analysis

Consider a set of n asset returns $\boldsymbol{r}$ and a set of portfolio weights $\boldsymbol{w}$. Let r_w denote the portfolio return associated with this particular set of portfolio weights. If we know that the portfolio weights are permanently fixed, then r_w can be treated as if it were a single asset return. We can analyze the risk of r_w without analyzing the numerous risk relationships among all the constituent asset returns. The focus of the book is on *portfolio* risk analysis, by which we mean either that we do not know the portfolio weights $\boldsymbol{w}$ when we build the risk analysis model or we are allowing $\boldsymbol{w}$ to vary. We need to create a risk analysis model for potential portfolios r_w that will be accurate across a wide range of portfolio weight vectors $\boldsymbol{w}$. This requires a risk model of all n asset returns $\boldsymbol{r}$ and their interdependencies, rather than just a model of a particular portfolio return r_w.

Financial Engineering

Financial engineering and derivatives-trading strategies pose especially difficult problems for risk analysis. Financial engineers are willing and able to trade, at an acceptable price, virtually any nonlinear function of any future asset price or price path. This transforms the risk analysis problem into a subdiscipline of financial engineering; the portfolio aspect diminishes in importance. There are many high-quality texts on risk analysis for financial engineering and derivatives trading;[2] we do not attempt to cover this material. Risk managers oriented toward derivatives will find that this book covers only one part of their problem: risk analysis for portfolios of primary assets not including any financially engineered securities.[3] This is an important component of risk analysis for financial engineering, but it is not the whole story.

Limits to Coverage of Research Literature

Although the general perspective in this book is strongly empirical, we generally do not attempt to replicate the vast array of empirical findings on portfolio risk analysis. Instead, we provide references to empirical findings in the research literature and incorporate them into our analysis without attempting to re-derive them from raw data. We provide empirical illustrations when it seems particularly illuminating to do so, to underscore major conceptual points in the analysis or to highlight counterintuitive empirical findings.

---

[2] Including, for example, Christoffersen (2003), Crouhy et al. (2001), Dowd (2005), and Jorion (2007).

[3] We allow for the simplest types of derivatives overlays such as equity index futures.

Chapter Summaries

Chapter 1 sets out basic measures of return and risk. It compares arithmetic and logarithmic returns and discusses the relative advantages of each. It introduces the key measures of portfolio risk including variance, value-at-risk, and expected shortfall. It discusses the objectives of portfolio risk management and its limitations.

Chapter 2 examines the estimation and use of unstructured return covariance matrices. It discusses the problem of estimation error in covariance matrices and the implications for their use in portfolio management. Chapter 3 examines industry–country component models. In these simple models the cross section of returns is divided into industry-related returns, country-related returns, and asset-specific (neither country- nor industry-related) returns. This simple decomposition is surprisingly powerful in explaining the common components in the cross section of equity returns, and also has growing relevance for corporate bond markets as they broaden and deepen internationally.

Factor models of security returns are typically categorized as statistical, economic, or characteristic-based. Chapter 4 describes factor models of security returns and discusses statistical factor analysis. Chapter 5 deals with macroeconomic factor models in which the pervasive factors in returns are observable economic time series, such as output, inflation, and interest rate changes. Chapter 6 treats characteristic-based factor models, in which the factor sensitivities of assets are tied to the corporate characteristics and/or cash flow characteristics of assets. Not all factor models fit neatly into one of these three categories. We also discuss "hybrid" factor models, which have features from more than one of these pure types. Chapter 7 analyzes foreign exchange risk.

An important design choice in risk model construction is the approach to integration of risk analysis across asset classes and across national borders. This problem of risk model integration is considered in chapter 8. This chapter also surveys research on the level and trend of cross-border capital market integration, which has obvious relevance for the choice of integrated versus segregated risk modeling.

Due to its analytical convenience, the first eight chapters of the book have an emphasis on unconditional portfolio return variance as a risk measure. Chapters 9–14 broaden the perspective, using many other risk metrics besides variance, and explicitly account for risk dynamics. Chapter 9 explores models of dynamic volatility and dynamic correlations, and the choice of forecast horizon. Chapter 10 considers density estimation and the related problem of tail estimation and value-at-risk measures. Chapter 11 discusses credit risk, and chapter 12 liquidity risk.

Chapter 13 looks at risk analysis for alternative asset classes such as hedge funds, venture capital, and commodities. Chapter 14 deals with the performance evaluation of portfolio risk–return realizations and also the performance evaluation of portfolio risk-forecasting models. Chapter 15 provides a brief conclusion.

Useful Background

Understanding the material in the book requires at least an intermediate-level background in statistics, linear algebra, and finance theory. Some sections require more advanced knowledge in statistics or finance theory. For those who wish to refresh their knowledge or study these topics independently, we suggest some appropriate finance and statistics texts.

Greene (2008) provides a solid foundation in statistics and econometrics appropriate for understanding the material covered in this book. Readers wanting a finance-focused treatment at a more advanced level may benefit from reading Campbell et al. (1997). For general finance background, Bodie et al. (2009) and Elton et al. (2010) are two possible references.

Approximations Used in the Book

Statistical approximations are very important in portfolio risk analysis. Diversification is a key principle of portfolio management, and by its nature it relies on statistical approximations. There are also useful approximations as the chosen return interval becomes short or as the sample used for risk model estimation becomes large.

We use a simple common notation for the different types of approximations used in the book. Most of the approximations rely on one of three limiting variables: either the number of assets n, the number of time periods T, or the return measurement interval Δ (monthly, weekly, daily, hourly, etc.). We take the limiting approximation for large n, or large T, or for small Δ, holding all other variables constant. Which of these three limiting variables is being used in the approximation is indicated by a superscript on the approximately equals symbol:

$$\overset{n}{\approx}, \quad \overset{T}{\approx}, \quad \overset{\Delta}{\approx}.$$

If f and g go to zero with Δ, but the difference goes to zero more quickly, in the sense that

$$\frac{f-g}{\Delta} \overset{\Delta}{\approx} 0,$$

we write

$$f \overset{o(\Delta)}{\approx} g,$$

meaning that $f - g$ goes to zero relative to the magnitude, or "order," of Δ. This is useful if we are looking at two returns over a short time interval and want to say that the returns are approximately the same, even though both are approximately zero. The symbol "$\approx$" has the standard definition from introductory calculus; those who received at least a "B" in their introductory calculus course do not need to read this long footnote, while those who received a "C" or worse will not want to, but we include it anyway for completeness.[4]

We also rely on the two basic statistical approximations: limit in probability and limit in distribution. We add the superscript "pr" for limit in probability and "di" for limit in distribution. So, for example, let $\hat{m}$ denote the sample mean from T independent observations of a random variable with a true mean of zero, a variance of one, and finite higher moments. Then

$$\hat{m} \overset{\mathrm{pr},T}{\approx} 0$$

is our notation for the law of large numbers (the sample mean approaches zero in probability) and

$$(T^{1/2})\hat{m} \overset{\mathrm{di},T}{\approx} N(0,1)$$

is our notation for the central limit theorem (the sample mean scaled by the square root of the number of observations is approximately normal in its distribution). Readers not familiar with these standard statistical approximations are referred to Greene (2008, appendix D) or any standard statistics textbook. In a few isolated places we use approximations that do not fit neatly into these simple categories; we use the notation $\overset{*}{\approx}$ in these cases, and give references outside the text.

---

[4] Recall from introductory calculus that

$$f \overset{T}{\approx} a$$

means that for any $\epsilon > 0$ there exists a T^* such that $|f(T) - a| < \epsilon$ for all $T > T^*$;

$$f \overset{n}{\approx} a$$

has the analogous definition with n replacing T as the limiting variable. Approximations based on the return interval differ in that the limiting approximation relies on a suitably small (rather than suitably large) value of the limiting variable:

$$f \overset{\Delta}{\approx} a$$

means that for any $\epsilon > 0$ there exists a δ such that $|f(\Delta) - a| < \epsilon$ for all $\Delta < \delta$.

Key Notation

This section gives some of the key notation that we use throughout the text. It is not a comprehensive list; it covers only the most commonly used symbols in the book. We use bold font for vectors and matrices and regular font for real values; so for example r is an individual asset or portfolio return and $\boldsymbol{r}$ is a vector of asset returns.

$\mathbf{0}^{n\times k}$	an $n \times k$ matrix of zeros
$\mathbf{1}^{n}$	an n-vector of ones
arg max	in an optimization problem this denotes the value of the choice variable that gives a maximum of the objective function
$\boldsymbol{B}$	the $n \times k$ matrix of the assets' exposures to the factors
$\boldsymbol{C}$	the $n \times n$ matrix of return covariances
$\boldsymbol{C}_f$	the $k \times k$ matrix of factor return covariances
$\boldsymbol{C}_\varepsilon$	the $n \times n$ matrix of asset-specific return covariances
$\mathrm{cum}(\cdot)$	the cumulative distribution function of an asset or portfolio return; hence $\mathrm{cum}(a) = \Pr(r \leqslant a)$
$\mathrm{cum}_{\mathrm{loss}}(\cdot)$	the cumulative distribution function of an asset or portfolio loss; $\mathrm{cum}_{\mathrm{loss}}(a) = \Pr(-r \leqslant a)$
$\mathrm{den}(\cdot)$	the density function of an asset or portfolio return
$\mathrm{Diag}[a_1, \dots, a_n]$	an $n \times n$ diagonal matrix with elements $a_1, \dots, a_n$ along the diagonal
$E[\cdot]$	the expectation operator for a random variable
$E^*[\cdot]$	the expectation operator for a random variable under the risk-neutral probability measure (see chapter 1 for a discussion)
$\mathrm{ES}(1-\alpha)$	the expected shortfall of an asset or portfolio, with confidence level $1-\alpha$ (see chapter 1 for a description)

$\boldsymbol{f}$	the k vector of factor returns
loss	minus the return on an asset or portfolio
$L(\cdot)$	the likelihood function of a sample of data for a set of estimated parameters (see chapter 1 for details)
n	the number of assets in the investment universe
p_i	the price of asset i
$\Pr(\cdot)$	the probability function of a set of events; so for example $\Pr(r_i > r_0)$ is the probability that the return to asset i, r_i, is larger than the riskless return, r_0
$Q(\alpha)$	the αth quantile of the cumulative probability distribution of a random return
r	the return on an individual asset or portfolio
$\boldsymbol{r}$	the n-vector of asset returns
$\boldsymbol{R}$	the $n \times T$ matrix of returns on n assets for a sample period of T periods
r_0	the riskless return
r_l	the logarithmic return on an asset or portfolio
r_w	the return on a portfolio $\boldsymbol{w}$
t	any particular time period
T	the total number of time periods; also the last time period, as in $t = 1, T$, or in continuous time $t \in [0, T]$
$\mathrm{VaR}(1-\alpha)$	the value-at-risk of an asset or portfolio with confidence level $1-\alpha$ (see chapter 1 for a detailed description)
$\boldsymbol{w}$	the n-vector of portfolio weights
x	the excess return on an individual asset or portfolio (return minus the riskless return)
$\boldsymbol{x}$	the n-vector of asset excess returns
$\boldsymbol{X}$	the $n \times T$ matrix of excess returns on n assets for a sample period of T periods
Δ	a small discrete unit of time

$\boldsymbol{\varepsilon}$	the n-vector of asset-specific or nonmarket returns
$\boldsymbol{\mu}$	the n-vector of expected returns
σ^2	the variance of a random variable; correspondingly σ is the standard deviation of a random variable
$\overset{n}{\approx}$	approximately equal for large n (see the introduction for a discussion)
$\overset{T}{\approx}$	approximately equal for large T (see the introduction for a discussion)
$\overset{\mathrm{pr},n}{\approx}$	the probability limit for large n (see the introduction for a discussion)
$\overset{\mathrm{pr},T}{\approx}$	the probability limit for large T (see the introduction for a discussion)
$\overset{\mathrm{di},n}{\approx}$	the distribution limit for large n (see the introduction for a discussion)
$\overset{\mathrm{di},T}{\approx}$	the distribution limit for large T (see the introduction for a discussion)
$\overset{o(\Delta)}{\approx}$	of smaller order, so that $a \overset{o(\Delta)}{\approx} b$ means that $a - b$ goes to zero relative to the magnitude of Δ for small Δ (see the introduction for a discussion)
$\overset{*}{\approx}$	approximately equal using some approximation measure other than the five shown above (see the introduction for a discussion)
$\sim N(\mu, \sigma^2)$	denotes that a random variable is normally distributed with mean μ and variance σ^2
$'$	the transpose of a vector or matrix; so for example if $\boldsymbol{a}$ and $\boldsymbol{b}$ are n-vectors, then $\boldsymbol{a}'\boldsymbol{b}$ is the inner product of the vectors

Portfolio Risk Analysis

1

Measures of Risk and Return

Section 1.1 gives definitions of portfolio return. Section 1.2 introduces some key portfolio risk measures used throughout the book. Section 1.3 discusses risk–return preferences and portfolio optimization. Section 1.4 discusses the capital asset pricing model (CAPM). In that section we relate the CAPM to the more general state-space pricing model, and critically assess its applications to portfolio risk management. Section 1.5 takes a broader perspective, discussing the institutional environment and overall objectives of portfolio risk management, and its fundamental limitations.

1.1 Measuring Return

Except where noted, throughout the book we work in terms of a unit investment, that is, an investment with an initial value of \$1. The analysis can be scaled up to cover an investment of any size.

1.1.1 Arithmetic and Logarithmic Return

We define the investment universe as the set of assets that are current or potential holdings in the portfolio. In many applications, the investment universe is very large since it includes individual stocks, bonds, commodities, and other assets from around the world. We use n to denote the number of assets in the investment universe.

We usually measure the random per-period payoff on an asset in terms of its *arithmetic return*, denoted by r. This is defined as the end-of-period price plus any end-of-period cash flow, divided by the beginning-of-period price, minus one. Intermediate cash flows can be artificially shifted to the end of the period using an appropriate reinvestment rate. The arithmetic return on a portfolio is defined analogously as the end-of-period value plus cash flow divided by the beginning-of-period value, minus one. Note that *return* is a random variable; its expected value is called the *expected return*.

The arithmetic portfolio return equals the weighted sum of constituent asset returns. We use $\boldsymbol{r}$ to denote the n-vector of asset returns on all the assets in the investment universe, and $\boldsymbol{w}$ the n-vector of portfolio weights. These weights give the proportion invested in each asset, and therefore sum to one. (In a typical application, the vast majority of portfolio weights are zero, since the number of assets in the investment universe tends to be much larger than the number held in nonzero amounts in the portfolio.) The portfolio return can be expressed as

$$r_w = \boldsymbol{w}'\boldsymbol{r}. \tag{1.1}$$

Arithmetic return supports subportfolio analysis: the arithmetic return on the portfolio equals the value-weighted sum of the returns on any complete collection of nonoverlapping subportfolios. We can apply (1.1) to nested subsets, first using it to find the returns to subportfolios, where $\boldsymbol{w}$ is the vector of asset weights within a subportfolio and $\boldsymbol{r}$ is the vector of assets in the subportfolio, and then to the aggregate portfolio, where $\boldsymbol{w}$ is the vector of weights in the subportfolios and $\boldsymbol{r}$ is the vector of subportfolio returns. At each step, the investment universe is defined appropriately. So, for example, consider a large diverse portfolio of common stocks, government bonds, corporate bonds, and real estate. Defining the investment universe as the collection of all individual assets in all the categories, the total portfolio return is the weighted sum of all the individual returns. Alternatively, if desired, we can first calculate the return on the common stock portfolio using the universe of common stocks as the set of assets and the total amount invested in common stocks as total value. From this we get a common stock portfolio return. Repeating this procedure for government bonds, then corporate bonds, and then real estate gives analogously a government bond portfolio return, a corporate bond portfolio return, and a real estate portfolio return. Now we redefine the investment universe as consisting of these four "assets" (our computed subportfolio returns) so that in the second step $n = 4$, and we can compute the total portfolio return as the weighted sum of these four asset returns.

Return is typically measured at daily, weekly, monthly, quarterly, and annual frequencies. However, the T single-period arithmetic returns do not add up to the arithmetic return over T periods. Instead, the T-period arithmetic return on an asset or portfolio is the compound product of the constituent one-period returns:

$$r_{0,T} = (1 + r_{0,1})(1 + r_{1,2}) \cdots (1 + r_{T-1,T}) - 1. \tag{1.2}$$

When written in this form, the T-period return is called the *compound return* to highlight the fact that it is a product of returns at higher frequency. If the intervening single-period returns are uncorrelated, then the expected compound return equals the product of the returns (each augmented by one) and then minus one:

$$E[r_{0,T}] = (1 + E[r_{0,1}])(1 + E[r_{1,2}]) \cdots (1 + E[r_{T-1,T}]) - 1.$$

If, in addition, the single-period returns are independent through time with constant mean and variance, then the variance of the compound return can be expressed in terms of the single-period mean and variance:

$$\operatorname{var}[r_{0,T}] = (1 + \operatorname{var}[r] + 2E[r] + E[r]^2)^T - (1 + E[r])^{2T}. \tag{1.3}$$

However, this relatively simple formula for variance (1.3) does not apply if the single-period mean or variance is time dependent.

Temporal analysis of return is simpler in the continuously compounded or logarithmic framework. The *log return* of an asset or portfolio is defined as the log of the end-of-period value plus cash flow minus the log of the beginning-of-period value. Mathematically, this is written

$$r_l = \log(1 + r).$$

Log returns add up over time. Letting $r_{l0,T}$ denote the log return over T periods,

$$r_{l0,T} = r_{l0,1} + r_{l1,2} + \cdots + r_{lT-1,T}. \tag{1.4}$$

Formula (1.4) facilitates temporal aggregation of risk. For example, if returns are uncorrelated, then the variance of the T-period log return is the sum of the variances of the one-period returns. Consequently, log returns often provide a better foundation for multiperiod and long-horizon risk–return analysis than arithmetic returns since the additive formula (1.4) is much more tractable than the multiplicative formula (1.2).

A significant drawback to log returns is that they do not satisfy the portfolio linearity property (1.1). In other words, the log return of a portfolio is not the value-weighted sum of the log returns of the constituent assets. Another drawback is that investment objectives are less naturally stated in terms of log return than arithmetic return. Thus, log and arithmetic returns have complementary strengths and weaknesses. In this book we will use both definitions; the term return without modifier will refer to arithmetic return.

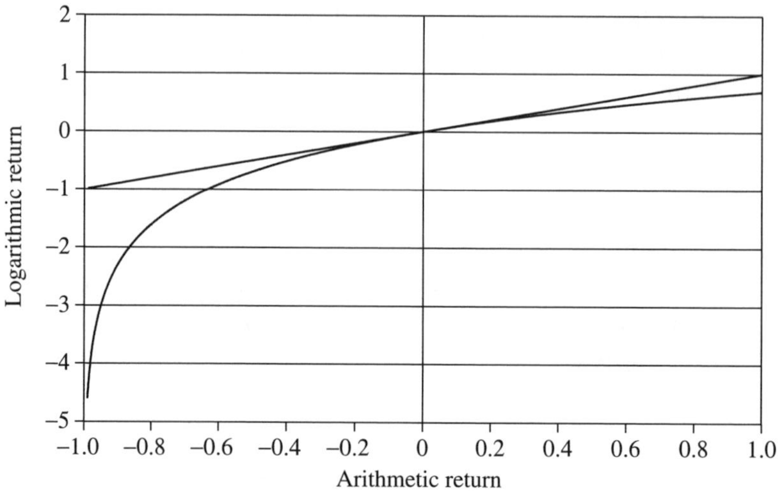

Figure 1.1. Comparison of logarithmic and arithmetic returns.

1.1.2 Approximate Relationships between Arithmetic and Log Returns

A second-order Taylor expansion[1] of $\log(1+r)$ evaluated at $r = 0$ gives a useful relationship between arithmetic and log returns:

$$r_l = \log(1+r) = r - \frac{r^2}{2(1+z)^2}, \quad z \in (0, r). \tag{1.5}$$

If r is small enough for $r^2/2(1+z)^2$ to be small relative to r, then the log and arithmetic returns are approximately equal. For high-frequency returns, this condition is often satisfied so there is little difference between the values of the two types of returns, relative to their size. Figure 1.1 compares log and arithmetic returns over the interval $r = (-0.99, 1.0)$; figure 1.2 shows the difference between them as a proportion of arithmetic return.

If the log return of a particular asset or portfolio has a normal distribution, then the moments of the arithmetic and log returns have exact analytical relationships. For the mean and variance,

$$E[r] = \exp(E[r_l] + \tfrac{1}{2}\operatorname{var}[r_l]) - 1,$$
$$\operatorname{var}[r] = (\exp(\operatorname{var}[r_l]) - 1)(\exp(2E[r_l] + \operatorname{var}[r_l])).$$

However, the assumption of normality for log asset returns implies that the log portfolio return is nonnormal. Formally, this limits the applicability of normal log returns in portfolio analysis. Campbell and Viceira

[1] A smooth function f evaluated at x can be expressed as $f(x) = f(0) + xf'(0) + \frac{1}{2}x^2 f''(z)$, where z is some point between 0 and x.

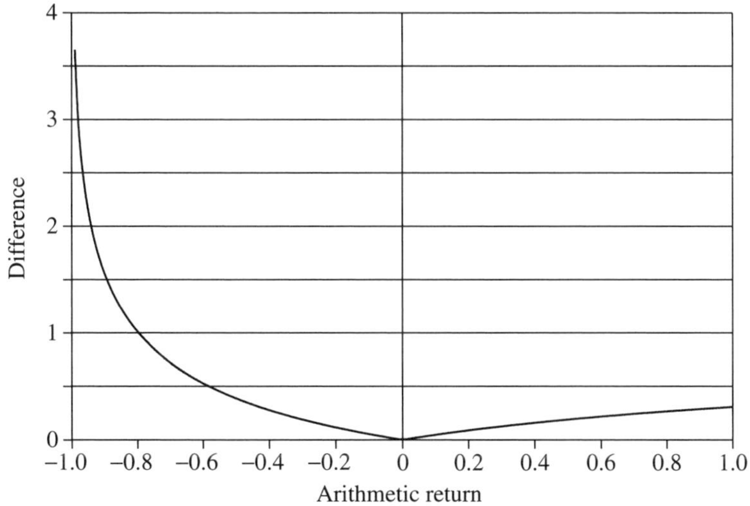

Figure 1.2. Difference between logarithmic and arithmetic returns as a proportion of the arithmetic return.

(1999, 2001) argue that the log return of a portfolio can be treated as approximately normal, based on the multivariate normality of the log returns of the constituent assets.

1.1.3 Excess Return, Active Return, and Long–Short Return

The *excess return* of an asset or portfolio is defined as the arithmetic return minus the riskless return. It is typically preferable in risk analysis to use excess return rather than total return since it removes the riskless component of the return.[2] Let $\boldsymbol{x} = \boldsymbol{r} - \mathbf{1}^n r_0$ denote the vector of asset excess returns, where $\mathbf{1}^n$ is an n-vector of ones and r_0 is the riskless return. There are several equivalent ways to express the excess return of a portfolio $\boldsymbol{w}$ in terms of its components:

$$x_w = \boldsymbol{w}'\boldsymbol{r} - r_0 = \boldsymbol{w}'\boldsymbol{x} = \begin{bmatrix} \boldsymbol{w} \\ -1 \end{bmatrix}' \begin{bmatrix} \boldsymbol{r} \\ r_0 \end{bmatrix}. \tag{1.6}$$

Note that in the final expression in (1.6) the $n + 1$ vector of portfolio weights (including the -1 weight in the riskless return) sums to zero rather than one. Excess log return is usually defined as $r_l - r_{l0}$, which is equal to $\log((1 + r)/(1 + r_0))$.

Large institutional investors typically allocate funds to more than one asset class and there may be a different manager for every class. Each

[2] Campbell and Viceira (2004) show that using excess return is not appropriate for very-long-horizon investors, due to reinvestment risk. We will discuss this in detail in chapter 9.

manager is typically benchmarked to an index portfolio appropriate to his asset class, and for that manager risk and return are measured relative to the assigned benchmark. The difference between the return to the manager's portfolio and the benchmark return is called the *active return.*

Letting $\boldsymbol{w}_{\mathrm{B}}$ denote the benchmark portfolio weights, we define the *active portfolio weights* by

$$\boldsymbol{w}_{\mathrm{A}} = \boldsymbol{w} - \boldsymbol{w}_{\mathrm{B}}. \tag{1.7}$$

In the active framework, a zero-cost constraint $\boldsymbol{w}_{\mathrm{A}}'\mathbf{1}^n = 0$ replaces the unit-cost constraint $\boldsymbol{w}'\mathbf{1}^n = 1$. Despite the fact that an active portfolio has zero cost, its return is well-defined due to formula (1.7), which implies that active return can be expressed as the difference between the return on two unit-cost portfolios.

The *long–short return* is a variation on active return. Many hedge fund investment portfolios consist of a collection of long positions and short positions split equally, supported by a cash account earning a riskless return (not included in the portfolio weights). Assume that the long and short positions have equal total value and scale the portfolio weights so that the sum of the long positions equals one and the sum of the short positions equals one. The difference between these long and short portfolio returns is called the long–short return.

Note that the total value of a long–short portfolio equals zero by construction. Typically, the cash position of the hedge fund will be significantly smaller than the total position, giving rise to a leverage effect. The *leverage ratio* (the ratio of the fund's position size to its cash value) has a big effect on the riskiness of the fund.

An increasingly popular product design in institutional portfolio management is "relaxed constraint" funds, sometimes called "130/30" funds. For this type of fund, the manager invests the value of the fund in securities and then short-sells securities with a total value equal to 30% of the fund value and invests the short-sale receipts in more security purchases. The return to the fund is measured as a proportion of the initial fund value. See Jacobs and Levy (2007) for a detailed overview of relaxed constraint funds.

1.2 The Key Portfolio Risk Measures

In this section we introduce some key risk measures used throughout the book.

1.2.1 Portfolio Risk Components

Jorion (2007) decomposes portfolio risk into market risk, liquidity risk, credit risk, operational risk, and legal risk. This book will cover the first three of these but not operational risks, which Jorion defines as "inadequate systems, management failure, faulty controls, fraud, or human error." In practical applications, systems for the measurement and control of operational risk are extremely important. However, they lie outside the scope of this book. We will only consider legal risks to the extent that they are related to the structure and maintenance of quantitative risk models. We also consider *model risk*, which we define as risk due to misspecification or estimation error in the risk analysis model.

In this first chapter we focus on *market risk*, which is risk stemming from the variation in the market prices of the assets in the portfolio.

1.2.2 Return Distribution and Moments

The most general notion of quantitative portfolio risk is the *return distribution* of r, which gives the cumulative probability $\mathrm{cum}(x)$ that an asset or portfolio return r is no larger than x for every fixed value of x:

$$\mathrm{cum}(x) = \Pr(r \leqslant x),$$

where $\Pr(\cdot)$ denotes the probability of a given set of events. A related concept is the *portfolio return density* $\mathrm{den}(\omega)$, which satisfies

$$\mathrm{cum}(x) = \int_{-\infty}^{x} \mathrm{den}(\omega)\,\mathrm{d}\omega \quad \text{for all } x.$$

In principle, all risk measures can be derived from the return distribution. However, as is often the case, generality comes at a cost. Without additional assumptions, the return distribution is difficult to estimate.

An alternative characterization of the return distribution $\mathrm{cum}(\cdot)$ is given by the moments of the distribution function. The first moment of a distribution is the mean. We denote mean return by μ and *demeaned return* by $\tilde{r} = r - \mu$. The kth central moment of the return distribution is the expected value of demeaned return raised to the power k. One widely used risk measure is *variance*, which is the second central moment:

$$\sigma^2 = E[\tilde{r}^2].$$

It is often convenient to take the square root of variance, which we will call *volatility*, denoting it by $\sigma = (E[\tilde{r}^2])^{1/2}$.

To separate out the effect of variance on the distribution, it is standard practice to scale demeaned return by volatility in the definition of moments for k greater than two. This scaled version of return, $\tilde{r}/\sigma$, is

Table 1.1. The first four moments of the four portfolios.

Period	Volatility	Skewness	Excess kurtosis
Stock market index			
1-day	1.04×10^{-4}	−1.2104	28.03
5-day	5.72×10^{-4}	−0.9837	14.13
20-day	2.02×10^{-3}	−0.6447	7.18
Bond market index			
1-day	2.83×10^{-3}	0.0108	4.82
5-day	3.98×10^{-5}	−0.0806	1.27
20-day	1.87×10^{-4}	−0.0214	1.37
Sterling–dollar foreign exchange return			
1-day	0	−0.1113	4.44
5-day	1.95×10^{-4}	−0.0900	3.19
20-day	8.71×10^{-4}	0.2555	1.80
Market insurance provision			
1-day	3.30×10^{-5}	−32.8600	1,994.09
5-day	1.12×10^{-4}	−14.5140	400.35
20-day	6.81×10^{-4}	−5.5170	117.35

called *standardized return*. *Skewness* is the third central moment of the standardized return,

$$E\left[\left(\frac{\tilde{r}}{\sigma}\right)^3\right],$$

and *kurtosis* is the fourth central moment of the standardized return:

$$E\left[\left(\frac{\tilde{r}}{\sigma}\right)^4\right].$$

If return is normally distributed, then return variance completely determines the distribution of demeaned return; the higher moments provide no additional information. In particular, in the case of normality all the moments equal zero for odd values of k, and the fourth moment (kurtosis) has a value of 3. Since the normal distribution serves as the benchmark case, it is useful to define *excess kurtosis* as raw kurtosis minus 3.

The plausibility of assuming that a return distribution is normal depends on the portfolio in question and the return horizon. Table 1.1 shows the variance, skewness, and excess kurtosis of four return series for three different return intervals (1-day, 5-day, and 20-day). In addition to a stock market index, a long-term bond index, and an exchange rate return, we show the return to an option-based portfolio that involves writing out-of-the-money put options on the stock market index combined with a cash account. We call this the *market insurance provision portfolio*, since the portfolio holder is essentially "selling insurance" against market declines, underwritten by his cash account. Lo (2001) uses this type of portfolio strategy to illustrate the dangers of using variance as a risk measure for derivatives-based investment strategies. Note the extreme negative skewness and positive excess kurtosis of the market insurance provision portfolio return.

Figure 1.3 shows estimated density functions for the stock, bond, and exchange rate return series using 1-day and 20-day return frequencies, along with a normal density (scaled to have the same mean and variance) for comparison. As a general rule, the use of a normal distribution for portfolio return is not reasonable for short-horizon (intradaily, daily, or weekly) return. As we will discuss in later chapters, there is conclusive evidence that returns over these short horizons have very high kurtosis relative to the normal distribution, and also, in many cases, negative skewness. Variance still has uses as a measure of return dispersion, but it is not a comprehensive measure of portfolio risk.

1.2.3 Portfolio Variance and the Asset Covariance Matrix

Now consider the case $n > 1$. Portfolio return variance is the expected value of squared demeaned portfolio return; using the additive property of portfolio weights,

$$\sigma_w^2 = E[(\boldsymbol{w}'\tilde{\boldsymbol{r}})^2] = \boldsymbol{w}'E[\tilde{\boldsymbol{r}}\tilde{\boldsymbol{r}}']\boldsymbol{w}.$$

Let $\boldsymbol{C}$ denote the $n \times n$ asset covariance matrix:

$$\boldsymbol{C} = E[\tilde{\boldsymbol{r}}\tilde{\boldsymbol{r}}'].$$

Note that portfolio variance is the quadratic product of the asset covariance matrix and the vector of portfolio weights:

$$\sigma_w^2 = \boldsymbol{w}'\boldsymbol{C}\boldsymbol{w}. \tag{1.8}$$

Thus, the problem of estimating portfolio return variance reduces to estimating the $n \times n$ asset covariance matrix $\boldsymbol{C}$. Note that (1.8) has the powerful and flexible property that once we have estimated $\boldsymbol{C}$ we can use this simple formula to analyze the variance of any portfolio $\boldsymbol{w}$.

1.2.4 Value-at-Risk and Expected Shortfall

In order to select measures that supplement variance in a meaningful way, it is important to understand how an empirical portfolio return

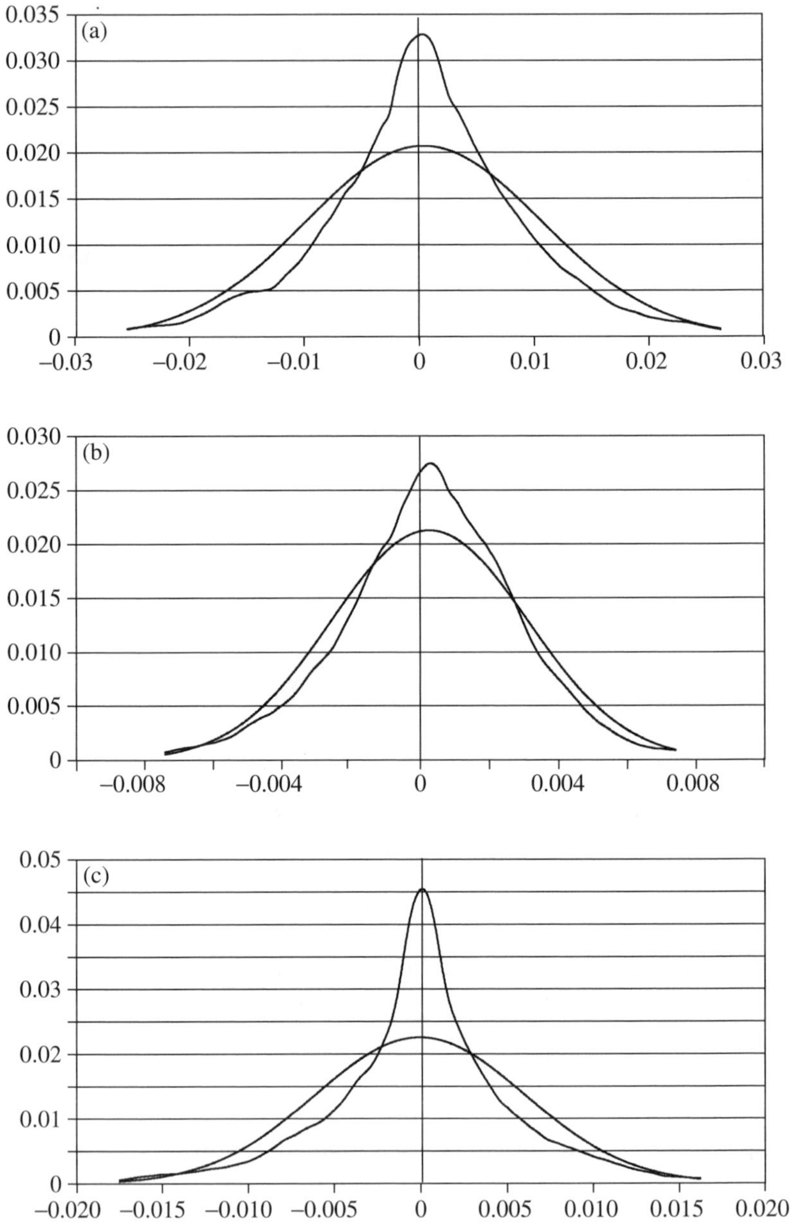

Figure 1.3. The estimated density functions for (a) the U.S. stock market index, (b) the U.S. bond market index, and (c) the sterling–dollar foreign exchange return for 1-day return frequencies, along with a normal density (scaled to have the same mean and variance) for comparison.

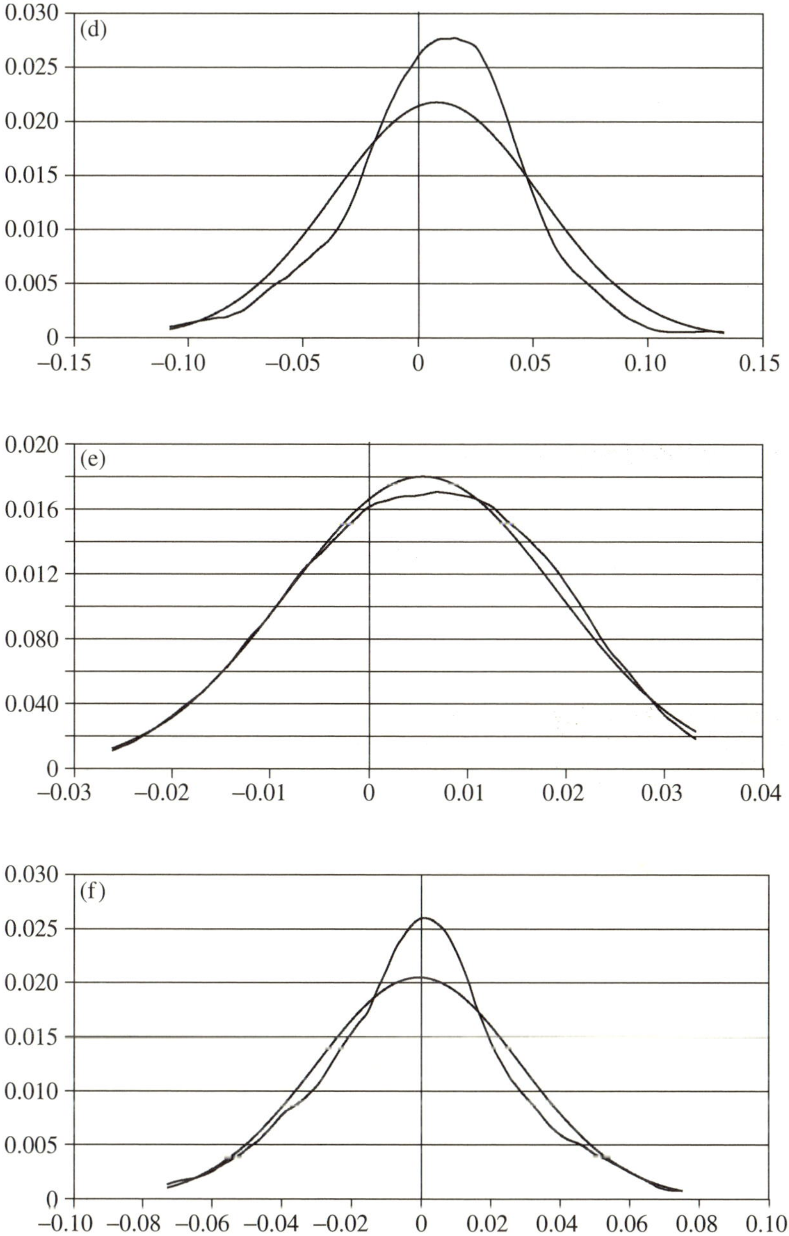

Figure 1.3. (*Cont.*) The estimated density functions for (d) the U.S. stock market index, (e) the U.S. bond market index, and (f) the sterling–dollar foreign exchange return for 20-day return frequencies, along with a normal density (scaled to have the same mean and variance) for comparison.

distribution deviates from normality. Observed portfolio returns tend to have too many inliers (demeaned returns close to zero) and outliers (extreme events) relative to a normal distribution with the same variance. Furthermore, large losses tend to outnumber large gains. These observations have led to the development of alternative risk measures including value-at-risk and expected shortfall.

Value-at-risk is parameterized by a *confidence level* usually set at either 95% or 99%. Given confidence level $1 - \alpha$ the *value-at-risk* (VaR) of a unit-cost portfolio is the level of (negative) return such that the cumulative probability of a larger-magnitude negative return equals α. Mathematically, this is written

$$\Pr(-r \geqslant \text{VaR}) = \alpha, \tag{1.9}$$

so that we have $1 - \alpha$ confidence that our loss will not exceed VaR in magnitude. Unlike volatility, value-at-risk takes account of any asymmetry between losses and gains.

Our definition of value-at-risk is based on a unit-cost investment. Often, value-at-risk is defined in units of total wealth, by taking our definition for a unit-cost portfolio (1.9) and multiplying by total initial investment. The total-wealth definition is convenient for hedge funds or other leveraged investment vehicles, since in that formulation value-at-risk depends only upon the absolute position size and not on the degree of leverage. It is trivial to switch between the two choices of scaling; the per-unit-cost scaling is more convenient for our analysis.

An important counterpart to value-at-risk is *expected shortfall* (ES), which is the expected loss given that a value-at-risk limit is breached:

$$\text{ES} = E[-r \mid -r \geqslant \text{VaR}].$$

By its definition, expected shortfall is always at least as large as value-at-risk. If the return is nonnormal, then expected shortfall can be substantially larger than value-at-risk.

Table 1.2 shows the estimated 95% and 99% confidence level value-at-risk and expected shortfall for the four return series mentioned above. The estimates in the first column are based on historical return frequencies and those in the second on a best-fit normal distribution.

1.3 Risk–Return Preferences and Portfolio Optimization

The best way to measure portfolio risk and to analyze the trade-off between risk and return depends on the investment objective. The simplest case is the static investment objective, in which the investor maximizes the one-period utility of wealth. Assume that an investor with

Table 1.2. Two estimates of 95% and 99% value-at-risk and expected shortfall for four return series.

Period	VaR^{95}	VaR^{95} normal	VaR^{99}	VaR^{99} normal	ES^{95}	ES^{95} normal	ES^{99}	ES^{99} normal
Stock market index								
1-day	0.0155	0.0164	0.0256	0.0233	0.0228	0.0207	0.0376	0.0269
5-day	0.0356	0.0373	0.0570	0.0536	0.0517	0.0473	0.0854	0.0619
20-day	0.0597	0.0658	0.1083	0.0965	0.0982	0.0846	0.1647	0.1121
Bond market index								
1-day	0.0044	0.0044	0.0074	0.0063	0.0063	0.0056	0.0095	0.0073
5-day	0.0872	0.0090	0.0152	0.0133	0.0126	0.0117	0.0179	0.0155
20-day	0.0166	0.0170	0.0261	0.0263	0.0233	0.0227	0.0356	0.0311
Sterling–dollar foreign exchange return								
1-day	0.0099	0.0100	0.0175	0.0141	0.0148	0.0125	0.0229	0.0163
5-day	0.0225	0.0232	0.0380	0.0327	0.0327	0.0290	0.0490	0.0376
20-day	0.0489	0.0493	0.0731	0.0694	0.0641	0.0616	0.0838	0.0797
Market insurance provision								
1-day	0.0028	0.0092	0.0081	0.0131	0.0083	0.0116	0.0233	0.0151
5-day	0.0055	0.0168	0.0177	0.0244	0.0187	0.0214	0.0543	0.0282
20-day	0.0004	0.0047	0.0025	0.0108	0.0030	0.0084	0.0104	0.0139

unit wealth at time zero has static, increasing, risk-averse preferences for wealth at time one. He seeks to maximize the expected utility of end-of-period wealth by selecting a unit-cost portfolio $\boldsymbol{w}$ using the n available assets, with random return vector $\boldsymbol{r}$. An algebraic statement of the static one-period maximization problem is

$$\max_{\{\boldsymbol{w} \mid \boldsymbol{w}'\mathbf{1}^n = 1\}} E[u(1 + \boldsymbol{w}'\boldsymbol{r})], \tag{1.10}$$

where $u(\cdot)$ is the investor's *utility function*. We assume that $u(\cdot)$ is increasing and concave to reflect the facts that most investors prefer more to less and are risk averse. We also assume that the utility function has a first derivative, denoted $u'(\cdot)$, and we refer to this as the *marginal utility function*.

1.3.1 Static, Dynamic, and Myopic Risk–Return Preferences

Most portfolio risk analysis systems rely at least partially on static risk measures. For example, the three risk measures described in sections 1.2.2 and 1.2.4—variance, value-at-risk, and expected shortfall—are all one-period, static measures. This despite the obvious fact that the true portfolio risk-management problem is long term and dynamic. Solving an intertemporal dynamic problem as if it were a sequence of static problems is called *myopic optimization.* Under some strict assumptions, myopic optimization can give the first-best solution. More realistically it is likely to be only a rough approximation to the true intertemporal dynamic solution.

A dynamic aspect can be added to the portfolio choice problem by allowing reinvestment over multiple periods, with preferences defined only in terms of wealth at the terminal date. An alternative dynamic formulation allows the investor to consume and save each period, and maximizes the discounted present value of expected utility over a T-period investment lifetime. In comparison with the static case (1.10) the dynamic models add an additional source of risk since the investor's realized utility depends upon the uncertain reinvestment opportunities each period. This extra source of uncertainty is called *reinvestment risk.*

Dynamic portfolio optimization problems can be restated as a series of single-period optimization problems of the form

$$\max_{\boldsymbol{w}_{t-1}} E[V_t(\boldsymbol{w}_{t-1}'\boldsymbol{r}_t, \boldsymbol{s}_t)], \tag{1.11}$$

where $V_t(\boldsymbol{w}_{t-1}'\boldsymbol{r}_t, \boldsymbol{s}_t)$ is the value function capturing the discounted expected value of all future utility from time t forward and $\boldsymbol{s}_t$ is a vector of state variables at time t capturing random changes in the risk–return opportunity set of the investor over time. This sequence of single-period representations of an intertemporal problem (1.11) differs from a true single-period problem (1.10) since the true single-period problem has no time subscript or time-varying state variables. A multiperiod investment strategy that ignores these differences is called *myopic.* In some cases, the sequence of myopic solutions is fully optimal, since the dynamic optimization problem is equivalent to a sequence of static optimization problems. Samuelson (1969) shows that if an investor has constant relative risk aversion and returns are independent and identically distributed (i.i.d.) through time, then the dynamic portfolio optimization problem has a myopic solution: it can be reduced to a series of static problems equivalent to (1.10). Merton (1971) shows that in the special case of logarithmic utility, the optimality of myopic behavior holds without the assumption that returns are i.i.d.

In his influential treatise on economic modeling, Milton Friedman (1953) argues that models are to be used, not believed. Portfolio risk analysis models often rely on myopic analysis even when it is not fully justified. While appreciating their simplicity, the analyst needs to be aware of the dangers and shortcomings of myopic risk modeling and adjust where necessary for dynamic and intertemporal effects. We will often rely on myopic risk modeling in this book, but we will be watchful for situations where this approach is not appropriate. The alert reader should do the same!

1.3.2 Static Mean–Variance Optimization

Consider the static portfolio problem (1.10). If asset returns are multivariate normal, then any portfolio return $\boldsymbol{w}'\boldsymbol{r}$ is normal and the expected utility of return can be written in the form

$$E[u(1+\boldsymbol{w}'\boldsymbol{r})] = g(\mu_w, \sigma_w^2),$$

where μ_w and σ_w^2 are the mean and variance of portfolio $\boldsymbol{w}$ and $g(\cdot,\cdot)$ is a two-variable function that is increasing in its first argument and decreasing in its second. We will assume that $g(\cdot,\cdot)$ has first derivatives in both arguments.

This portfolio optimization problem can be restated in several ways that are useful in different contexts. The most general formulation is as a mean–variance optimization problem with a nonlinear objective function:

$$\max_{\{\boldsymbol{w}|\boldsymbol{w}'\mathbf{1}^n=1\}} g(\mu_w, \sigma_w^2). \tag{1.12}$$

Formula (1.12) can be reexpressed in three ways. If the optimal variance $\bar{\sigma}^2$ is specified, then (1.12) reduces to the *constrained return-maximization problem*:

$$\max_{\{\boldsymbol{w}|\boldsymbol{w}'\mathbf{1}^n=1,\, \boldsymbol{w}'\boldsymbol{C}\boldsymbol{w}=\bar{\sigma}^2\}} \boldsymbol{w}'\boldsymbol{\mu}. \tag{1.13}$$

This formulation provides the basis for risk budgeting, discussed in section 1.3.7 below.

If the optimal expected return μ^* is specified, then the optimization (1.12) reduces to the *constrained risk-minimization problem*:

$$\min_{\{\boldsymbol{w}|\boldsymbol{w}'\mathbf{1}^n=1,\, \boldsymbol{w}'\boldsymbol{\mu}=\mu^*\}} \boldsymbol{w}'\boldsymbol{C}\boldsymbol{w}. \tag{1.14}$$

In applications, (1.14) can also be used to find the optimal portfolio when the investor cannot fully express his preference function. The analyst solves for the minimum variance via (1.14) over a grid of candidate values μ^* and then the investor selects the most appealing mean–variance pair from among these trial optima.

A third formulation of (1.12) relies on the assumption that $g(\mu_w, \sigma_w^2)$ is a smooth concave function. By simple calculus applied to the constrained maximization problem (1.12) there exists a scalar λ^* such that the solution to (1.12) equals the solution to

$$\max_{\{\boldsymbol{w}|\boldsymbol{w}'\mathbf{1}^n=1\}} \boldsymbol{w}'\boldsymbol{\mu} - \tfrac{1}{2}\lambda^* \boldsymbol{w}'\boldsymbol{C}\boldsymbol{w}, \tag{1.15}$$

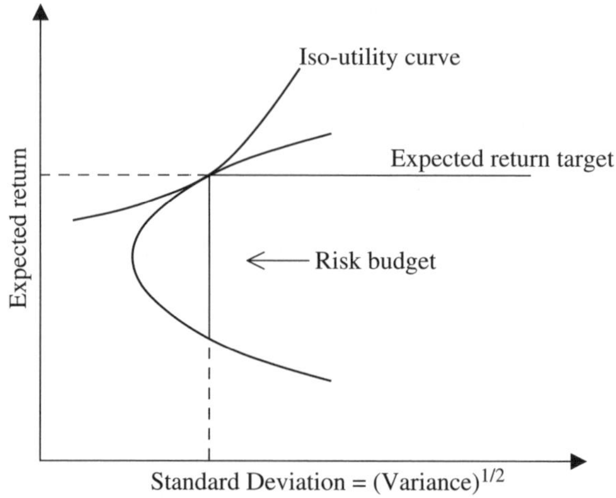

Figure 1.4. Three equivalent statements of the mean-variance optimization problem.

which is known as the *linear mean-variance optimization problem.* The value of λ^* can be found from the optimal values of μ_w, σ_w^2, in particular:

$$\lambda^* = -2\frac{\partial g(\mu_w, \sigma_w^2)}{\partial \mu_w} \bigg/ \frac{\partial g(\mu_w, \sigma_w^2)}{\partial \sigma_w^2}.$$

These three simpler formulations of the general mean-variance problem—constrained return maximization (1.13), constrained risk minimization (1.14), and linear mean-variance optimization (1.15)—have the theoretical drawback that to apply them we must first find the optimal values of μ_w, σ_w^2. However they are often useful in applications, employing external information to set the missing parameter or selecting the missing parameter by choosing the best solution from a grid of trial values. Figure 1.4 illustrates the three equivalent statements of the mean-variance optimization problem.

1.3.3 Linear Mean-Variance Preferences

The parameter λ in the optimization problem (1.15) can be interpreted as a measure of investor risk aversion. An important special case is an investor with constant absolute risk aversion (CARA). In this case, his utility function can be expressed as

$$u(x) = -\exp(-\lambda x). \tag{1.16}$$

Assuming CARA utility and return normality, the linear mean-variance optimization problem (1.15) has a very useful interpretation. Using the properties of the normal distribution gives

$$\begin{aligned} E[u(1+\boldsymbol{w}'\boldsymbol{r})] &= -\exp(-\lambda\mu_w + \tfrac{1}{2}\lambda^2\sigma_w^2) \\ &= -a\exp(\mu_w - \tfrac{1}{2}\lambda\sigma_w^2) \end{aligned}$$

for a constant $a > 0$. Applying an order-preserving transformation to the objective of the optimization problem (1.12), we find that the optimal portfolio is

$$\begin{aligned} \boldsymbol{w} &= \operatorname*{arg\,max}_{\{\boldsymbol{w}\mid\boldsymbol{w}'\mathbf{1}^n=1\}} E[u(1+\boldsymbol{w}'\boldsymbol{r})] \\ &= \operatorname*{arg\,max}_{\{\boldsymbol{w}\mid\boldsymbol{w}'\mathbf{1}^n=1\}} \mu_w - \tfrac{1}{2}\lambda\sigma_w^2 \\ &= \operatorname*{arg\,max}_{\{\boldsymbol{w}\mid\boldsymbol{w}'\mathbf{1}^n=1\}} \boldsymbol{w}'\boldsymbol{\mu} - \tfrac{1}{2}\lambda\boldsymbol{w}'\boldsymbol{C}\boldsymbol{w}. \end{aligned} \tag{1.17}$$

From (1.17) we see that in the special case of normal returns and CARA, the nonlinear optimization problem (1.12) reduces directly to the linear mean–variance optimization (1.15) with the constant λ equal to the absolute risk aversion of the investor.

The linear mean–variance setting (1.17) corresponding to the CARA-normal return model is a very useful tool for portfolio risk analysis. It is common practice to apply this simple portfolio model first and subsequently make adjustments for deviations from normality and non-CARA preferences at appropriate stages of the risk forecasting and portfolio management process. Computerized portfolio optimization routines tend to rely heavily on (1.17). Note as a caveat that this linear model is very unreliable for portfolios including options (see, for example, Lo (2001) for a discussion). It relies on the restrictive assumptions of CARA preferences and normally distributed returns.

1.3.4 Interpreting the Linear Risk–Return Preference Parameter

A closed-form solution to the linear mean–variance problem (1.15) is

$$\boldsymbol{w} = \frac{1}{\lambda}\boldsymbol{C}^{-1}(\boldsymbol{\mu} - \gamma\mathbf{1}^n), \tag{1.18}$$

where

$$\gamma = \left(\frac{\boldsymbol{\mu}'\boldsymbol{C}\mathbf{1}^n - \lambda}{\mathbf{1}^{n\prime}\boldsymbol{C}\mathbf{1}^n}\right).$$

If an investor has chosen his portfolio optimally and there are no short-sale constraints, then at the margin, any change in asset positions that preserves the budget constraint gives a zero change in expected utility. This leads to an illuminating interpretation of the parameter λ. Suppose we artificially add a position in the riskless asset into the portfolio but give it a portfolio weight $w_0 = 0$ so that the portfolio is unchanged. Changing the weight in the riskless asset away from zero must give a marginal change in expected utility of zero. The weight on the risky assets is $(1 - w_0) = \boldsymbol{w}'\boldsymbol{1}^n$, in order for the budget constraint to hold. Let r_0 denote the return to the riskless asset and let r_w, μ_w, and σ_w^2 denote the return, expected return, and variance of the optimal solution to (1.18). The marginal change in utility from adding the riskless asset must be zero so that

$$\frac{\partial}{\partial w_0}\bigg|_{w_0=0} E[u(w_0 r_0 + (1 - w_0)r_w)] = 0. \tag{1.19}$$

Combining (1.19) and (1.17) and rearranging the expression gives

$$\lambda = \frac{\mu_w - r_0}{\sigma_w^2}. \tag{1.20}$$

If we can measure the expected excess return and volatility of the investor's chosen portfolio, then (1.20) provides an observable, nonsubjective measure of the investor's risk aversion. So, for example, suppose that the investor holds a portfolio with mean excess return of 0.06 and a variance of 0.04. Then applying (1.20) it follows that the investor has $\lambda = 1.5$.

It is sometimes convenient in portfolio risk analysis to restate risk-reducing or risk-increasing changes to the portfolio in units of expected return. For example, suppose that by diversifying internationally a fund can lower its return variance from 0.09 to 0.08 per annum. If the investor has linear risk-aversion parameter $\lambda = 1.5$, then at the margin the reduced risk from this diversification is value-equivalent to an increase in portfolio expected return of $(1.5)(0.01) = 0.015$, that is, 150 basis points of equivalent mean return increase.

The simple formula (1.18) only holds when the set of assets has a nonsingular covariance matrix, which means that the set of assets does not include a riskless asset. Including a riskless asset in the set of assets (but excluding it from the covariance matrix so that the matrix in nonsingular) the optimal portfolio is the solution to

$$\max_{\boldsymbol{w}}(1 - \boldsymbol{w}'\boldsymbol{1}^n)r_0 + \boldsymbol{w}'\boldsymbol{\mu} - \tfrac{1}{2}\lambda\boldsymbol{w}'\boldsymbol{C}\boldsymbol{w}. \tag{1.21}$$

Letting $\boldsymbol{\mu}_x = \boldsymbol{\mu} - \boldsymbol{1}^n r_0$ denote the excess expected returns of the assets, a simple closed-form solution to optimization problem (1.21) is given by

$$\boldsymbol{w} = \frac{1}{\lambda}\boldsymbol{C}^{-1}\boldsymbol{\mu}_x. \tag{1.22}$$

In (1.22) the portfolio weights do not sum to one and instead the holding in the riskless asset is implicitly defined by the unit-sum condition.

1.3.5 Active Risk–Return Preferences

As discussed in section 1.1.3, many investors allocate their investments across a collection of institutional portfolio managers assigned to separate asset classes and benchmarks. As noted earlier, the difference between the manager's individual portfolio return and his benchmark return is called the active return. Active risk refers to the uncertainty of demeaned active return. Each manager can restate the portfolio management problem from his perspective as active return–active risk optimization of his subportfolio.

Roll (1992a) shows that active risk–return optimization by multiple managers assigned distinct benchmarks is suboptimal from a first-best perspective. The managers' individual active risk–return incentives do not aggregate to consistent total risk–return incentives for the primary investor. This type of subportfolio benchmarking system can be justified only from a second-best perspective. It allows the primary investor to allocate wealth across investment classes while exploiting the specialized security selection ability of the managers within asset classes.

Letting $\boldsymbol{w}_{\mathrm{B}}$ denote the benchmark weights, a portfolio manager's investment problem is expressed in terms of the active weights $\boldsymbol{w}_{\mathrm{A}} = \boldsymbol{w} - \boldsymbol{w}_{\mathrm{B}}$. The active-return equivalent of the linear mean–variance model (1.15) is often used by managers:

$$\max_{\{\boldsymbol{w}_{\mathrm{A}} \mid \boldsymbol{w}_{\mathrm{A}}'\mathbf{1}^n = 0\}} \boldsymbol{w}_{\mathrm{A}}'\boldsymbol{\mu} - \tfrac{1}{2}\lambda_{\mathrm{A}}\boldsymbol{w}_{\mathrm{A}}'\boldsymbol{C}\boldsymbol{w}_{\mathrm{A}}. \tag{1.23}$$

It is possible to center the active optimization problem (1.23) around benchmark expected return $r_{\mathrm{B}} = \boldsymbol{w}_{\mathrm{B}}'\boldsymbol{\mu}$ so that the unit-cost constraint on portfolio weights is explicit. Let $r_{\mathrm{A}} = \boldsymbol{r} - r_{\mathrm{B}}\mathbf{1}^n$ denote the active return, let $\boldsymbol{\mu}_{\mathrm{A}} = \boldsymbol{\mu} - (\boldsymbol{w}_{\mathrm{B}}'\boldsymbol{\mu})\mathbf{1}^n$ be the active mean, and let

$$\boldsymbol{C}_{\mathrm{A}} = \boldsymbol{C} + (\boldsymbol{w}_{\mathrm{B}}'\boldsymbol{C}\boldsymbol{w}_{\mathrm{B}})\mathbf{1}^n\mathbf{1}^{n\prime} - \mathbf{1}^n\boldsymbol{w}_{\mathrm{B}}'\boldsymbol{C} - \boldsymbol{C}\boldsymbol{w}_{\mathrm{B}}\mathbf{1}^{n\prime}$$

be the active covariance matrix. Then (1.23) can be reformulated as

$$\max_{\{\boldsymbol{w} \mid \boldsymbol{w}'\mathbf{1}^n = 1\}} \boldsymbol{w}'\boldsymbol{\mu}_{\mathrm{A}} - \tfrac{1}{2}\lambda_{\mathrm{A}}\boldsymbol{w}'\boldsymbol{C}_{\mathrm{A}}\boldsymbol{w}.$$

The algebra of active risk analysis is very similar to that of total risk analysis. However, the statistical distribution of active risk can be quite different.

In the case of total return with linear mean–variance optimization, formula (1.20) provides an observable proxy for an investor's risk aversion coefficient, λ. The same analysis reveals the risk preferences of an active investor. Let μ_{A}, σ_{A}^2 denote the active mean return and active variance of the investor's optimal portfolio from solving (1.23). Note that for any $\gamma \geqslant 0$, $(\gamma\mu_A, \gamma^2\sigma_A^2)$ is the return to a feasible portfolio and the maximum occurs at $\gamma = 1$. Taking the first-order condition at $\gamma = 1$ and setting it to zero,

$$\left.\frac{\partial}{\partial\gamma}\right|_{\gamma=1}[\gamma\mu_A - \tfrac{1}{2}\lambda_A\gamma^2\sigma_A^2] = 0,$$

gives

$$\lambda_A = \mu_A/\sigma_A^2,$$

so the formula is analogous to that in the total-return case.

Active risk analysis focuses on the difference between the managed portfolio $\boldsymbol{w}$ and the benchmark portfolio $\boldsymbol{w}_B$. The resulting active portfolio $\boldsymbol{w}_A$ has zero cost, but return is well-defined since the active portfolio is the difference between the return on two unit-cost portfolios. In other cases of zero-cost portfolios, the definition of the per-unit return can be ambiguous. The simplest procedure (and the one analogous to the active portfolio analysis) is to scale the units of return for the portfolio so that the sum of the long weights equals one, and therefore the sum of the short weights will equal minus one. Note that this is the same as the units of the active portfolio as long as both the managed and benchmark portfolios have all nonnegative weights.

1.3.6 Marginal Contributions to Risk

A *portfolio tilt* is a deliberate overweighting or underweighting of securities of a certain type relative to a benchmark portfolio. Portfolio tilts are intermediate between asset allocation and security selection. Some commonly employed tilt portfolios are those based on an industry, a country or region, or a style such as value, growth, size, or yield (such as for tax strategies). One important function of a portfolio risk model is to provide the marginal risk contributions of portfolio tilts.

Let $\boldsymbol{w}$ denote the current portfolio and let $\boldsymbol{v}$ denote a unit-cost portfolio reflecting an intended direction of change in $\boldsymbol{w}$, that is, a prospective portfolio tilt. The marginal contribution to risk of a tilt in vector direction $\boldsymbol{v}$ for current portfolio $\boldsymbol{w}$ is the change in portfolio standard deviation σ_w caused by a marginal change in direction $\boldsymbol{v}$:

$$\begin{aligned}\frac{\partial\sigma_w}{\partial v} &= \left.\frac{\partial}{\partial\gamma}\right|_{\gamma=0}[(\boldsymbol{w}+\gamma\boldsymbol{v})'\boldsymbol{C}(\boldsymbol{w}+\gamma\boldsymbol{v})]^{1/2}\\ &= \frac{1}{\sigma_w}\boldsymbol{v}'\boldsymbol{C}\boldsymbol{w}.\end{aligned} \tag{1.24}$$

Implicit in this definition is the assumption that an offsetting negative position of $-y$ is taken in the riskless asset, so that the unit-cost constraint $\boldsymbol{w}'\mathbf{1}^n = 1$ continues to hold along the vector gradient. The directional portfolio $\boldsymbol{v}$ is often designed to capture some prominent feature such as an industry factor, style, or other labeled factor.

The marginal risk contribution MCR_i of the ith asset can be obtained by setting the tilt portfolio equal to a vector with a one in the ith position and zeros elsewhere. The marginal risk of an asset can be negative.

1.3.7 Risk Budgeting

Risk budgeting maximizes expected return subject to a risk constraint. The risk budgeting constraint can be expressed in terms of total or active variance or value-at-risk. If variance is used as the measure of risk, then risk budgeting amounts to the dual statement of the mean–variance problem (1.13) discussed earlier. Risk can be budgeted to qualitatively defined asset classes, or to a set of portfolio managers who will manage subportfolios, or to a set of trading desks. Alternatively, it can be budgeted to quantitatively defined categories, such as maturity bands for a fixed-income portfolio.

We consider the case of portfolio total variance as the budget constraint. The investor allocates his funds to n risky assets and a riskless asset. We modify the formulation (1.13) of the mean–variance optimization problem to include a riskless asset:

$$\max_{\{\boldsymbol{w}|\boldsymbol{w}'\boldsymbol{C}\boldsymbol{w}=\bar{\sigma}^2\}} (1 - \boldsymbol{w}'\mathbf{1}^n)r_0 + \boldsymbol{w}'\boldsymbol{\mu}.$$

Defining expected excess returns $\boldsymbol{\mu}_X = \boldsymbol{\mu} - r_0\mathbf{1}^n$, this becomes

$$\max_{\{\boldsymbol{w}|\boldsymbol{w}'\boldsymbol{C}\boldsymbol{w}=\bar{\sigma}^2\}} \boldsymbol{w}'\boldsymbol{\mu}_X. \tag{1.25}$$

In risk budgeting we view (1.25) as a problem of maximizing expected return by allocating the total risk $\bar{\sigma}^2$ across the n assets. Sharpe (2002) notes that risk budgeting does not have the commonsense meaning of a fixed sum to be allocated across budget items since risk is not additive. The budget is nonlinear; in the mean–variance application, more specifically, the budget constraint is quadratic in the portfolio weights. As we explain below, the optimal portfolio weights do follow a linear equation, but are written in units of marginal risk.

1.3.8 The Value-Additivity of Marginal Contributions

Although the risk budgeting problem is not linear, the marginal contributions to portfolio risk are linear in the allocations to budget items:

$$\frac{\partial(\boldsymbol{w}'\boldsymbol{C}\boldsymbol{w})}{\partial\boldsymbol{w}} = 2\boldsymbol{C}\boldsymbol{w}. \tag{1.26}$$

This means that the change in variance due to a small change in risk allocation is a linear function of the allocation weights.

Since (1.25) is a smooth function of the allocation weights, at the optimum the marginal changes in expected return must be proportional to the marginal changes in the risk constraint $\boldsymbol{w}'\boldsymbol{C}\boldsymbol{w}$ for some constant of proportionality λ:

$$\frac{\partial(\boldsymbol{w}'\boldsymbol{\mu})}{\partial\boldsymbol{w}} = \mu^* = \lambda\frac{\partial(\boldsymbol{w}'\boldsymbol{C}\boldsymbol{w})}{\partial\boldsymbol{w}}. \tag{1.27}$$

Condition (1.27) combined with the linear marginal risk expression (1.26) can be used to rationally allocate capital across assets or subportfolios. For example, Sharpe (2002) gives a detailed application to investment fund planning. Sharpe highlights the case in which the covariance matrix $\boldsymbol{C}$ is estimated using a factor model. In this case, the marginal contributions to variance can be expressed in terms of the components of the factor model:

$$\frac{\partial(\boldsymbol{w}'\boldsymbol{C}\boldsymbol{w})}{\partial\boldsymbol{w}} = \frac{\partial}{\partial\boldsymbol{w}}(\boldsymbol{w}'\boldsymbol{B}\boldsymbol{C}_f\boldsymbol{B}\boldsymbol{w} + \boldsymbol{w}'\boldsymbol{C}_\varepsilon\boldsymbol{w}),$$

where $\boldsymbol{C}_f$ is the factor covariance matrix, $\boldsymbol{B}$ is the $n \times k$ factor beta matrix, and $\boldsymbol{C}_\varepsilon$ is the diagonal matrix of asset-specific risks. Sharpe (2002) considers a pension fund allocating capital across n asset classes with return vector $\boldsymbol{r}$ using the usual linear mean–variance objective function:

$$\max_{\{\boldsymbol{w} \mid \boldsymbol{w}'\boldsymbol{1}^n = 1\}} \boldsymbol{w}'\boldsymbol{\mu} - \tfrac{1}{2}\lambda\boldsymbol{w}'\boldsymbol{C}\boldsymbol{w}. \tag{1.28}$$

Using the portfolio optimality condition applied to (1.28), Sharpe notes that each asset class must have expected excess return proportional to its portfolio variance contribution in (1.26). That is, setting the vector derivative of (1.28) with respect to $\boldsymbol{w}$ to zero gives

$$\boldsymbol{\mu}_x = \lambda\boldsymbol{C}\boldsymbol{w}.$$

Litterman (1996) stresses the importance of applying multiple risk budgeting perspectives in (1.26) and (1.27) for a given portfolio. For example, it may be appropriate to consider risk allocation across countries, calculate marginal contributions (1.26) for each country allocation and check that they obey (1.27), then switch to risk allocation across fixed-income maturity buckets, recalculate marginal contributions (1.26) for each allocation to a bucket and check (1.27), then switch to asset type allocations, etc. This requires a flexible risk analysis model that can support the calculation of marginal contributions from these multiple perspectives. Litterman's purpose is to find large-magnitude marginal risk contributions in (1.26) that are not matched in terms of contribution to expected excess return in (1.27) and to adjust the risk-budgeted positions accordingly. Note that a position with a large negative marginal contribution can have a negative expected excess return and still make a net positive contribution to portfolio risk–return optimality.

1.4 The Capital Asset Pricing Model and Its Applications to Risk Analysis

Theories of the equilibrium relationship between portfolio risk and asset expected return, known as *asset pricing theories*, have obvious relevance to the study of portfolio risk analysis. This section reviews the foundational asset pricing theory of the modern era, the Sharpe–Lintner–Mossin capital asset pricing model (CAPM) and its applications to portfolio risk analysis. We will consider some alternatives to the CAPM in later chapters of the book.

If all investors have one-period mean–variance preferences, then each of them will solve an optimization problem like (1.12). Throughout this section we assume this and also that all investors have the same beliefs about the expected return vector $\boldsymbol{\mu}$ and covariance matrix $\boldsymbol{C}$.

1.4.1 Mean–Variance Efficiency of the Market Portfolio

For convenience we will detail the case in which there is no riskless asset; including a riskless asset just adds a minor complication to the notation. Rearranging the first-order condition from the constrained risk-minimization version (1.14) of the general mean–variance problem (1.12) gives

$$\boldsymbol{w} = \boldsymbol{C}^{-1}(\gamma_1 \mathbf{1}^n + \gamma_2 \boldsymbol{\mu}) \quad \text{for some } \gamma_1, \gamma_2 > 0, \tag{1.29}$$

and this condition is both necessary and sufficient for a portfolio $\boldsymbol{w}$ to be mean–variance efficient. The particular values of the parameters γ_1 and γ_2 depend upon the preferences of the individual investor j. However, note (as is easy to show) that the set of mean–variance efficient portfolios solving (1.29) is convex: that is, if it holds for two portfolios, then it holds for any convex combination[3] of them.

Define the *market portfolio* as the value-weighted portfolio of all assets in the investment universe. Note that in theory this investment universe

[3] A convex combination of a set of vectors is a linear combination of them that has positive linear weights that sum to one.

should include all assets held by investors, not just the assets whose returns are readily observable. In equilibrium, by supply–demand clearing, the wealth-weighted sum of all investors' portfolio holdings must equal the market portfolio (this is just a simple adding-up condition, since every share of every asset must be held by someone). Recall also that every investor (in our simple world) chooses to hold a mean–variance efficient portfolio. From (1.29) we have seen that the set of mean–variance efficient portfolios is convex; hence if everyone holds one, and the market portfolio is a wealth-weighted combination of their holdings, then the market portfolio must be mean–variance efficient by this convexity property.

The result on the centrality of the market portfolio is strengthened if we add a riskless asset. Assume that there is a riskless borrowing/lending opportunity in zero net supply (so that its weight in the market portfolio is zero). The market portfolio will then be the only mean–variance efficient portfolio of risky assets. All other mean–variance efficient portfolios will consist of a position in the market portfolio combined with riskless lending or borrowing.

1.4.2 Passive Benchmarks and the CAPM

One of the key implications of the CAPM is that the market portfolio is mean–variance efficient. This means that the market portfolio solves the linear mean–variance problem (1.15) for some value of the risk aversion parameter λ. In the presence of a riskless asset the market portfolio solves the problem for *all* values of λ, since all efficient portfolios are combinations of the market portfolio and riskless borrowing or lending.

Note that to solve the mean–variance problem directly we need a valuation model that provides mean returns $\boldsymbol{\mu}$ for all n assets in the investment universe and a risk model giving the full covariance matrix $\boldsymbol{C}$. The CAPM provides a simple alternative to developing return and risk forecasts for all assets: hold the market portfolio combined with some appropriate degree of borrowing and lending. This passive investment strategy avoids the need to perform valuation modeling to get $\boldsymbol{\mu}$ and risk modeling to get $\boldsymbol{C}$. The passive investor uses the fact that other investors are correctly valuing assets and ensuring that the CAPM pricing relationship sets expected returns so that the market portfolio is optimal. The passive investor then mimics their optimal behavior by holding the market portfolio.

The efficiency of the market portfolio justifies the use of the market portfolio as the benchmark in active risk analysis. A portfolio manager attempting to use information to create investment value can be compared with the market portfolio, which is an information-less but efficient alternative investment choice. It means that we need not construct a full valuation model to judge the performance of an active manager; we simply compare his risk–return performance with that of the passive CAPM benchmark.

1.4.3 Expected Returns in the CAPM

In addition to establishing the market portfolio as a performance benchmark, the CAPM gives a simple and elegant model for asset expected returns. Rearranging the first-order condition for the mean–variance efficiency of the market portfolio using the constrained risk-minimization version (1.14) gives

$$\boldsymbol{\mu} = \lambda_1 \boldsymbol{C}^{-1}\boldsymbol{w}_{\mathrm{m}} + \lambda_2 \mathbf{1}^n. \tag{1.30}$$

Let $\mu_0 = \boldsymbol{w}_0'\boldsymbol{\mu}$ denote the expected return on a portfolio $\boldsymbol{w}_0$ that has zero covariance with the market portfolio (that is, $\boldsymbol{w}_0'\boldsymbol{C}\boldsymbol{w}_{\mathrm{m}} = 0$). Multiplying (1.30) by $\boldsymbol{w}_0'$ and also by $\boldsymbol{w}_{\mathrm{m}}'$ and using the resulting two expressions to solve for λ_1 and λ_2 in (1.30) gives

$$\boldsymbol{\mu} = \mu_0 \mathbf{1}^n + \boldsymbol{\beta}(\mu_{\mathrm{m}} - \mu_0), \tag{1.31}$$

where

$$\boldsymbol{\beta} = \left(\frac{1}{\boldsymbol{w}_{\mathrm{m}}'\boldsymbol{C}\boldsymbol{w}_{\mathrm{m}}}\right)\boldsymbol{C}\boldsymbol{w}_{\mathrm{m}} = \left(\frac{1}{\mathrm{var}(r_{\mathrm{m}})}\right)\mathrm{cov}(\boldsymbol{r}, r_{\mathrm{m}}). \tag{1.32}$$

This is the standard statement of the CAPM in the absence of a riskless rate. If there is a riskless asset, then we can substitute its return for μ_0 in (1.31), giving

$$\boldsymbol{\mu} = r_0 \mathbf{1}^n + \boldsymbol{\beta}(\mu_{\mathrm{m}} - r_0), \tag{1.33}$$

so that assets' expected excess returns are linear in the market betas, with linear coefficient equal to the expected excess return on the market portfolio.

1.4.4 Risk Modeling Using Market Betas

In addition to its role as a risk measure, the market beta of an asset measures the market-related return of the asset. The *market model* is the description of excess returns as an additive sum of a vector of constants, market-related returns (betas times market return), and nonmarket returns:

$$\boldsymbol{x} = \boldsymbol{a} + \boldsymbol{\beta} x_{\mathrm{m}} + \boldsymbol{\varepsilon}, \tag{1.34}$$

where the nonmarket return is simply the residual, which ensures that the equality holds exactly. It follows from the definition of $\boldsymbol{\beta}$ that

$\text{cov}(\boldsymbol{\varepsilon}, x_{\text{m}}) = \mathbf{0}^n$, as the reader can easily verify. The market model imposes no assumptions on returns except finite variances. It is a decomposition of returns rather than a restriction on returns and does not require that the CAPM holds.

The market beta coefficients in (1.32) can be estimated by time-series regression using the market model. Suppose that we observe a time series of excess returns for asset i for periods $t = 1, T$ as well as the market portfolio excess returns. Running time-series ordinary least squares on the market model for asset i gives an estimated beta, and nonmarket returns as regression residuals:

$$x_{it} = \hat{a}_i + \hat{\beta}_i x_{\text{m}t} + \hat{\varepsilon}_{it}.$$

Let $\hat{\boldsymbol{\beta}}$ denote the n-vector of betas from estimating the market model for each of the n assets, and $\hat{\boldsymbol{\varepsilon}}$ the $n \times T$ matrix of nonmarket returns. The nonmarket return covariance matrix can be estimated by the sample covariance matrix of these regression-based nonmarket returns: $\hat{\boldsymbol{C}}_\varepsilon = (1/T)\hat{\boldsymbol{\varepsilon}}\hat{\boldsymbol{\varepsilon}}'$. This gives a full covariance matrix estimate:

$$\hat{\boldsymbol{C}} = \sigma_{\text{m}}^2 \hat{\boldsymbol{\beta}}\hat{\boldsymbol{\beta}}' + \hat{\boldsymbol{C}}_\varepsilon. \tag{1.35}$$

This does not alter the estimation of $\hat{\boldsymbol{C}}$: since $\hat{\boldsymbol{C}}_\varepsilon$ is unrestricted, the right-hand side of (1.35) does not affect the estimation of $\hat{\boldsymbol{C}}$ on the left-hand side. However, (1.35) does give us a useful decomposition of the covariance matrix into market-related and nonmarket components.

The diagonal-market model is a restricted version of the market model in which the nonmarket returns are assumed to be uncorrelated:

$$\boldsymbol{C}_\varepsilon = E[\boldsymbol{\varepsilon}\boldsymbol{\varepsilon}'] = \text{Diag}[\sigma_{\varepsilon_1}^2, \dots, \sigma_{\varepsilon_n}^2]. \tag{1.36}$$

There is a minor conflict between (1.36) and (1.31) if the sample of assets in (1.36) includes all the assets in the market portfolio. The reason for this is that the market portfolio $\boldsymbol{w}_{\text{m}}$ has no nonmarket risk and in particular $\boldsymbol{w}_{\text{m}}' \boldsymbol{C}_\varepsilon \boldsymbol{w}_{\text{m}} = 0$. This implies that the covariance matrix of nonmarket returns is singular and so cannot be diagonal. This singularity is only a "small-n" problem, which approximately disappears as the number of assets in the market portfolio grows large.[4] A simple expedient, which is harmless in most cases, is to assume that the set of assets whose returns are measured in the diagonal-market model (1.36) does not encompass all of the assets in the market portfolio in (1.31). This allows $\boldsymbol{C}_\varepsilon$ to be nonsingular without generating an internal inconsistency in the model.

[4] As the number of assets grows large we can have $\boldsymbol{w}_{\text{m}}' \boldsymbol{C}_\varepsilon \boldsymbol{w}_{\text{m}} \overset{n}{\approx} 0$ with $\boldsymbol{C}_\varepsilon$ diagonal and positive definite.

Imposing the diagonal-market model does not change the individual market model regression estimates, but it does change the implied return covariance matrix estimate. In place of (1.35) we have

$$\hat{C} = \sigma_{\mathrm{m}}^2 \hat{\boldsymbol{\beta}}\hat{\boldsymbol{\beta}}' + \mathrm{Diag}[\hat{\sigma}_{\varepsilon_1}^2, \dots, \hat{\sigma}_{\varepsilon_n}^2].$$

1.4.5 Marginal Contributions to Risk and Market Betas

There is an interesting connection between marginal contributions to risk and the market model decomposition (1.34). Decompose returns into market-related and nonmarket components using the current portfolio $\boldsymbol{w}$ as the "market" portfolio:

$$\left.\begin{aligned} x_i &= a_i + \beta_i^{\boldsymbol{w}} x_w + \varepsilon_i, \\ \beta_i^{\boldsymbol{w}} &= \frac{\mathrm{cov}(r_i, r_b)}{\mathrm{var}(r_b)} = \frac{\boldsymbol{e}^{i\prime} \boldsymbol{C} \boldsymbol{w}_b}{\boldsymbol{w}_b{}' \boldsymbol{C} \boldsymbol{w}_b}, \end{aligned}\right\} \tag{1.37}$$

where $\boldsymbol{e}^i$ denotes an n-vector with a one for its ith component and zeros elsewhere. Note that (1.37) is just a return decomposition that holds by definition and does not require that the current portfolio has any features of a market portfolio. Note the value-weighted linearity of portfolio betas, $\beta_d^{\boldsymbol{w}} = \boldsymbol{d}'\boldsymbol{\beta}^w$. Using betas calculated treating the current portfolio as the "market," and combining (1.34) and (1.24), the marginal contribution to risk for any portfolio direction $\boldsymbol{d}$ is "beta" (using the current portfolio as the regressor) multiplied by current portfolio volatility:

$$\mathrm{MCR}_d^{\boldsymbol{w}} = \sigma_w \beta_d^{\boldsymbol{w}}.$$

In the general mean–variance problem this implies that if $\boldsymbol{w}$ is an optimal portfolio then the marginal contribution to risk of any asset or portfolio must be proportional to its mean excess return, with proportionality parameter λ from (1.15):

$$\lambda\,\mathrm{MCR}_d^{\boldsymbol{w}} = \mu_{xd}. \tag{1.38}$$

In rebalancing the existing portfolio, the portfolio manager's job is to find directions $\boldsymbol{d}$ such that the right-hand "return" side of (1.38) exceeds the left-hand "risk" side.

1.4.6 State Price Densities and Risk-Neutral Probabilities

In this subsection we consider the asset pricing implications of the general portfolio optimization problem (1.10). This is a useful exercise in its own right, and comparing this general equilibrium asset pricing condition with the special case of the CAPM allows us to analyze more clearly the limitations of the CAPM.

For this subsection we drop the assumption that all asset returns are normally distributed (we return to it in the next subsection). Consider a unit-wealth, one-period investor who has solved the general static optimization problem (1.10) and chosen an optimal portfolio $\boldsymbol{w}$. The random consumption that he receives at the end of the period depends on the return on his chosen portfolio according to the rule $c = (1 + r_w)$ and this random consumption gives him a realized utility of $u(c)$. Note that consumption is a random variable; we write it as $c = c(\omega)$, where ω denotes a random outcome from the full set of possible random outcomes. Consider the return r_i to any traded asset i, and note that it is also a random variable $r_i(\omega)$. We also assume that there is a riskless asset with return r_0.

Since the investor has already chosen optimally, increasing or decreasing his holding in any asset i, financed by riskless borrowing, cannot increase expected utility. In particular, this implies that given that the optimal portfolio has been chosen, the marginal expected utility of the excess return $r_i - r_0$ must equal zero:

$$E[u'(c)(r_i - r_0)] = 0. \tag{1.39}$$

Recall the definition of the probability density from section 1.2.2. We assume that the set of random outcomes encompassing both asset return $r_i(\omega)$ and the investor's random consumption $c(\omega)$ are the set of real numbers $\omega \in (-\infty, \infty)$. Rewriting the expectation in (1.39) using the probability density of the random variables c and r_i gives us

$$E[u'(c)(r_i - r_0)] = \int_{-\infty}^{\infty} \mathrm{den}(\omega)u'(c(\omega))(r_i(\omega) - r_0)\,\mathrm{d}\omega = 0.$$

This expression simply takes the definition of the expectation and writes it out as an integral over all random outcomes. To analyze the asset pricing implications of this expression we define a new hypothetical "probability density" called the *risk-neutral density*, $\mathrm{den}^*(\cdot)$, by multiplying the true probability density by the marginal utility of consumption in each random state:

$$\mathrm{den}^*(\omega) = k(\mathrm{den}(\omega)u'(c(\omega))), \tag{1.40}$$

where the constant k is chosen so that the "probability density" $\mathrm{den}^*(\omega)$ has a cumulative probability of one (a necessary property of a probability density): that is, $\int_{-\infty}^{\infty} \mathrm{den}^*(\omega)\,\mathrm{d}\omega = 1$. The risk-neutral probability density is not the true probability density of the outcomes ω but rather a risk-adjusted variant, which puts more probability weight on the more needy states (those in which marginal utility is high) and less weight on less needy states (where marginal utility is low). The important feature of the risk-neutral probability density is that if we use it in place of the true probability to take expectations, then the expected return on any asset equals the riskless return. The reader can quickly verify using (1.40) and (1.39) that

$$E^*[r_i] = r_0, \tag{1.41}$$

where $E^*[r_i]$ denotes the expectation using the risk-neutral density in place of the true one.

The risk-neutral pricing rule (1.41) holds with great generality. It can easily be extended to a multiperiod context or to a continuous-time environment. Unlike the CAPM or similar linear-beta models, the risk-neutral pricing theory does not make strong assumptions on return distributions.

1.4.7 Limits to the Applicability of the CAPM in Portfolio Risk Management

The CAPM and associated mean–variance analysis provide simple and powerful tools for portfolio risk management and portfolio risk–return evaluation. However, it is important for the analyst to understand the limits to the applicability of this framework. It relies on strong assumptions about asset returns and investor preferences.

The generality of the risk-neutral pricing model can be used to illustrate the weaknesses of the CAPM. Consider the special case in which all investors have identical single-period CARA preferences and the primary asset returns (those assets in positive net supply) are multivariate normal. Assume that in addition to the primary assets, investors can freely trade derivatives on the primary assets; these derivatives are in zero net supply so they do not appear in the market portfolio. The CAPM applies in this market to the primary assets but not to the derivative assets.

We calibrate this artificial economy so that the stock market index has an annualized volatility of 20% and an expected return of 8%; the annualized riskless return is set at 4%. One period (the economy is a static one-period economy) is calibrated to equal one quarter of a year. Figure 1.5 illustrates the true general equilibrium prices of three-month stock market index options in this economy, along with the incorrect prices that would be calculated if one applied the CAPM to these options. The CAPM substantially underprices out-of-the-money put options and out-of-the-money call options. Note that in this economy the CAPM is (by construction) the correct pricing model for equities; it just does not apply to options.

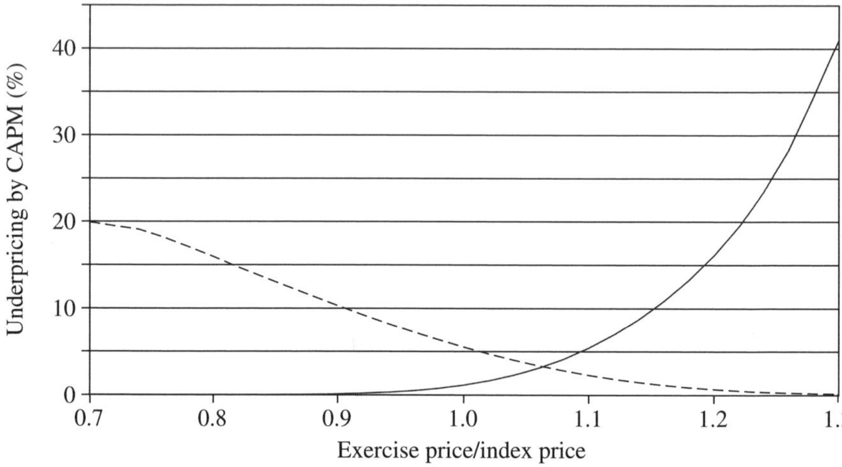

Figure 1.5. Percentage differences between true general equilibrium prices of three-month stock market index options and the incorrect prices that would be calculated by applying the CAPM to these options: dashed line, market index put options; solid line, market index call options.

1.4.8 Excess Volatility, the Risk Premium Puzzle, and Nonstandard Preferences

Shiller (1981) and Leroy and Porter (1981) argue that U.S. equity market volatility is too high relative to variations in equity cash flows (dividends) to be explained by standard equilibrium asset pricing models. In addition, Mehra and Prescott (1985) show that the long-run average risk premium of the U.S. equity market is too high relative to the volatility of equity cash flows to be consistent with standard pricing models. These papers (and the large number of subsequent papers) led to a fundamental reevaluation of standard pricing models. One alternative to the standard model is to impose nonseparable time preferences. Another related approach is to jettison rational preference maximization and instead allow psychological biases to affect investor behavior and thereby affect market-wide price equilibrium. Since the purpose of portfolio risk analysis is to provide clear and reliable information for rational decision making, it is difficult to embed these irrational-behavior models into the analysis. (However, Ariely (2008) describes how an individual can acknowledge his irrational biases in investment decision making and still use rational analysis to try to "improve" his own behavior.) Even if we choose to model our own investment behavior as rational, it is important not to assume that security markets will always conform to rational-equilibrium predictions, particularly in crisis conditions.

1.5 The Objectives and Limitations of Portfolio Risk Analysis

1.5.1 Varied Institutional Settings

There are a wide variety of institutional settings for portfolio risk analysis. The particular setting can have a substantial influence on risk model design and on risk-management best practice. In this subsection we briefly describe some relevant institutional environments.

In *traditional investment management*, an investment sponsor such as a pension fund provides control over a pool of capital to an investment management firm, together with an investment mandate including an agreed benchmark portfolio. The investment mandate describes the allowable set of assets, any limitations on portfolio weights of individual holdings or of subportfolio categories, any short-sale or derivative constraints, upper bounds on the forecast active risk of the portfolio, and reporting periods and reporting requirements of the investment manager to the sponsor.

Hedge funds are an alternative or supplement to traditional investment management. They manage pools of capital for sponsors, but the risk control and risk reporting oversight by sponsors is more limited. A typical hedge fund contract has no benchmark portfolio, and the investment mandate provides very limited input by the sponsor and limited reporting by the manager to the sponsor about investment strategy or holdings. Also, a typical hedge fund is a highly leveraged investment vehicle where internal risk control plays a central role in maintaining the stability and sustainability of the fund. Risk horizons tend to be shorter than for traditional investment management, and total return rather than active return is the focal return scale. We will discuss hedge funds in detail in chapter 13.

A third canonical setting for portfolio risk analysis is a *trading desk*. It differs from the previous two settings in that the pool of capital is provided from within the same firm that makes the day-to-day investment and risk-management decisions. Hence the risk-management team mostly reports intrafirm, though in many cases subject to government regulatory guidelines. Risk horizons can be as short as fifteen minutes; daily risk management is of paramount concern. Types of trading desks include *broker–dealer desks* (providing a market-making and brokerage service for clients), *financial engineering desks* (creating bespoke derivatives products for customers), and *proprietary trading desks* (using intrafirm capital to speculate on profitable trading strategies).

1.5.2 The Separate Identity of Portfolio Risk Management

In the portfolio management process and in the minds of portfolio managers, risk and return are intertwined. Nonetheless, it is often preferable to model and manage risk separately. In this subsection we consider some of the reasons why portfolio risk management has a separate identity from general portfolio management.

1.5.2.1 Institutional Separation of Portfolio Risk and Portfolio Return Management

The main reason for the separation of risk management from portfolio management relates to regulatory and management issues. An individual in charge of both activities might be tempted to modify his risk analysis to support his return forecasts. Also, risk management serves as an independent oversight of the portfolio management process. If a rogue portfolio manager attempts to violate the investment mandate of his client or his firm, an independent risk manager can prevent this. Particularly in traditional investment management and trading desk environments, the two functional reporting lines (trading/portfolio management versus risk management) are usually formally separated.

Traders working for large institutions effectively own a call option on their trading portfolio, since they earn a proportion of the positive profits from their trading, as reflected in performance-related salaries and bonuses, but have only limited exposure to large losses on the portfolio (they can be fired, nothing worse). The *trader option* is an informal term denoting the ability of traders to "walk away" from large losses, with limited damage to their personal wealth or career prospects. A separated risk-management function, with salaries and bonuses not tightly linked to trading desk performance, ameliorates the moral hazard problem associated with the trader option.[5]

In a traditional investment management environment, the separation of portfolio risk management from portfolio return management can act as a powerful control on legal risk. Just as in the trading desk environment, a separate risk-management function ensures an independent oversight with exclusive focus on risk-management issues, and also on

[5] The moral hazard problem associated with the trader options applies to any individual whose salary and bonus are closely tied to portfolio return, and this often includes senior managers. Hence the separation of the risk-management function needs to be implemented throughout the corporate command chain, including at the most senior levels.

ensuring that the investment mandate is scrupulously followed, avoiding exposure to the large reputational and legal costs associated with investor lawsuits.

1.5.2.2 Differences between Risk and Return Forecasting

Another reason for the separation of portfolio risk management stems from differences in quantitative techniques for forecasting risk versus those for forecasting return. Efficient markets contain a self-correcting mechanism that eliminates any large predictable difference in expected return between assets or over time.[6] The demand–supply price pressure of investors eager to profit from an observable difference is inconsistent with survival of the difference. There is no analogous effect with respect to risk: revealing a forecastable risk pattern does not generate profit-making pressure that eliminates the pattern. So removing expected return from the forecasting objective removes the direct profit-making potential, and resolves the efficient-markets paradox. Forecasting return is a constant, shifting battle against the competitive pressures of efficient market pricing. This is not true for risk forecasting.

A related phenomenon is that return forecasting models tend to be unreliable and quickly varying. Researchers find and publish expected return differences that subsequently disappear, reverse, or are shown to have never been there in the first place. Risk-management models generally produce more stable and reliable predictions.

An important caveat to the separate modeling of risk and expected return is that it is not always possible to completely isolate expected return from risk. The decomposition of return into expected return and demeaned return varies with the conditioning set. Furthermore, in market equilibrium there is a trade-off between portfolio risk and return, so that riskier portfolios tend to have slightly higher expected returns.

1.5.2.3 The Limited Impact of Expected Return on Risk Forecasting

In theory, it is not possible to fully separate risk forecasting from expected return forecasting. Recall that subtracting mean return μ from the random portfolio return r gives demeaned return $\tilde{r}$, hence demeaned return (the key variate in risk management) implicitly depends on expected return. However, in most practical applications, expected return has a negligible impact on risk measures, except for the case of long-horizon risk management.

[6] See Samuelson (1965). There can be small differences associated with differences in equilibrium risk-adjusted expected return.

In order to analyze the effect of expected return on risk across varying return horizons it is preferable to use log returns, which allow the return horizon to be varied easily. Let portfolio log return r_1 have a constant annualized mean of μ and a variance of σ^2. Note that mean-squared return, $E[r_1^2]$, which combines expected return and variance, equals $\mu^2 + \sigma^2$. If the return is measured at frequency Δ, then it has per-period mean $\Delta\mu$, variance $\Delta\sigma^2$, and mean-squared return $\Delta\sigma^2 + \Delta^2\mu^2$. Note that for small Δ, the mean-related term $\Delta^2\mu^2$ is negligible in its contribution to mean-squared return.

1.5.3 The Limits to Quantitative Risk Analysis

This book deals almost exclusively with quantitative risk analysis. It is important to understand and appreciate the limits to this quantitative approach.

In essence, quantitative risk models assign known or estimated probabilities to portfolio return outcomes. These probabilities are derived from statistical analysis of the existing historical record, structured by economic theory. The use of historical data as a representation of future risk is problematic, particularly in analyzing low-probability tail events, such as in the calculation of value-at-risk and expected shortfall. There are fundamental limits to how much information can be gleaned from the historical record, no matter how long that record, regarding the true future probability of low-probability events. Increasing the length of the historical record does not always result in an improvement, since the changing nature of financial markets means that older data is less relevant for future predictions. Constant innovations in portfolio management mean that risk managers are in a never-ending game of catch-up: the next market crisis will often stem from an instrument or trading strategy that did not even exist at the time of the previous market crisis.

Rebonato (2007) gives a detailed treatment of the limits to quantitative risk models in the context of bank trading desks. He argues that these models, used naively, can worsen rather than improve bank decision making. The developer of a quantitative risk model is likely to understand the weaknesses of the model as an approximation to reality, and he is likely to also understand the magnitude of the estimation error in the calibration of the model. Users of the model, however, may take its forecasts as equivalent to true risk probabilities. This can lead to worse risk-management decisions than having no quantitative model at all.

Recall from section 1.2.1 that model risk is the risk associated with misestimation or misspecification of the model used for risk forecasting and analysis. Since financial markets are constantly evolving (and are also subject to sudden, unpredictable structural changes), model risk can never be fully eliminated.

In some of our analysis we treat the risk model as known and exact, despite its empirical derivation from a finite sample of data. In chapter 2 we will discuss the Bayesian approach to model estimation, in which we combine the estimated parameters of the model with prior beliefs about financial market risk relationships. As we will see, Bayesian methods are a powerful tool in portfolio risk modeling, but they are not a complete solution. Nothing can completely eliminate model risk.

The notable failures of mortgage security credit-scoring models during the subprime mortgage meltdown of 2007–8 provide a telling example of how overreliance on statistical analysis of historical patterns can lead to severe risk-management errors. A major researcher from one of the ratings agencies explained in U.S. Congressional testimony that the poor performance of their statistical models could be traced back to "ahistorical behavior modes" by the mortgage debtors.[7] It now seems clear (with the benefit of twenty–twenty hindsight, and some recent research such as Ben-David (2008)) that the nature of the pool of mortgage debtors in 2006–7 was materially different from that of earlier periods. The history-based statistical models used by the ratings agencies and banks performed poorly in predicting mortgage payment deliquency and default rates in this new, very different, mortgage environment. It is now clear (after the fact) that the credit-scoring agencies and banks should have adjusted their statistical models to account for this changing market environment. Statistical analysis based on historical data, not sufficiently tempered by wise economic analysis, can contribute to financial disaster by giving a false impression of scientific certainty. This book will delve deeply into the statistical methods useful in portfolio risk management; it is up to the reader to add the appropriate wisdom in their application!

[7] Vickie A. Tillman, Executive Vice President of Standard & Poor's Credit Market Service, appearing before the Committee on Banking, Housing, and Urban Affairs on September 26, 2007. Quoted in Lowenstein (2008).

2
Unstructured Covariance Matrices

This chapter considers the estimation and use of return covariance matrices without any factor structure imposed upon them. Following this, in chapters 3–6, we consider structured covariance matrices.

Section 2.1 discusses the estimation of return covariance matrices using classical statistical methods. Section 2.2 describes the error-maximization problem in portfolio management and its implications for risk modeling. Section 2.3 treats portfolio risk management as a problem in decision making under uncertainty, and considers the Bayesian approach to covariance matrix estimation.

2.1 Estimating Return Covariance Matrices

This chapter is concerned with the estimation of the $n \times n$ covariance matrix of returns or excess returns. Since, by definition, the riskless rate has no variance, there is theoretically no difference between the total and excess return covariance matrices:

$$\boldsymbol{C} = [\mathrm{cov}(r_i, r_j)]_{i,j=1,n} = [\mathrm{cov}(x_i, x_j)]_{i,j=1,n}.$$

Although the riskless rate is known one period ahead, there is variation in its value over time, so that time-series-based estimates of $\mathrm{cov}(r_i, r_j)$ and $\mathrm{cov}(x_i, x_j)$ can differ. In most circumstances it is best practice to use excess returns in the estimation of $\boldsymbol{C}$. The resulting estimate can be thought of as measuring the covariance matrix of total returns, conditional upon knowing the riskless return.

For notational simplicity, we will not differentiate between the return frequency of the data set and the risk horizon used for risk analysis. In practice, the return frequency used in estimation can differ from the return frequency used in risk analysis. So, for example, the analyst may use a daily return frequency to measure the covariance matrix even though the analyst mostly cares about portfolio risk at the monthly return frequency. Or the analyst may use monthly returns to analyze risk at the annual frequency. We will discuss switching between estimation and forecasting return frequencies in chapter 9.

Let $\boldsymbol{X}$ denote the dimension $n \times T$ matrix of sample excess returns for n assets over a time-series sample of T periods. We assume that $\boldsymbol{X}$ is a *balanced* panel data set, which means that there are observations for all n returns in each time period. The simplest estimate of the covariance matrix is the sample moment estimate

$$\hat{\boldsymbol{C}} = \frac{1}{T}\tilde{\boldsymbol{X}}\tilde{\boldsymbol{X}}' \tag{2.1}$$

where $\tilde{\boldsymbol{X}}$ is the matrix of demeaned excess returns, using the vector of sample mean estimates

$$\tilde{\boldsymbol{X}} = \boldsymbol{X} - \hat{\boldsymbol{\mu}}(\mathbf{1}^T)' = \boldsymbol{X} - \left(\frac{1}{T}\boldsymbol{X}\mathbf{1}^T\right)(\mathbf{1}^T)'.$$

If the returns are multivariate normal and i.i.d. through time, then this estimate of $\boldsymbol{C}$ has a Wishart distribution. It is biased in small samples due to the use of the sample means, but for reasonably sized T the bias is negligible. Under weak conditions not requiring multivariate normality the estimate is T-consistent: that is,

$$\hat{\boldsymbol{C}} \overset{\text{pr},T}{\approx} \boldsymbol{C}.$$

Note that n is held fixed and must be small relative to T for this asymptotic result to be accurate.

2.1.1 Moment-Based and Maximum-Likelihood Estimation Methods

A common method for estimating a parameterized distribution is *maximum likelihood.* The likelihood function $L(\Theta \mid x_t,\ t = 1, T)$ of a given sample x_t, $t = 1, T$, for a chosen set of estimated parameters Θ is the joint density of the observations of x_t, $t = 1, T$, treating the estimated parameter values as the true parameters of the distribution. If the observations are independent, the likelihood function equals the product of the return densities of each of the observed sample values:

$$L(\Theta \mid \boldsymbol{X}) = \prod_{t=1}^{T} \text{den}_{\Theta}(x_t),$$

where $\text{den}_{\Theta}(x_t)$ is the probability density of x_t given that the chosen parameter values Θ are the true ones. The maximum-likelihood parameter estimates are those that maximize the likelihood of the observed sample. If returns are multivariate normal and we do not impose any restrictions on $\boldsymbol{C}$, then the maximum-likelihood estimate equals the sample moment estimate (2.1).

2.1.2 Unbalanced Panels and the Expectation–Maximization Algorithm

Asset return databases are often *unbalanced*, meaning that the sample of observed asset returns changes from one time period to the next. The simplest way to derive a balanced panel from an unbalanced one is to delete all assets that have missing observations. However, this creates a sample selection bias. Firms with lower realized returns over the early sample are most likely to be deleted before the end of the sample due to bankruptcy or delisting by the securities exchange. Also, there may be an induced selection bias against less liquid assets, which have more checkered trading records. Another concern is the substantial waste of information from deleting a nonnegligible proportion of the cross-sectional sample.

An alternative to the deletion of assets from an unbalanced panel is to apply the expectation–maximization (EM) algorithm (Dempster et al. 1977). In its general form, the EM algorithm estimates the parameters θ of a distribution from data series Z, Y, where Z is observed and Y is missing. There are two steps to the EM algorithm. The M-step performs maximum-likelihood estimation of θ based on data series Z, Y, replacing Y with its conditional expected value given Z and $\theta = \hat{\theta}$. The E-step finds the conditional expected value of Y given Z and $\theta = \hat{\theta}$. The algorithm iterates the two steps until a fixed point of the EM estimate $\hat{\theta}$ is found.

In the case of an unbalanced return panel we can use the EM algorithm to fill in the missing returns for those assets that have incomplete records. To begin, we need an initial estimate $\hat{C}$, found for example by using the data over a shorter, balanced subperiod and an observation for at least one asset in every period. Let x_t^{o} and x_t^{u} denote the vectors of observed and unobserved asset returns in period t. Let $\hat{C}^{\mathrm{o,u}}$ denote the submatrix of covariances between observed and unobserved asset returns and let $\hat{C}^{\mathrm{o,o}}$ denote the covariance matrix of the observed returns. Let $\hat{X}$ denote the matrix of demeaned excess returns in which the missing observations are replaced by their expected values from the E-step. The EM algorithm is as follows:

(1) E-Step: $\hat{X}_t^{\mathrm{u}} = \hat{C}^{\mathrm{o,u}}(\hat{C}^{\mathrm{o,o}})^{-1}X_t^{\mathrm{o}}$;

(2) M-Step: $\hat{C} = (1/T)\hat{X}(\hat{X})'$.

The steps are repeated until $\hat{C}$ is unchanged by the iteration. Stambaugh (1997) considers the case in which the sample of asset returns within the sample differ only in their starting dates; all assets have complete histories from their various starting dates to the final date T. In this case an EM-type iteration terminates in a fixed, finite number of steps if it is reordered to perform the estimation starting with the longest-lived assets and ending with the shortest-lived ones. Stambaugh also considers the iterative estimation of mean returns $\boldsymbol{\mu}$. See Ruud (1991) for extensions and applications of the EM algorithm.

2.1.3 Shrinking the Cross-Sectional Sample

In many applications the number of assets n is too large relative to the number of time periods T to produce a reliable estimate of the asset covariance matrix. This has led to the development of techniques that reduce the cross-sectional dimension n of the data set. The most common approaches are portfolio grouping and subsample analysis.

Suppose that the length T of our data history is adequate to estimate a covariance matrix whose dimension is no greater than k where $k < n$. The portfolio grouping technique assembles the assets into k groups corresponding to different market segments or styles. It is easiest to think of the groups as disjoint so that each asset belongs to exactly one group, but this is not necessary. For each group j, we specify a weight vector $\boldsymbol{g}_j$ of dimension n. The ith entry of $\boldsymbol{g}_j$ is the weight of asset i in group j, and the weights in each group must sum to one so that $\boldsymbol{g}_j'\mathbf{1}^n = 1$. Let $\boldsymbol{G}$ denote the $n \times k$ matrix whose columns are the group weight vectors $\boldsymbol{g}_j$, $j = 1, k$. Letting $\tilde{\boldsymbol{X}}$ denote the $n \times T$ matrix of demeaned asset returns, we set $\tilde{\boldsymbol{X}}_G = \boldsymbol{G}'\tilde{\boldsymbol{X}}$ to be the $k \times T$ matrix of demeaned excess returns to the groups. We can construct a dimension-k group covariance matrix as

$$\begin{aligned}\tilde{\boldsymbol{C}}_G &= \frac{1}{T}\tilde{\boldsymbol{X}}_G\tilde{\boldsymbol{X}}_G' \\ &= \frac{1}{T}\boldsymbol{G}'\tilde{\boldsymbol{X}}\tilde{\boldsymbol{X}}'\boldsymbol{G}.\end{aligned}$$

The membership of an asset in a group is determined by an indexing variable, which takes a value of zero or one for each pair of indices (i, j). For example, an industry decomposition of the set of n assets into k disjoint groups generates the indexing variable

$$G_{ij} = \begin{cases} 1 & \text{asset } i \text{ is in industry } j, \\ 0 & \text{otherwise.} \end{cases}$$

Similarly, a specific characteristic can be used to sort assets into fractile portfolios. Examples include market capitalization and return-based statistics such as volatility or momentum. One restriction is that the portfolio indexing variable must distinguish assets by their returns, in order to prevent the reduced-sample covariance matrix from being nearly singular (if assets are sorted into portfolios randomly, the correlation between portfolio returns approaches one for large cross-sectional sample sizes). Note that in using any return-related index the indexing variable should be based on a period prior to the one used for covariance matrix estimation.

Fixed income and equity characteristics tend to differ, and their indexing variables differ accordingly. Standard choices of fixed-income indexing variables are duration, time to maturity, and credit quality.

Indices can be combined to generate more complicated procedures for sorting. For example, we can divide stocks into five portfolios based on market capitalization and then divide each portfolio into five based on book-to-price ratios, giving $5 \times 5 = 25$ portfolios in total. Note that the order in which the indexing variables are applied affects the outcome in such a case.

The second step in the construction of $\boldsymbol{G}$ is to determine nonzero weights to assign within each group. An equal-weighting scheme minimizes the sum of squared portfolio weights. In a capitalization-weighting scheme the weight for asset i in group j equals the capitalization of asset i divided by the sum of the capitalizations of all the assets in group j. The returns generated by this scheme make economic sense. For example, capitalization-weighted industry portfolios are "investable" portfolios, whereas equally weighted industry portfolios may have a large proportion of funds in illiquid securities. One disadvantage of capitalization weighting is that it tends to produce unbalanced portfolio weights, with a few very large capitalization stocks having most of the weight.

Since markets are dynamic, it is important to recompute the portfolio groups at regular calendar intervals. Nevertheless, the resulting portfolio return series can be treated as having a time-constant covariance matrix. Portfolio group returns tend to have more stable covariance estimates than individual assets, and so this technique allows longer time-series samples to be used. This is especially important for fixed-income securities, since time decay of bond maturities otherwise invalidates long time-series samples for estimating covariance matrices.

Portfolio grouping has the drawback that it hides any source of return variation that is unrelated to the indexing variable. Suppose, for example, that stocks with similar dividend yields move in tandem, yet we base our portfolio grouping strictly on industries. If dividend yield and industry classification are independent, the portfolio covariance matrix will not reflect the return variability associated with dividend yield since all the industry portfolios will have roughly equal dividend yields.

By contrast to grouping, subsample analysis does not eliminate any sources of return variation. To apply this method, we randomly subdivide the cross-sectional sample into n/k subsamples with k assets each and estimate the $k \times k$ covariance matrix of each subsample separately. No indexing variable is required. Each subsample covariance matrix reflects all sources of return variation within its subset of assets. See Roll and Ross (1980) for a classic application. The difficulty with this method is that there is no general way to aggregate the findings or to draw inferences about the full cross-sectional covariance matrix. Thus, the popularity of the subsample methods has declined in recent years, as analysts have become more adept at choosing good portfolio grouping schemes or working with the full covariance matrix using large-n methods.

2.1.4 Increasing the Time-Series Sample

Many portfolio construction methods such as mean–variance optimization involve matrix inversion, which requires a nonsingular matrix. An $n \times n$ covariance matrix is symmetric and therefore has $n(n-1)/2$ parameters. Even with aggressive portfolio grouping, it is difficult to have a cross-sectional dimension n less than 10. To get a sufficiently detailed picture of return covariance that describes, for example, comovements of industries, we may need n in the range to 20–50. A 10×10 covariance matrix requires 45 estimated parameters and a 50×50 matrix requires 1,225.

Some asset return series extend back to the mid-nineteenth century (see, for example, Goetzmann et al. 2005). However, increasing T by lengthening the sample period is often impossible and in other cases may create problems due to changes in security market relationships over time. Parameter stability depends on a modest-duration time period to justify ignoring the slow accumulation of changes to the true covariances.

An alternative way to increase the time-series sample size is to increase the data frequency. There is a theoretical basis for this. Assuming time homogeneity of returns, the estimated covariance matrix for a given fixed-length sample period approaches the true matrix as the return measurement approaches zero. Consequently, for a given sample length, the higher the return frequency, the more accurate the covariance matrix estimate is.

Much of the classical research on portfolio risk is based on monthly returns. As analysts have become more adept at estimating variances and covariances using higher-frequency data, the balance has shifted toward weekly and daily returns, at least for the most liquid markets such as the U.S. and European equity and government bond markets.

2.1.5 Adjusting for Stale Prices and Other Sources of Autocorrelation

When using returns more frequent than monthly, it is critical to adjust for autocorrelation and cross-correlation. Standard, fixed-frequency returns are typically based on the last trade price of each asset in the interval. Since actual trades occur asynchronously, returns are measured over different, but overlapping, intervals. It is useful to define *shadow returns*, which are the hypothetical unobserved returns that would apply if true prices were observed continuously through time. Since measured returns tend to have positive correlations with each other, it is reasonable to assume that the shadow returns of securities are also positively correlated across securities. This cross-sectional positive correlation between shadow returns, together with the use of asynchronous trade prices to calculate measured returns, induces a positive cross-correlation between fixed-frequency measured returns. It also creates positive autocorrelation in measured returns to portfolios, since the portfolio constituent returns are recorded at overlapping periods during consecutive time intervals. These so-called stale-price effects are magnified for less liquid securities and for higher-frequency measurement intervals. See Campbell et al. (1997) for a careful empirical analysis of these effects for the case of U.S. equity returns.

Return covariance matrices can be adjusted for autocorrelation and cross-correlation with the Cohen et al. (1983) procedure, which we describe next. For any lag l, define the cross-covariance matrix of returns and l-period lagged returns

$$\hat{C}_{t,t-l} = \widehat{\operatorname{cov}}(\boldsymbol{x}_t, \boldsymbol{x}_{t-l}).$$

Note that $\hat{C}_{t,t-l}$ is the transpose of $\hat{C}_{t-l,t}$. In order to have a consistent covariance matrix estimate it is necessary to choose a lag length l that is sufficient to capture all the nonzero cross correlations between returns. The estimated covariance matrix is equal to the sum of the contemporaneous estimate and all the lagged estimates through lag l:

$$\hat{C} = \hat{C}_{t,t} + \hat{C}_{t,t-1} + \hat{C}_{t-1,t} + \cdots + \hat{C}_{t,t-l} + \hat{C}_{t-l,t}. \tag{2.2}$$

A value of l that is too high does not bias the estimator since the expected value of $\hat{C}_{t-l,t}$ is a zero matrix if all of the cross-correlations are zero for this lag length. However, it adds unnecessary sample noise to the estimate.

There are two interpretations of the covariance matrix estimate in formula (2.2). The original, from Cohen et al. (1983), is that this estimate captures the true contemporaneous covariance matrix adjusted for stale-price effects. In this interpretation, the recorded price of each security at time t reflects the most recent transaction for that security, which may have occurred before time t. Shadow returns, if observed contemporaneously, would have zero cross-correlation. In an alternative interpretation of formula (2.2), changes in true transaction price are cross-correlated, due for example to incomplete or delayed responses to information. Lo and MacKinlay (1990) show that the first interpretation is inadequate to explain the level of cross-correlation in observed prices. At least some of the cross-correlation is due to traded prices responding slowly to new information.

The two interpretations of the autocorrelation correction (2.2) impart different meanings to the resulting covariance matrix estimate. If autocorrelations are due only to stale prices, then the covariance matrix estimate is being corrected only for measurement errors in prices. The corrected covariance matrix is an unbiased estimate of the true one-period covariance matrix of shadow returns. If the autocorrelation comes from a slow response of traded prices to new information, then the covariance matrix (2.2) is not the one-period covariance matrix of true returns; it is the "long-run" covariance matrix that takes account of all short-run dynamic effects. More precisely, let l denote the longest nontrivial lag. Then (2.2) is an estimate of the covariance matrix of compound returns from 0 to l divided by l.

Covariance matrices involving assets traded on different exchanges, or on a common electronic exchange platform but in different time zones, suffer from the closely related problem of different daily closing times across countries and time zones. This is a special case of the stale-price problem and can be addressed using the same correction (2.2); see Martens and Poon (2001) for a careful examination of this problem in the context of world equity markets. Table 2.1 shows the contemporaneous and lagged correlations of a set of MSCI national equity index returns together with the corrected standard errors and correlations using (2.2). Note that the measured correlation between the U.S. and Japanese indices jumps from 0.082 using only contemporaneous returns to 0.3285 when we account for the lagged and led cross-correlations. This reflects the very strong cross-correlation between the lagged U.S. return and the Japanese return. Among these G7 markets, the Japanese market closes first each calendar day, so its daily return is strongly correlated with the previous day's return on the other markets (see panel (b) of the table). See Martens and Poon (2001) for a careful comparison of various

Table 2.1. The contemporaneous and lagged correlations of a set of MSCI National Equity Index returns (CAN, Canada; FR, France; GER, Germany; IT, Italy; JAP, Japan; Vol., Volatility).

(a) Uncorrected contemporaneous correlations and volatilities

	CAN	FR	GER	IT	JAP	U.K.	U.S.	Vol.
CAN	1	0.35	0.35	0.23	0.18	0.39	0.61	0.010
FR		1	0.66	0.48	0.27	0.59	0.29	0.013
GER			1	0.47	0.29	0.53	0.29	0.014
IT				1	0.21	0.4	0.18	0.014
JAP					1	0.28	0.08	0.014
U.K.						1	0.31	0.011
U.S.							1	0.010

(b) MSCI national indices of G7 countries, lagged correlations

	CAN	FR	GER	IT	JAP	U.K.	U.S.
CAN	0.1251	0.0544	0.0331	0.0367	−0.0182	0.0552	0.1765
FR	0.1487	0.0685	0.0506	0.0108	−0.0294	0.0464	0.2609
GER	0.1396	0.0439	0.0013	0.0163	−0.0341	0.0539	0.2721
IT	0.0989	0.0739	0.0493	0.1049	−0.0146	0.0626	0.1689
JAP	0.1844	0.1612	0.1459	0.0891	0.0593	0.1557	0.2652
U.K.	0.1465	0.0188	0.0224	0.0151	−0.0347	0.0527	0.2654
U.S.	−0.0039	−0.0038	−0.0115	0.0119	−0.0256	−0.0009	0.0165

(c) Contemporaneous correlations and volatilities corrected for autocorrelation and lagged cross-correlation

	CAN	FR	GER	IT	JAP	U.K.	U.S.	Vol.
CAN	1	0.4651	0.4613	0.3174	0.2981	0.5090	0.6993	0.0115
FR		1	0.6730	0.4765	0.3499	0.5490	0.5018	0.0134
GER			1	0.4899	0.3666	0.5544	0.5221	0.0132
IT				1	0.2547	0.4326	0.3408	0.0155
JAP					1	0.3583	0.3285	0.0142
U.K.						1	0.5136	0.0117
U.S.							1	0.0101

alternative corrections to contemporaneous-covariance matrices of daily equity index returns to account for these nonsynchronous price effects.

2.1.6 Diversification Curves

What proportion of the risk in the covariance matrix is diversifiable? One informative way to address this question is to impose a factor structure on returns and we will consider this in later chapters. However, it is possible to get a limited answer to the question without imposing a factor structure. In an influential paper, Solnik (1971) develops a graphical technique to describe the proportion of diversifiable and nondiversifiable risk in a covariance matrix. Beginning with a total universe of n assets, Solnik calculates the sample variance of a randomly selected, equally weighted portfolio of m assets, for $m = 1, \dots, n^* < n$. Solnik repeats the exercise for a large number of randomly selected portfolios and for each m takes an average over the variances of the randomly chosen portfolios. He calls the resulting graph a *diversification curve*. The curve is steeply downward sloping for small m and then flattens, showing that the risk-reduction benefits of diversification dampen after a relatively small number of assets are included. Solnik's empirical finding is part of the motivation for the popular *twenty-stock rule*: the claim that a randomly selected, equally weighted portfolio of twenty stocks has near-complete diversification of asset-specific risk. However, Campbell et al. (2001) use diversification curves to show that the same level of diversification achievable by a twenty-stock portfolio in the 1960s required fifty stocks during the 1990s, due to the large secular increase in asset-specific variance.

Solnik's estimator $S(m)$ is subject to simulation noise, which is the random variation due to the particular asset combinations chosen by the computer's random number generator. This can be eliminated with some additional analysis and high-speed computer processing. First, note that there are exactly $n!/m!(n-m)!$ equally weighted portfolios of m assets chosen from a universe of n assets. A straightforward but computation-intensive procedure that completely eliminates the simulation noise is to sample every portfolio exactly once. However, sampling the full set of combinations is unnecessarily time consuming. Each asset variance and paired asset covariance will be drawn equally often in the full set of combinations. Hence the exact value of the diversification curve for all $m \leqslant n$ can be derived from two sample values: the average of all variances and the average of all covariances,

$$S(m) = \frac{1}{m}\bar{\sigma}_i^2 + \left(1 - \frac{1}{m}\right)\bar{\sigma}_{ij}, \tag{2.3}$$

$$\bar{\sigma}_i^2 = \frac{1}{n}\sum_{i=1}^{n} \operatorname{var}(x_i),$$

$$\bar{\sigma}_{ij} = \frac{2}{n(n-1)}\sum_{j \neq i}^{n}\sum_{i=1}^{n} \operatorname{cov}(x_i, x_j). \tag{2.4}$$

Table 2.2. Average variances and covariances for U.S. equity returns for 1950–2005.

		Average variance	Average covariance
1950s	Total	0.0058	0.0011
	Active	0.0050	0.0003
1960s	Total	0.0140	0.0027
	Active	0.0122	0.0009
1970s	Total	0.0261	0.0045
	Active	0.0233	0.0018
1980s	Total	0.0343	0.0028
	Active	0.0322	0.0008
1990s	Total	0.0495	0.0025
	Active	0.0484	0.0013
2000s	Total	0.0524	0.0051
	Active	0.0501	0.0027

Even for large n it is easy to compute (2.4); for example, with $n = 5{,}000$ this requires taking the average of $n(n-1)/2 = 12{,}497{,}500$ covariances, which is a reasonably quick computation.

A reinterpretation of the diversification curve can be created by treating the cross section of assets as a sample from a random population of assets. Taking the expectation both over assets (treated as random draws from a cross-sectional population) and over returns, and letting $\tilde{r}_i$ denote the demeaned return of asset i, gives

$$\begin{aligned} S(m) &= E[\operatorname{var}(r_{w^{\mathrm{e}}})] \\ &= E\bigg[\bigg(\sum_{i=1}^{n} w_i^{\mathrm{e}} \tilde{r}_i\bigg)^2\bigg] \\ &= E\bigg[\sum_{i=1}^{n}\sum_{j=1}^{n} w_i^{\mathrm{e}} w_j^{\mathrm{e}} \tilde{r}_i \tilde{r}_j\bigg] \\ &= \frac{1}{m} \underset{i}{E}[\operatorname{var}(r_i)] + \bigg(1 - \frac{1}{m}\bigg) \underset{i \neq j}{E}[\operatorname{cov}(r_i, r_j)], \end{aligned} \tag{2.5}$$

where the expectation is over randomly chosen equally weighted portfolios $\boldsymbol{w}^{\mathrm{e}}$. Note that this formulation gives the same value as with (2.3), only the statistical interpretation changes, since now the cross-sectional averages are treated as estimates of underlying true population values. An advantage of this interpretation (2.5) is that it is easy to extend the diversification curve to take account of capitalization weighting. This can

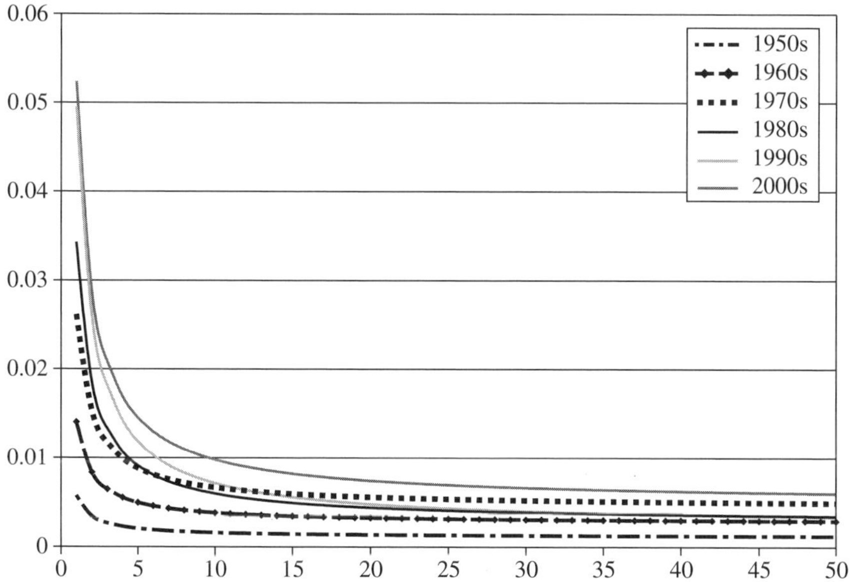

Figure 2.1. The diversification curves for monthly U.S. equity returns for the 1950s, the 1960s, the 1970s, the 1980s, the 1990s, and for the 2000–2005 period.

be done by using capitalization weights as probabilities in the definitions of $E[\text{var}(r_i)]$ and $E[\text{cov}(r_i, r_j)]$.

Note that it is straightforward to estimate diversification curves for active returns by subtracting a market benchmark. This does not change any of the analytics, just the definition of return.

Table 2.2 shows the intercepts, asymptotes, and their ratio for diversification curves using active and total returns for each of the 1950s, the 1960s, the 1970s, the 1980s, the 1990s, and the period 2000–2005. Figure 2.1 displays the diversification curves for total returns.

2.2 The Error-Maximization Problem

The mean–variance portfolio optimization problem described in chapter 1 is not implementable unless $\boldsymbol{\mu}$ and $\boldsymbol{C}$ are observed. Proceeding with a straightforward (if naive) practical implementation we can solve for an "optimal" portfolio using estimates $\hat{\boldsymbol{\mu}}$, $\hat{\boldsymbol{C}}$ as proxies for the unknown true values. The linear mean–variance problem with estimated proxies is

$$\begin{aligned}\max_{\boldsymbol{w}'1^n=1} \; & \boldsymbol{w}'\hat{\boldsymbol{\mu}} - \tfrac{1}{2}\lambda \boldsymbol{w}'\hat{\boldsymbol{C}}\boldsymbol{w} \\ &= \max_{\boldsymbol{w}'1^n=1} \boldsymbol{w}'\boldsymbol{\mu} - \tfrac{1}{2}\lambda \boldsymbol{w}'\boldsymbol{C}\boldsymbol{w} + [\boldsymbol{w}'(\hat{\boldsymbol{\mu}} - \boldsymbol{\mu}) - \lambda \boldsymbol{w}'(\hat{\boldsymbol{C}} - \boldsymbol{C})\boldsymbol{w}]. \quad (2.6)\end{aligned}$$

The presence of the bracketed term in (2.6) distorts the problem in two ways. Instead of trading off true expected return $\boldsymbol{w}'\boldsymbol{\mu}$ against true variance $\boldsymbol{w}'\boldsymbol{C}\boldsymbol{w}$, we are trading off expected return plus the unobserved estimation error $\boldsymbol{w}'(\hat{\boldsymbol{\mu}} - \boldsymbol{\mu})$ against true variance plus estimation error $\boldsymbol{w}'(\hat{\boldsymbol{C}} - \boldsymbol{C})\boldsymbol{w}$.

To give a sense of the magnitudes involved we utilize a simulation model of international equity returns—in particular a calibrated model of the dollar-based returns to the MSCI Barra equity market indices of the G7 countries. For the purposes of the simulation we set the true covariance matrix of these returns equal to the estimated covariance matrix from table 2.1, calibrated to a monthly return frequency. We set the expected returns on the indices so that the wealth-weighted portfolio is the true optimal portfolio. The average market weights of these seven indices, Canada, France, Germany, Italy, Japan, the United Kingdom, and the United States, are 2.3%, 4.8%, 4.8%, 2.9%, 17.0%, 10.7%, and 58.2%, respectively. We assume that the annual riskless return is 4% and that the representative investor has linear mean–variance preference with a risk-aversion parameter of 1.5. Recall from chapter 1 the equation giving the optimal portfolio choice for an investor with linear mean–variance preferences:

$$\boldsymbol{w} = \frac{1}{\lambda}\boldsymbol{C}^{-1}\boldsymbol{\mu}_x, \qquad w_0 = 1 - \boldsymbol{w}'\mathbf{1}^n, \tag{2.7}$$

where $\boldsymbol{w}$ is the n-vector of optimal weights in the risky assets and w_0 is the optimal position in the riskless asset. Solving (2.7) backward (setting the optimal portfolio equal to the market weights and inferring expected returns) gives annual expected returns equal to 6.78%, 6.94%, 6.99%, 6.46%, 6.89%, 6.70%, and 7.14% for the seven countries, respectively.[1] Note that, by construction, the optimal portfolio of the representative investor equals the capitalization-weighted portfolio, with zero net borrowing/lending.

Next we consider an investor who does not know the true means and covariances of the assets but instead must estimate them from sample data. We assume that the investor observes ten years of monthly returns. Since we know the true values we can simulate the estimation error in the investor's derived estimates. To do this, we draw 120-month samples repeatedly and illustrate the range of sample outcomes for the means, variances, and covariances (see table 2.3).

---

[1] Black and Litterman (1990) pioneered the method of using the assumed mean–variance optimal choice of the representative investor to infer expected returns from the market weights. They call the expected returns derived in this way the "implied market views."

Table 2.3. Simulation of estimation error in asset expected returns and covariances using 120-month samples.

(a) Expected returns

	True value	Average estimated value	Standard deviation of estimated value	25% fractile of estimated values	75% fractile of estimated values
Canada	0.0023	0.0023	0.0048	−0.0009	0.0056
France	0.0025	0.0024	0.0056	−0.0013	0.0061
Germany	0.0025	0.0025	0.0055	−0.0012	0.0062
Italy	0.0021	0.0021	0.0064	−0.0023	0.0065
Japan	0.0024	0.0024	0.0059	0.0016	0.0063
U.K.	0.0023	0.0022	0.0049	−0.0011	0.0055
U.S.	0.0026	0.0026	0.0042	0.0002	0.0055

(b) Return volatilities

	True value	Average estimated value	Standard deviation of estimated value	25% fractile of estimated values	75% fractile of estimated values
Canada	0.0527	0.0526	0.0034	0.0502	0.0549
France	0.0612	0.0611	0.0039	0.0584	0.0637
Germany	0.0604	0.0602	0.0039	0.0575	0.0629
Italy	0.0709	0.0707	0.0046	0.0675	0.0737
Japan	0.0649	0.0647	0.0042	0.0618	0.0675
U.K.	0.0535	0.0534	0.0035	0.0511	0.0557
U.S.	0.0462	0.0461	0.0030	0.0441	0.0481

(c) Return correlations with U.S. index

	True value	Average estimated value	Standard deviation of estimated value	25% fractile of estimated values	75% fractile of estimated values
Canada	0.6993	0.6979	0.0473	0.6677	0.7317
France	0.5018	0.5007	0.0687	0.4560	0.5490
Germany	0.5221	0.5205	0.0678	0.4770	0.5679
Italy	0.3408	0.3386	0.0812	0.2849	0.3949
Japan	0.3285	0.3277	0.0809	0.2754	0.3838
U.K.	0.5136	0.5120	0.0678	0.4685	0.5596

Note that there are two distinct sources of estimation error, in the mean vector and in the covariance matrix, and they both interact with the true values. To better analyze the error-maximization problem it is

Table 2.4. Simulation of error maximization in portfolio choice using estimated expected returns in place of true values.

	True optimal value	Average chosen value	Standard deviation of chosen value	25% fractile of chosen values	75% fractile of chosen values
Riskless asset weight	0.0000	0.0072	1.5115	−1.3323	1.0095
Canada	0.0230	0.0292	1.6744	−1.0992	1.1269
France	0.0480	0.0170	1.4541	−0.9562	1.0234
Germany	0.0480	0.0724	1.5052	−0.9434	1.0675
Italy	0.0290	0.0362	1.0219	−0.6622	0.7203
Japan	0.1700	0.1624	1.0492	−0.5375	0.8782
U.K.	0.1070	0.0963	1.5258	−0.9355	1.1282
U.S.	0.5815	0.5794	1.9610	−0.7600	1.9037
Portfolio variance		0.0275	0.0148	0.0167	0.0355
Portfolio expected return		0.0025	0.0037	0.0000	0.0050
Estimated portfolio expected return		0.0413	0.0223	0.0250	0.0532

useful to consider two special cases: first the case of estimation error only in the mean vector, and then the case of estimation error only in the covariance matrix.

2.2.1 The True Covariance Matrix and Estimated Means

Suppose that the covariance matrix is observed without error but that there is estimation error in the means. This special case has practical relevance in many situations. Strictly speaking, an error in mean return comes from an expected return model rather than a risk model, but it impinges on the risk-management problem in numerous ways and so we consider it in detail.

We return to our simulation experiment from the last subsection and let an investor improperly use the sample mean returns in place of true means, and find the "optimal" portfolio from (2.7). Here we assume that he knows the true covariance matrix exactly (we will drop this assumption in the next subsection). Table 2.4 simulates the estimation

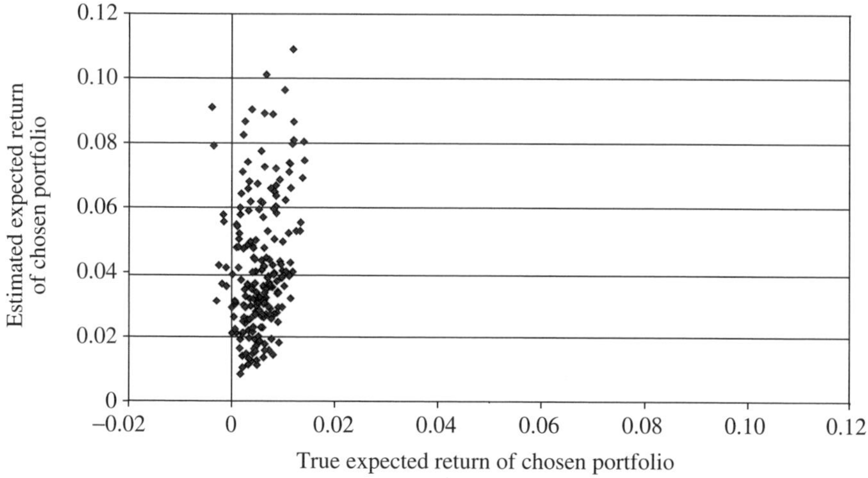

Figure 2.2. A comparison of the true and estimated expected returns of the chosen portfolios from the first 100 simulations (see table 2.5).

error in mean–variance optimal portfolios when the mean return vector is estimated and the covariance matrix is known. Note the large positive bias in the expected mean return of the optimal portfolio. This is the *error-maximization effect*: the investor overweights the assets whose mean return is overestimated, leading to a positive mean return forecast bias. This also leads to a bias toward a higher-risk portfolio: the manager has an exaggerated perception of the marginal increase in expected return per unit of risk and so chooses a portfolio that is riskier than optimal. See figure 2.2 for this induced overoptimism effect; it compares the true and (incorrectly) estimated expected returns of the chosen portfolios from the simulations.

2.2.2 Risk Minimization

A different simplification is to consider risk minimization with no control on expected return. This case has practical relevance when the model is used solely to control risk rather than to optimize a risk–return tradeoff. An application example is a basket trader who wants to hedge a package trade and knows that he can reasonably ignore expected return differences between individual assets, which are likely to be small over his time horizon. Similarly, a manager of an index-tracking fund trying to minimize risk relative to his benchmark may ignore purported mean return differences between individual assets. A portfolio manager whose active or total portfolio risk is too high might use optimization to find trades that lower risk. In all these cases the optimization does not make use of expected return so the only source of estimation error is in the covariance matrix.

Another reason for considering pure risk minimization is that the error in estimated mean return swamps covariance estimation error in most optimization problems. Pure risk minimization isolates the effect of covariance estimation error and thereby allows for a clearer analysis of it.

In table 2.5 we repeat the optimization exercise but this time we assume that the investor knows the true expected returns but uses a sample estimate of the covariance matrix. In this case, the "error-maximization problem" leads to an underestimation of portfolio variance, but the effect is not as dramatic as the overestimation of expected return in table 2.4.

Assuming that there is no riskless asset (otherwise the solution is trivial, $\boldsymbol{w} = \mathbf{0}_n$), the minimum-risk portfolio is defined by

$$\min_{\boldsymbol{w}'1^n=1} \boldsymbol{w}'\boldsymbol{C}\boldsymbol{w}. \tag{2.8}$$

Taking the derivative and rearranging gives

$$\boldsymbol{w} = \gamma \boldsymbol{C}^{-1}\mathbf{1}^n, \tag{2.9}$$

where γ is set so that $\boldsymbol{w}'\mathbf{1}^n = 1$. If $\hat{\boldsymbol{C}}$ is used in place of $\boldsymbol{C}$ in (2.8), the solution (2.9) is in terms of the inverse of the estimated covariance matrix as opposed to the actual estimated covariance matrix. Table 2.6 uses the same simulation data as is used in tables 2.3–2.5 and compares the minimum-variance portfolios using the true and estimated covariance matrices.

The effect of the estimation error in $\hat{\boldsymbol{C}}$ on the chosen minimum-risk portfolio depends on the estimation error, which is the difference $(\boldsymbol{C}^{-1} - (\hat{\boldsymbol{C}})^{-1})$. Therefore it is useful to understand the effect of matrix inversion on estimation error. A standard analysis, followed by Ledoit (1996), takes account of the quotient of the largest eigenvalue $\hat{\lambda}_1$ of the estimated covariance matrix to the smallest, $\hat{\lambda}_n$. The ratio $\hat{\phi} = \hat{\lambda}_1/\hat{\lambda}_n$ is called the *condition number* of the sample matrix and it provides an upper bound for the magnification of estimation error that occurs when the sample covariance matrix is inverted. When $\hat{\boldsymbol{C}}$ is ill-conditioned, which means that its condition number $\hat{\phi}$ is much greater than one, inversion is not recommended since it can tremendously amplify estimation error.

Table 2.5. Simulation of error maximization in portfolio weights using an estimated covariance matrix.

	True optimal value	Average chosen value	Standard deviation of chosen value	25% fractile of chosen values	75% fractile of chosen values
Riskless asset weight	0.0000	−0.0721	0.1471	−0.1626	0.0326
Canada	0.0230	0.0244	0.1145	−0.0501	0.0994
France	0.0480	0.0511	0.0985	−0.0141	0.1154
Germany	0.0480	0.0511	0.1040	−0.0161	0.1184
Italy	0.0290	0.0258	0.0709	−0.0211	0.0721
Japan	0.1700	0.1816	0.0724	0.1319	0.2273
U.K.	0.1070	0.1144	0.1063	0.0430	0.1832
U.S.	0.5815	0.6236	0.1472	0.5236	0.7139
Portfolio expected return		0.0026	0.0039	0.0000	0.0053
Portfolio variance		0.0021	0.0006	0.0017	0.0024
Estimated portfolio variance		0.0018	0.0002	0.0016	0.0019

Table 2.6. Simulation of error maximization in minimum-variance portfolio weights using an estimated covariance matrix.

	True optimal value	Average chosen value	Standard deviation of chosen value	25% fractile of chosen values	75% fractile of chosen values
Canada	0.1240	0.1237	0.1036	0.0542	0.1917
France	0.0241	0.0241	0.0895	−0.0363	0.0843
Germany	0.0097	0.0089	0.0943	−0.0534	0.0722
Italy	0.0913	0.0926	0.0640	0.0498	0.1348
Japan	0.1712	0.1711	0.0623	0.1283	0.2130
U.K.	0.1749	0.1741	0.0943	0.1103	0.2373
U.S.	0.4048	0.4055	0.1149	0.3284	0.4826
Portfolio variance		0.0017	0.0001	0.0017	0.0017
Estimated portfolio variance		0.0015	0.0002	0.0014	0.0017

2.3 Portfolio Choice as Decision Making under Uncertainty

In this section we first briefly discuss the difference between classical and Bayesian statistical methods and then describe some applications of Bayesian methods to portfolio risk management.

To implement a classical hypothesis test, the empirical researcher assumes a value for the parameter being estimated. Then he asks whether the sample estimate is unusually far from the assumed value in a precise statistical sense. If so, he rejects the hypothesis that the assumed value is correct: some other value must be the right one for the parameter. The alternative outcome is that the difference between the sample estimate and the assumed value is not too large so the hypothesis is not rejected. Logically, however, this does not mean that the assumed value is correct.

Classical hypothesis testing is not perfectly aligned with the needs of portfolio risk analysis. Portfolio risk managers are faced with the problem of making decisions under uncertainty. The model builder is not looking to reject his risk model in favor of an unknown alternative. Instead, he is estimating parameters, and the degree of uncertainty in those parameter estimates, for a model that he will use to make decisions.

One distinction between classical statistical methods and the needs of portfolio risk managers concerns parameter bias. In classical statistics, good parameter estimates are *unbiased*, which means that the expected value of the estimator is equal to the value of the parameter being estimated. For example, a sample estimate $\hat{\boldsymbol{C}}$ of a covariance matrix $\boldsymbol{C}$ is unbiased if

$$E[\hat{\boldsymbol{C}} \mid \boldsymbol{C}] = \boldsymbol{C}.$$

However, bias may not be relevant for the decision maker under uncertainty since he does not know $\boldsymbol{C}$. He may prefer an estimator that is biased for some particular values of $\boldsymbol{C}$ but has other desirable properties. Bayesian methods differ from classical methods in that they treat a parameter to be estimated as a random variable with a prior probability distribution. The prior distribution is updated using the sample data to produce a posterior distribution.

2.3.1 Bayesian Expected Returns

In this subsection we consider the case in which the covariance matrix $\boldsymbol{C}$ is known but the vector of expected returns $\boldsymbol{\mu}$ must be estimated. Bayesian methods provide an elegant and powerful solution to the error-maximization problem for expected returns. Alternative methods, if they have a firm theoretical foundation, typically use some features of the Bayesian framework.

The investor begins with a Bayesian prior distribution for the likely values of μ_i. This prior distribution is assumed to be normal with a known mean and variance, $\mu_i \sim N(\bar{\mu}_i, \sigma^2_{\mu_i})$. The investor also has independent sample information on μ_i, which takes the form of an unbiased estimate with normally distributed estimation error, $\hat{\mu}_i \sim N(\mu_i, \sigma^2_{\hat{\mu}_i})$. It is straightforward to mix the two normal distributions to obtain the posterior distribution for μ_i:

$$\mu_i \sim N(\hat{\hat{\mu}}_i, \sigma^{2*}_{\mu_i}),$$

$$\hat{\hat{\mu}}_i = (1 - \theta)\bar{\mu}_i + \theta\hat{\mu}_i, \tag{2.10}$$

$$\theta = \frac{\sigma^2_{\mu_i}}{\sigma^2_{\mu_i} + \sigma^2_{\hat{\mu}_i}}. \tag{2.11}$$

The shrinkage coefficient $0 < \theta < 1$ gives the proportional weight assigned to the prior and sample information; note that it depends in a simple way on their relative variances. In order to apply (2.11) we need values for $\bar{\mu}_i$ and $\sigma^2_{\mu_i}$ along with the estimation variance $\sigma^2_{\hat{\mu}_i}$.

Jorion (1985) suggests an empirical Bayesian approach, using the average of the estimated means as the proxy for the prior mean of all assets,

$$\bar{\mu}_i = \bar{\mu} = \frac{1}{n}\sum_{i=1}^{n} \hat{\mu}_i,$$

and the cross-sectional variability of the estimated means as a proxy for the prior variance,

$$\sigma^2_{\mu_i} = \sigma^2_{\mu} = \frac{1}{n}\sum_{i=1}^{n} (\hat{\mu}_i - \bar{\mu})^2.$$

Under general conditions, the estimated sample mean vector is an unbiased estimate of the true mean vector $\boldsymbol{\mu}$. However, this estimate is subject to significant estimation variance. Consider instead the empirical Bayesian estimate that Jorion uses as the prior mean vector: $\bar{\boldsymbol{\mu}} = \bar{\mu}\mathbf{1}^n$. This is a biased estimate since the high-mean assets will have estimates that are too low and the low-mean assets will have estimates that are too high. This type of bias is called specification error: the specification that we have imposed on the vector of means is too restrictive since it does not have enough estimable parameters. The advantage of this estimate is that it has low estimation variance because it is so structured: there is only one estimated parameter rather than n. The empirical Bayesian method finds the optimal combination of the unstructured, unbiased, high-variance estimate and the structured, biased, low-variance estimate.

The mixing or shrinkage coefficient θ in the convex combination (2.10) sets the relative weights on the prior and sample values.

The trade-off between specification error and estimation error is a pervasive issue in the development of portfolio risk models: we will confront this trade-off in many other contexts throughout the book. The trade-off is made clear using Bayesian methods, but it also applies in the classical framework.

Black and Litterman (1992) replace Jorion's empirical Bayesian approach with a theoretical approach to setting priors. They propose that the investor's prior mean for an asset is the expected return predicted by the CAPM. This gives $\bar{\mu}_i = r_0 + \beta_i(\mu_{\rm m} - r_0)$, where β_i is the CAPM beta of asset i. Black and Litterman retain formula (2.10) for the estimated mean, but they do not use formula (2.11). Instead, they rebrand θ as the "degree of confidence" that the investor has in his sample mean return estimates relative to the CAPM-based prior values. If the investor has no confidence in his sample estimates, then $\hat{\mu}_i = r_0 + \beta_i(\mu_{\rm m} - r_0)$ and the investor will choose to hold the market portfolio, which is the optimal portfolio given that the CAPM holds. The deviations of the investor's optimal portfolio from the market portfolio depends on his degree of confidence in his estimates.

Grinold (1994) restates the problem as a return forecasting problem as opposed to a mean return estimation problem. Define the abnormal return on asset i as its excess return x_i minus the excess return of the market portfolio $x_{\rm m}$. Grinold assumes that the security's abnormal return is normally distributed with mean zero:

$$x_i - \beta_i x_{\rm m} \sim N(0, \sigma_{x_i}^2).$$

The investor observes a valuation signal, or "estimated alpha," $\hat{\alpha}_i$, predicting the abnormal return on asset i; the signal is normally distributed and is positively correlated with abnormal return:

$$\hat{\alpha}_i \sim N(0, \sigma_{\hat{\alpha}_i}^2),$$
$$\operatorname{corr}(\hat{\alpha}_i, x_i - \beta_i x_{\rm m}) \geqslant 0.$$

Defining the information coefficient $\mathrm{IC}_i = \operatorname{corr}(\hat{\alpha}_i, x_i - \beta_i x_{\rm m})$ gives Grinold's version of the Bayesian shrinkage formula:

$$\hat{\alpha}_i^* = (\mathrm{IC}_i)(\sigma_{xi})\left(\frac{\hat{\alpha}_i}{\sigma_{\hat{\alpha}}}\right).$$

The Black–Litterman and Grinold approaches are very similar and with appropriate choices of parameter inputs they give identical predictions. The reader can verify that by setting the Black–Litterman degree of confidence θ equal to $(\mathrm{IC}_i)(\sigma_{xi}/\sigma_{\hat{\alpha}})$, the predictions of the two models are made identical. So they differ in how the analyst chooses to set the shrinkage coefficient θ, either by directly setting it in the Black–Litterman approach or deriving by it from the information coefficient, asset return volatility, and signal volatility in Grinold's formulation.

2.3.2 Bayesian Expected Returns and Equilibrium Models

The analysis in the last subsection is essentially normative, suggesting how portfolio managers ought to behave in making decisions under uncertainty. A related branch of the Bayesian portfolio management literature focuses on positive research questions: what type of investment behavior are we likely to observe from portfolio managers, given the types and levels of decision-making uncertainty that they face, and what are the implications of this predicted behavior for price equilibrium in securities markets? A major theme in this literature is the impact of results from empirical asset pricing research on investor behavior.

McCulloch and Rossi (1990, 1991) test whether a Bayesian investor, faced with the available sample return data, would assign a substantially higher probability to the arbitrage pricing theory (APT) or the CAPM as the correct model of expected return. (Arbitrage pricing theory will be discussed further in chapter 4.) McCulloch and Rossi also consider a utility-based metric: would an investor benefit in terms of expected utility from using the correct pricing model (APT or CAPM) versus the incorrect one? Or is the difference between the two models insubstantial in terms of its relevance for the individual investor's optimal portfolio? Pástor and Stambaugh (2000) is a similar study but compares two multi beta pricing models: the APT, based on statistical factors (which will be discussed in chapter 4), and an alternative model based on security characteristics (which will be discussed in chapter 6). Kandel and Stambaugh (1996) ask whether sample return data provides any useful information for a Bayesian investor making dynamic asset allocation between equities and cash, relying on standard predictive variables for stock market returns.

2.3.3 A Bayesian Covariance Matrix

This subsection considers the case in which we need only estimate the covariance matrix. This could be either because we seek to minimize risk with no constraints on expected return or because we treat the expected return vector as if it were measured without error. As above, the main idea of Bayesian estimation is to mix a biased, low-variance, structured estimate with an unbiased, high-variance, unstructured estimate.

Ledoit and Wolf (2003, 2004) suggest four specifications for the prior expectation of the covariance matrix: a diagonal matrix, the constant-correlation matrix, the diagonal-market model, and a strict factor model,

$$C^* = \mathrm{Diag}(\sigma_1^2, \sigma_2^2, \dots, \sigma_n^2), \tag{2.12}$$

$$C^* = \mathrm{Diag}(\sigma_1, \sigma_2, \dots, \sigma_n)\,\mathrm{corr}(\rho)\,\mathrm{Diag}(\sigma_1, \sigma_2, \dots, \sigma_n), \tag{2.13}$$

$$C^* = \sigma_{\mathrm{m}}^2 \beta\beta' + \mathrm{Diag}(\sigma_{\varepsilon_1}^2, \sigma_{\varepsilon_2}^2, \dots, \sigma_{\varepsilon_n}^2), \tag{2.14}$$

$$C^* = BC_fB' + \mathrm{Diag}(\sigma_{\varepsilon_1}^2, \sigma_{\varepsilon_2}^2, \dots, \sigma_{\varepsilon_n}^2), \tag{2.15}$$

where $\mathrm{corr}(\rho)$ is a correlation matrix whose entries are all equal to ρ.

These four specifications (2.12)–(2.15) differ in the amount of structure imparted to the covariance matrix, in the number of estimated parameters, and, consequently, in the amount of bias they introduce into the individual covariance estimates. The diagonal model (2.12) has only n parameters: it is very structured and very biased. The constant-correlation model (2.13) adds one additional parameter. The diagonal-market model (2.14) has $2n + 1$ parameters. It is a compelling choice in some contexts, providing a reasonable trade-off between specification error and estimation error. A weakness is that it misses the "extra-market" components of return. For example, if two assets are in the same industry, they tend to have higher covariance than is implied by their market betas. Or if two assets share other factor-related characteristics (such as a similar capitalization or price-to-earnings ratio), then (2.14) tends to underestimate their covariance.

The factor model (2.15) has up to $(nk + \frac{1}{2}k(k+1) + n)$ parameters to estimate, with the exact number depending on the type of factor model (see chapter 6 for more discussion). Correspondingly, this model imposes the least structure and the smallest specification error. It provides the greatest flexibility of these four models and the greatest number of parameters to estimate. The remaining estimation bias depends on the type of factor model used.

Ledoit and Wolf (2003) develop a Bayesian framework for mixing the prior distribution for C with the sample estimate $\hat{C}$. The underlying analysis is more complicated than for Bayesian expected returns because we cannot use independent normality of the prior and sample distributions to generate a normally distributed posterior. Ledoit and Wolf provide a large-sample approximation for the expected covariance matrix given a restricted prior of the form (2.12), (2.13), (2.14), or (2.15). As in the case of Bayesian means, the posterior covariance matrix takes the form of a convex combination of the prior covariance matrix and the sample estimate, with shrinkage coefficient θ:

$$\hat{C}^* = (1-\theta)\bar{C} + \theta\hat{C}.$$

Ledoit and Wolf show that their Bayesian estimated covariance matrix substantially outperforms a classically estimated, unstructured covariance matrix for the purpose of mean–variance portfolio optimization (both for total-return mean–variance optimization and for active-return optimization).

Briner and Connor (2008) compare the performance of unstructured, factor-structured, and Ledoit–Wolf-type Bayesian estimates of the covariance matrix of U.S. equities. Briner and Connor find that both the factor-structured and Bayesian methods substantially outperform the unstructured approach. However, the relative performance of the Bayesian and factor-structured estimates is less clear-cut in their tests.

2.3.4 Position Limits as Estimation Error Control

A popular ad hoc method for controlling error maximization is the use of position limits. Letting α denote a moderately small positive number that serves as an upper bound on individual asset weights, the problem becomes

$$\max_{\boldsymbol{w}} E[u(1 + \boldsymbol{w}'\boldsymbol{r})] \quad \text{such that } \boldsymbol{w}'\mathbf{1}^n = 1 \text{ and } 0 \leqslant w_i \leqslant \alpha. \tag{2.16}$$

Solutions to the mean–variance optimization problem with position limits have practical value since the limits are often imposed by institutional mandates. Note that the lower bound of zero for the weights enforces short-sale constraints as a type of position limit. Importantly, position limits prevent large estimation error in individual mean return from having an undue influence on the chosen portfolio. Jagannathan and Ma (2003) show that an analogous cap applies to covariance matrix estimation error. Large positions taken to hedge covariance risk may include large estimation error in asset covariances and position limits moderate the overreaction of portfolio weights to the error. Jagannathan and Ma show empirically that position limits are surprisingly effective in muting the error-maximization problem for covariance matrix estimation error. The performance of position limits in muting mean-return estimation error is less clear from their findings.

In addition, Jagannathan and Ma explain how to view position limits as a type of shrinkage estimator. Suppose that we have solved the variance-minimization problem subject to the position limits $0 \leqslant w_i \leqslant \alpha$ for each asset. For an asset at the upper or lower boundary, we can find the Lagrange multiplier for the binding constraint and measure its effect on the chosen portfolio. For an asset with optimal weight strictly between 0 and α, the constraint is nonbinding and the Lagrange multiplier equals zero. Let $\boldsymbol{\phi}$ denote the vector of Lagrange multipliers for the constraints

$0 \leqslant w_i$ and let $\boldsymbol{\zeta}$ denote the vector of Lagrange multipliers for the constraints $w_i \leqslant \alpha$. Combine the sample covariance matrix estimate with outer-product matrices of these Lagrangian multipliers and a unit vector:

$$\hat{C}^* = \hat{C} + (\boldsymbol{\phi}\mathbf{1}^{n\prime} + \mathbf{1}^n\boldsymbol{\phi}') - (\boldsymbol{\zeta}\mathbf{1}^{n\prime} + \mathbf{1}^n\boldsymbol{\zeta}'). \tag{2.17}$$

Jagannathan and Ma show that using $C = \hat{C}^*$ in the original unconstrained variance-minimization problem gives the same answer as using $C = \hat{C}$ in the position-constrained problem. Therefore, applying constraints is equivalent to covariance matrix shrinkage using formula (2.17).

Michaud (1998) proposes a resampling method that extends optimization with position limits. He suggests solving the portfolio optimization problem repeatedly, each time replacing the estimated sample mean vector and the sample covariance matrix with bootstrap resampled estimates. The optimal portfolio is recalculated for the new mean vector and covariance matrix input. The average over the bootstrap draws of the resampled optimal portfolios serves as the "resampled optimal" portfolio. Scherer (2002) shows that Michaud's resampling technique depends on the use of the position-limited version of the portfolio optimization problem (2.16). Applying Michaud's resampling to the portfolio optimization problem without position limits (2.6) adds no value since the only difference between the resampled optimum portfolio and the original optimum portfolio comes from simulation noise. So the theoretical justification for Michaud's technique relies on the assumption that position limits provide a good control for error maximization.

3
Industry and Country Risk

Estimating country and industry risk factors is of paramount importance in the design and implementation of portfolio risk models. Country and industry allocations are a major determinant of the riskiness of a global equity portfolio, particularly when risk is measured relative to a standard benchmark portfolio. The expansion of the corporate bond market to a wider range of countries has led to an emergent interest in country–industry factors in corporate bond returns.

Country–industry models typically have a very simple structure, with each security having a unit exposure to exactly one industry and one country. Despite their simplicity, these models are surprisingly powerful empirically.

Section 3.1 discusses industry–country factor component models. Section 3.2 examines the relative importance of industry and country factors in explaining equity returns. Section 3.3 discusses industry–country models of corporate bond returns.

3.1 Industry–Country Component Models

Table 3.1 shows the correlation matrix of monthly returns for ten developed market equity indices. Table 3.2 shows the correlation matrix of ten industry indices for U.S. equities. The correlations between U.S. industry portfolios are somewhat higher on average than those between the national indices. The examination of correlation matrices of country-based indices and industry-based indices is on its own insufficient to evaluate the magnitude of industry and country factors due to the problem of cross-effects. Two country indices could be highly correlated because a large proportion of their index components come from a particular industry; alternatively, two industry portfolios could be correlated because they both have large proportions of stocks from a particular country. To fully understand country and industry risk it is necessary to construct "pure" industry and country factors.

Table 3.1. Correlations of national equity index returns (AU, Australia; FR, France; GER, Germany; HK, Hong Kong; IT, Italy; JAP, Japan; SP, Spain; SW, Switzerland).

	AU	FR	GER	HK	IT	JAP	SP	SW	U.K.	U.S.
AU	1.00	0.42	0.37	0.46	0.30	0.32	0.39	0.44	0.51	0.49
FR	0.42	1.00	0.67	0.35	0.52	0.41	0.51	0.62	0.58	0.52
GER	0.39	0.66	1.00	0.38	0.48	0.35	0.51	0.70	0.51	0.50
HK	0.44	0.33	0.38	1.00	0.30	0.29	0.32	0.42	0.47	0.44
IT	0.31	0.53	0.49	0.29	1.00	0.35	0.49	0.41	0.42	0.35
JAP	0.30	0.38	0.34	0.26	0.36	1.00	0.38	0.43	0.38	0.31
SP	0.38	0.50	0.52	0.33	0.50	0.38	1.00	0.44	0.43	0.42
SW	0.47	0.61	0.71	0.43	0.45	0.39	0.49	1.00	0.61	0.52
U.K.	0.51	0.55	0.49	0.46	0.43	0.34	0.41	0.61	1.00	0.55
U.S.	0.53	0.57	0.55	0.44	0.38	0.38	0.47	0.62	0.61	1.00

The correlations above the diagonal use returns stated in U.S. dollars, whereas those below the diagonal are the correlations of returns in local currency units. Monthly data covering the period January 1975 to December 2007. Data courtesy of Ken French.

Table 3.2. Correlations of U.S. industry portfolio returns (NDs, nondurables; Dur., durables; Man., manufacturing; En., energy; Tel., telecom; Util., utilities).

	NDs	Dur.	Man.	En.	HiTec	Tel.	Shops	Health	Util.	Other
NDs	1.00	0.42	0.39	0.44	0.31	0.3	0.38	0.47	0.51	0.53
Dur.		1.00	0.66	0.33	0.53	0.38	0.5	0.61	0.55	0.57
Man.			1.00	0.38	0.49	0.34	0.52	0.71	0.49	0.55
En.				1.00	0.29	0.26	0.33	0.43	0.46	0.44
HiTec					1.00	0.36	0.5	0.45	0.43	0.38
Tel.						1.00	0.38	0.39	0.34	0.38
Shops							1.00	0.49	0.41	0.47
Health								1.00	0.61	0.62
Util.									1.00	0.61
Other										1.00

Monthly data covering the period January 1975 to December 2007. Data courtesy of Ken French. See http://mba.tuck.dartmouth.edu/pages/faculty/ken.french/data_library.html for details of industry portfolio construction.

We consider the case in which the only common factors in returns are industry and country factors. A pure industry factor is the return to an industry corrected for the influence of differing country weightings across industries. Analogously, a pure country factor is the return to a country index corrected for the effect of its particular industry weightings.

Roll (1992b) demonstrates that, at least in theory, pure industry and country factors can be inferred from country index returns given that the analyst also has industry weightings data. Roll works with a data set of twenty-four country index daily returns and a set of seven industry weights for each country, describing the proportion of the index in each of the industries. Roll implements cross-sectional regression of a day's twenty-four-element vector of country index returns on the set of seven industry weights for each country. The coefficients from this regression can be interpreted as the global industry returns for the industry for that day. Repeating the cross-sectional regression day by day gives a time series of implied global industry returns. The country-specific time series of residuals from the cross-sectional regressions are the associated country-only returns. These residuals capture the part of the country index return that is unrelated to industry decomposition. Aggregating and evaluating the results from these cross-sectional regressions, Roll argues that industry factors are very strong in explaining the cross-sectional dispersion of country index returns. Roll notes that this estimation methodology is indirect, necessitated by data limitations in the absence of firm-by-firm returns in all the national markets.

Econometric advances often follow from data improvements. The increasing size and easier accessibility of global asset return databases, containing individual security returns linked with industry and country identifiers, have dramatically changed empirical work on industry–country risk. They have also altered the conventional empirical findings. Whereas Roll posited a dominant role for industry effects, subsequent studies, relying on more extensive asset-by-asset databases, have typically found stronger country-related effects and weaker industry effects.

We will assume that we have a panel data set of individual asset returns in which each individual asset is assigned to one industry and one country. We will start with the case of an industry-only model:

$$x_{it} = \sum_{j-1}^{k} \delta_{ij} f_{jt} + \varepsilon_{it}, \tag{3.1}$$

where $\delta_{ij} = 1$ if security i is in industry j and $\delta_{ij} = 0$ otherwise. The ε_{it}, $t = 1, T$, are the asset-specific returns with $E[\boldsymbol{\varepsilon} \mid \boldsymbol{f}] = \mathbf{0}_n$. For simplicity we assume that there are no firm-specific intercepts in (3.1) so that the expected returns of securities only depend on their industry exposures (this will be generalized later). In vector–matrix notation we will write (3.1) as $\boldsymbol{x}_t = \boldsymbol{B}\boldsymbol{f}_t + \boldsymbol{\varepsilon}_t$, where $\boldsymbol{B}$ is the $n \times k$ matrix of industry dummies.

For interpretability and to embed the industry model into more complex models it is often useful to isolate the "market factor" by rearranging the k factor returns into one market factor plus k extra-market industry factors:

$$x_{it} = f_{0t} + \sum_{j=1}^{k} \delta_{ij} f_{jt}^{*} + \varepsilon_{it}, \tag{3.2}$$

$$\text{subject to} \sum_{j=1}^{k} w_j f_{jt}^{*} = 0 \text{ for every } t. \tag{3.3}$$

The adding-up constraint (3.3) is necessary to avoid the trap of having a full set of dummy variables plus a cross-sectional constant in the regression model, giving rise to a singularity. In most contexts (such as least-squares estimation), (3.1) and (3.2) are effectively identical and choosing between them is merely a question of interpretability. By far the strongest commonality in stock returns is their tendency to move together as a group, so the market factor f_{0t} will be the dominant factor if it is included. Although statistically innocuous, including the market factor f_{0t} can have an enormous effect on interpretation. Suppose, for example, that we are measuring the ability of industry factors to explain returns. If we use (3.1), then the industry factors will prove very powerful. If we use (3.2), then the "extra-market" industry factors will be much less impressive.

For the adding-up constraint (3.3) some analysts use equal weighting $w_j = 1/k$, others use weighting by the number of firms in each industry $w_j = n_j/n$, where n_j is the number of firms in industry j, and others use capitalization weighting, where w_j is the proportion of total market value in industry j. The weighting choice affects the interpretation of the market factor and through this the interpretation of the extra-market industry factors.

Including country factors just requires a second set of dummy variables and a second adding-up constraint to avoid the dummy variable trap:

$$\left.\begin{aligned} x_{it} &= f_{0t} + \sum_{j=1}^{k_{\mathrm{I}}} \delta_{ij}^{\mathrm{I}} f_{jt}^{\mathrm{I}} + \sum_{j=1}^{k_{\mathrm{C}}} \delta_{ij}^{\mathrm{C}} f_{jt}^{\mathrm{C}} + \varepsilon_{it}, \\ \text{subject to} &\sum_{j=1}^{k_{\mathrm{I}}} w_j^{\mathrm{I}} f_{jt}^{\mathrm{I}} = 0 \text{ and } \sum_{j=1}^{k_{\mathrm{C}}} w_j^{\mathrm{C}} f_{jt}^{\mathrm{C}} = 0 \text{ for every } t. \end{aligned}\right\} \tag{3.4}$$

Here the intercept-related factor f_{0t} represents the global market factor (the empirically strong tendency for stocks worldwide to move together), the f_{jt}^{I} are the global industry factors, and the f_{jt}^{C} are the "pure" country factors (that is, the country factors adjusted for the influence of differing industrial weightings across nations). With this improved asset-by-asset data, there is no need for Roll's indirect method to find country and industry influences from industrial weights and the returns on country index portfolios. We still have that the returns on the country and industry index portfolios will be weighted combinations of the appropriate pure country and industry factors in (3.4) but we do not need to use indirect methods to infer them. We can directly estimate the pure factor returns using (3.4) applied to individual returns data. If wanted, we can confirm the accuracy of these estimates by comparing the index portfolio returns with weighted combinations of the estimated pure factor returns.

3.1.1 The Random Coefficients Perspective on Industry–Country Component Models

The random coefficient model is a very useful econometric framework for industry–country component models. In this model the factor returns $\boldsymbol{f}_t$ are treated as random variables through time, while from an estimation perspective they are treated as coefficients in a linear cross-sectional model of returns. The random coefficient model allows us to switch consistently between the risk problem (country and industry factors as random variables) and the estimation problem (factor returns as estimable parameters). Also, the random coefficient model links industry–country component models to characteristic-based factor models. This is important since characteristic-based factors can be incorporated into the industry country model to create a full-fledged portfolio risk model.

We will work with (3.1) in this subsection for simplicity, but the same methodology applies to the other industry–country component models. As we will see below, in some contexts nothing is lost by treating a component model such as (3.1) as a series of seemingly unrelated cross-sectional regression models with fixed coefficients. This is best understood as a conditioned version of the random coefficient model, where we have conditioned on a particular realization of the factor returns. At a later stage, when we wish to use the estimated factor returns to build a risk model, we will need to remove the conditioning on a particular realization of $\boldsymbol{f}_t$.

Writing (3.1) as a random coefficient model, we add distributional assumptions for the random variables (rather than fixed coefficients) $\boldsymbol{f}_t$, treating them as a k vector of random variables i.i.d. through time:

$$\boldsymbol{f}_t \sim N(\boldsymbol{\pi}_f, \boldsymbol{C}_f).$$

In the random coefficient application for standard panel data problems the main focus is on estimating the means of the random coefficients; in our case, these correspond to the industry factor risk premia, $\boldsymbol{\pi}_f$. For risk model estimation, the focus is somewhat different. In building a risk model the most important estimable parameter set is the factor covariance matrix $\boldsymbol{C}_f$. The econometrician may choose to ignore the means of the random coefficients or set them to zero.

The random coefficient model can be transformed into a seemingly unrelated regression model by conditioning on the realized factor returns, f_{jt}, $j = 1, k$, $t = 1, T$. If we condition on the realized values, thereby treating them as fixed coefficients, then (3.1) becomes a set of seemingly unrelated cross-sectional regression models with no cross-equation restrictions. Period-by-period generalized least-squares estimation of each of these cross-sectional regressions gives best linear unbiased estimation of the conditionally fixed values of $\boldsymbol{f}_t$:

$$\hat{\boldsymbol{f}}_t = (\boldsymbol{B}'\boldsymbol{C}_\varepsilon^{-1}\boldsymbol{B})^{-1}\boldsymbol{B}'\boldsymbol{C}_\varepsilon^{-1}\boldsymbol{x}_t. \tag{3.5}$$

In many applications, consistent but inefficient ordinary least squares is used instead, replacing $\boldsymbol{C}_\varepsilon^{-1}$ in (3.5) with the identity matrix I; we will discuss this and various other regression weighting choices in section 3.1.4.

3.1.2 Estimated Covariance Matrices

Having estimated $\hat{\boldsymbol{f}}_t$, $t = 1, T$, from (3.5), we want to derive an estimate of the factor covariance matrix, $\boldsymbol{C}_f$. Here, the random coefficients perspective becomes crucial to the correct definition of the covariance matrix.

There are three covariance matrices associated with $\hat{\boldsymbol{f}}$. First, at each t there is the covariance matrix of the least-squares estimates, $E_t[(\hat{\boldsymbol{f}}_t - \boldsymbol{f}_t)(\hat{\boldsymbol{f}}_t - \boldsymbol{f}_t)' \mid \boldsymbol{f}_t]$; second, there is the unconditional covariance matrix of the estimated factors, $E_0[\hat{\boldsymbol{f}}_t\hat{\boldsymbol{f}}_t']$, where the expectation is taken over t and is not conditioned on the random factor realizations, $\boldsymbol{f}_t$; and, third, there is the covariance matrix of the random factor returns, $\boldsymbol{C}_f$. The first and second can be estimated simply, and the third of these, which is what we need for the risk model, equals the second minus the first.

To estimate the covariance matrix $E_t[(\hat{\boldsymbol{f}}_t - \boldsymbol{f}_t)(\hat{\boldsymbol{f}}_t - \boldsymbol{f}_t)' \mid \boldsymbol{f}_t]$, where we are conditioning on the realized factors, we just invoke the standard formula for the covariance matrix of a generalized least-squares regression with nonrandom coefficients:

$$E_t[(\hat{\boldsymbol{f}}_t - \boldsymbol{f}_t)(\hat{\boldsymbol{f}}_t - \boldsymbol{f}_t)' \mid \boldsymbol{f}_t] = (\boldsymbol{B}'\boldsymbol{C}_\varepsilon^{-1}\boldsymbol{B})^{-1}. \tag{3.6}$$

Note that this covariance matrix is constant over t, if the panel of assets, their industry exposures, and the asset-specific covariance matrix do not change through time.

An obvious estimate for the covariance matrix of estimated factor returns is the sample moment matrix of their values over the T realizations. Under general conditions this provides a T-consistent estimate of the true unconditional covariance matrix of $\hat{\boldsymbol{f}}_t$:

$$\frac{1}{T}\sum_{t=1}^{T}\hat{\boldsymbol{f}}_t\hat{\boldsymbol{f}}_t' \overset{\text{pr},T}{\approx} E[\hat{\boldsymbol{f}}\hat{\boldsymbol{f}}']. \tag{3.7}$$

For notational simplicity we have imposed the condition $\boldsymbol{\pi}_f = \mathbf{0}_k$, otherwise the sample means must be subtracted in (3.7).

Next we derive the true factor covariance matrix, which equals the difference between the previous two covariance matrices, using the standard result from generalized least squares that $(\hat{\boldsymbol{f}}_t - \boldsymbol{f}_t)$ is orthogonal to $\boldsymbol{f}_t$:

$$\boldsymbol{C}_f = E[\hat{\boldsymbol{f}}_t\hat{\boldsymbol{f}}_t'] - E[(\hat{\boldsymbol{f}}_t - \boldsymbol{f}_t)(\hat{\boldsymbol{f}}_t - \boldsymbol{f}_t)' \mid \boldsymbol{f}_t]. \tag{3.8}$$

Note from (3.8) that the true value $\boldsymbol{C}_f$ equals the true value $E[\hat{\boldsymbol{f}}_t\hat{\boldsymbol{f}}_t']$ minus the true value $E[(\hat{\boldsymbol{f}}_t - \boldsymbol{f}_t)(\hat{\boldsymbol{f}}_t - \boldsymbol{f}_t)' \mid \boldsymbol{f}_t]$. Since we have estimates for both of the covariance matrices on the right-hand side we can estimate $\boldsymbol{C}_f$ as the difference between the estimated values of $E[\hat{\boldsymbol{f}}_t\hat{\boldsymbol{f}}_t']$ and $E[(\hat{\boldsymbol{f}}_t - \boldsymbol{f}_t)(\hat{\boldsymbol{f}}_t - \boldsymbol{f}_t)' \mid \boldsymbol{f}_t]$:

$$\hat{\boldsymbol{C}}_f = \frac{1}{T}\left(\sum_{t=1}^{T}\hat{\boldsymbol{f}}_t\hat{\boldsymbol{f}}_t' - (\boldsymbol{B}'\boldsymbol{C}_\varepsilon^{-1}\boldsymbol{B})^{-1}\right).$$

This estimate has the potential drawback that there is no guarantee that $\hat{\boldsymbol{C}}_f$ will be positive definite; Baltagi (1995) suggests using

$$\hat{\boldsymbol{C}}_f = \frac{1}{T}\sum_{t=1}^{T}\hat{\boldsymbol{f}}_t\hat{\boldsymbol{f}}_t'$$

instead, which is always positive definite.

Note that the limit of (3.6) is a zero matrix independent of T and that the limit in (3.7) is independent of n. From this we have a consistency result taking both n and T to infinity without a restriction on their relative speed of increase:

$$\frac{1}{T}\left(\sum_{t=1}^{T}\hat{\boldsymbol{f}}_t\hat{\boldsymbol{f}}_t' - (\boldsymbol{B}'\boldsymbol{C}_\varepsilon^{-1}\boldsymbol{B})^{-1}\right) \overset{\text{pr},n,T}{\approx} \boldsymbol{C}_f. \tag{3.9}$$

For this consistency result it is not strictly necessary to subtract $(1/T)(\boldsymbol{B}'\boldsymbol{C}_\varepsilon^{-1}\boldsymbol{B})^{-1}$ since this term equals zero in the limit $T \to \infty$.

3.1.3 Testing for the Size and Significance of Industry and Country Factors

The random coefficients perspective is important when testing whether a particular factor or group of factors has an economically or statistically significant effect. Consider the series of cross-sectional regressions to estimate industry factor returns (3.1) for $t = 1, T$. To test the significance of a particular industry factor in a particular cross-sectional regression at date t (that is, testing whether one of the cross-sectional regression coefficients equals zero) we can use the standard regression Student's t-test. If we wish to test for the significance of a set of factors at a particular date t, then the standard F-test can be applied.

Neither of these tests used alone provides much value in our context, since they apply only to a single date t and are conditional upon the time-t returns of the factors. The finding that a particular factor return is not significantly different from zero in one particular month is not that informative. We expect the true factor returns to vary widely through time; often they will have true values near zero by chance. We need a test that can be applied across the full time series of estimated factor returns so we can test whether the factor returns are *always* close to zero, not just in a particular month.

The random coefficients literature focuses chiefly on testing whether the *mean* of a random coefficient differs from zero (see Hsiao and Pesaran (2004) for a review of this literature). These tests are not very relevant to the context of industry–country models. Since these factors have high volatility relative to their means it could take a hundred years or more of data to reliably test whether the mean returns differ from zero. We want to test whether the random realizations are often significantly different from zero, by aggregating the one-month significance tests. The contribution of country and industry factors to cross-sectional volatility, not their expected returns, is the key issue in the context of a portfolio risk model.

There are a variety of ways to aggregate the one-month t-statistics and F-statistics across months. A robust method is to count the percentage of significant t-statistics for each individual factor return. Suppose that we use a 5% significance level. Then under the null hypothesis that the true factor return equals zero every period, the percentage of significant t-statistics over T periods has a binomial distribution. This has the advantage that one or two extremely large t-statistics will not distort the overall finding.

An alternative metric for the importance of particular industry and/ or country factors comes directly from their estimated covariance matrix $\hat{C}_f$. Since the factor exposures are zero/one dummies, the factor return variances provide a direct measure of the importance of a factor in explaining returns. In this case it is important to subtract the covariance matrix of estimation error, as in (3.9), otherwise estimation error will increase rather than decrease the perceived importance of the factor returns.

3.1.4 Regression Weighting Schemes

In the cross-sectional regression used to estimate the factor returns (3.5) we treated C_ε as known. If C_ε is not known, it can be replaced with a consistent estimate. Typically, it is assumed that C_ε is diagonal, although this is not fully in keeping with the empirical evidence. Given diagonality, one procedure is first to set C_ε^0 equal to I, then to find the panel of estimated residual returns from the full set of ordinary least-squares cross-sectional regressions, then to calculate time-series standard errors from these residuals, and then to repeat the regression estimation using these for the diagonal values in C_ε: $C_{\varepsilon ii}^1 = \hat{\sigma}_i^2$. If necessary, the iteration can be repeated, using the new residuals to calculate $C_{\varepsilon ii}^2$ and then rerunning the cross-sectional regressions. This is a version of feasible weighted least squares.

Although feasible weighted least squares has superficial appeal, it may or may not be superior to ordinary least squares in this environment. The potential problem with it comes from the estimation errors in $\hat{\sigma}_i^2$ and their effects on estimation quality given the typical dimensions of this panel data problem (very large n, moderately large T).

An alternative weighting scheme is root-capitalization-weighted regression. This can be treated as a weighted least-squares scheme by assuming that true asset-specific variances are proportional to a negative power of securities' market capitalization:

$$C_{\varepsilon ii} = a(\mathrm{MV}_i)^{-\alpha}, \tag{3.10}$$

where MV_i denotes the market value of security i at the beginning of the estimation period and a is a constant that drops out of the regression weighting. The exponent α can be estimated by computing the first-iteration ordinary least squares based variance estimates as above and writing (3.10) as a log-linear cross-sectional regression problem:

$$\log(\hat{\sigma}_{\varepsilon i}^2) = \log(a) - \alpha\log(\mathrm{MV}_i) + u_i.$$

This capitalization-based weighting scheme (3.10) captures in a simple way the empirical property that large firms tend to have lower asset-specific variances than small firms. It also has another desirable property: it puts greatly increased regression weight on the high-capitalization securities. From an economic perspective, these are the securities that matter most in analyzing the risk factors in the capital market. Some analysts have found that low-capitalization securities have different industry factor returns from high-capitalization securities. Obviously, if this is true then the simple factor model with one set of industry factors is not strictly true, and it would be better, if it were feasible, to include separate industry factors for the high-capitalization and low-capitalization sectors. If this is not feasible, then using (3.10) is a second-best method which puts higher weight on the factors associated with the (much more economically important) high-capitalization stocks.

So far we have assumed that the weighting matrix in (3.5) is the true asset-specific covariance matrix or a consistent estimate thereof. This assumption is not necessary and is often inappropriate. Suppose, for example, that we have chosen to use capitalization weights in the regression, even though we find that these are not close proxies for asset-specific variances. The resulting cross-sectional regression estimates are no longer efficient, but they remain consistent. It is only necessary to correct the estimated covariance matrix. So we can replace the cross-sectional regression formula (3.5) with

$$\hat{\boldsymbol{f}}_t = (\boldsymbol{B}'\boldsymbol{V}\boldsymbol{B})^{-1}\boldsymbol{B}'\boldsymbol{V}\boldsymbol{x}_t, \tag{3.11}$$

and the factor estimates are still n-consistent as long as

$$(\boldsymbol{B}'\boldsymbol{V}\boldsymbol{B})^{-1} \overset{n}{\approx} \boldsymbol{0}^{k\times k}. \tag{3.12}$$

However, the covariance matrix of the estimated factors must be adjusted. Instead of (3.6) the formula becomes a bit messy:

$$E_t[(\hat{\boldsymbol{f}}_t - \boldsymbol{f}_t)(\hat{\boldsymbol{f}}_t - \boldsymbol{f}_t)' \mid \boldsymbol{f}_t] = (\boldsymbol{B}'\boldsymbol{V}\boldsymbol{B})^{-1}\boldsymbol{B}'\boldsymbol{V}\boldsymbol{C}_\varepsilon\boldsymbol{V}\boldsymbol{B}(\boldsymbol{B}'\boldsymbol{V}\boldsymbol{B})^{-1}.$$

The unknown value for $\boldsymbol{C}_\varepsilon$ in the middle of this formula can be proxied using the White and Domowitz (1984) technique.

3.1.5 Interpreting Estimated Factor Returns as Portfolio Returns

Because all the independent variables in industry–country component models are zero–one dummies, the estimated coefficients will be simple weighted combinations of the underlying asset returns. We can interpret them as the returns to weighted index portfolios, as shown next.

First we start with the industry-only model without a market factor (3.1). Using the partitioning properties of the matrix of dummy variables, the weighted least-squares estimate of each factor return is just the weighted average return of the assets within that industry:

$$\left.\begin{aligned} \hat{f}_{jt} &= \frac{1}{\mathrm{Sum}_j} \sum_{i=1}^{n} \delta_{ij} V_{ii} x_{it}, \\ \mathrm{Sum}_j &= \sum_{i=1}^{n} \delta_{ij} V_{ii}. \end{aligned}\right\} \quad (3.13)$$

Adding the market factor and the constraint $\sum_{j=1}^{k} \phi_j f_{jt}^* = 0$ rearranges the factor returns to include a market-wide factor return without affecting the fit of the model. It is simplest if the weighting scheme is consistent with the regression weighting: that is, if $\phi_j = \mathrm{Sum}_j$. Then it follows that

$$\hat{f}_{0t} = \frac{1}{\mathrm{Sum}} \sum_{j=1}^{k} \mathrm{Sum}_j \hat{f}_{jt} = \frac{1}{\mathrm{Sum}} \sum_{i=1}^{n} V_{ii} x_i.$$

Consider the case $V = I$. The market factor return is then simply the return to the equally weighted portfolio. Each industry factor return is simply the return to an equally weighted portfolio of stocks in the industry, minus the market factor return. In fact, we do not really need to use least squares to find the estimates in this case, we can just find the returns to the appropriate weighted-index portfolios.

Next consider the case of the country–industry model with a market factor. Again the trick is to use partitioned regression to simplify the analysis. First take the regression-estimated country factor returns and subtract the appropriate country factor return from each asset return. This gives the same industry factor model as above but with returns minus country factor returns as the dependent variable. The industry factor returns are the weighted averages of the "market-adjusted country-adjusted" asset returns. The same steps can be applied to describe the country factor returns as weighted averages of the "market-adjusted industry-adjusted" asset returns.

3.1.6 Capitalization Weighting in Concentrated Markets

Given the simple interpretation of factor returns as weighted-index returns (3.13), the analyst might be tempted to use simple capitalization weighting in regression (3.11). The market factor return estimate is then the value-weighted market portfolio return, and the other factor return estimates are simple linear combinations of value-weighted country and industry indices. Note, however, that the least-squares consistency condition (3.12) might not prove innocuous in this case. This condition requires that the chosen weights are spread in small proportions not only across the full set of assets but also in small *relative* proportions within each country and industry grouping. In many markets, the heavy concentration of market capitalization in the top few firms, both across the whole equity market and within industrial sectors, makes capitalization weighting a problematic choice.

Curds (2004) shows that, in the U.K. market, even weighting by the square root of capitalization ($\alpha = \frac{1}{2}$ in (3.10)) creates difficulties due to size concentration. Recall that the weighted sum of regression residuals equals zero:

$$\frac{1}{\text{Sum}} \sum_{i=1}^{n} V_{ii}\hat{\varepsilon}_{it} = 0.$$

This induces a usually mild negative correlation between the estimated residuals, since the final residual equals minus the weighted sum of the preceding ones. We have the additional property that weighted sums of residuals within each industry and within each country sum to zero:

$$\frac{1}{\text{Sum}_j} \sum_{i=1}^{n} V_{ii}\delta_{ij}\hat{\varepsilon}_{it} = 0.$$

Note that this induces negative autocorrelation between the residuals *within* each industry and country. If the weights $V_{ii}/\,\text{Sum}_j$ are substantial for one or two firms within an industry, then the factor returns will be estimated with considerable error, and the estimated asset-specific returns of the large-capitalization assets will have large negative correlations. Suppose, for example, that a particular industry has only two firms and each has $V_{ii}/\,\text{Sum}_j = \frac{1}{2}$. The estimated industry return will be the average of these two asset returns and the estimated asset-specific returns will be the difference of each return from this average.

3.1.7 Multiple Industry and Country Weightings

The model above assumes that each firm operates in only one industry and one country—not a great assumption in a world full of multinational conglomerates! Econometrically, it is trivial to extend the model to allow multiple industry and country weightings. Instead of a dummy variable for industry and country identifiers, each asset has a set of nonnegative industry weights summing to one, and likewise for country weights. The weight proportions capture the linear exposures of the asset to the pure industry and country factors. The econometric analysis from previous sections carries through virtually unchanged after this minor enhancement. But this assumes that we know the weights!

There are two approaches to setting multiple industry and country weightings. One is to set weights based on accounting data, giving the split of sales, profits, or corporate balance sheet assets across industries and/or countries. The second approach is to estimate the exposures using time-series regressions of each asset return on industry and country factors. This requires a preliminary step using the unit-dummy model to estimate initial industry and country factors. The multiple exposures for asset i are then estimated via time-series regression:

$$x_{it} = \hat{\beta}_i f_{0t} + \sum_{j \in S_{\mathrm{I}i}} \hat{\delta}^{\mathrm{I}}_{ij} f^{\mathrm{I}}_{jt} + \sum_{j \in S_{\mathrm{C}i}} \hat{\delta}^{\mathrm{C}}_{ij} f^{\mathrm{C}}_{jt} + \hat{\varepsilon}_{it}, \quad \text{such that}$$

$$\sum_{j \in S_{\mathrm{I}i}} \hat{\delta}^{\mathrm{I}}_{ij} = 1, \quad \sum_{j \in S_{\mathrm{C}i}} \hat{\delta}^{\mathrm{C}}_{ij} = 1, \quad \hat{\delta}^{\mathrm{I}}_{ij} \geqslant 0, \quad \hat{\delta}^{\mathrm{C}}_{ij} \geqslant 0.$$

Each asset must be allocated a small set of potential nonzero industry and country exposures, $S_{\mathrm{I}i}$ and $S_{\mathrm{C}i}$. For generality we have allowed the market factor exposures to vary as well, adding the estimable parameter $\hat{\beta}_i$. The number of free parameters to include depends upon the specification error/estimation error trade-off for the particular context in which the model will be used. As a general rule, multiple industry and country exposures estimated in this way are very noisy, so this trade-off is severe. For this reason many risk analysts prefer the unit-exposures model even in the presence of many firms that are obviously conglomerates and/or multinationals.

3.2 Empirical Evidence on the Relative Magnitudes of Country and Industry Risks

Lessard (1974, 1976) uses an extended market model regression to measure industry–country factor integration. In order to maximize the explanatory power of the world market index return (subscript "mw"), each of the sixteen national market indices, $r_{\mathrm{m}j}$, $j = 1, 16$, and each of the thirty global industry indices, $r_{\mathrm{I}h}$, $h = 1, 30$, is first regressed individually on the world market index and then the residuals from each regression are used in place of the raw variable:

$$\begin{aligned} r_{\mathrm{m}j} &= \hat{a} + \hat{b}_{\mathrm{mw}} + \hat{\varepsilon}_{\mathrm{m}j}, \\ r^{\mathrm{o}}_{\mathrm{m}j} &= \hat{\varepsilon}_{\mathrm{m}j}, \\ r_{\mathrm{I}h} &= \hat{a} + \hat{b}_{\mathrm{mw}} + \hat{\varepsilon}_{\mathrm{I}h}, \\ r^{\mathrm{o}}_{\mathrm{I}h} &= \hat{\varepsilon}_{\mathrm{I}h}. \end{aligned}$$

This "orthogonalization" process is a common preliminary step in risk modeling when two or more risk sources are highly correlated. It assigns all of the common variation to one of the risk sources (in this case, the world market index). Each individual equity is then regressed on the world market index, its orthogonalized national market index, $r^{\mathrm{o}}_{\mathrm{m}j}$, and its orthogonalized global industry index, $r^{\mathrm{o}}_{\mathrm{I}h}$. Using a capitalization-weighted global market index in all these regressions, and taking an average across all assets in all countries, the average explained variance of the global market index is 7%, the national market indices explain 33%, and the global industry indices explain 12%. Replacing the capitalization-weighted world market index with an equally weighted average of the national indices, these percentages change to 20%, 22%, and 6%, respectively.

Heston and Rouwenhorst (1994) is the first paper to use cross-sectional regression subject to linear constraints (3.3) to isolate industry and country effects. This eliminates the need for Lessard's two-step regression procedure. Heston and Rouwenhorst apply the technique to European data and find that, contrary to the earlier work of Roll (1992b) using index-only data, country factors account for a much larger percentage of return variance than industry factors. Country factors explain 18% of equity return variance and industry factors explain only 3%.

Griffin and Karolyi (1998) confirm and extend the Heston and Rouwenhorst findings, using a worldwide collection of equity markets and a more detailed set of industry classifications. Griffin and Karolyi note that, by applying the properties of cross-sectional regression coefficients in dummy variable models, it is possible to apply the Heston–Rouwenhorst cross-sectional regression methodology using appropriately weighted country and industry index returns (see the discussion above, and particularly equation (3.13) for the intuition behind this result). Griffin and Karolyi find that smaller countries tend to have relatively larger country factors, and that industries producing internationally traded goods such as automobiles and oil tend to account for more industry factor variance than domestically oriented industries.

Puchkov et al. (2005) estimate an equity factor model for forty-one developing and emerging markets using data from January 1992 to February 2004. The authors find that global industries and styles increase in importance during the second half of the 1990s, and that industry effects surpassed country effects in developed markets between 1999 and 2002. In emerging markets, however, country effects dominate throughout the study period.

Due to its high level of market and political integration, Europe has been a particular focus for studies of industry and country factor integration. This is particularly relevant for member states of the European Union (EU); there has been a long program of regulatory reform aimed at increasing the free flow of labor, products, and capital across national borders within the EU. We will discuss European fixed-income and currency market integration in later chapters; in this section we focus only on country–industry decomposition of European equity markets. Heston and Rouwenhorst influenced a number of subsequent papers with their surprising finding that, even within the highly integrated market environment of Western Europe, country factors are more important than regional industry factors. Drummen and Zimmerman (1992) address this same measurement problem using alternative methodologies (statistical factor analysis and time-series-based regression models). They find that within Europe, country factors explain 19% of individual stock variance and regional industry factors explain 9%. Unlike Heston and Rouwenhorst they also measure the factors associated with the worldwide and Europe-wide market factors, which explain 11% and 9% of asset variance, respectively. Because Drummen and Zimmerman use time-series regression, the variance contributions of the factors are not additive and, as they note, the worldwide and market factors have particularly high correlation, making their separate contributions difficult to measure accurately. Like Heston and Rouwenhorst, Drummen and Zimmerman find that currency effects are relatively small in European equity markets, explaining only 2% of the variance of a typical stock.

Beckers et al. (1996) look both at Europe as a region and (separately) at a global collection of markets. Their European findings are similar to those of Heston and Rouwenhorst and Drummen and Zimmerman. They find that European equity markets are more integrated than global markets, in terms of higher proportional variance due to the market-wide factor and industry factors.

Hopkins and Miller (2001) apply a Heston–Rouwenhorst-type model to a more detailed industry classification data set and a larger set of countries. They follow Rouwenhorst (1999) in using mean absolute return rather than squared return to compare the importance of country and industry factors. They confirm the Griffin–Karolyi findings that smaller countries and more export-oriented industries tend to have larger factor return magnitudes. Hopkins and Miller also note that the fineness of the industry classifications has an influence on the results, with a more detailed industry classification increasing the explanatory power of the industry components. This same point is made by Heckman et al. (2001). Hopkins and Miller find a larger industry component than some of the earlier studies, using data up to the end of December 2000.

3.2.1 Industry–Country Factor Integration Trends

Many of the papers on industry–country factor integration also test for time-series trends, reflecting the belief that increased globalization has led to a secular increase in market integration. The most common approach to measuring country–industry factor integration trends is to calculate the period-by-period variance contribution of the factor categories and examine them for time trends. Consider the model (3.4) applied to an individual asset i that is in industry j and country h. Eliminating all the other industry and country factors, since this asset has zero exposure to them, gives a simple additive decomposition of return:

$$x_{it} = f_{0t} + f^{\mathrm{I}}_{jt} + f^{\mathrm{C}}_{ht} + \varepsilon_{it}.$$

The explained variance (EV) attributed to each category at time t can be found by finding the mean-squared factor return within each category:

$$\left.\begin{aligned} \mathrm{EV}_{\mathrm{m}t} &= (f_{0t})^2, \\ \mathrm{EV}_{\mathrm{I}t} &= \frac{1}{k_{\mathrm{I}}}\sum_{j=1}^{k_{\mathrm{I}}} (f^{\mathrm{I}}_{jt})^2, \\ \mathrm{EV}_{\mathrm{C}t} &= \frac{1}{k_{\mathrm{C}}}\sum_{j=1}^{k_{\mathrm{C}}} (f^{\mathrm{C}}_{jt})^2. \end{aligned}\right\} \tag{3.14}$$

Then we can test whether, as predicted by the increasing integration hypothesis, the country component $\mathrm{EV}_{\mathrm{C}t}$ declines over time and/or the industry or global market components $\mathrm{EV}_{\mathrm{I}t}$, $\mathrm{EV}_{\mathrm{m}t}$ increase. Technically these mean-squared factor variances should be corrected for the estimation variance in the factor returns, but this is never done. Cavaglia et al. (2000) and Hopkins and Miller (2001) use mean absolute rather than mean-squared factor returns. Mean absolute returns have the advantage that they put relatively less weight on the extreme factor return observations.

There is evidence for increasing relative importance of global industry factors relative to country factors in the late 1990s and 2000s. In particular, Cavaglia et al. (2000), L'Her et al. (2002), and Hopkins and Miller (2001) all provide evidence for this trend. Brooks and Del Negro (2004) argue that this finding might at least partly reflect the temporary influence of the late-1990s technology bubble.

Rouwenhorst (1999) examines European data and finds an integration trend in the late 1980s and very early 1990s but the trend flattens and then reverses during the mid 1990s. He argues that, even if there is a modest integration trend during this period, it is not sufficiently strong to reverse the basic conclusion from Heston and Rouwenhorst (1994) that country factors are much stronger than industry factors. He contrasts this with valuation modeling as typically practiced in the portfolio analysis industry, where standard practice has moved noticeably toward industry-based rather than country-based analysis. Since the objectives are not identical, the best modeling approach for valuation need not be the same as the best modeling approach for risk analysis.

3.3 Sector–Currency Models of Corporate Bond Returns

Research on industry–country decompositions of corporate bond returns has lagged behind that on equity returns due to a lack of good data. Until recently, corporate bond markets outside of the United States were not sufficiently liquid with reliable price records to support industry–country decompositions. This has changed since the late 1990s, particularly with the growth of the European corporate bond market.

Bond market analysts tend to use "sectors" rather than "industries"—meaning broadly defined rather than narrowly defined industry categories. Large global corporations often issue corporate bonds in several currencies, and these are best categorized by their currency numeraires, rather than by the national location of the headquarters of the issuing firm. Hence the currency of the fixed-income claim substitutes for the country designation used in equity industry–country models.

Kercheval et al. (2002, 2003) sort a large database of corporate bonds by investment grade, sector, and currency (euro, British pound sterling, and U.S. dollar). They form equally weighted portfolio returns within each grade–sector–currency class (called a "bucket" in fixed-income parlance). To remove term-structure factors and focus on bond default risk factors they use spread return, defined as the return to a corporate bond minus the return to a portfolio of government bonds of the same currency denomination and duration.

Kercheval et al. examine the correlations of spread returns across investment grades, sectors, and currencies. They find a very high degree of national segmentation of the spread-return components. Within each country, all the sector and grade bucket spread returns are strongly correlated. On the other hand, equivalent sector and grade bucket spread returns have very weak correlation across countries. Their evidence mimics perhaps even more strongly the evidence of industry–country segmentation in equity returns. They give an illuminating example by considering in detail the case of Toyota corporate bonds, which have been issued in all three currencies. The monthly spread returns to these Toyota bonds differ remarkably across euro-, dollar-, and pound sterling-denominated bonds, often having opposite signs in the same month, and with an average correlation close to zero. Clearly, it is currency-specific risk premia, not changing default probabilities, that explain these spread returns—Toyota bonds are unlikely to have different contemporaneous changes in the probability of default across currency denominations.

4

Statistical Factor Analysis

The three types of factor models are statistical, macroeconomic and characteristic based. This chapter considers statistical factor models, which are the most technically difficult of the three classic types but also the most fundamental.

Section 4.1 describes the basic types of statistical factor models. Section 4.2 looks at approximate factor models, which impose an approximate structure on the covariance matrix as the number of assets becomes large. Section 4.3 discusses the arbitrage pricing theory and its applications to portfolio risk management. Section 4.4 considers "small-n" factor model estimation techniques, in which the number of assets is small relative to the number of time periods. Section 4.5 considers "large-n" techniques, in which the number of assets is large. Section 4.6 discusses techniques to determine the number of pervasive factors in returns.

4.1 Types of Factor Models

4.1.1 The Linear Factor Decomposition

Before defining a factor model it is useful to simply divide the returns on all assets into two parts: the part of the return correlated to a set of factors and the remaining (uncorrelated) part. The *linear factor decomposition* expresses the vector of asset excess returns as a linear combination of factor returns and a vector of asset-specific returns:

$$\boldsymbol{x} = \boldsymbol{a} + \boldsymbol{B}\boldsymbol{f} + \boldsymbol{\varepsilon}, \tag{4.1}$$

where $\boldsymbol{B}$ is an $n \times k$ matrix of factor betas, $\boldsymbol{f}$ is a random vector of factor returns, and $\boldsymbol{\varepsilon}$ is an n-vector of asset-specific returns. The vector of coefficients $\boldsymbol{a}$ is set so that $E[\boldsymbol{\varepsilon}] = \boldsymbol{0}^n$. By defining $\boldsymbol{B}$ appropriately, in particular $\boldsymbol{B} = \operatorname{cov}(\boldsymbol{x}, \boldsymbol{f})\boldsymbol{C}_f^{-1}$, it follows that $\operatorname{cov}(\boldsymbol{f}, \boldsymbol{\varepsilon}) = \boldsymbol{0}^{k \times n}$.

Note that the linear factor decomposition (4.1) on its own is completely unrestrictive on returns: it only requires that $\boldsymbol{x}$ and $\boldsymbol{f}$ have finite variances. The assumption that $\boldsymbol{C}_f$ is nonsingular is unrestrictive since otherwise at least one factor can be eliminated without changing the fit of the model. Given any vector of asset excess returns $\boldsymbol{x}$ and any chosen factors $\boldsymbol{f}$ (which need have no particular connection to returns) we can create a linear factor decomposition. In statistical terminology, it is just the linear projection of $\boldsymbol{x}$ on $(1, \boldsymbol{f})$ and it puts no restrictions on returns (except finite variances).

Although it does not restrict returns, the linear factor decomposition provides a useful decomposition of returns, due to the zero correlations between $\boldsymbol{f}$ and $\boldsymbol{\varepsilon}$. The covariance matrix of returns decomposes into two parts, usually called common factor risk and idiosyncratic risk,

$$\boldsymbol{C} = \boldsymbol{B}\boldsymbol{C}_f\boldsymbol{B}' + \boldsymbol{C}_{\boldsymbol{\varepsilon}},$$

and analogously portfolio variance can be decomposed into common factor variance and idiosyncratic variance,

$$\operatorname{var}(x_w) = \boldsymbol{w}'\boldsymbol{B}\boldsymbol{C}_f\boldsymbol{B}'\boldsymbol{w} + \boldsymbol{w}'\boldsymbol{C}_{\boldsymbol{\varepsilon}}\boldsymbol{w}.$$

4.1.2 The Strict Factor Model

The strict factor model is the original factor model specification and is used heavily in psychometric research. It takes the linear factor decomposition (4.1) and adds the assumption that the idiosyncratic returns are cross-sectionally uncorrelated:

$$\boldsymbol{C}_\varepsilon = \operatorname{Diag}[\sigma^2_{\varepsilon_1}, \dots, \sigma^2_{\varepsilon_n}], \tag{4.2}$$

where $\boldsymbol{C}_\varepsilon$ is the $n \times n$ covariance matrix of $\boldsymbol{\varepsilon}$ and σ^2_ε is the n-vector of asset-specific variances. Combining (4.1) and (4.2) gives a key representation of the return covariance matrix as the sum of a matrix of rank k and a diagonal matrix:

$$\boldsymbol{C} = \boldsymbol{B}\boldsymbol{C}_f\boldsymbol{B}' + \boldsymbol{C}_\varepsilon.$$

In a classic paper, Ross (1976) had the powerful insight that a strict factor model is a useful device for separating pervasive and diversifiable risk in asset returns. In addition to imposing a strict factor model, Ross assumes that the number of assets n is large and imposes an upper bound on the individual elements of $\boldsymbol{C}_\varepsilon = \operatorname{Diag}[\sigma^2_{\varepsilon_1}, \dots, \sigma^2_{\varepsilon_n}]$.

Define a *well-spread portfolio* as a portfolio with weights near zero: that is, $\boldsymbol{w}'\boldsymbol{w} \overset{n}{\approx} 0$. As Ross notes, in a strict factor model, well-spread portfolios will have approximately zero asset-specific risk: that is, $\boldsymbol{w}'\boldsymbol{C}_\varepsilon\boldsymbol{w} \leqslant \boldsymbol{w}'\boldsymbol{w}\max\{\sigma^2_{\varepsilon_1}, \dots, \sigma^2_{\varepsilon_n}\} \overset{n}{\approx} 0$, since $\max\{\sigma^2_{\varepsilon_1}, \dots, \sigma^2_{\varepsilon_n}\}$ is bounded above by assumption. So the idiosyncratic returns in a strict factor model represent diversifiable risk: it is the part of individual-asset risk that is eliminated from any well-spread portfolio.

4.1.3 Scalar and Noiseless Factor Models

One special case of a strict factor model is a *scalar factor model.* Here we eliminate the heteroskedasticity of asset-specific risks, setting all asset-specific variances equal to a single value:

$$C_\varepsilon = \sigma_\varepsilon^2 I.$$

The advantage of the scalar factor model over the strict factor model is the large decrease in the number of free parameters. The model has one rather than n asset-specific variances to estimate. In some applications the simplicity of the scalar model compensates for its decreased accuracy. For example, as we will see, imposing this restriction simplifies the estimation algorithm for statistical factor analysis.

In some cases it is convenient to impose the very restrictive case of a *noiseless factor model,* in which $\boldsymbol{\varepsilon} \equiv \mathbf{0}^n$:

$$\boldsymbol{x} = \boldsymbol{a} + \boldsymbol{B}\boldsymbol{f}. \tag{4.3}$$

In this case the covariance matrix is the quadratic product of the beta matrix $\boldsymbol{B}$ and the covariance matrix of the factors,

$$\boldsymbol{C} = \boldsymbol{B}\boldsymbol{C}_f\boldsymbol{B}',$$

and the return variance of any portfolio $\boldsymbol{w}$ is completely identified by its factor betas $\boldsymbol{b}_w' = \boldsymbol{w}'\boldsymbol{B}$ since $\operatorname{var}(r_w) = \boldsymbol{b}_w'\boldsymbol{C}_f\boldsymbol{b}_w$. Similarly, the covariance between any two portfolio returns depends only on their factor betas: $\operatorname{cov}(r_w, r_{w*}) = \boldsymbol{b}_w'\boldsymbol{C}_f\boldsymbol{b}_{w*}$. The same applies for any risk metric, not just portfolio variance: the de-meaned distribution of any portfolio return is completely determined by the portfolio betas $\boldsymbol{b}_w$ and the distribution of the factors $\boldsymbol{f}$.

4.1.4 Rotational Indeterminacy

In the classic approach to factor modeling both the beta matrix $\boldsymbol{B}$ and the factor realizations $\boldsymbol{f}$ are estimated freely from return data without any restrictions on values. Since only the product $\boldsymbol{B}\boldsymbol{f}$ affects returns, in this case the factor model specification has a *rotational indeterminacy.* Let $\boldsymbol{L}$ be a nonsingular $k \times k$ matrix. We can replace the factors $\boldsymbol{f}$ with alternative factors $\boldsymbol{f}^* = \boldsymbol{L}\boldsymbol{f}$ without affecting the empirical fit of the factor model. We simply undo the linear transformation by applying its inverse to the beta matrix. Replacing $\boldsymbol{f}$ and $\boldsymbol{B}$ with $\boldsymbol{f}^* = \boldsymbol{L}\boldsymbol{f}$ and $\boldsymbol{B}^* = \boldsymbol{B}\boldsymbol{L}^{-1}$ gives a statistically identical factor model of returns. In order to identify the model we need to arbitrarily choose one $\boldsymbol{f}$, $\boldsymbol{B}$ pair from all these equivalent pairs. This is called choosing the rotation. One common and convenient choice is to set the covariance matrix of the factor returns equal to an identity matrix, $E[\boldsymbol{f}\boldsymbol{f}'] = \boldsymbol{I}_k$. This does not completely eliminate the rotational indeterminacy (note, for example, that we can still transpose the ordering of any of the factors) but it is usually enough to proceed with estimation.

In many security market applications, the identity of the factors and/or the identity of the factor betas is fixed beforehand. For example, we may prespecify that the factors are particular macroeconomic shocks—such as inflation shocks, interest rate shocks, exchange rate shocks—or we may prespecify that the factor betas are observable quantities—such as the industry exposures of the firms or security characteristics like book-to-price ratios or share price momentum. In this case the rotational indeterminacy of the model is reduced or eliminated.

4.2 Approximate Factor Models

A key feature of factor models in financial applications is that well-spread portfolios have near-zero asset-specific variance. The strict factor model assumption (plus a bound on the n diagonal elements of $\boldsymbol{C}_\varepsilon$) is sufficient for this result, but not necessary.

In an important paper, Chamberlain and Rothschild (1983) introduce an approximate factor model, which weakens the strict factor model assumption but keeps the key feature that well-spread portfolios have near-zero asset-specific variance. It uses a "large-n" modeling approach: the restrictions on the covariance matrix need only hold approximately, with the approximation depending upon the number of assets n being sufficiently large.

Let $\text{eigval}_j(\boldsymbol{A})$ denote the jth largest eigenvalue of a symmetric positive semidefinite[1] matrix A. A useful property of the first eigenvalue is that $\max_{\boldsymbol{w}'\boldsymbol{w}=1} \boldsymbol{w}'A\boldsymbol{w} = \text{eigval}_1(\boldsymbol{A})$. If we think of A as a return covariance matrix and of $\boldsymbol{w}$ as a portfolio vector, then this relates the variance of the portfolio return to the largest eigenvalue of the covariance matrix. The level of "spread" of the portfolio weights is fixed by the condition $\boldsymbol{w}'\boldsymbol{w} = 1$.

[1] The symmetric positive semidefinite condition on A ensures that its eigenvalues are real, so that they can be ordered.

Chamberlain and Rothschild show that the existence of an approximate factor model with k factors is equivalent to an upper bound on the $(k+1)$st eigenvalue of the covariance matrix for large n. Subsequent work shows that if all k factors are pervasive in the economy, then the kth eigenvalue must be unbounded for large n. (We give a technical definition of "pervasive" factors below.) This gives a very precise defining condition for an approximate factor model. Returns obey an approximate factor model if and only if the kth eigenvalue of the covariance matrix is unbounded and the $(k+1)$st eigenvalue is bounded for large n. We will briefly review the intuition behind their result.

Given finite variance excess returns $\boldsymbol{x}$ and any random vector $\boldsymbol{f}$ one can always create a linear decomposition of $\boldsymbol{x}$ with uncorrelated residuals $\boldsymbol{\varepsilon}$:

$$\boldsymbol{x} = \boldsymbol{a} + \boldsymbol{B}\boldsymbol{f} + \boldsymbol{\varepsilon} \quad \text{with } E[\boldsymbol{f}\boldsymbol{\varepsilon}'] = \boldsymbol{0}^{k\times n},$$
$$\boldsymbol{C} = \boldsymbol{B}\boldsymbol{B}' + \boldsymbol{C}_{\varepsilon}.$$

Consider a "well-spread" n-vector of portfolio weights $\boldsymbol{w}$: i.e., $\boldsymbol{w}'\boldsymbol{w} \overset{n}{\approx} 0$. If asset-specific returns $\boldsymbol{\varepsilon}$ capture diversifiable risk only, then by the definition of diversifiable risk, $\boldsymbol{w}'\boldsymbol{C}_{\varepsilon}\boldsymbol{w} \overset{n}{\approx} 0$ for any well-spread portfolio. It is easy to show that $\boldsymbol{w}'\boldsymbol{C}_{\varepsilon}\boldsymbol{w} \overset{n}{\approx} 0$ for all well-spread portfolios $\boldsymbol{w}$ if and only if $\text{eigval}_1[\boldsymbol{C}_{\varepsilon}]$ is bounded above for all n. Chamberlain and Rothschild impose the condition that $\text{eigval}_1(\boldsymbol{C}_{\varepsilon})$ is bounded above for all n. This is the necessary and sufficient condition to ensure that if $\boldsymbol{w}'\boldsymbol{w} \overset{n}{\approx} 0$, then $\boldsymbol{w}'\boldsymbol{C}_{\varepsilon}\boldsymbol{w} \overset{n}{\approx} 0$, so it is an appropriate defining condition for referring to $\boldsymbol{\varepsilon}$ as diversifiable risk.

A symmetric argument can be used to guarantee that all the factors capture pervasive risk. A factor f_j is defined as pervasive if there exists a well-spread portfolio $\boldsymbol{w}$ such that $\boldsymbol{w}'\boldsymbol{B}\boldsymbol{B}'\boldsymbol{w} = \boldsymbol{e}^j$, where $\boldsymbol{e}^j$ denotes a vector with a one in the jth component and zeros elsewhere. It is easy to show that this pervasiveness condition holds for each $j = 1, \dots, k$ if and only if $\text{eigval}_k(\boldsymbol{B}'\boldsymbol{B})$ goes to infinity with n.

Taking these conditions together we can then define an approximate factor model as a linear projection on returns such that $\text{eigval}_1[\boldsymbol{C}_{\varepsilon}]$ is bounded and $\text{eigval}_k(\boldsymbol{B}'\boldsymbol{B})$ goes to infinity. Chamberlain and Rothschild prove the elegant result that these conditions are equivalent to requiring that $\text{eigval}_{k+1}(\boldsymbol{C})$ is bounded and $\text{eigval}_k(\boldsymbol{C})$ goes to infinity. So in order for an approximate factor model to hold, there must be a sharp drop in moving from the kth to the $(k+1)$st eigenvalue of the covariance matrix.

4.2.1 The Pervasive/Idiosyncratic Risk Dichotomy

Let us consider more carefully what we mean when we say that the covariance matrix of asset-specific returns has bounded eigenvalues.

Intuitively it means that after removing the common effects from a small number of factors, the remaining asset-specific returns should be "mostly" uncorrelated. A classic example is an industry-based model with a large number of industries. Each industry has a relatively small number of firms (for simplicity, assume that there are m firms in each industry) and the number of industries, $n^* = n/m$, is large. The covariances of asset-specific returns within each industry are unrestricted but the asset-specific returns are uncorrelated between industry blocks. It is important to note that, unlike in the estimated industry components model discussed in chapter 3, we do not need to observe the industry identifiers, or even know what the industries are, in order to use this assumption. We only need to assume that some underlying industry structure restricts the covariances between asset-specific returns in this way. So although we assume that $\boldsymbol{C}_\varepsilon$ has the block-diagonal form, we need not know how to "index" the firms to get this simple structure. The only important feature is the prevalence of zeros in $\boldsymbol{C}_\varepsilon$ given this assumed structure. The covariance matrix has $n^2 - n^*m^2$ zeros, which is a large fraction of its total of n^2 elements, as long as m is small relative to n.

Another example of an approximate factor model is one in which each asset has nonnegligible correlation with "nearby" assets but the correlation declines exponentially. That is, for any asset i and any integer s, $\operatorname{corr}(x_i, x_{i+s}) = \rho^s$ for a fixed ρ such that $0 \leqslant \rho < 1$. For simplicity of notation let all the asset variances equal one, in which case the covariance matrix can be written

$$\boldsymbol{C}_\varepsilon = \begin{bmatrix} 1 & \rho & \cdots & \cdots & \rho^{n-1} \\ \rho & 1 & \rho & \cdots & \rho^{n-2} \\ \vdots & & & & \vdots \\ \rho^{n-1} & \cdots & \cdots & \rho & 1 \end{bmatrix}.$$

As long as ρ is less than one and n is large, most of the elements of this matrix will be very close to zero (since they equal ρ raised to a high power). Here again it is important to note that the analyst does not need to observe the proper indexing order $i = 1, \dots, n$ that induces this correlation structure. We only need to assume that there is some way to reorder the assets so that this model applies. The particular ordering that we use in estimation procedures has no relevance to the estimation results.

Some standard time-series methods are not implementable with cross-sectional data for which the index determining the structure of the covariance matrix is unknown. In time-series estimation it is often standard to correct for covariances by allowing nonzero correlation of "nearby" observations while imposing zero correlation on "distant" observations (e.g., White-Domowitz autocorrelation-consistent standard errors). These techniques do not work for cross-sectional data if the indexing variable is not known. There is no way to determine which assets are "near" each other if we do not observe the indexing variable.

4.2.2 Additional Conditions for Empirical Analysis

Approximate factor models provide a very convenient framework for empirical analysis since their structure is very similar to the structure used for large-sample methods in econometrics. Often, a few technical conditions are added to the approximate factor model assumptions to make them more amenable to large-sample statistical methods.

Recall from the description of the generic factor model that without loss of generality we can impose the condition $E[\boldsymbol{f}\boldsymbol{\varepsilon}'] = \mathbf{0}^{k\times n}$, since this is just part of the return decomposition. To apply a factor model empirically we often need to strengthen this zero correlation condition slightly. We replace it with the slightly stronger conditionally unbiased assumption $E[\boldsymbol{\varepsilon} \mid \boldsymbol{f}] = \mathbf{0}^n$. Most analysts treat the distinction between $E[\boldsymbol{f}\boldsymbol{\varepsilon}'] = \mathbf{0}^{k\times n}$ and $E[\boldsymbol{\varepsilon} \mid \boldsymbol{f}] = \mathbf{0}^n$ as a technical difference only.

Suppose that we plan to use the matrix of factor betas, $\boldsymbol{B}$, as the matrix of independent variables in a cross-sectional regression. In order to guarantee consistent estimates for large n, we need to impose the standard regression condition on the matrix of independent variables:

$$\left(\frac{1}{n}\boldsymbol{B}'\boldsymbol{B}\right) \overset{n}{\approx} M, \quad \text{a nonsingular matrix.} \tag{4.4}$$

The condition (4.4) is a slight strengthening of the unbounded eigenvalue condition: rather than only requiring that all the eigenvalues of $\boldsymbol{B}'\boldsymbol{B}$ increase unboundedly with n (rate of increase not specified), it requires that all the eigenvalues increase at rate n.

Another technical adjustment is needed to invoke the central limit theorem. Recall from the last section that bounded eigenvalues of $\boldsymbol{C}_\varepsilon$ are enough for Ross's diversification argument. However, in addition to requiring that weighted averages of idiosyncratic returns go to zero in probability, we often want to invoke the result that scaling these weighted averages by $\sqrt{n}$ gives an approximately normal random variable. The central limit theorem requires slightly stronger restrictions on the lack of interdependence between asset-specific returns. We have imposed limits on interdependence between asset-specific returns purely in terms of their covariances. In order to use the central limit theorem it is necessary to strengthen this slightly, so as to also restrict higher-moment dependencies between them. This is typically stated in terms of mixing conditions on the joint probability distribution of the vector of asset-specific returns: see, for example, Stock and Watson (2002a,b) for technical details on this.

4.3 The Arbitrage Pricing Theory

The arbitrage pricing theory (APT) was originally developed by Stephen Ross (1976). One of Ross's insights was to use portfolio risk modeling as a foundation for asset pricing theory. Portfolio risk modelers have returned the compliment, by using the APT as a key pricing reference in much of their analysis.

4.3.1 Statistical Arbitrage

Ross introduced the notion of *statistical arbitrage*. Statistical arbitrage has subsequently become very important in the hedge fund industry, so Ross's 1976 analysis was prescient. Given a factor model of returns, a *statistical arbitrage portfolio* is defined by three conditions: it is well-diversified (4.5), it has zero cost (4.6), and it has zero betas against all k factors (4.7):

$$\boldsymbol{w}'C_{\varepsilon}\boldsymbol{w} \overset{n}{\approx} 0, \tag{4.5}$$

$$\boldsymbol{w}'\mathbf{1}^n = 0, \tag{4.6}$$

$$\boldsymbol{w}'B = \mathbf{0}^k. \tag{4.7}$$

If a statistical arbitrage portfolio has nonnegligible mean return (that is, if $\mu_w \neq 0$), the investor can make a positive profit at zero cost and with negligible risk. If the mean return is positive, go long this portfolio to earn a positive profit with near-zero risk; if the mean is negative, go short. To create a fully invested portfolio, combine the statistical arbitrage portfolio with a unit position in the riskless return, creating a long–short portfolio (see chapter 1). By increasing the leverage ratio of the position the manager can earn any level of expected excess return with negligible risk.

When used in practice by hedge fund managers and trading desks, statistical arbitrage is less straightforward. The "large-n approximation" $\boldsymbol{w}'C_{\varepsilon}\boldsymbol{w} \overset{n}{\approx} 0$ is not exact, and so some portfolio risk always remains. Also, the statistical arbitrageur needs to ensure that the factor model he is using is sufficiently comprehensive for the zero-beta condition (4.7) to truly eliminate all pervasive sources of risk. If there are hidden factor exposures in the portfolio due to factors that are missing from the estimated factor model, this can lead to nasty surprises. There is some anecdotal evidence that it was just this type of factor model misspecification that led to the spectacular collapse of Long Term Capital Management in 1998. The fund had a carefully crafted statistical arbitrage portfolio spanning a wide variety of asset classes around the world, combined with a high leverage ratio to maximize profitability. The risk model used to impose (4.5) and (4.7) did not adequately account for liquidity risk as a pervasive risk factor. When liquidity premia rose sharply and unexpectedly worldwide, the portfolio suffered enormous losses.

4.3.2 Expected Returns in the APT

The APT pricing restriction is analogous to that from the CAPM, but with multiple factor betas rather than one market beta. It states that expected excess returns on assets are linear in factor betas of the assets:

$$\boldsymbol{\mu} = \mathbf{1}^n r_0 + \boldsymbol{B}\boldsymbol{\pi}, \tag{4.8}$$

where $\boldsymbol{\pi}$ is a k vector of factor risk premia. It is simplest to derive the APT in the case of a noiseless factor model and we begin with this case.

Suppose that returns obey a noiseless factor model. Consider the projection of the n-vector of expected returns on an intercept and the $n \times k$ matrix of factor betas:

$$\boldsymbol{\mu} = \mathbf{1}^n \pi_0 + \boldsymbol{B}\boldsymbol{\pi} + \boldsymbol{\eta}, \tag{4.9}$$

where $\boldsymbol{\pi}^* = (\pi_0, \boldsymbol{\pi})$ are the least-squares projection coefficients, e.g.,

$$\boldsymbol{\pi}^* = ([\mathbf{1}^n : \boldsymbol{B}]'[\mathbf{1}^n : \boldsymbol{B}])^{-1}[\mathbf{1}^n : \boldsymbol{B}]'\boldsymbol{\mu},$$

and $\boldsymbol{\eta}$ is the n-vector of residuals. Unless this vector of residuals is a zero vector (we will consider this case below) rescale the vector so that the sum of the long weights equals one, giving $\boldsymbol{\eta}^* = a\boldsymbol{\eta}$. The interested reader can easily show that the portfolio $\boldsymbol{\eta}^*$ has zero cost (4.6) and zero factor exposures (4.7). It has exactly zero asset-specific risk (4.5) since in the case of a noiseless factor model $\boldsymbol{C}_\varepsilon$ is a zero matrix. So this portfolio is costless and completely risk free. Unless the portfolio has exactly zero expected return, it provides a pure arbitrage opportunity, since the holder can generate infinite profits at no cost and with no risk by taking a large position in the portfolio. The expected return on the portfolio is

$$\boldsymbol{\eta}^{*\prime}\boldsymbol{\mu} = a\boldsymbol{\eta}'\boldsymbol{\eta},$$

which is greater than zero unless $\boldsymbol{\eta}$ is the zero vector. So this ensures that $\boldsymbol{\eta} = \mathbf{0}^n$ in (4.9). This shows that unless there is a pure arbitrage opportunity, the condition $\boldsymbol{\mu} = \mathbf{1}^n \pi_0 + \boldsymbol{B\pi}$ must hold. To complete the derivation of (4.8) it is only necessary to show that $\pi_0 = r_0$. This is easy to show since otherwise any unit-cost portfolio $\boldsymbol{w}$ with $\boldsymbol{w}'\boldsymbol{B} = \mathbf{0}^k$ is risk free but does not earn the riskless return, giving rise to pure arbitrage.

The absence of statistical arbitrage implies that all well-diversified portfolios will have mean returns that are linear in the riskless return and their factor betas:

$$\mu_w \overset{n}{\approx} r_0 + \boldsymbol{b}'_w \boldsymbol{\pi}. \tag{4.10}$$

The argument is analogous to that in the noiseless factor model case. Unless the approximation holds, a combination of well-diversified portfolios can be found that will constitute an approximate arbitrage portfolio.

4.4 Small-n Estimation Methods

4.4.1 Psychometric versus Financial Applications

Factor modeling was originally developed for applications in psychology, and many of the existing statistical methods reflect this history. In a typical psychometric application, the researcher has data on a set of n test results for a large sample of T subjects. So, for example, in a typical data set the researcher may have $n = 15$ cognitive or personality test results for $T = 600$ college students. The number of students tested, T, tends to be substantially larger than the number of test results, n, provided by each individual student. So the standard statistical methods used in psychometrics apply the approximation that n is fixed and that $T \to \infty$ to reflect these relative magnitudes. Relating the standard psychometric application to the return modeling problem, the number of "test results" n corresponds to the number of securities, and the number of "student subjects" T corresponds to the number of time periods of returns. It is less natural to impose the approximation that n is fixed and that $T \to \infty$ in return modeling, since typically we have n equal to several thousand, whereas T can be as small as 60. Nonetheless, small-n methods can be useful in many financial applications.

4.4.2 Principal Components

Note that for any symmetric positive-definite matrix $\boldsymbol{C}$ (such as a covariance matrix) we can perform the eigenvector decomposition $\boldsymbol{C} = \boldsymbol{V\Lambda V}'$, where $\boldsymbol{\Lambda}$ is the $n \times n$ diagonal matrix of eigenvalues (ordered from largest to smallest) and $\boldsymbol{V}$ is the $n \times n$ matrix of eigenvectors with the property that $V'V = I_n$. If the $n \times n$ matrix C is positive semidefinite with rank k, then we can write it in the same form, but with only k eigenvalues and vectors: $C = V\Lambda V'$, where Λ is the $k \times k$ diagonal matrix of eigenvalues and V is the $n \times k$ matrix of eigenvectors with the property that $V'V = I_k$.

The first k eigenvectors scaled by the square roots of their eigenvalues, $B^* = V_k \Lambda_k^{1/2}$, are called the k *principal components* of the covariance matrix. In portfolio risk applications, the principal components can be viewed as estimates of the factor betas in a factor model decomposition of the covariance matrix. However, the principal components have meaning even if returns do not obey any factor model restriction. In many scientific and engineering fields, principal-components analysis is used simply as a data reduction technique. The principal components isolate the largest eigenvectors of the covariance matrix. In this way they give a lower-dimensional approximation to this matrix. The principal components maximize fit in the sense that they provide a k-dimensional matrix that best approximates the sample covariance matrix:

$$\hat{B}^* = \arg\min \|\hat{C} - \hat{B}^* \hat{B}^{*\prime}\|$$

under the Euclidian norm on square matrices, $\|X\| = \max \operatorname{abs}(y'Xy)$ such that $y'y = 1$.

In portfolio risk applications, principal-components analysis is usually combined with a factor model restriction on returns. Suppose that the true covariance matrix C obeys a noiseless factor model. Consider the eigenvector decomposition and the factor model decomposition of the true (not estimated) covariance matrix in this case:

$$C = BB', \tag{4.11}$$

$$C = V\Lambda V'. \tag{4.12}$$

Setting the right-hand sides of equations (4.11) and (4.12) equal we have $V\Lambda^{1/2} = BL$, where L is a nonsingular $k \times k$ matrix (in particular, $L = (B'B)^{-1}B'V\Lambda^{1/2}$). The matrix L reflects the rotational indeterminacy of the factor model that will appear in any estimate. So we have shown that in the case of a noiseless factor model, the principal components are valid estimates of the factor betas, since the principal components of the covariance matrix equal the factor betas adjusted for the rotational indeterminacy.

The principal-components approach is also valid in the case of a scalar factor model. To see this, consider the eigenvector decomposition of the true covariance matrix for a scalar factor model:

$$\operatorname{eigvec}_k(C) = \operatorname{eigvec}_k(BB' + \sigma_\varepsilon^2 I).$$

Scalar matrices have the property that any vector is an eigenvector of a scalar matrix, with eigenvalue equal to the diagonal element. From this, it is straightforward to show that the first k eigenvectors of $\text{eigvec}(\boldsymbol{C})$ equal the k eigenvectors of $\boldsymbol{BB}'$. The first k eigenvalues equal the eigenvalues of $\boldsymbol{BB}'$ plus σ_ε^2:

$$\left.\begin{aligned} \text{eigvec}_k(\boldsymbol{C}) &= \text{eigvec}_k(\boldsymbol{BB}'), \\ \text{eigval}_k(\boldsymbol{C}) &= \text{eigval}_k(\boldsymbol{BB}') + \sigma_\varepsilon^2. \end{aligned}\right\} \tag{4.13}$$

So the principal components of $\boldsymbol{C}$ equal $\boldsymbol{BL}$, with only the definition of the arbitrary rotation $\boldsymbol{L}$ changing slightly from the noiseless case. Note from (4.13) that the first k eigenvalues of $\boldsymbol{C}$ equal those of $\boldsymbol{BB}'$ plus the constant σ_ε^2.

Replacing $\boldsymbol{C}$ with the sample covariance matrix $\hat{\boldsymbol{C}}$ means that the principal components are estimates of the first k eigenvectors based on the sample covariance matrix. The estimation error in the covariance matrix goes to zero for large T:

$$\hat{\boldsymbol{C}} \overset{\text{pr},T}{\approx} \boldsymbol{C}. \tag{4.14}$$

Sample eigenvectors and eigenvalues are smooth nonlinear functions of the sample covariance matrix. Hence we can use (4.14) plus the result that the approximation $\overset{\text{pr},T}{\approx}$ is preserved under smooth nonlinear transformations to get the same consistency result for the ordered eigenvectors and eigenvalues:

$$\text{eigvec}_j(\hat{\boldsymbol{C}}) \overset{\text{pr},T}{\approx} \text{eigvec}_j(\boldsymbol{C}), \quad j = 1, n, \tag{4.15}$$

$$\text{eigval}_j(\hat{\boldsymbol{C}}) \overset{\text{pr},T}{\approx} \text{eigval}_j(\boldsymbol{C}), \quad j = 1, n. \tag{4.16}$$

Note that the estimated eigenvectors are ordered based on the corresponding estimated eigenvalues. So the eigenvector convergence result (4.15) relies implicitly on the eigenvalue convergence result (4.16). Due to the rotational indeterminacy it is not necessary to estimate each individual eigenvector correctly. Rather it is only necessary that the set of the first k estimated eigenvectors converges (up to a nonsingular rotation L) to the set of the first k true eigenvectors.

4.4.3 Maximum-Likelihood Estimation

In this subsection we assume that excess returns obey a strict factor model. We assume that $\{\boldsymbol{f}, \boldsymbol{\varepsilon}\}$ has a multivariate normal distribution, which implies that $\boldsymbol{x}$ is also multivariate normal. Maintaining the small-n approach, we assume that $T > n > k$.

Recall from section 4.4.2 that if returns obey a scalar factor model, then the k principal components are valid estimates of the factor betas.

Now consider the case of a strict factor model in which C_ε is diagonal but not scalar. To provide the basic intuition we first suppose that both C and C_ε are observed without error. Calculate the weighted covariance matrix $C^* = C_\varepsilon^{-1/2} C C_\varepsilon^{-1/2}$ and note that $C^* = C_\varepsilon^{-1/2} BB' C_\varepsilon^{-1/2} + I$. So by pre- and post-multiplying the covariance matrix by $C_\varepsilon^{-1/2}$ we create a scalar factor model. Recall from section 4.4.2 that with a scalar covariance matrix the first k scaled eigenvectors are valid estimates of the factor betas. It follows immediately that the first k scaled eigenvectors of C^* equal $C_\varepsilon^{-1/2} BL$ for some rotation L. Pre-multiplying by $C_\varepsilon^{1/2}$ we have $C_\varepsilon^{-1/2} V_k^* = BL$. These are the essential steps of statistical factor analysis for the case of a strict factor model. We begin with (estimates of) C and diagonal matrix C_ε, find the first k eigenvectors of $C^* = C_\varepsilon^{-1/2} C C_\varepsilon^{-1/2}$, scale the eigenvectors by $(\Lambda_k - I_k)^{1/2}$, and pre-multiply these scaled eigenvectors by $C_\varepsilon^{1/2}$ to get the estimates of B.

The last paragraph gave a full description of statistical factor analysis if we could begin by observing C and C_ε exactly. Now we need to fill in some details since both of these matrices must be estimated as part of the methodology.

First define $\hat{C}$ as the sample moment estimate of C:

$$\hat{C} = \frac{1}{T} \tilde{R}' \tilde{R}.$$

Note that even if true returns follow a strict factor model, the sample moment estimate $\hat{C}$ will not follow a strict factor model, in the sense that we cannot write it in the form $BB' + C_\varepsilon$, where B is an $n \times k$ matrix and C_ε is a diagonal matrix. The sample moment estimate $\hat{C}$ is not a maximum-likelihood estimate of the covariance matrix given the factor model restriction since it does not reflect the fact that the true covariance matrix obeys a strict factor model. The maximum-likelihood estimate will have the form $\hat{\hat{C}} = \hat{B}\hat{B}' + \hat{C}_\varepsilon$. To find $\hat{\hat{C}}$ we need $\hat{B}$ and $\hat{C}_\varepsilon$; to find $\hat{B}$ we need $\hat{\hat{C}}$ and $\hat{C}_\varepsilon$; and to find $\hat{C}_\varepsilon$ we need $\hat{\hat{C}} - \hat{B}\hat{B}'$. The trick is to begin with a guess for each and then iterate between the estimation of each one using the others. We describe next the Joreskog algorithm for finding the maximum-likelihood estimates by a fairly simple iterative scheme.

(1) Compute the principal components of the sample moment covariance matrix $\hat{C}$. Take these as the initial estimates of the beta matrix $\hat{B}$.

(2) Estimate the diagonal covariance matrix of asset-specific returns using the difference between $\hat{C}$ and $\hat{B}\hat{B}'$: $\hat{C}_\varepsilon = \text{Diag}(\hat{C}) - \text{Diag}(\hat{B}\hat{B}')$.

(3) Calculate the weighted sample covariance matrix

$$\hat{C}^* = \hat{C}_\varepsilon^{-1/2}\hat{C}\hat{C}_\varepsilon^{-1/2}$$

and compute its eigenvector decomposition

$$\hat{C}^* = V\Lambda V'.$$

Set

$$\hat{B} = \hat{C}_\varepsilon^{1/2}V_k(\Lambda_k - I_k).$$

(4) Repeat steps (2) and (3) until $\hat{C}_\varepsilon$ converges to a fixed point (that is, the matrix does not change from one iteration to the next).

The convergent solution to this algorithm is a solution to the equations defining the maximum-likelihood estimation of $\hat{B}$, $\hat{C}$, and $\hat{C}_\varepsilon$.

One technical concern (which often becomes a practical concern) is that these equations ignore the constraint that the diagonal components of the asset-specific covariance matrix, $C_{\varepsilon jj}$, must be nonnegative for the solution to have meaning. The Joreskog algorithm does not take account of this constraint. This missing condition is often a real problem, and the resulting solution to the algorithm gives the meaningless estimates $\hat{C}_\varepsilon$, where one or more entries (asset-specific variances) are negative. A solution with $\hat{C}_{\varepsilon jj} < 0$ for some j is called a Heywood case. Various fix-ups have been proposed for Heywood cases, such as deleting the offending asset j with $\hat{C}_{\varepsilon jj} < 0$ and then rerunning the estimation procedure.

4.4.4 Testing the Fit of the Model

The maximum-likelihood procedure described in the last subsection produces a restricted estimate of the covariance matrix $\hat{\hat{C}} = \hat{B}\hat{B}' + \hat{C}_\varepsilon$. If we drop the strict factor model assumption, then the maximum-likelihood estimate of the covariance matrix is the sample moment matrix $\hat{C}$. We can test the null hypothesis that returns obey a strict factor model using a likelihood ratio statistic to compare the likelihood of $\hat{\hat{C}}$ with that of $\hat{C}$. There are $\frac{1}{2}n(n-1)$ estimated parameters in the unconstrained sample covariance matrix $\hat{C}$ and $n + nk$ in the constrained estimate $\hat{\hat{C}}$. Under the null hypothesis that returns obey a factor model we can use a chi-squared test of the factor model restriction:

$$\ln(L(\hat{\hat{C}})/L(\hat{C})) \overset{\text{di},T}{\approx} \chi^2(\tfrac{1}{2}n(n-1) - (n + nk)),$$

where $L(\cdot)$ is the likelihood function. This provides a formal test, but often more important are statistical measures of the fit of the factor model. The ratio of explained variance to total variance is the sum of the diagonal elements of BB' divided by the sum of the diagonal elements of C.

4.5 Large-n Estimation Methods

4.5.1 Approximate Factor Models

As discussed earlier, Chamberlain and Rothschild (1983) introduced the approximate factor model, which imposes assumptions on the covariance matrix as the number of assets grows large. Standard factor analysis methods, however, rely on a fixed value of n that is small relative to the number of time periods T. Financial econometricians have developed new methods to deal with the estimation of large-n covariance matrices.

4.5.2 Asymptotic Principal Components

The technique of asymptotic principal components gives direct estimates of the time-series sample of factor returns, rather than (as with standard principal components) the factor beta matrix (Connor and Korajczyk 1986). Let $\boldsymbol{x}_t$ denote the n-vector of excess returns on n assets at time t. It is convenient to absorb the expected returns on the assets into the expected returns of the factors by imposing a multi-beta pricing relation. Recall the factor model decomposition $\boldsymbol{x} = \boldsymbol{a} + \boldsymbol{B}\boldsymbol{f} + \boldsymbol{\varepsilon}$. Setting $\boldsymbol{a} = \boldsymbol{B}\boldsymbol{\pi}$, where $\boldsymbol{\pi}$ is a k vector of constants capturing the risk premia associated with the factors, is equivalent to assuming that the expected excess returns on assets are linear in their factor betas. For most return measurement frequencies, such as monthly, daily, or weekly, this restriction on $\boldsymbol{a}$ has little discernible effect on risk measurement, since volatilities tend to dominate means except at very low (e.g., annual) return frequencies. This expected return restriction is convenient in terms of notation since it allows us to absorb $\boldsymbol{a}$ into the factor return term in the factor decomposition:

$$\boldsymbol{x} = \boldsymbol{B}(\boldsymbol{f} + \boldsymbol{\pi}) + \boldsymbol{\varepsilon}.$$

Assume that returns follow an approximate factor model with fixed $n \times k$ exposure matrix $\boldsymbol{B}$, k random factors $\boldsymbol{f}_t$, and n asset-specific returns $\boldsymbol{\varepsilon}_t$:

$$\left.\begin{aligned} E[\boldsymbol{\varepsilon}_t \mid \boldsymbol{f}_\tau] = \boldsymbol{0}^n \quad & \text{for all } t, \tau, \\ \frac{1}{n}\boldsymbol{B}'\boldsymbol{B} \overset{n}{\approx} \boldsymbol{M} \quad & \text{a nonsingular matrix}, \\ \|E[\boldsymbol{\varepsilon}_t \boldsymbol{\varepsilon}_t']\| \overset{n}{\approx} c < \infty. & \end{aligned}\right\} \tag{4.17}$$

Assume that the law of large numbers holds for averages of asset-specific returns:

$$\frac{1}{n}\boldsymbol{\varepsilon}_t'\boldsymbol{\varepsilon}_\tau \overset{\mathrm{pr},n}{\approx} \begin{cases} 0 & \text{for } \tau \neq t, \\ \sigma_\varepsilon^2 > 0 & \text{for } \tau = t. \end{cases} \tag{4.18}$$

Let $\boldsymbol{X}$ denote the $n \times T$ sample of excess returns data that we will use to estimate the factor returns. Let $\boldsymbol{F}$ denote the $k \times T$ matrix of factor returns, including the risk premia π, and let $\boldsymbol{\Xi}$ denote the $n \times T$ matrix of asset-specific returns. Writing out the data matrix in terms of the unobserved $\boldsymbol{B}$, $\boldsymbol{F}$, and $\boldsymbol{\Xi}$:

$$\boldsymbol{X} = \boldsymbol{BF} + \boldsymbol{\Xi}. \tag{4.19}$$

The trick in the asymptotic principal-components technique is to perform an eigenvector decomposition on the $T \times T$ cross-product matrix of returns rather than on the $n \times n$ covariance matrix of returns. Define the cross-product matrix as follows:

$$\boldsymbol{\Omega} = \frac{1}{n}\boldsymbol{X}'\boldsymbol{X}. \tag{4.20}$$

Writing out (4.20) using (4.19) gives

$$\boldsymbol{\Omega} = \boldsymbol{F}\left(\frac{1}{n}\boldsymbol{B}'\boldsymbol{B}\right)\boldsymbol{F} + \frac{1}{n}\boldsymbol{\Xi}'\boldsymbol{\Xi} + \frac{1}{n}\text{ cross products},$$

where it is straightforward to show that

$$\frac{1}{n}\text{ cross products} \overset{\text{pr},n}{\approx} \boldsymbol{0}^{T\times T}.$$

Note that

$$\frac{1}{n}\boldsymbol{B}'\boldsymbol{B} \overset{n}{\approx} \boldsymbol{M}$$

by assumption (4.17) above. Using assumption (4.18) we have

$$\frac{1}{n}\boldsymbol{\Xi}'\boldsymbol{\Xi} \overset{\text{pr},n}{\approx} \sigma_\varepsilon^2 \boldsymbol{I}_T.$$

Putting all these together and taking the probability limit of the cross-product matrix as n goes to infinity gives

$$p \lim_{n\to\infty} \boldsymbol{\Omega} \overset{\text{pr},n}{\approx} \boldsymbol{F}'\boldsymbol{MF} + \sigma_\varepsilon^2 \boldsymbol{I}_T.$$

Note that $\boldsymbol{F}'\boldsymbol{MF}$ has k eigenvectors, which are equal to $\boldsymbol{LF}$ for some nonsingular $k \times k$ matrix $\boldsymbol{L}$. Also note that the first k eigenvectors of $\boldsymbol{F}'\boldsymbol{MF} + \sigma_\varepsilon^2 \boldsymbol{I}_T$ equal the eigenvectors of $\boldsymbol{F}'\boldsymbol{MF}$. This result was used earlier in the discussion of standard principal-components analysis.

Using the fact that the eigenvector function is a smooth function of a nonsingular matrix, we obtain

$$\text{eigvec}_k[\boldsymbol{\Omega}] \overset{\text{pr},n}{\approx} \boldsymbol{LF}.$$

This suggests a very simple estimation algorithm. Simply calculate the cross-product matrix of returns $\boldsymbol{\Omega}$ and use its first k eigenvectors as the estimates of the factor returns, including the factor risk premia $\boldsymbol{\pi}$. The resulting factor return estimates will be consistent for large n.

Note that the direct output from asymptotic principal-components analysis is the $k \times T$ matrix of factor returns, $\hat{\boldsymbol{F}}$. This contrasts with the small-n methods that give the $n \times K$ matrix $\hat{\boldsymbol{B}}$ directly. However, in either case the other component ($\hat{\boldsymbol{F}}$ or $\hat{\boldsymbol{B}}$) can be recovered in a second-step estimation.

4.5.3 Asymptotic Principal Components for Unbalanced Panels

The treatment so far of asymptotic principal-components analysis assumes a balanced panel. There are two ways to proceed with asymptotic principal-components analysis using an unbalanced panel. One is to perform the cross-product operation defining $\boldsymbol{\Omega}$ element by element, each time using only the set of securities that have returns in both of the time dates:

$$\Omega_{t\tau} = \frac{1}{n_{t\tau}} \sum_{i=1}^{n_{t\tau}} x_{it} x_{i\tau}, \quad t, \tau = 1, \dots, T, \tag{4.21}$$

where $n_{t\tau}$ is the number of assets with returns in both period t and period τ and the sum runs only over these assets (Connor and Korajczyk 1987).

Using (4.21) increases the amount of data being utilized but it can create small-sample biases in the estimates. An alternative to (4.21) is the expectation–maximization (EM) procedure suggested by Stock and Watson (2002a). Here, we substitute in the conditionally expected return for each missing asset return. The algorithm is analogous to the EM algorithm for the estimated covariance matrix discussed in chapter 2:

$$\left.\begin{aligned} \boldsymbol{\Omega}^* &= \frac{1}{n} \boldsymbol{X}^{*\prime} \boldsymbol{X}^*, \\ \hat{\boldsymbol{F}} &= \text{eigvec}_k(\boldsymbol{\Omega}^*), \\ \hat{\boldsymbol{B}}_i &= \boldsymbol{X}_i \hat{\boldsymbol{F}}_{t/i} (\hat{\boldsymbol{F}}'_{t/i} \hat{\boldsymbol{F}}_{t/i})^{-1}, \\ \boldsymbol{X}^*_{it} &= \begin{cases} \boldsymbol{X}_{it} & \text{if return observed for asset } i \text{ at time } t, \\ \hat{\boldsymbol{B}}_i \hat{\boldsymbol{F}}_t & \text{otherwise.} \end{cases} \end{aligned}\right\} \tag{4.22}$$

The time-series regression to estimate $\boldsymbol{B}_i$ (4.22) is run only over the sample of time periods for which asset i has observed returns, and so $\hat{\boldsymbol{F}}_{t/i}$ denotes the estimated factor return matrix restricted to this subsample. Also note that when applying the EM algorithm to estimate $\boldsymbol{B}$ and $\boldsymbol{F}$, we must use the true returns only for estimating $\sigma^2_{\varepsilon t}$:

$$\hat{\sigma}^2_{\varepsilon t} = \frac{1}{n_t} \sum_{i=1}^{n_t} \hat{\varepsilon}^2_{it},$$

where the $\hat{\varepsilon}_{it}$ are the time-t asset-specific returns of the assets that have observed returns in that period.

4.5.4 Correcting for Time-Varying Asset-Specific Return Dispersion

The analysis so far makes the seemingly reasonable assumption that the cross-sectional variance of asset-specific returns, $\sigma^2_{\varepsilon t}$, is constant through time. Recent literature shows, surprisingly, that this is not an appropriate characterization of security returns data: see, for example, Campbell et al. (2001), who show, using a simple market-plus-industry factor model of monthly U.S. equity returns, that $\sigma^2_{\varepsilon t}$ has both long-term secular trends and short-term variation linked to business conditions. Jones (2001) gives a similar finding using a statistical factor model (again applied to monthly U.S. equity returns). Connor et al. (2006) extend the Jones analysis, describing the secular and short-term dynamics in $\sigma^2_{\varepsilon t}$ for a statistical factor model of monthly U.S. equity returns.

The asymptotic principal-components method described in the last section relies on $\sigma^2_{\varepsilon t}$ being constant through time. Jones generalized the asymptotic principal-components method to allow for time-varying $\sigma^2_{\varepsilon t}$. Rather than the limit of the cross-product matrix of asset-specific returns being a scalar matrix as in (4.18) it is assumed to be diagonal:

$$\frac{1}{n}\boldsymbol{\varepsilon}_t'\boldsymbol{\varepsilon}_\tau \overset{\mathrm{pr},n}{\approx} \begin{cases} 0 & \text{for } \tau \neq t, \\ \sigma^2_{\varepsilon t} > 0 & \text{for } \tau = t. \end{cases}$$

Suppose that we observe this diagonal (rather than scalar) matrix of cross-sectional mean asset-specific variances $\mathrm{Diag}[\boldsymbol{S}]$, where $\boldsymbol{S} = [\sigma^2_{\varepsilon 1}, \dots, \sigma^2_{\varepsilon T}]$, then we have

$$\boldsymbol{\Omega} \overset{\mathrm{pr},n}{\approx} \boldsymbol{F}'\boldsymbol{M}\boldsymbol{F} + \mathrm{Diag}[\sigma_{\varepsilon 1}, \dots, \sigma_{\varepsilon T}].$$

At this stage, Jones applies an iterative procedure similar to the Joreskog algorithm used for maximum-likelihood factor analysis. We begin by performing asymptotic principal-components analysis without any correction for time-varying variances. This estimation gives starting values for the idiosyncratic variances $\sigma_{\varepsilon 1}, \dots, \sigma_{\varepsilon T}$. Next we apply asymptotic principal-components analysis to a scaled version of the cross-product matrix $\boldsymbol{\Omega}$, giving scaled estimates of the factor return matrix $\boldsymbol{F}$ and updated estimates of the idiosyncratic variances $\sigma_{\varepsilon 1}, \dots, \sigma_{\varepsilon T}$. The iteration is repeated until convergence (which in practice is quite quick; typically less than ten iterations).

The convergent solution to this iterative procedure is a set of consistent estimates for the factor return matrix and the time series of idiosyncratic variances. As is usual the estimates of the factor returns

Table 4.1. Explanatory power of five statistical factors for monthly U.S. equity returns.

Subsample estimation period	Average asset-specific variance	One minus (average asset-specific variance/average total variance)	Total number of securities
01/1926–12/1930	0.0091	0.40	551
01/1931–12/1935	0.0172	0.69	686
01/1936–12/1940	0.0066	0.67	756
01/1941–12/1945	0.0049	0.45	786
01/1946–12/1950	0.0031	0.50	930
01/1951–12/1955	0.0025	0.35	1,019
01/1956–12/1960	0.0031	0.34	1,032
01/1961–12/1965	0.0051	0.29	1,860
01/1966–12/1970	0.0075	0.39	1,990
01/1971–12/1975	0.0092	0.44	4,186
01/1976–12/1980	0.0104	0.32	4,392
01/1981–12/1985	0.0133	0.23	4,708
01/1986–12/1990	0.0163	0.27	5,441
01/1991–12/1995	0.0177	0.15	5,564
01/1996–12/2000	0.0208	0.24	6,515

are subject to a rotational indeterminacy captured by a nonsingular $k \times k$ matrix $\boldsymbol{L}$:

$$\begin{aligned}
&\operatorname{eigvec}_k\{\operatorname{Diag}[\boldsymbol{S}]^{-1/2}\boldsymbol{\Omega}\operatorname{Diag}[\boldsymbol{S}]^{-1/2}\}\operatorname{Diag}[\boldsymbol{S}]^{1/2}\\
&\quad\overset{\mathrm{pr},n}{\approx}\operatorname{eigvec}_k\{\operatorname{Diag}[\boldsymbol{S}]^{-1/2}\boldsymbol{F}'\boldsymbol{M}\boldsymbol{F}\operatorname{Diag}[\boldsymbol{S}]^{-1/2}+\boldsymbol{I}_T\}\operatorname{Diag}[\boldsymbol{S}]^{1/2}\\
&\quad=\boldsymbol{L}\boldsymbol{F}.
\end{aligned}$$

It is clear that time-varying dispersion of asset-specific returns is an important component of the security market risk environment. So an estimation procedure that gives separate time-series values of $\sigma^2_{\varepsilon t}$ has a potentially important advantage for portfolio risk modeling and forecasting.

Table 4.1 shows the results from asymptotic principal-components analysis (with the Jones correction) of U.S. equity returns for the period 1926–2000, using sixty-month subsamples and setting the number of statistical factors equal to five. It is notable that the average idiosyncratic variance trends upward over time, and the proportion of variance explained by the factors (captured by one minus the ratio of average idiosyncratic variance to average total variance) trends downward. The secular trend toward higher average idiosyncratic variance in the U.S. equity market will be discussed further in chapter 9.

4.6 Number of Factors

All of the analysis so far has assumed that there is a fixed known number of factors. However, the number k of factors is something that in practice must be determined from the data. There are a variety of approaches and we will discuss some of them in this section.

For the small-n maximum-likelihood estimation of factor models we can use a variant of the same test used to test the factor modeling assumption. Now instead of comparing the factor-model-based covariance matrix estimate with the unrestricted estimate, we compare two factor model estimates, one with k factors and one with $k+1$ factors. We compare the log likelihood of the restricted estimates of the covariance matrices using k and $k+1$ factors:

$$\ln(h(\hat{\hat{C}}_k)/h(\hat{\hat{C}}_{k+1})) \overset{\text{di},T}{\approx} \chi^2(n). \tag{4.23}$$

In applications to returns data this standard test (4.23) has had, at best, mixed success. Dhrymes et al. (1984) find that the number of securities used in this test tends to affect the number of factors found (the larger n is, the larger the estimated value for k is). Conway and Reinganum (1988) show that there is a tendency to find too many factors in small-T samples. Shanken (1987) shows that correcting for nonsynchronous trading (if daily data is used) substantially alters the number of factors found. There is also the difficulty that the test relies too heavily on the strict factor model assumption, since it simply tests whether the asset-specific covariance matrix is diagonal. The assumption of a diagonal matrix is a convenient fiction in many circumstances, but when taken literally in this way it is a poor representation of security market returns.

Given the inadequacy and mixed empirical performance of the standard small-n test, analysts have naturally turned to large-n tests. A straightforward if naive approach to find k in the case of an approximate factor model hinges on the behavior of the eigenvalues of the return covariance matrix. However, Brown (1989) shows that the empirical properties of these sample eigenvalues are notably different from the theoretical properties of the true eigenvalues. In particular, the first estimated eigenvalue tends to dominate and all the other sample eigenvalues tend to increase as the cross section n increases. Connor and Korajczyk (1993) expand on Brown's result, examining the properties of the eigenvalues as n grows holding T fixed. The sample eigenvalues are complicated nonlinear functions of the sample covariance matrix. The sampling behavior of the ordered eigenvalues has not proved useful for determining k.

Given that the strict factor model conditions are not really necessary for most modern estimation techniques, a more natural approach to determining k is to focus on the pervasiveness condition (4.17) of an approximate factor model. This condition requires that only k factors have a pervasive ability to explain the cross section of random returns. Connor and Korajczyk (1993) suggest comparing the cross-sectional average asset-specific variance estimated using k factors with that estimated using $k + 1$ factors. If there are only k true factors, then adding the $(k + 1)$st factor (or pseudo-factor) should have a negligible effect on the cross-sectional average asset-specific variance. Connor and Korajczyk estimate cross-sectional asset-specific variance $\sigma_{\varepsilon t}^2$ with k factors on the odd months, t, and with $k + 1$ factors on the even months, τ, and test whether the difference $\sigma_{\varepsilon t}^2 - \sigma_{\varepsilon\tau}^2$ is significantly different from zero. Jones's (2001) evidence on the time variation in $\sigma_{\varepsilon t}^2$ creates problems for the Connor–Korajczyk test of the number of factors since the test requires that $\sigma_{\varepsilon t}^2$ is constant over time.

Bai and Ng (2002) set up the factor number determination problem as a model selection problem. This approach makes clear that determining the number of factors involves a trade-off between model parsimony and good fit to the data. They generalize the standard approximation by allowing both n and T to increase. Their tests are variations on Akaike- and Bayesian-information-criterion-based tests. Essentially, the tests examine the decrease in time-series/cross-sectional average asset-specific variance with the addition of a $(k + 1)$st factor, subtracting a penalty function to correct for the lost degrees of freedom when the extra factor is added to the estimation set. Note that whereas Connor and Korajczyk rely on the cross-sectional average variance calculated separately at each date, Bai and Ng take the full panel data set average variance:

$$\sigma_\varepsilon^2 = \frac{1}{T}\sum_{t-1}^{T} \sigma_{\varepsilon t}^2.$$

Their test uses a penalty function PC that depends on the number of estimated factors employed in the calculation of σ_ε^2:

$$PC(k) = \sigma_\varepsilon^2 + kg(n, T), \tag{4.24}$$

where $g(n, T)$ is a penalty function that depends on the dimension of the returns data set (both the n and T dimensions). The penalty is to adjust for possible overfitting of the model by using too many factors. The optimal value of k is the value that maximizes $PC(k)$. Bai and Ng offer a variety of specifications for the penalty function $g(n, T)$ that guarantee the correct choice of k as n and T both grow large. Choosing between the particular specifications depends on simulation evidence of their behavior for finite sample sizes. One penalty function specification that performs well according to their simulation evidence is

$$g(n,T) = \sigma_{\varepsilon}^{2}\left(\frac{n+T}{nT}\right)\ln\left(\frac{nT}{n+T}\right). \tag{4.25}$$

Applied to monthly U.S. equity returns data, they find that two factors is the optimal number by their criterion.

5
The Macroeconomy and Portfolio Risk

Factor models of security returns divide returns into components that are specific to individual assets or small groups of assets and components that are common and pervasive across many assets. The pervasive components are caused by new information or events that affect most or all assets. In many cases these pervasive shocks can be traced to new realizations or changes in expectations about macroeconomic variables. Understanding the relationships between asset returns and the macroeconomy gives the analyst a deeper understanding of the pervasive risks in security markets.

Section 5.1 discusses the estimation of macroeconomic factor models. Section 5.2 analyzes the empirical links between macroeconomic announcements and security returns. Section 5.3 considers how government macroeconomic policy rules can affect the link between macroeconomic variables and asset returns. Section 5.4 looks at dynamic market betas and their connections to the business cycle. Section 5.5 assesses the overall value and contribution of macroeconomic models in portfolio risk analysis applications.

5.1 Estimating Macroeconomic Factor Models

5.1.1 Definition of a Macroeconomic Factor Model

Recall that an approximate factor model is a set of linear relations between excess returns $\boldsymbol{x}$ and k observable factors $\boldsymbol{f}$ with uncorrelated or weakly correlated residuals $\boldsymbol{\varepsilon}$. In a *macroeconomic factor model* the factors driving returns are observed time series.

The realized return on an asset depends on the realized cash payments on the asset and capital gains or losses, which, in turn, are determined by changes in expected future cash payments and changes in discount rates. From the definition of return we have

$$r_{it} = \frac{\mathrm{CF}_{it} + p_{it}}{p_{it-1}} - 1, \tag{5.1}$$

where CF_{it} is the cash payment on asset i at time t and p_{it} is the price of asset i at time t. Some of the earliest work on macroeconomic factor models can be found in Chan et al. (1985) and Chen et al. (1986). To motivate their macroeconomic factor model, Chen et al. (1986) consider the unexpected part of return, $\tilde{r}_{it} = r_{it} - E_{t-1}[r_{it}]$, using (5.1):

$$\tilde{r}_{it} = \frac{\widetilde{\mathrm{CF}}_{it} + \tilde{p}_{it}}{p_{it-1}},$$

noting that $E_{t-1}[p_{it-1}] = p_{it-1}$. Hence realized return is necessarily a function of the shocks to cash flows $\widetilde{\mathrm{CF}}_{it}$ and prices $\tilde{p}_{it}$. The authors also note that the price innovation $\tilde{p}_{it}$ will reflect new information about future cash flows and changes in required return. All three of these fundamental variates that drive realized returns—cash flow innovations, new information about future cash flows, and changes in required returns—will respond to a considerable degree to macroeconomic variables. Chen et al. make the assumption that returns are linearly related to the innovations in a set of macroeconomic variables $\boldsymbol{m}_t$:

$$r_{it} = a_i + \boldsymbol{B}_i \boldsymbol{f}_t + \varepsilon_{it}, \tag{5.2}$$

$$\boldsymbol{f}_t = \boldsymbol{m}_t - E_{t-1}[\boldsymbol{m}_t], \tag{5.3}$$

where the asset-specific returns are uncorrelated or weakly correlated, and are uncorrelated with the factors.

The return equation (5.1) can be written using log return: in particular, $r_{\mathrm{l}t} = \log(\mathrm{CF}_{it} + p_{it}) - \log(p_{it-1})$. This yields an approximate linear relationship between unexpected return and changes in expected cash payments (that is, dividends) and discount rates (Campbell and Shiller 1989; Campbell 1991):

$$\begin{aligned}\tilde{r}_{\mathrm{l}t} &= r_{\mathrm{l}t} - E_{t-1}[r_{\mathrm{l}t}] \\ &\overset{*}{\approx} (E_t - E_{t-1}) \sum_{j=0}^{\infty} \phi^j (\mathrm{DEX}_{t+j}) - (E_t - E_{t-1}) \sum_{j=0}^{\infty} \phi^j r_{\mathrm{l}t+j},\end{aligned} \tag{5.4}$$

where $\tilde{r}_{\mathrm{l}t}$ is the unexpected log return on the asset from $t-1$ to t, $(E_t - E_{t-1})$ is the change in the expected value of the argument, DEX_{t+j} is the change, from $t+j-1$ to $t+j$, in the expected log dividend, and ϕ is a parameter slightly smaller than one.

Campbell and Shiller (1989) and Campbell (1991) apply the approximate relation (5.4) to aggregate stock indices. A literal application of equation (5.4) to individual assets is problematic since many firms do not pay dividends, hence log dividend is undefined. Nonetheless, the approximation is useful in the search for macroeconomic factors. The macroeconomic variables driving returns will either explain changing expectations about future dividends (captured in the term $(E_t - E_{t-1}) \sum_{j=0}^{\infty} \phi^j(\mathrm{DEX}_{t+j})$) or changing expectations about future discount rates (captured in the term $(E_t - E_{t-1}) \sum_{j=0}^{\infty} \phi^j r_{1t+j}$) or both.

5.1.2 Identifying Macroeconomic Innovations

Accurately identifying the macroeconomic variables driving asset returns presents some significant hurdles. One problem is that the observation intervals of asset prices and macroeconomic series are often very different. Asset prices can be observed at high frequencies, such as daily or intra-daily, whereas macroeconomic series are typically observed monthly, quarterly, annually, or at even longer frequencies. Another problem is that it is often difficult for the econometrician to know when the historical macroeconomic data were impounded into asset returns. If a macroeconomic time series is reported with a lag or revised *ex post*, then the time-t macrovariate might be linked with subsequent returns rather than contemporaneous returns. On the other hand, asset returns will be linked to the unanticipated component of the macroeconomic variable not the time-t level of the variate. If investors have some ability to forecast the levels of the macroeconomic variables, then the time-t macroeconomic variable might be linked to returns in an earlier period. So, in theory, the link between asset returns and macroeconomic variables can be contemporaneous, lagging, or leading. Overall, empirical evidence is that asset returns tend to lead changes in macroeconomic time series (see, for example, Fama 1981).

Note that for estimation of $\boldsymbol{B}$ in (5.2) by time-series regressions of returns on the factors, the innovation $\boldsymbol{f}_t$ must be filtered from the raw macrovariates $\boldsymbol{m}_t$ as in (5.3). If the filtered values of $\boldsymbol{f}_t$ contain measurement error, this creates an errors-in-variables (EIV) problem in the regression-based estimation of the factor exposures in (5.2). There are three potential sources of errors-in-variables in $\boldsymbol{f}_t$. The first is that the observed macroeconomic series, $\boldsymbol{m}_t$, might be a noisy estimate of the true underlying macroeconomic variables that actually drive returns. The second is that economic agents may use a finer information set in setting expectations, $E_{t-1}[\boldsymbol{m}_t]$, than is available to the econometrician. The third is that the econometrician may not know exactly when $\boldsymbol{m}_t$ is known by market participants or whether the currently reported value of $\boldsymbol{m}_t$ has been revised from an initially reported value. These errors-in-variables problems are potentially large and can lead to estimated exposure coefficients $\hat{\boldsymbol{B}}$ being inconsistent, with bias of unknown sign.

Another confounding difficulty is the reverse causality from asset returns to macroeconomic variables. Note, for example, that the S&P 500 index is a component of the leading economic indicators of Stock and Watson (1989) and of the Conference Board.[1] Thus, the dynamics between asset returns and macroeconomic time series are likely to be complicated, with causality in both directions.

5.1.3 Empirical Findings

Chan et al. (1985) and Chen et al. (1986) specify the vector of macroeconomic variables, $\boldsymbol{m}_t$, to be

(a) the monthly percentage change in industrial production (led by one period);

(b) a measure of unexpected inflation;

(c) the change in expected inflation;

(d) the difference in returns on low-grade (Baa and under) corporate bonds and long-term government bonds; and

(e) the difference in returns on long-term government bonds and short-term Treasury bills.[2]

These two studies are mainly interested in studying whether these variables explain risk premia in the cross section of expected returns, rather than studying their ability to explain the time-series variability of $\tilde{\boldsymbol{x}}_t$. It is this latter concern that is critically important for portfolio risk modeling. Nonetheless, these studies are important for understanding the role of the macroeconomic analysis in portfolio risk analysis.

Note that industrial production is led by one month in both these studies. Using the lead of industrial production is motivated by the fact that industrial production for month t is the sum of daily industrial production flows over the entire month, where, ideally, we would like to measure the flow at the end of the month. Another reason for leading this variable is the fact, as stated above, that asset prices and returns tend to lead macroeconomic variables since they embody changes in expectation (as in equation (5.4)). Both these studies adjust for the annual seasonal pattern in the monthly industrial production data.

Expected real returns on Treasury bills are estimated using a time-series model from Fama and Gibbons (1984) and are subtracted from the Treasury bill rate to estimate expected inflation. The measure of unexpected inflation is actual inflation minus expected inflation. The change in expected inflation variable is just the change in the one-month-ahead estimate of expected inflation.

---

[1] See www.conference-board.org/economics/bci/pressrelease_output.cfm?cid=1.

[2] Berry et al. (1988) use a similar set of macroeconomic factors.

Sixty months of time-series observations are used to estimate assets' betas relative to the prespecified factors. Given these estimates of the factor sensitivities, $\hat{\boldsymbol{B}}_i$, cross-sectional regressions of returns on $\hat{\boldsymbol{B}}_i$ provide estimates of the returns on factor-mimicking portfolios, which are discussed in detail in section 6.2.3. As in Fama and MacBeth (1973), portfolios rather than individual assets are used in these second-stage regressions in order to reduce the errors-in-variables (EIV) problem caused by the use of $\hat{\boldsymbol{B}}_i$ rather than $\boldsymbol{B}_i$. Chen et al. (1986) form twenty portfolios on the basis of firm size (market capitalization of equity) at the beginning of the particular test period. The average risk premia are estimated for the full sample period (January 1958–December 1984) as well as for three subperiods.

The average factor risk premia are statistically significant over the entire sample period for the industrial production, unexpected inflation, and low-grade bond factors. The factor premium is marginally significant for the term-spread factor. To check how robust the results are to changes in the prespecified factors, Chen et al. (1986) perform the above exercise with the change in industrial production factor replaced by several alternative factors.

In the CAPM, the appropriate measure of risk is an asset's beta with respect to a market portfolio. Therefore, one logical alternative candidate as a factor would be a market portfolio proxy. The above analysis is conducted with the annual industrial production factor replaced by a market portfolio factor (either the equal-weighted or the value-weighted New York Stock Exchange (NYSE) portfolio). They find that the risk premia of the market factors are not statistically significant when the other factors are included in the regression.

Consumption-based asset pricing models (see, for example, Lucas 1978; Breeden 1979) imply that risk premia are determined by assets' covariance with agents' intertemporal marginal rate of substitution in consumption. This can be approximated by assets' covariance with changes in consumption. The growth rate in per capita real consumption is added as a factor (to replace the market portfolios). This growth rate is actually led by one period to reflect the fact that there are lags in data collection. The risk premium on the consumption factor is not significant when the other five prespecified factors are included.

The last alternative factor analyzed by Chen et al. (1986) is the percentage change in the price of oil. The same analysis as above is performed with the beta of assets' returns with respect to changes in oil prices replacing the other alternative factors. The estimated risk premium associated with oil price shocks is statistically insignificant for the full period and for two of the three subperiods. The subperiod in which the premium is statistically significant is that between 1958 and 1967.

Chen et al. (1986) conclude that the five prespecified factors provide a reasonable specification of the sources of systematic and priced risk in the economy. This conclusion is based largely on their results that suggest that, after controlling for factor risk, other measures of risk (such as market betas or consumption betas) do not seem to be priced.

Chan et al. (1985) seek to determine whether cross-sectional differences in factor risk are enough to explain the size anomaly evident in the literature. For each test year from 1958 to 1977, an estimation period is defined as the previous five-year interval (i.e., 1953–1957 is the estimation period for 1958, 1954–1958 is the estimation period for 1959, etc.). The sample consists of all NYSE firms that exist at the beginning of the estimation period and have price data at the end of the estimation period. Firm size is defined as the market capitalization of the firm's equity at the end of the estimation period. Each firm is ranked by firm size and assigned to one of twenty portfolios.

Chan et al. (1985) estimate the factor sensitivities of the twenty size-based portfolios relative to the prespecified factors and the equal-weighted NYSE portfolio over the estimation period. In the subsequent test year, cross-sectional regressions of portfolio returns on the estimated factor sensitivities are run each month. This is repeated for each test year and yields a monthly time series of returns on factor-mimicking portfolios from January 1958 to December 1977.

If the risk premia from the factor model explain the size anomaly, then the time-series averages of the residuals from the cross-sectional regression should be zero. Chan et al. (1985) use paired Student's t-tests and Hotelling T^2 tests to determine if the residuals have the same means across different size portfolios.

Chan et al. (1985) find that the risk premium for the equal-weighted market portfolio is positive in each subperiod but is not statistically significant. Over the entire period they find significant premia for the industrial production factor, the unexpected inflation factor, and the low-grade bond spread factor. They find that the average residuals are not significantly different across portfolios and that the difference in the average residuals between the portfolio of the smallest firms and the portfolio of the largest firms, while positive, is not significantly different from zero.

Since the focus of Chan et al. (1985) and Chen et al. (1986) is the pricing of macroeconomic risk in the cross section, there is little discussion of the explanatory power of the macroeconomic shocks, $\boldsymbol{f}_t$, in explaining the realization of $\tilde{\boldsymbol{x}}_t$. Connor and Korajczyk (1991) use a set of macroeconomic variables similar in spirit to those in Chan et al. (1985) and Chen et al. (1986). They study all of the macroeconomic series of the two previous studies except one: the change in expected inflation, which is replaced by unexpected unemployment. They also include equal- and value-weighted stock indices. They study the relationship between the macroeconomic series and factors extracted from monthly equity returns using the asymptotic principal-components procedure (discussed in chapter 4). In particular, they seek a rotation of the statistical factors so that they can be interpreted as shocks to the prespecified macroeconomic series. This rotation is inferred from a multivariate regression of the macroeconomic series on the factor portfolio returns. They report the adjusted coefficient of determination, $\bar{R}^2$, values of these regressions in their table 6.1. The macroeconomic series that are defined as excess returns on asset classes are reasonably correlated with the five statistical factors. The equal- and value-weighted stock indices have $\bar{R}^2$ values of 99.4% and 95.4%. The long-term versus short-term bond return has an $\bar{R}^2$ value of 20.2%. The low-grade versus high-grade bond return has an $\bar{R}^2$ value of 9.9%. By contrast, the purely macroeconomic series have very low values of $\bar{R}^2$. Unexpected unemployment has a value of 8.6%, unexpected inflation has a value of 6.3%, and unexpected industrial production has a value of 1.6%.

Thus, at a monthly frequency, there does not seem to be a strong relation between asset returns and the macroeconomic series studied in Chan et al. (1985) and Chen et al. (1986). Similar results are found by Cutler et al. (1989) and Chan et al. (1998). This might be due to the problems mentioned above: lead–lag mismatches, incorrect prewhitening, temporal aggregation, mismeasurement, and, possibly, an incorrect choice of macroeconomic factors. Given the low correlation of asset returns and macroeconomic series at monthly frequencies, it seems that using these macroeconomic factor models for building risk models and structuring portfolios to either hedge or take bets on macroeconomic fluctuations will not yield very precise estimates of appropriate hedge ratios. Papers that address the effect of misspecified factors on risk premia estimates include Jagannathan and Wang (1998), Kan and Zhang (1999), and Kan et al. (2009).

The Campbell–Shiller log-linear approximation in equation (5.4) is written in terms of dividends. However, there is an equivalence between present-value relations expressed in terms of dividends, cash flows, or earnings (see Fama and Miller 1972, pp. 86–89). Ball et al. (2009) suggest working with earnings rather than dividends since dividends are generally smoothed by management and may not give an accurate picture of the underlying cash flows of the firm. They scale earnings by the level of assets on the balance sheet to obtain return on assets (ROA). They apply the asymptotic principal-components procedure of Connor and Korajczyk (1986, 1987) to annual ROA for equities traded on the NYSE and the American stock exchanges (AMEX) with fiscal year-ends of December 31. They extract five common factors for ROA and five common factors for stock returns. The five earnings factors explain almost 60% of the variation in an average firm's ROA. Thus, earnings have important common undiversifiable shocks.

Ball et al. (2009) also apply the asymptotic principal-components procedure to annual percent return, where returns are measured from the beginning of April to the end of March. They chose differing annual periods for earnings and returns because December 31 earnings are not publicly known until some time in the following year. The U.S. Securities and Exchange Commission requires that firms report earnings within ninety days of their fiscal year-end and most firms comply (Alford et al. 1994). Therefore, the change in price from April to March corresponds to the period over which agents learn about changes in earnings. The five return factors also explain almost 60% of the variation in an average firm's annual stock return.

The contemporaneous correlation between the first earnings factor and the first return factor is -0.21 (where contemporaneous means earnings for January 1 to December 31 of year t and returns are measured from April of year t to March of year $t + 1$). Given the fact that changes in asset prices reflect news about current and future cash flows, returns may reasonably be expected to lead earnings changes (Fama 1981). Ball et al. (2009) report that the correlation between the first earnings factor for next year and the first return factor is 0.34 (i.e., the correlation between the earnings factor for January 1 to December 31 of year $t + 1$ and returns measured from April of year t to March of year $t + 1$). This positive correlation is what one would expect given the linearized present-value relation in equation (5.4).

The return and earnings factors are significantly correlated with macroeconomic aggregates: industrial production growth, real gross domestic product (GDP) growth, unemployment, and inflation. The first return factor has correlations of 0.23, 0.38, 0.40, and -0.19 with industrial production growth, real GDP growth, unemployment, and inflation, respectively. The corresponding correlations with the macroeconomic series are 0.25, 0.04, -0.71, and 0.08 for the first contemporaneous earnings factor and 0.58, 0.67, 0.14, and -0.25 for the first lead earnings factor. It is interesting that industrial production and GDP growth have higher correlations with the lead earnings factor than with the contemporaneous earnings factor. The first canonical correlation of the four macroeconomic series with the five systematic factors is 0.68 for returns, 0.76 for contemporaneous earnings, and 0.75 for lead earnings.

The results of Ball et al. (2009) show a strong relation between macroeconomic aggregates and asset returns (the left-hand side of equation (5.4)) at an annual frequency. A large component of that relation is due to the correlation of the macroeconomic series with current and future cash flows (the first set of terms on the right-hand side of equation (5.4)). Part of the increased explanatory power over monthly observation intervals may be due to a higher signal-to-noise ratio in the lead–lag relation between returns and macroeconomic series at an annual frequency. This poses some difficulties for estimating macroeconomic risk models for individual assets. We can estimate the systematic factors for long periods even though any individual asset may have a shorter sample period. However, many individual assets do not have a sufficiently long time series to estimate the relation between their annual returns and macroeconomic series with reasonable accuracy.

5.1.4 Identifying Macroeconomic Shocks by Statistical Factor Analysis

So far the studies we have cited have all specified, *ex ante*, the macroeconomic variables' to use in the risk models. An alternative approach is to select the components that are common across a large set of macroeconomic series. Stock and Watson (1998, 2002a,b) extend the method of asymptotic principal components to address this problem. They accommodate dynamic models in which the idiosyncratic error terms can be autocorrelated and variables can have differing observation intervals. In Stock and Watson (2002a), the relative performance of several approaches to forecasting industrial production over the next year is studied. One of the forecasting models is based on the factors extracted from a large set of macroeconomic series (149 series are used). The macroeconomic factor model outperforms univariate autoregressive, vector autoregressive (VAR), and leading indicator models in terms of lower mean-squared error.

In Stock and Watson (2002b) factors extracted from 215 monthly macroeconomic series are used to forecast eight series: industrial production, real personal income (less transfers), real manufacturing and trade sales, number of employees on nonagricultural payrolls, and four price indices. They evaluate models of the form

$$\hat{y}_{t+h} = \hat{\alpha}_h + \sum_{j=1}^{m} \hat{\beta}_{h,j}\hat{F}_{t+1-j} + \sum_{j=1}^{p} \hat{\gamma}_{h,j}y_{t+1-j}, \tag{5.5}$$

which allow the forecast to depend on current and lagged macroeconomic factors as well as on lagged values of the variable being forecasted. Univariate autoregressive specifications set the βs to zero, macro-factor models set the γs to zero, and hybrid models allow all parameters to be nonzero. For forecasting the real variables above, using the macroeconomic factor model or the hybrid model with two factors captures most of the forecasting improvement over a univariate autoregressive model. Interestingly, including lags of the macroeconomic factors, $\hat{\boldsymbol{F}}$, does not improve forecasts. This implies that the predictable dynamics of the series are explained by the contemporaneous macroeconomic factors. In contrast, for the price-level variables, including autoregressive terms always improves the forecasts. Again, the dynamics of the variables are picked up by the contemporaneous macroeconomic factors, and added factors do not improve forecasts.

The results in Stock and Watson (1998, 2002a,b) indicate that applying asymptotic principal components to macroeconomic time series provides useful factors for forecasting other macroeconomic variables. We know of no study that incorporates these macroeconomic factors into a portfolio risk model. However, the forecasting results give some hope that these factors will have more explanatory power for asset returns than some of the prespecified macroeconomic series used in previous studies.

5.2 Event Studies of Macroeconomic Announcements

The weakness in the observed correlation between asset returns and macroeconomic time series is partly due to the fact that anticipation of future macroeconomic variables is impounded in asset prices as information becomes available rather than as the macroeconomic series are announced. While agents do not know the exact number before it is reported for variates like industrial production, unemployment, or inflation, they learn about these variables through the media or by direct observation (e.g., some brokerage analysts sample prices of goods and services directly). From equation (5.4), asset returns this period are based on the change in expectations in cash flows and required returns. Those changes in expectations may have weak correlations with contemporaneous changes in macroeconomic series due to this timing mismatch.

One approach to alleviating the associated EIV problem is to perform an "event study" in which one isolates periods in which macroeconomic announcements take place. The event study is a common approach to isolating the effects of various corporate announcements. The approach requires the researcher to develop a forecasting model for the macroeconomic time series based on publicly available information, yielding the forecasts $\boldsymbol{m}_t^*$. While time-series models are often used, there is a growing literature that uses survey data to measure expectations. As in any forecasting model, $\boldsymbol{m}_t^*$ is based on an assumed information set that is a subset of information available to agents, so $\boldsymbol{m}_t^*$ is an error-prone measure of expectations, $E_{t-1}[\boldsymbol{m}_t]$.

In addition to the forecasting model, we need to determine when the macroeconomic announcement is made and the actual observation announced, $\boldsymbol{m}_t$. Thus, we need the original announcement and a subsequently revised value, although the asset price reaction to the announcement can help us predict what those revisions will be (Gilbert 2007).

Given the announcement-date factor innovation,

$$\boldsymbol{f}_t = \boldsymbol{m}_t - \boldsymbol{m}_t^*,$$

we can estimate the relationship between excess returns and $\boldsymbol{f}_t$:

$$\boldsymbol{x}_t = \boldsymbol{\xi}\boldsymbol{f}_t + \boldsymbol{v}_t. \tag{5.6}$$

McQueen and Roley (1993) find that, while interest rates exhibit statistically significant reactions to announcements of macroeconomic data, stock prices do not. In fact, the S&P 500 index falls on news of an unexpected increase in industrial production.

Rigobon and Sack (2006) discuss the EIV problem (i.e., that we observe $\boldsymbol{f}_t^* = \boldsymbol{f}_t + \boldsymbol{u}_t$ rather than $\boldsymbol{f}_t$) encountered in estimating equation (5.6). The EIV problem leads to a downward bias in ordinary least-squares estimates of $\boldsymbol{\xi}$. They suggest an approach to identification that relies on the assumption that the nonannouncement component of asset returns, $\boldsymbol{v}_t$, is either homoskedastic or we have a model to predict the variance of $\boldsymbol{v}_t$. Under the assumption of homoskedasticity, and considering the univariate case for simplicity, their estimator is

$$\hat{\xi} = \frac{\hat{\sigma}_{\mathrm{AD}}^2(r_t) - \hat{\sigma}^2(r_t)}{\widehat{\mathrm{cov}}(r_t, f_t^*)}, \tag{5.7}$$

where $\hat{\sigma}_{\mathrm{AD}}^2(r_t)$ is the return variance in announcement periods and $\hat{\sigma}^2(r_t)$ is the return variance in nonannouncement periods. They study the reaction of interest rates and equity returns to thirteen different types of macroeconomic announcements using thirty-minute intraday announcement periods. Using the unadjusted event study approach (5.6), they find strong evidence of reaction to announcements in bond prices but a much weaker reaction in equity prices. One explanation offered is that the announcements have offsetting effects on cash flows and discount rates in equation (5.4). However, the EIV-corrected estimates, equation (5.7), are substantially larger than the event study estimates.

McQueen and Roley (1993) consider the possibility that the unconditional response coefficients, ξ in equation (5.6) or the corrected version in equation (5.7), mask significant responses that differ across the business cycle. This is discussed further in the next section.

5.3 Macroeconomic Policy Endogeneity

A difficulty in measuring the links between the macroeconomy and financial market returns comes from feedback effects of government macroeconomic policy on financial markets. Central banks set monetary policy with an eye on the macroeconomy, including the level of interest rates, equity prices, foreign exchange rates, and real estate values. One of the most important control variates of central banks is the short-term borrowing rate. Central banks can also influence the exchange rate to some degree. Therefore, asset prices influence monetary policy and, in turn, are partly determined by monetary policy. Macroeconomic policy, asset prices, and economic shocks are simultaneously determined and causality among them is multidirectional.

The endogeneity of macroeconomic policy variates with respect to asset returns implies that the factor model specification for one sample period may perform poorly out of sample. Macroeconomic factor models, as in equation (5.2), are essentially reduced-form models that do not explicitly model the endogeneity of the macro-factors and asset returns. A theoretically consistent model will include a simultaneous equation for the central bank policy function.

An oft-used representation of central bank policy is the "Taylor rule" (Taylor 1993), in which interest rates are a linear function of inflation and gross national product (GNP). Thus, interest rates (and, therefore, bond prices) are policy variables rather than exogenous variables in this model. This can be used to analyze the modeling errors induced in reduced-form models, which ignore policy feedback. For example, Clarida and Waldman (2007) argue that bad news about inflation can be good news for the exchange rate if the monetary authority is following a Taylor rule (contrary to the classical reduced-form model in which inflation causes currency depreciation). This is precisely because the bad news about inflation causes the monetary authority to take actions that lead to anticipated currency appreciation.

Stock market price changes can also influence central bank policy. Rigobon and Sack (2003) estimate the influence of stock market price movements on monetary policy and conclude that a 5% rise in the stock market leads to a 50% increase in the probability of a tightening of monetary policy, which in turn leads to a 0.25% increase in interest rates.

McQueen and Roley (1993) argue that macroeconomic policy endogeneity explains the poor explanatory power of economic factors for security returns. They argue that unconditional factor betas are close to zero due to offsetting responses during different phases of the business cycle. Recall that macroeconomic shocks influence both the cash flow and discount rate components that determine returns in equation (5.4). McQueen and Roley argue that the relative importance of the cash flow/discount rate components shift over the business cycle. During periods of high economic activity (measured as deviations from trend) good news about the economy is associated with declines in the stock market. On the other hand, during periods of low economic activity good news about the economy is associated with increases in the stock market. They find that the differences in the response coefficient, ξ in equation (5.6), across phases of the business cycle are statistically significant. In a related study, Boyd et al. (2005) empirically analyze the relationship between unemployment news and stock market returns. Similar to the findings of McQueen and Roley (1993), Boyd et al. find that an announcement of rising unemployment is good news for stocks during economic expansions and bad news during economic contractions. They argue that discount rate information is the dominant announcement news during expansions, with good economic news being associated with higher discount rates. By equation (5.4) this leads to lower stock prices. Conversely, during economic contractions the dominant news is about cash flows. In contractions, good economic news is good for stocks since the positive cash flow news dominates the negative discount rate effect.

Macroeconomic policy rules sometimes change. A classic example is exchange rate regimes switching between pegged and floating rate systems. Another example of a functional shift in policy is the shift in monetary policy in the United States at the end of the 1970s. The U.S. Federal Reserve Board shifted from targeting interest rates to targeting money supply. This was associated with a large change in the level and volatility of interest rates.

These types of regime shifts have direct implications for macroeconomic factor models. Let us look at the effect of the Federal Reserve Board regime switch on some of the Chan et al. (1985) and Chen et al. (1986) economic factors. Before 1979 monetary policy was well-approximated as an attempt to hold the short-run real rate constant

(Fama 1975, 1976):

$$r_{0t} = r_0^* + E_{t-1}[i_t],$$

where r_{0t} is the nominal interest rate, r_0^* is the expected real interest rate, and i_t is inflation.

In this regime, *ex post* real interest rates depend upon the difference between expected and realized inflation:

$$r_{0t}^* = r_0^* - (i_t - E_{t-1}[i_t]).$$

A related specification in Fama and Gibbons (1982, 1984) assumes that the real return follows a random walk but that the variance of the innovation in real return is small relative to the variance of unexpected inflation. They derive expected inflation from realized inflation and observed nominal short-term rates using a Kalman filter. The unexpected inflation factor in Chan et al. (1985) and in Chen et al. (1986) relies on the Fama–Gibbons filter.

Paul Volker's 1979 Federal Reserve Board policy change to a money-supply-only policy function had significant effects on inflation and interest rates. The money-supply-based policy function was subsequently changed to an inflation-focused target under Alan Greenspan. Evans and Wachtel (1992, 1993) and others show that there is a clearly discernible regime break in inflation expectations and bond market behavior during the period 1979–84.

Campbell et al. (2003) apply a vector autoregression model to stock and bond index returns and several state variables using either quarterly data from 1952 to 1999 or annual data from 1890 to 1998. They find that the long-horizon inflation-adjusted risk contribution of long-term bonds and short-term bonds is critically dependent upon the monetary policy regime. Before 1979, a period of real-rate targeting, nominal long-term bonds were very risky and optimal portfolios had large short positions in these assets (see Campbell et al.'s figure 3). In the inflation-targeting regime, nominal long-term bonds are low risk and rolled-over short term bonds have increased risk. Thus, long-horizon portfolio risk modeling is critically dependent upon the assumed monetary regime.

Using reduced-form factor models to study the relation between macroeconomic variables and asset returns has advantages in terms of ease of implementation and the amount of data that can be brought to bear on the analysis. However, endogeneity of the relations among variables and the possibility of large regime shifts have clear implications for these approaches. Reduced-form models can run afoul of the Lucas critique (Lucas 1976) and perform poorly out of sample.

5.4 Business Cycle Betas

Single-factor risk models with dynamic betas, where the dynamic movements of the betas are linked to macroeconomic variables, are an alternative to multiple-beta macroeconomic factors models. Consider a conditional one-factor model of excess returns,

$$\boldsymbol{x}_t = \boldsymbol{a} + \boldsymbol{\beta}_{t-1} x_{\mathrm{m}t} + \boldsymbol{\varepsilon}_t, \tag{5.8}$$

recalling that $x_{\mathrm{m}t}$ is the excess return to the market portfolio, and let the n-vector of conditional betas functionally depend upon a vector of macroeconomic variables $\boldsymbol{m}_t$:

$$\boldsymbol{\beta}_{t-1} = f(\boldsymbol{m}_{t-1}). \tag{5.9}$$

There is a substantial body of evidence showing that market factor betas vary across the business cycle (see, for example, Keim and Stambaugh 1986; Fama and French 1989; Chen 1991). In many studies the exact functional form in (5.9) is not estimated; rather, the time-series returns data is sorted into "good" and "bad" macroeconomic states and then (5.8) is estimated separately on the two subsamples. Significant differences in the beta estimates are indicative of a connection between the macroeconomy and asset betas.

Business-cycle-related dynamics in betas mean that unconditional betas cannot be used to compare the appropriate risk premia of assets. Assets that have higher betas when macroeconomic conditions are poor will typically command larger risk premia than assets with constant unconditional betas of the same magnitude. Perez-Quiros and Timmermann (2000) estimate a regime-switching model in which stocks' risk sensitivities depend on the regime. They find that small-capitalization stocks have more asymmetric responses to the state of the business cycle. They suggest that this risk asymmetry could explain the high expected returns of small stocks relative to their unconditional betas. Jagannathan and Wang (1996) show that the covariation of dynamic betas with the dynamic market risk premium affects the risk-adjusted returns of assets. Since the market risk premium is higher during recessions, assets whose betas are higher in recessions will have higher unconditional expected returns.

Campbell and Vuolteenaho (2004) use a dynamic single-beta model and highlight the differential risk premia associated with cash-flow-related beta and discount-rate-related beta. That is, they use (5.4) to decompose the return on the market portfolio and differentiate between an asset's covariance with the two separate parts of the market portfolio's random return. They argue that covariance of an asset's return with discount rate news will have a substantially larger risk premium (in a dynamic version of the CAPM) than covariance with cash flow news.

5.5 Empirical Fit and the Relative Value of Macroeconomic Factor Models

In terms of parsimonious description of the covariance matrix of asset returns, the fundamental characteristic and statistical factor models tend to outperform macroeconomic factor models (see Connor 1995; Cochrane 2005). For most risk-management applications, this fact would lead us to prefer these two approaches to the macroeconomic factor model approach.

However, for pricing implications, Cochrane (2005) argues that the macroeconomic approach places discipline on the "fishing expedition" of asset pricing models. Risk premia should accrue to those assets who pay off well in good times and pay off poorly in bad times. We should be seeking pricing models for which the definition of good/bad times makes sense in the context of a macroeconomic model. There is a huge literature in finance and macroeconomics that studies asset pricing within the macroeconomy. We have explicitly chosen not to emphasize the pricing implication of risk models here and we refer the interested reader to the excellent survey of that literature in Cochrane (2005). However, ignoring macroeconomic models when building portfolio risk models opens up the possibility of overfitting past empirical relations across assets and missing the changes in those relations due to temporal changes in the nature of the state variables driving the economy.

6 Security Characteristics and Pervasive Risk Factors

Observable characteristics of equities—such as market capitalization, book-to-price ratio and other accounting ratios, and return-based characteristics such as momentum and volatility—have surprisingly strong power in explaining the comovements of individual equity returns. Similarly (but less surprisingly), cash flow and credit characteristics explain the comovements of individual bonds. This chapter explores the empirical link between security characteristics and return comovements and discusses how best to incorporate them into portfolio risk analysis models. Section 6.1 discusses some of the stock and bond market characteristics with empirical links to return comovements. Section 6.2 introduces Rosenberg's approach to factor modeling of security returns, in which suitably normalized security characteristics serve as factor exposures. Section 6.3 examines the Fama–French factor model of stock and bond returns, a time-series regression-based alternative to Rosenberg's model. Section 6.4 considers semiparametric characteristic-based factor models, which combine elements of the Rosenberg and Fama–French approaches.

6.1 Equity and Fixed-Income Characteristics

6.1.1 Characteristics of Default-Free Fixed-Income Securities

The dominant source of risk for a default-free fixed-income security is changes in the term structure of interest rates. As a consequence, characteristic-based risk measures for default-free fixed-income securities rely on models of term-structure shocks.

6.1.1.1 Term-Structure Shocks

The term structure of interest rates is defined as the set of long rates $y = (y_1, y_2, \ldots, y_T)$, where y_τ is the internal rate of return[1] on a

[1] The internal rate of return is the constant interest rate that sets the present value of future cash flows equal to the current price of the bond.

τ-period pure-discount[2] bond with maturity τ. Since internal rates of return and yields are identical for pure-discount bonds, the term structure is also called the *yield curve.* As a first approximation, interest rates at different maturities tend to move approximately in parallel: that is, a drop in the one-year long rate is generally accompanied by a roughly equal drop in long rates at all other maturities. Sensitivity to such a parallel shift in the term structure is the dominant risk factor in fixed-income securities. This observation is borne out by empirical analysis. Litterman and Scheinkman (1991) fit a three-factor interest rate risk model using weekly observations of U.S. treasury prices between January 1984 and June 1988. The dominant risk factor is a parallel shift of the term structure and it explains roughly 90% of the term-structure variation.

Duration is the exposure of a bond to the risk of a parallel shift in the term structure. It is the most basic fixed-income characteristic. Duration can be expressed as the weighted-average time to maturity of the bond's repayments, as we show next.

By nonarbitrage principles, the price of any T-period default-free bond can be written as the discounted sum of its cash flows using the current T vector of long rates, $\boldsymbol{y} = (y_1, y_2, \dots, y_T)$:

$$p_i(\boldsymbol{y}) = \sum_{\tau=1}^{T} \frac{\mathrm{CF}_{i\tau}}{(1+y_\tau)^\tau}, \tag{6.1}$$

where p_i is the price of the ith bond, $\mathrm{CF}_{i\tau}$ is the τth future cash flow of bond i, and y_τ is the yield on a τ-period pure-discount bond. The bond price, collection of future cash flows, and the vector of yields are all dependent on the time t of analysis. We suppress this dependence in the notation for readability. Suppose that we shift the τth yield as follows:

$$y_\tau(s) = y_\tau - s(1+y_\tau), \tag{6.2}$$

so that $y_\tau(0) = y_\tau$. This is an approximate parallel shift in rates, designed to make the algebra work out neatly. We define the shift sensitivity of the bond to term-structure shock $\mathrm{d}s$ as the derivative of $p_i(y(s))$ at $s = 0$ divided by p_i:

$$\mathrm{Shift}_i = \frac{1}{p_i}\left(\frac{\partial p_i(y(s))}{\partial s}\right). \tag{6.3}$$

This is a sensible definition of return sensitivity since if there is a very small parallel shock to long rates, as in (6.2) with $s = \mathrm{d}s$ for small $\mathrm{d}s$, then the bond return over a short time interval will be well-approximated by

[2] A pure-discount bond has only one cash flow; the cash flow is paid at its maturity date τ.

(6.3) times ds. Calculating the scaled derivative (6.3) using the present-value formula gives shift sensitivity:

$$\text{Shift}_i = \frac{1}{p_i}\sum_{\tau=1}^{T}\tau\left[\frac{\text{CF}_{i\tau}}{(1+y_\tau)^\tau}\right]. \tag{6.4}$$

The formula for shift sensitivity (6.4) is also the formula for bond duration, the weighted average time to maturity of the bond, with weight at time τ equal to $\text{CF}_{i\tau}/(1+y_\tau)^\tau$, which is the proportion of bond value paid that period.

While shift risk is the dominant component of interest rate risk, there are other significant risk factors. The second most important component of interest rate risk is a term-structure *twist*, which is a steepening or flattening of the yield curve: the long and short ends move in opposite directions. As for the shift, there are varied forms of this factor in the literature. A neat formulation is in terms of a swivel point, which can be chosen to be a middle vertex t_{mid}. In the specification below, longer rates decrease as a linear function of distance from t_{mid}, while shorter rates increase:

$$y(s) = y_\tau[(1 - s(t - t_{\text{mid}}))].$$

Taking the scaled derivative of (6.1) with respect to s at $s = 0$ gives the twist sensitivity of the bond:

$$\begin{aligned}\text{Twist}_i &= \frac{1}{p_i}\left(\frac{\partial p_i(y(s))}{\partial s}\right)\\ &= \frac{1}{p_i}\sum_{\tau=1}^{T}(\tau - \tau_{\text{mid}})\frac{\text{CF}_{i\tau}}{(1+y_\tau)^\tau}.\end{aligned} \tag{6.5}$$

The next most important interest rate risk factor is a change in the curvature of the term structure. This factor is commonly known as a *butterfly* shock, since the two "ends" of the term structure move in opposite directions like the wings of a butterfly in flight. The shocks to the long and short ends of the yield curve are opposite, while the shock at the swivel point is zero. See figure 6.1 for a graphical depiction of the shift, twist, and butterfly shocks. Adding the butterfly shock into the model of long rates,

$$y_\tau(s) = y_\tau[(1 - s|\tau - \tau_{\text{mid}}|)], \tag{6.6}$$

taking the scaled derivative with respect to b, and setting $s = 0$,

$$\begin{aligned}\text{Butterfly}_i &= \frac{1}{p_i}\left(\frac{\partial p_i(y(s))}{\partial s}\right)\\ &= \frac{1}{p_i}\sum_{\tau=1}^{T}|\tau - \tau_{\text{mid}}|\frac{\text{CF}_{i\tau}}{(1+y_\tau)^\tau}.\end{aligned} \tag{6.7}$$

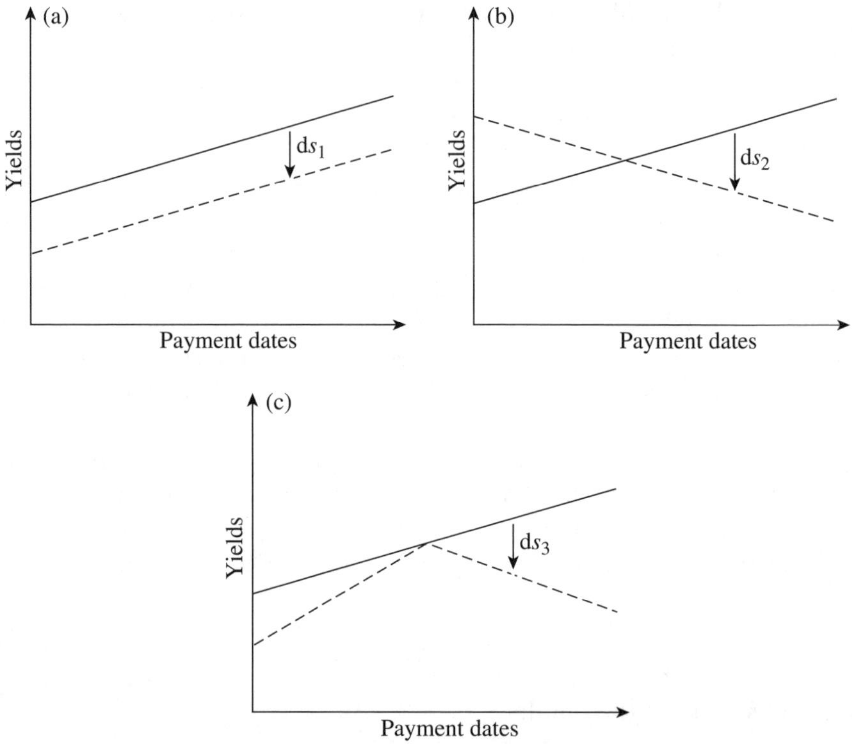

Figure 6.1. A graphical depiction of three term-structure shocks: (a) shift, (b) twist, and (c) butterfly shocks.

Note that it is simple to combine the three term-structure shock functions into a three-variable function $y_\tau(s_1, s_2, s_3)$. Define the $n \times 3$ matrix of factor exposures $\boldsymbol{B} = [\text{Shift}, \text{Twist}, \text{Butterfly}]$ and the 3 vector of characteristic-based factors $\boldsymbol{f} = (\mathrm{d}s_1, \mathrm{d}s_2, \mathrm{d}s_3)$. Treating the term-structure innovations $(\mathrm{d}s_1, \mathrm{d}s_2, \mathrm{d}s_3)$ as small enough for a first-order Taylor expansion to provide a useful approximation gives a three-factor model of the vector of bond returns:

$$\boldsymbol{r} = \boldsymbol{a} + \boldsymbol{B}\boldsymbol{f} + \boldsymbol{\varepsilon}, \tag{6.8}$$

where we can view the idiosyncratic returns $\boldsymbol{\varepsilon}$ as arising from missing features such as pricing errors, or tax and liquidity considerations. The vector of constant terms $\boldsymbol{a}$ serves to capture the predictable returns on the bonds. The three characteristic-based risk exposures—shift (6.4), twist (6.5), and butterfly (6.7)—are easily calculated using the promised cash flows of each bond and the current term structure of interest rates. Since the factor betas in (6.8) do not need to be estimated from returns but instead can be directly calculated from the characteristics of the asset (in particular the bond's schedule of promised cash flows), this is called a *characteristic-based factor model.*

The shift–twist–butterfly, three-factor model of default-free fixed-income securities fits the data well. Litterman and Scheinkman (1991) find that this model explains an average of 98.4% of the term-structure variance in the U.S. market between January 1984 and June 1988. Chaumeton et al. (1996) apply the two-factor version (shift and twist) to the monthly excess returns of government bonds from twelve developed markets, using nation-specific models and also a global model. They find that this two-factor model has an average explanatory power of 95.7% when estimated separately on each national market. When all the bonds are treated as belonging to an integrated global market with only two worldwide term-structure factors, this simple model still has explanatory power of 60.3%.

6.1.1.2 Convexity

The shift–twist–butterfly return approximation in (6.8) is valid only for suitably small term-structure shocks, since it relies on a first-order Taylor expansion in the vector equation for yields. Taylor expansion approximations can be made more accurate by including higher-order terms. *Convexity* is the second-order term in the Taylor expansion of price as a function of the parallel shift, ds. Taking the second derivative of price as a function of $y(s)$ from (6.2) evaluated at $s = 0$, and dividing by p_i, gives

$$\begin{aligned}\text{Convex}_i &= \frac{1}{p_i}\frac{\partial^2 p_i}{\partial s^2} \\ &= \frac{1}{p_i}\sum_{\tau=1}^{T}\tau^2\frac{\text{CF}_{i\tau}}{(1+y_\tau)^\tau}.\end{aligned} \tag{6.9}$$

Including both shift sensitivity and convexity gives a quadratic (not linear) model of term-structure risk:

$$r_i = a + \text{Shift}_i\ \mathrm{d}s + \text{Convex}_i(\mathrm{d}s)^2 + \varepsilon.$$

Convexity is particularly important if the cash flows of the bonds are functionally dependent on the term structure. The classic example of this is a mortgage-backed security, where mortgage repayment rates respond to term-structure changes. For a bond with term-structure-dependent cash flows, convexity can be a very strong component of risk.

An important extension of the three-factor bond model is the inclusion of characteristics that measure the default-risk sensitivities of the bonds. We will defer the issue of fixed-income default risk to a dedicated chapter on credit risk (chapter 11).

6.2 Characteristic-Based Factor Models of Equities

6.2.1 Equity Characteristics and Empirical Comovements

For equities it is sometimes difficult to explain theoretically the link between security characteristics and the common risk factors in returns. Nonetheless, security characteristics are surprisingly powerful in describing the comovements of individual equities. Table 6.1 lists some of the attributes that have been used in characteristic-based factor models of stock returns, how they are measured, and research references that include them in estimation.

6.2.2 Rosenberg's Linear Specification

Consider a factor model of an n-vector of excess returns with k factors:

$$\boldsymbol{x} = \boldsymbol{B}\boldsymbol{f} + \boldsymbol{\varepsilon}. \tag{6.10}$$

In a statistical factor model (see chapter 4) both the exposure matrix $\boldsymbol{B}$ and the factor returns $\boldsymbol{f}$ are estimated from the panel data set of returns. In an economic factor model (see chapter 5) the factor returns are observed as economic time series. The factor exposure matrix is estimated from time-series regression using the factor returns and the panel data set of asset returns.

Rosenberg (1974) suggests a characteristic-based factor model of equity returns, in which the factor exposure matrix in (6.10) is linearly related to a set of asset characteristics:

$$\boldsymbol{B} = \boldsymbol{A}\boldsymbol{L}, \tag{6.11}$$

where $\boldsymbol{A}$ is the $n \times k$ matrix of characteristics, giving the k characteristics for each of the n assets, and $\boldsymbol{L}$ is a nonsingular $k \times k$ matrix. Since the factor model has a rotational indeterminacy, it is simplest to set $\boldsymbol{L} = \boldsymbol{I}$. This choice also has the benefit that the factors now have a meaningful rotation, since they are tied to the characteristics.

Rosenberg's assumption that the factor betas are linear in a set of characteristics (6.11) seems quite arbitrary for most equity-model characteristics. The linear form of the relationship between characteristics and betas should be viewed as a fairly standard empirical approximation: linear models are used extensively in economic and financial research even when theory imposes only a nonlinear relationship. More troubling, the characteristics and betas may not be tied together by any explicit theory in the case of equity models, even allowing for a nonlinear relationship. The link between characteristics and factor betas is usually motivated

Table 6.1. Some attributes used in characteristic-based factor models.

Attribute	How measured	References
Industry and country dummies	Zero/one dummies or percent of revenue by industry/ country	Heston and Rouwenhorst (1994); Cavaglia et al. (2000); Hopkins and Miller (2001); L'Her et al. (2002)
Size	Log of market capitalization or log of book value of assets	Banz (1981); Daniel and Titman (1997, 1998); Dowen and Bauman (1986)
Value	Earnings-to-price ratio or book-to-price ratio	Reinganum (1981); Daniel and Titman (1997, 1998); Dowen and Bauman (1986)
Return momentum	Last twelve months (or three months) cumulative return	Jegadeesh and Titman (1993); Chan et al. (1996); Carhart (1997); Wu (2002)
Long-term reversal	Cumulative returns over thirty-six months	DeBondt and Thaler (1985)
Recent individual-stock volatility	Sixty-month or twelve-month sample variance of returns	Ang et al. (2006)
Liquidity, tradability	Bid–ask spread or price reaction to trading volume or trading volume	Amihud and Mendelson (1986); Datar et al. (1998); Amihud (2002); Pástor and Stambaugh (2003); Chen and Tu (2000); Holmström and Tirole (2001)
Dividend yield	Annual dividends over the price	Keim (1985); Brennan (1970); Litzenberger and Ramaswamy (1979); Miller and Scholes (1978)
Index membership	Zero/one dummies	Brennan et al. (1998)
Leverage ratio	Debt to assets or debt to equity	Bhandari (1988)
Currency exposure	Change in exchange rate	Adler and Dumas (1984); Hodder (1982); Jorion (1990)

Table 6.1. *Cont.*

Attribute	How measured	References
Institutional ownership	Natural logarithm of the proportion of the stock held by institutions	Dowen and Bauman (1986); Brennan et al. (1998)
Analyst evaluations	Variation of analysts' earnings estimates for the current year (following year), revision of earnings on one- (three-) month basis	Brennan et al. (1998)

by empirical findings: it works well empirically, but may not have a firm theoretical justification.

The industry–country model discussed in chapter 3 is a simple special case of Rosenberg's characteristic-based factor model, with exposures set equal to zero/one dummy variables. Rosenberg's estimation strategy is to combine an industry dummy-variable model (he is studying the case of U.S. equities, so there are no country dummies) with a set of corporate characteristics to capture style characteristics such as size, value, and momentum. Since the industry dummies serve to capture the dominant market-related factor, the corporate-characteristic-related factors capture only the "extra-market" risk factors.

Let $\boldsymbol{A}_j$ denote the n-vector of the jth security characteristic for the n assets, but not one of the zero/one industry dummies. Without loss of generality it is possible to linearly transform the jth characteristics so that the cross section of exposures has a mean of zero and a standard deviation of one:

$$A^*_{ij} = A_{ij} - \frac{1}{n}\sum_{i=1}^{n} A_{ij}, \tag{6.12}$$

$$B_{ij} = \frac{n^{1/2}A^*_{ij}}{(\sum_{i=1}^{n} A^{*2}_{ij})^{1/2}}. \tag{6.13}$$

This standardization can be applied to all the characteristics except the industry zero/one dummies. The presence of a full set of industry dummies in the model allows the average exposure of the other characteristics to be set to zero via (6.12) without affecting the fit of the model; this transformation merely shifts the mean-related return effect onto the industry factors. Similarly, the scaling of the characteristics (6.13) scales the factor returns by an exactly offsetting amount, leaving the fit of the factor model (6.10) unaffected. This provides a useful interpretation of the exposure to the characteristic as a standardized deviation from the average.

Let w_{m} denote the market portfolio. Rosenberg suggests replacing the equally weighted mean

$$\frac{1}{n}\sum_{i=1}^{n} A_{ij}$$

in formula (6.12) with the capitalization-weighted mean

$$\sum_{i=1}^{n} w_{\mathrm{m}i} A_{ij}.$$

This makes the factor exposures easier to interpret for the analyst who wants to measure the factor exposure of a particular asset or portfolio relative to the corresponding factor exposure of the market portfolio. Consider a portfolio $\boldsymbol{w}$ whose exposure to characteristic j happens to be $\frac{1}{2}$, so that

$$b_{wj} = \boldsymbol{w}'[\boldsymbol{B}]_{\bullet j} = \tfrac{1}{2}.$$

If the capitalization-weighted mean is used in the definition (6.13) of $\boldsymbol{B}$, then the exposure of portfolio $\boldsymbol{w}$ to characteristic j exceeds the exposure of the market portfolio to characteristic j by one-half the cross-sectional standard deviation of the asset exposures. If the portfolio has a characteristic exposure of zero, it is market neutral with respect to this factor.

Once the scaling of the characteristic-based factor exposures has been chosen, the factor returns can be estimated as random coefficients in a series of period-by-period cross-sectional regressions. The estimation problem mirrors that in the case of industry–country models (see chapter 3). Given the time-t vector of excess returns $\boldsymbol{x}_t$ and the matrix of factor exposures $\boldsymbol{B}$, the time-t factor returns can be estimated by cross-sectional regression applied to (6.10), treating the factor exposures as explanatory variables and the factor returns as random time-t coefficients to be estimated:

$$\hat{\boldsymbol{f}}_t = (\boldsymbol{B}'\boldsymbol{C}_\varepsilon^{-1}\boldsymbol{B})^{-1}\boldsymbol{B}'\boldsymbol{C}_\varepsilon^{-1}\boldsymbol{x}_t, \tag{6.14}$$

where $\boldsymbol{C}_\varepsilon$ is the covariance matrix of idiosyncratic returns. The covariance matrix of the estimated factors is given by

$$\operatorname{cov}(\hat{\boldsymbol{f}}_t - \boldsymbol{f}_t, \hat{\boldsymbol{f}}_t' - \boldsymbol{f}_t') = (\boldsymbol{B}'\boldsymbol{C}_\varepsilon^{-1}\boldsymbol{B})^{-1}. \tag{6.15}$$

The square roots of the diagonal elements give the standard errors of the estimated factor returns:

$$\sigma_{\hat{f}_{jt}} = ([\operatorname{cov}(\hat{\boldsymbol{f}}_t - \boldsymbol{f}_t, \hat{\boldsymbol{f}}_t' - \boldsymbol{f}_t')]_{jj})^{1/2}.$$

Here we are assuming that C_ε is known. In practice we must either estimate it or use the consistent but inefficient ordinary least-squares estimates (artificially setting the term C_ε^{-1} in (6.14) equal to an identity matrix) instead. See Greene (2008, chapter 8) for a good discussion of the use of ordinary least squares in the presence of heteroskedasticity and correlation between residuals.

6.2.3 Factor-Mimicking Portfolios

Fama and MacBeth (1973) note that estimated coefficients from cross-sectional regressions on returns can be interpreted as portfolio returns, since they are linear functions of the dependent variable, the n-vector of returns. This is critically important in the context of characteristic-based factor models. Consider the ordinary least-squares estimation of the characteristic-based factor model:

$$\hat{f}_t = (B'B)^{-1}B'x_t,$$

where x_t is the n-vector of excess returns at time t. Define the $n \times k$ matrix

$$W = B(B'B)^{-1}.$$

Since $\hat{f}_t = W'x_t$, we can interpret the matrix B as a set of k portfolio vectors with the jth estimated factor equal to the excess return on the jth portfolio. These k factor-mimicking portfolios have the property that their k-set of factor exposure vectors equals a $k \times k$ identity matrix:

$$W'B = B'B(B'B)^{-1} = I_k.$$

The jth factor-mimicking portfolio has unit exposure to factor j and zero exposure to the other $k - 1$ factors.

Suppose that the model includes j^* industry dummies and that they are listed first. For $j \leqslant j^*$ the factor-mimicking portfolio will have a unit-cost position in industry j and a net-zero-cost position in every other industry. For $j > j^*$ the factor-mimicking portfolio will have a net-zero-cost position in every industry (and so a total cost of zero). These are called style-neutral industry portfolios for $j \leqslant j^*$ and industry-neutral style portfolios for $j > j^*$.

If the characteristic-based factor model obeys the conditions necessary for an approximate factor model, then the regression-based factor-mimicking portfolio weights are well spread across the n assets and have idiosyncratic returns that tend to zero as n becomes large. The sum of squared portfolio weights equals the diagonal elements of the matrix

$$W'W = (B'B)^{-1}B'B(B'B)^{-1} = (B'B)^{-1}.$$

One of the defining features of an approximate factor model is that all the eigenvalues of $\boldsymbol{B}'\boldsymbol{B}$ tend to infinity with n. The eigenvalues of $(\boldsymbol{B}'\boldsymbol{B})^{-1}$ equal the reciprocals of the eigenvalues of $\boldsymbol{B}'\boldsymbol{B}$, and so all the eigenvalues of $(\boldsymbol{B}'\boldsymbol{B})^{-1}$ go to zero. This guarantees that

$$\mathrm{Diag}[\boldsymbol{W}'\boldsymbol{W}] = \mathrm{Diag}[(\boldsymbol{B}'\boldsymbol{B})^{-1}] \to \boldsymbol{0}^k$$

with n. It is then easy to show that $\boldsymbol{W}_j'\boldsymbol{C}_\varepsilon\boldsymbol{W}_j \to 0$ for each j, using the property that $\boldsymbol{C}_\varepsilon$ has bounded eigenvalues. The proof is left to the interested reader.

The factor-mimicking portfolios created by cross-sectional regression are easy to compute and use, but they are suboptimal as investment vehicles. The style portfolios are invested in every stock in the cross section and have high implied turnover and many illiquid positions.

Numerical portfolio optimization provides an alternative to cross-sectional regression as a method to create factor-mimicking portfolios. Rather than rely on the Fama–MacBeth properties of regression coefficients interpreted as mimicking portfolio returns, we can directly search for portfolios that have the desired properties. A *factor-mimicking portfolio* for factor j is a well-diversified portfolio that has unit exposure to factor j and zero exposures to the other factors:

$$\boldsymbol{w}'\boldsymbol{C}_\varepsilon\boldsymbol{w} \approx 0,$$
$$\boldsymbol{w}'\boldsymbol{B} = [0 \cdots 1 \cdots 0].$$

See Lehmann and Modest (2005) for an example of an optimization algorithm designed to compute factor-mimicking portfolios without using regression methods.

6.2.4 Relative Explanatory Power of Characteristic-Based versus Macroeconomic and Statistical Factor Models

It is an interesting empirical exercise to compare the fit of the three types of factor models—economic, statistical, and characteristic based—applied to the same asset universe. Connor (1995) compares the three models for U.S. equities. He finds that the economic model performs much more poorly than the statistical and characteristic-based models in terms of explanatory power. The characteristic-based model slightly outperforms the statistical model. This result may be surprising at first since this comparison is in-sample and the statistical factor model is estimated by maximizing in-sample fit. The explanation for the better performance of the characteristic-based model is the larger number of factors on which it is based.[3] A statistical factor model is forced to

[3] The industry factors make an especially important contribution.

identify both factor exposures and factor returns from the returns data set alone. This imposes a strict limit on the number of usable factors. With the assistance of massively larger databases of characteristics and industry identifiers, characteristic-based factor models can outperform statistical models even in-sample.

Suppose that there are n assets and k factors and we have T time periods of data. Of the three standard types of factor models—macroeconomic, characteristic based, and statistical—the characteristic-based ones have the fewest parameters to estimate when n is large relative to T. Impose a strict factor model (of whichever type) so that the idiosyncratic return covariance matrix $\boldsymbol{C}_\varepsilon$ has n estimable parameters. A statistical factor model requires estimation of $\boldsymbol{B}$, $\boldsymbol{f}$, $\boldsymbol{C}_f$, and $\boldsymbol{C}_\varepsilon$, which amounts to

$$nk + kT + \tfrac{1}{2}k(k+1) + n$$

parameters, using the nT panel data set of returns. An economic factor model requires estimation of $\boldsymbol{B}$, $\boldsymbol{C}_f$, and $\boldsymbol{C}_\varepsilon$, which results in

$$nk + \tfrac{1}{2}k(k+1) + n$$

parameters, using the nT panel data set of returns and the kT set of macroeconomic factor innovations. A characteristic-based factor model requires estimation of $\boldsymbol{f}$, $\boldsymbol{C}_f$, and $\boldsymbol{C}_\varepsilon$, which results in

$$kT + \tfrac{1}{2}k(k+1) + n$$

parameters, using the nT panel data set of returns and the nk set of security characteristics. For large n, the characteristic-based model has the fewest parameters by far. In contrast, it uses the most data, since the nk-dimensional cross section of characteristics is typically larger than the kT-dimensional sample of macroeconomic factors. This means that if we count data points and parameters, the characteristic-based factor models have the most information per parameter by a large margin, when n is large relative to T.

A hybrid factor model combines two or more types of factor models. Connor considers all six two-type hybrids. In each case, one type is used as the primary factor model in a first stage and a second is used to explain the first-stage residuals (that is, the asset-specific returns). The macroeconomic model is substantially improved by hybridization with the characteristic-based or statistical model, whereas those two types are not significantly improved by including macroeconomic factors. The statistical and characteristic-based models are not strictly ordered: each has some explanatory power for the first-stage residual returns produced by the other model.

An especially useful type of hybrid factor model begins with a characteristic-based model and then applies statistical factor analysis to the residual returns from this first-stage model. Let $\boldsymbol{B}^*$, $\boldsymbol{f}^*$, ε^* denote the factor betas, factor returns, and asset-specific returns from a first-stage characteristic-based factor model:

$$\boldsymbol{C} = \boldsymbol{B}^* \boldsymbol{C}_{f^*} \boldsymbol{B}^{*\prime} + \boldsymbol{C}_{\varepsilon^*}. \tag{6.16}$$

However, suppose that there are factors missing from this decomposition so that $\boldsymbol{C}_{\varepsilon^*}$ is not diagonal and contains pervasive risk components. Apply statistical factor analysis to the cross-product matrix of the asset-specific returns to estimate a factor model of the asset-specific covariance matrix:

$$\boldsymbol{C}_{\varepsilon^*} = \boldsymbol{B}^{**} \boldsymbol{C}_{f^{**}} \boldsymbol{B}^{**\prime} + \boldsymbol{C}_{\varepsilon}.$$

The final covariance matrix estimate is the sum of the labeled common factor component, the statistical common factor component, and the asset-specific variances:

$$\boldsymbol{C} = \boldsymbol{B}^* \boldsymbol{C}_{f^*} \boldsymbol{B}^{*\prime} + \boldsymbol{B}^{**} \boldsymbol{C}_{f^{**}} \boldsymbol{B}^{**\prime} + \boldsymbol{C}_{\varepsilon}. \tag{6.17}$$

Note that with finite data the hybrid model including statistical factors (6.17) need not outperform the simpler characteristic-based factor model (6.16) which excludes them. Miller (2006) provides a methodology for deciding whether statistical factor models add risk-forecasting value using a hybrid model like (6.17). He draws a distinction between *structural* and *statistical* errors in risk-forecasting models. Characteristic-based factor models are prone to structural errors since the model builder assumes he knows the source of all the pervasive risks in the capital market in order to build the model. For example, if the industry categories used in building the model are not the correct ones, the resulting risk model will have a structural error. Statistical factor models impose minimal structure but compensate through large statistical errors. Effective estimation of factors and exposures from returns data alone requires a data set that is large relative to the number of estimation parameters. As a consequence, even a substantially flawed characteristic-based model can outperform a statistical model due to the inability of purely statistical methods to reliably identify factors and factor betas based on limited samples of returns data. For more details on estimating hybrid factor models, see Stroyny (2005).

Miller notes that statistical factor models, or hybrid models including statistical factors, can increase risk-forecasting accuracy when there have been unobserved changes in the market risk factors causing structural errors in a characteristic-based model. Miller uses simulation methods to argue that at weekly or monthly return frequencies, statistical factor modeling is not competitive with characteristic-based modeling for the purposes of building equity risk-forecasting models of equities. However, at a daily frequency, a hybrid model can potentially add value. He gives an example where the addition of a daily second-stage statistical factor model improves the risk forecasts of a characteristic-based factor model of Japanese equities.

6.3 The Fama–French Model and Extensions

In a very influential paper, Fama and French (1992) find that time-series estimated market betas are not very good at explaining cross-sectional differences in the mean returns of U.S. equities. On the other hand, two security characteristics, market capitalization and book-to-price ratio, are strongly correlated with the difference in mean returns across securities. Stocks with smaller capitalization and those with higher book-to-price ratios have higher mean returns. There are analogous findings for many other equity markets, but the result remains controversial nevertheless. Note that this finding in Fama and French (1992) concerns mean returns, not return comovements or portfolio risk.

Fama and French (1993) complement the mean-return model of their earlier paper with an analysis of the role of size and value in portfolio risk. Returns to large firms comove with each other, and likewise for returns to small firms. This creates a nondiversifiable risk associated with the size characteristic, and the same holds for the value characteristic.

Fama and French use characteristic-based portfolios and time-series regression to capture the pervasive factors and factor exposures. First, they double-sort all U.S. equities into six portfolios, sorting them according to two size categories (big and small) and three value categories (high, medium, and low book-to-price (BTP) ratio). Judiciously chosen return differences between these sorted portfolios serve as the estimated factor returns. For the size factor, they use a combination portfolio that they call the small minus big (SMB) portfolio:

$$\begin{aligned}
\text{SMB} &= \frac{1}{3}\bigg[\bigg(\frac{\text{large size}}{\text{high BTP portfolio return}} - \frac{\text{small size}}{\text{high BTP portfolio return}}\bigg) \\
&\quad + \bigg(\frac{\text{large size}}{\text{medium BTP portfolio return}} - \frac{\text{small size}}{\text{medium BTP portfolio return}}\bigg) \\
&\quad + \bigg(\frac{\text{large size}}{\text{low BTP portfolio return}} - \frac{\text{small size}}{\text{low BTP portfolio return}}\bigg)\bigg].
\end{aligned}$$

The value factor is represented by the high minus low (HML) portfolio, a different combination portfolio of the same six double-sorted portfolios:

$$\text{HML} = \frac{1}{2}\left[\left(\frac{\text{large size}}{\text{high BTP portfolio return}} - \frac{\text{large size}}{\text{low BTP portfolio return}}\right) + \left(\frac{\text{small size}}{\text{high BTP portfolio return}} - \frac{\text{small size}}{\text{low BTP portfolio return}}\right)\right].$$

Fama and French use these two factor portfolios, together with the value-weighted market index (called MKT), to explain the returns on a finer collection of size and book-to-price sorted portfolios. For the fine-sort portfolios they use twenty-five portfolios based on a five-category sort for both size and book-to-price. The excess returns on the fine-sort portfolio, x_{jt}, are regressed on the three-factor portfolio returns and a constant. This time-series regression is used to estimate the fine-sort portfolio's factor exposures and asset-specific return:

$$x_{jt} = \hat{\alpha}_j + \hat{\beta}_{\text{MKT},j}\,\text{MKT}_t + \hat{\beta}_{\text{SMB},j}\,\text{SMB}_t + \hat{\beta}_{\text{HML},j}\,\text{HML}_t + \hat{\varepsilon}_{j,t}. \tag{6.18}$$

Each of the three factors shows economically and statistically significant explanatory power across the set of fine-sort portfolios. Although a few estimated factor exposures fall close to zero (as one would expect), the vast majority of coefficients have very high t-statistics. There is an EIV bias in these regressions since the imperfectly estimated factor returns serve as independent variables, but this bias is unlikely to be large enough to completely explain the findings. Fama and French also employ other sort variables (dividend yield and earnings-to-price ratio) to construct the fine-sort portfolios and then estimate their factor exposures via (6.18).

One important finding from the Fama–French factor exposure estimation (6.18) is the very narrow spread of estimated market betas, $\hat{\beta}_{\text{MKT},j}$, $j = 1, \dots, 25$, in this three-factor model. The estimated coefficients differ only negligibly from 1.0. As Fama and French note, this throws considerable light on their earlier finding in Fama and French (1992) that market betas show little ability to explain the cross section of mean returns in a model including size and value characteristics. Tests for the marginal difference in mean returns associated with market beta suffer from a range-restriction problem: since the market betas of equities barely differ from 1.0 across the full range of equities it is empirically difficult to isolate the associated risk premium. Fama and French note that adding fixed-income securities (which tend to have market betas far below 1.0) gives a significantly positive measured risk premium.

The tight spread of market betas around 1.0 has implications for the structure of portfolio risk-forecasting models, in light of the key noise-versus-bias trade-off (see chapter 2). Fixing all the market betas at 1.0, rather than estimating them freely, is generally preferable if this is true.

Define the momentum of a stock as the difference between its lagged twelve-month cumulative return and the cumulative return on the market index over the same period. Jegadeesh and Titman (1993, 2001) show that the momentum characteristic is cross-sectionally associated with mean returns: high-momentum stocks subsequently outperform the market index and low-momentum stocks underperform. Carhart (1997) shows that standardized twelve-month relative momentum has similar properties to the size and value characteristics: it helps explains the cross section of mean returns on managed portfolios (having a role independent of market, size, and value) and serves as a source of covariability across stocks. Carhart extends the Fama–French market-size–value model by adding an additional factor-mimicking portfolio to represent the momentum factor. Adding the momentum factor to the Fama–French market-size–value factor model improves the explanatory power of the model for a sample of mutual fund portfolio returns, and eliminates the observed outperformance of the funds with positive momentum exposures. One can construct a mimicking portfolio for this factor return as the difference between a positive-momentum and a negative-momentum sort portfolio, often called the UMD (up-minus-down) portfolio, analogous to the SMB and HML portfolios of Fama–French.

Size and value tend to change only slowly, whereas the momentum characteristic of an individual equity will typically vary quite rapidly over time. There is a need for frequent rebalancing of sort portfolios in order to treat their momentum factor exposures as (approximately) fixed.

6.4 The Semiparametric Approach to Characteristic-Based Factor Models

Connor and Linton (2007) propose a model that combines elements of Rosenberg's linear-characteristic factor model and the Fama–French model. In place of Rosenberg's linearity assumption, Connor and Linton assume that the factor exposures are smooth univariate functions of observable characteristics:

$$r_{it} = f_{zt} + \sum_{j=1}^{k} g_j(c_{ij}) f_{jt} + \varepsilon_{it}, \tag{6.19}$$

where c_{ij} is the jth characteristic of asset i and the $g_j(\cdot)$ functions need not be linear. There is a rotational indeterminacy in (6.19) so, without loss of generality, Connor and Linton set $g_j(1) = 1$ and impose the assumption $g_j(0) = 0$, which only requires that $g_j(0) \neq g_j(1)$. These identification constraints, $g_j(0) = 0$ and $g_j(1) = 1$, are given intuitive content by standardizing the characteristics to have zero mean and unit variance. The intercept in (6.19) captures the market-related factor return.

In place of Fama and French's set of six characteristic-sorted portfolios for factor construction and twenty-five sorted portfolios for exposure estimation, Connor and Linton use a semiparametric regression method to optimally construct mimicking portfolios for a large set of value–size target vectors. They then use bilinear regression to estimate the characteristic-exposure functions $g_j(\cdot)$ and factor returns f_{jt} simultaneously for all time periods and for the full set of target vectors.

7

Measuring and Hedging Foreign Exchange Risk

Foreign exchange risk is an important component of international portfolio risk. In this chapter we study the empirical properties of currency risk and develop risk model architecture that includes it.

Section 7.1 describes an approximation method for decomposing the total return on a foreign investment into currency-unrelated return (called local return) and currency-only return. This decomposition can be employed in building a portfolio risk model with three components: a local risk component, a currency risk component, and a component measuring the covariances between local and currency returns. Section 7.2 discusses currency hedging models from both short-horizon and long-horizon investment perspectives. Section 7.3 reviews empirical research on the covariances between currency returns and pervasive factor returns in stock and bond markets. Section 7.4 discusses the relationships between macroeconomic variables and currency returns.

Economic researchers use the term "peso problem" to refer to any situation in which the true relationship between economic variables is difficult to measure accurately because one or more of the variables is subject to large, infrequent jumps. The term has its origins in economic research on currency markets (in particular, the Mexican peso–U.S. dollar foreign exchange market (see Lewis 1995)). Currency markets, particularly those under pegged exchange rates, are the classic case of an economic environment subject to"peso problems," where reliable inference requires historical samples of unfeasible length. Short-term currency risk management is reasonably well understood, but for long-horizon investors there are many open questions about optimal risk-management policies.

7.1 Definitions of Foreign Exchange Risk

7.1.1 Local and Currency-Translated Returns

Suppose that our home currency is the U.S. dollar, so we measure risk and return in dollar units. In this case the U.S. dollar is called our *numeraire currency*. Let $p_t^{£\$}$ denote the current exchange rate for the immediate delivery of one British pound sterling paid for in U.S. dollars. If the dollar is our numeraire currency, then this is called the *direct exchange rate* for the British pound, since it states the dollar price of a British pound just as one would state the dollar price of any other commodity for sale. Alternatively, exchange rates can be quoted as the number of units of foreign currency received per unit of home currency; this is called the *indirect exchange rate*. Hence, $1/p_t^{£\$} = p_t^{\$£}$ is the indirect exchange rate for the pound when the numeraire currency is the dollar; this gives the number of British pounds received per dollar.

From the perspective of a foreign-based investor the direct and indirect exchange rates are exactly reversed. The direct exchange rate of the U.S. dollar using a British pound numeraire is $1/p_t^{£\$}$ and the indirect exchange rate is $p_t^{£\$}$. For concreteness we will state exchange rates as direct exchange rates from the perspective of a U.S. dollar-based investor.

Note that the exchange rate $p_t^{£\$}$ is a random variable at time $t-1$. Define the *currency return* as the random dollar return for holding a British pound for one period (without interest) and then exchanging it back into U.S. dollars:

$$r_{ct}^{£\$} = \frac{p_t^{£\$}}{p_{t-1}^{£\$}} - 1.$$

An institutional investor holding foreign currency almost always places it in an interest-bearing account. Let the riskless interest rate for deposits in British pounds be $r_{0t}^{£}$. The riskless rate $r_{0t}^{£}$ applies from time $t-1$ to time t, but unlike $p_t^{£\$}$ the value of $r_{0t}^{£}$ is known at time $t-1$ since it is riskless. The *foreign cash return* is the return from holding a riskless foreign deposit for one period. This is affected by the exchange rate since the deposit is made at the time-$(t-1)$ exchange rate and the repatriation of cash is at the time-t rate:

$$r_{0t}^{£\$} = (1 + r_{0t}^{£})\frac{p_t^{£\$}}{p_{t-1}^{£\$}} - 1.$$

This cash asset has a riskless return from a pound sterling numeraire but a risky return from a dollar numeraire due to varying exchange rates.

Suppose that we have an investment in the Financial Times and London Stock Exchange (FTSE) index. Let $r_{\text{FTSE}}^{£}$ denote the *local* return on the FTSE: that is, its random return stated in its home currency of British pounds. Translated into dollars, the random return on the FTSE index is

$$r_{\text{FTSE}t}^{\$} = (1 + r_{\text{FTSE}t}^{£})\frac{p_t^{£\$}}{p_{t-1}^{£\$}} - 1.$$

Note that the dollar return on the FTSE is the product of its gross local return and gross currency return, minus one:

$$r^{\$}_{\mathrm{FTSE}t} = (1 + r^{£}_{\mathrm{FTSE}t})(1 + r^{£\$}_{\mathrm{c}t}) - 1 \tag{7.1}$$

$$= r^{£}_{\mathrm{FTSE}t} + r^{£\$}_{\mathrm{c}t} + r^{£}_{\mathrm{FTSE}t} r^{£\$}_{\mathrm{c}t}, \tag{7.2}$$

so the foreign return equals the sum of the local return plus the currency return plus the product of these two returns.

7.1.2 Linear Approximations of Foreign Investment Returns

The multiplicative product of random returns in (7.1) makes risk analysis of foreign returns difficult. For example, the variance of the U.S. dollar return to the FTSE depends nonlinearly on the joint probability distributions of the local return $r^{£}_{\mathrm{FTSE}t+1}$ and currency return $r^{£\$}_{\mathrm{c}t+1}$.

There are two methods for simplifying the risk analysis of foreign investments. One method is to switch to log returns, so that the relationship between foreign return, local return, and currency return is exactly additive. Adding one to both sides of equation (7.1) and taking logarithms, we obtain

$$r^{\$}_{\mathrm{l}t} = r^{£}_{\mathrm{l}t} + r^{£\$}_{\mathrm{lc}t}.$$

Therefore, if we use log returns, there is an exact additive relationship between local, currency, and foreign asset returns. However, we encounter the usual difficulty that log portfolio returns are not additive in the constituent asset log returns.

The second method is to use a small-return approximation to the product in (7.2). If both local return and currency return are small over a short time interval Δ, then their product is small relative to their sum: that is,

$$r^{£}_{t} \times r^{£\$}_{\mathrm{c}t} \overset{\Delta}{\approx} 0. \tag{7.3}$$

Applying the approximation (7.3) to the expression for the foreign asset return (7.2) gives

$$r^{\$}_{t} \overset{o(\Delta)}{\approx} r^{£}_{t} + r^{£\$}_{\mathrm{c}t}, \tag{7.4}$$

so the foreign asset return approximately equals the simple sum of the local return and the currency return, under the assumption that both these returns are reasonably small. We will call the decomposition (7.4) the *approximate linear model*. The approximate linear model works best when the risk forecasting horizon is short, since in this case it is reasonable to ignore the return product (7.3) as negligible. The approximation is far from perfect and the portfolio risk analyst must remain cognizant of its weaknesses. Note, for example, that in a currency crisis, both local returns and currency returns can be substantial even for short horizons, making the approximation (7.4) inappropriate.

7.1.3 Negative Symmetry of Translated Currency Returns

Currency returns, when translated across numeraires, have negative symmetry. By this we mean that the domestic investor's log return on the "foreign" currency equals minus the foreign investor's log return on the "home" currency. For example, the currency return on the British pound from a dollar numeraire equals minus the dollar return from a British pound numeraire:

$$r_{\text{lc}t}^{£\$} = -r_{\text{lc}t}^{\$£}. \tag{7.5}$$

The same relationship holds for arithmetic returns using the approximate linear model. This negative symmetry differentiates currencies from other types of returns, and affects the structural design of currency risk models. Many problems in portfolio risk analysis involve modeling differences between positive and negative return realizations. For example, there is evidence (discussed in chapter 10) that for many asset classes, returns have negative skewness, meaning that negative realized returns tend to be larger in magnitude than positive realized returns. In light of equation (7.5), this cannot apply to returns to every currency from the perspective of every numeraire. Similarly, the empirical property (discussed in chapter 9 for some asset classes) that variances and correlations tend to increase following a negative return cannot hold universally for currencies. Note that there is no negative symmetry when the numeraire is a basket consisting of more than one currency. The *effective currency return* for a given numeraire is the weighted sum of the returns to all foreign currencies from that perspective, usually relying on import-export trade weights for the weighting scheme. See Chinn (2006) for a discussion.

7.1.4 Covered Interest Rate Parity

As above, we let $r_{0t}^{\$}$ and $r_{0t}^{£}$ denote the riskless rates for the time interval from time $t-1$ to t, in dollar-denominated accounts and pound sterling-denominated accounts, respectively. Let $F_{t-1}^{£\$}$ denote the forward rate for the delivery of one pound at t, paid for in dollars at time t but at a rate set at $t-1$. This is the *forward exchange rate*. There is an important relationship between the current (or spot) exchange rate, the forward exchange rate, and the two local riskless interest rates. In particular,

$$F_{t-1}^{£\$} = p_{t-1}^{£\$}\left(\frac{1+r_{0t}^{\$}}{1+r_{0t}^{£}}\right). \tag{7.6}$$

The equality holds by simple arbitrage. If the right-hand side of (7.6) exceeds the left-hand side, an arbitrageur can go long $1+r_{0t}^{£}$ units of the forward contract, borrow £1 at rate $r_{0t}^{£}$, exchange the borrowed pound for dollars at spot rate $p_{t-1}^{£\$}$, and then lend the dollars at rate $r_{0t}^{\$}$. At the end of the month, the arbitrageur would have $p_{t-1}^{£\$}(1 + r_{0t}^{\$})$ dollars to deliver on the forward contract, which only requires $F_{t-1}^{£\$}(1 + r_{0t}^{£})$ dollars: since the former is larger, this leaves a riskless profit at no initial cost. If the left-hand side exceeds the right-hand side, the same strategy in reverse makes a riskless costless profit (short the forward contract, borrow dollars, exchange now for pounds, lend the pounds). Rewriting (7.6) in log returns gives

$$\log(F_{t-1}^{£\$}) - \log(p_{t-1}^{£\$}) = r_{10t}^{\$} - r_{10t}^{£}.$$

Consider a dollar-based investor who goes short $1/F_t^{£\$}$ units of the British pound forward contract. At the end of the period he must deliver $1/F_t^{£\$}$ pounds and he receives \$1 in payment. The spot exchange rate for pounds is $p_{t-1}^{£\$}$, and using covered interest rate parity to find the forward rate gives a total dollar payout of

$$1 - \frac{p_t^{£\$}}{F_{t-1}^{£\$}} = 1 - \frac{p_t^{£\$}}{p_{t-1}^{£\$}}\left(\frac{1 + r_{0t}^{£}}{1 + r_{0t}^{\$}}\right) = 1 - (1 + r_{ct}^{£\$})\left(\frac{1 + r_{0t}^{£}}{1 + r_{0t}^{\$}}\right) \tag{7.7}$$

$$\overset{\Delta}{\approx} -r_{ct}^{£\$} + (r_{0t}^{\$} - r_{0t}^{£}). \tag{7.8}$$

Note that the random portion of the return to a short position in the forward contract is minus the random currency return in the dollar return to a foreign asset (7.4). So an investor holding a foreign asset can hedge his currency exposure by taking an offsetting short position in currency forward contracts.

An investor can get the equivalent of a short forward contract by borrowing in the foreign currency and lending the equivalent amount in the domestic currency. Suppose we borrow $1/F_{t-1}^{£\$}(1+r_{0t}^{£})$ British pounds at the riskless rate $r_{0t}^{£}$, exchange the borrowed pounds and save the resulting $p_{t-1}^{£\$}/F_{t-1}^{£\$}(1+r_{0t}^{£})$ dollars for one period. At the end of the period we are holding one borrowed dollar, since formula (7.6) for covered interest rate parity implies that

$$\frac{p_{t-1}^{£\$}(1 + r_{0t}^{\$})}{F_{t-1}^{£\$}(1 + r_{0t}^{£})} = 1.$$

On the other hand, we have to repay the borrowed pounds plus interest. This amounts to

$$\frac{(1 + r_{0t}^{£})}{F_{t-1}^{£\$}(1 + r_{0t}^{£})}$$

pounds. After exchanging dollars and repaying the loan, what remains is exactly

$$1 - \frac{p_t^{£\$}}{p_{t-1}^{£\$}}\left(\frac{1+r_{0t}^{£}}{1+r_{0t}^{\$}}\right),$$

which is identical to the payoff of a short position in the forward contract shown in formula (7.7). This equivalence between forward contracts and foreign/domestic cash positions is a consequence of covered interest rate parity. It is useful in risk model architecture, as we discuss in the next section.

7.1.5 The Interest Cost of Currency Hedging

The linear model (7.4) approximates foreign portfolio return as a sum of local market return and currency exchange rate return. A portfolio is *currency hedged* if it is short a forward contract in the foreign currency. As a concrete example, consider again the purchase of the FTSE index with U.S. dollars, which was discussed in section 7.1.1. Adding the short forward payoff (7.8) to the approximate return (7.4) to the unhedged portfolio,[1] we obtain the hedged portfolio return:

$$r_{\text{FTSE}}^{\text{hedged}\,\$} \overset{o(\Delta)}{\approx} r_{\text{FTSE}}^{£} + (r_0^{\$} - r_0^{£}), \tag{7.9}$$

so the hedged foreign investor receives the local return plus the difference between the domestic and foreign interest rates. The *interest cost of hedging*, $r_0^{£} - r_0^{\$}$, is positive for low-interest-rate currency numeraires and negative for high interest rate numeraires. If the home currency has a low interest rate, then the hedging investor pays a premium to hedge; if it has a high interest rate, then the hedging investor receives a discount to hedge.

Consider from the dollar perspective the hedged excess return to holding the FTSE, from (7.9):

$$r_{\text{FTSE}}^{\text{hedged}\,\$} - r_0^{\$} \overset{o(\Delta)}{\approx} r_{\text{FTSE}}^{£} - r_0^{£},$$

so the hedged excess return from a foreign-numeraire perspective equals the local excess return. Importantly, this means that the hedged excess return is the same from the perspective of any currency, and it always equals the local excess return.

---

[1] Since the value of the forward contract at inception is zero, we can add arbitrary multiples of the payoff to the return without changing the initial value of the portfolio. The extent of the hedge depends on the multiple. In formula (7.9), we have fully hedged the currency return.

7.1.6 The Local Return/Cash Return Decomposition

In order to compartmentalize the theoretically separate elements of portfolio risk, it is useful to decompose the risk of each foreign asset into its local asset risk and the implicit currency risk associated with holding the asset. To do this, each unhedged foreign investment holding must be restated as the excess return to a hedged investment in the foreign asset, plus long–short holdings of foreign cash/domestic cash to offset the artificial hedge. For example, consider a dollar-numeraire portfolio with a third of its value in each of the S&P 500 index, the FTSE index, and the German DAX. Both foreign positions are unhedged. Using the approximate linear model and covered interest rate parity, this is equivalent to a portfolio with weight $\frac{1}{3}$ in each of the S&P 500 index, the hedged FTSE index, the hedged DAX, a pound sterling cash account and a euro cash account, and a short position with weight $-\frac{2}{3}$ in a dollar cash account. An advantage of this second representation is that the excess hedged returns to the foreign equities are equivalent to their local excess returns.

Although the portfolio has no explicit cash holdings, the unhedged positions in the FTSE and the DAX generate implicit holdings in foreign cash when we restate the foreign asset positions using hedged equivalents. Total cash holdings in each currency equal the sum of any explicit cash holdings and implicit cash holdings generated by asset positions. Note that any existing currency forward contract positions can also be restated as foreign/domestic cash holdings, using covered interest rate parity.

7.1.7 Constructing a Covariance Matrix with Currency Factors

Suppose that there are n assets in the investment universe, each denominated in one of $m + 1$ currencies (including the numeraire currency, which we take to be the dollar). The global covariance matrix has three blocks. The first is the currency covariance matrix, denoted by $\boldsymbol{C}_{\mathrm{c}}^{\$}$. Since there is no risk in the home currency, it seems natural to exclude it from the set of risk factors, resulting in an $(m \times m)$-dimensional currency block that is generally nonsingular. This is a preferable risk model representation for portfolio optimization and risk management and we will use it through most of the chapter. If the home currency is included, the matrix has dimension $(m + 1) \times (m + 1)$, and it is necessarily singular since the row and column corresponding to the home currency are populated with zeros.[2]

[2] As we show in section 7.1.8, in some special circumstances there is an advantage to including the home currency in the risk model; in particular, the inclusion of the zero row and column is useful for a change-of-numeraire transformation of the matrix.

The second block is the $n \times n$ covariance matrix of local asset return covariances, $\boldsymbol{C}_{\mathrm{a}}$. The variances and covariances are based on returns measured in local currencies. For example, the covariance between the FTSE and the DAX is the covariance between the return to the FTSE in British pounds and the return to the DAX in euros. This block can be thought of as the covariance matrix of local excess returns. Since local cash returns have no one-period volatility, there is no real difference between total and excess returns for measuring these covariances. Finally, assuming the home currency is not included as a risk factor, there is the $n \times m$ matrix of covariances between local asset returns and currency returns, $\boldsymbol{C}^{\$}_{\mathrm{ac}}$. The full covariance matrix is the $((n + m) \times (n + m))$-partitioned combination of these three matrices:

$$\boldsymbol{C}^{\$} = \begin{pmatrix} \boldsymbol{C}_{\mathrm{a}} & \boldsymbol{C}^{\$}_{\mathrm{ac}} \\ \boldsymbol{C}^{\$\prime}_{\mathrm{ac}} & \boldsymbol{C}^{\$}_{\mathrm{c}} \end{pmatrix}. \tag{7.10}$$

7.1.8 Change of Numeraire

In this section only, we include the (riskless) home currency in the covariance matrix, adding a row and column of zeros to the currency covariance matrix. This enables one to derive the covariance matrix from the perspective of any numeraire in the model from the dollar numeraire matrix, $\boldsymbol{C}^{\$}$, by a matrix transformation. The inclusion of the home currency means that the global covariance matrix given in formula (7.10) has size $(n + m + 1) \times (n + m + 1)$, since the currency block $\boldsymbol{C}^{\$}_{\mathrm{c}}$ has size $(m + 1) \times (m + 1)$.

Suppose that we switch from a dollar perspective to a pound sterling perspective. Under the approximate linear model (or using log returns),

$$r_{\mathrm{c}}^{£\$} = -r_{\mathrm{c}}^{\$£}$$

and

$$r_{\mathrm{c}}^{¥£} = r_{\mathrm{c}}^{¥\$} - r_{\mathrm{c}}^{£\$},$$

where ¥ denotes another currency, say the yen. As a consequence, the covariance between the returns to two currencies ¥ and € from a pound perspective can be expressed in terms of the covariance between linear combinations of dollar-perspective returns to ¥, € and the pound:

$$\operatorname{cov}(r_{\mathrm{c}}^{¥£}, r_{\mathrm{c}}^{€£}) = \operatorname{cov}(r_{\mathrm{c}}^{¥\$} - r_{\mathrm{c}}^{£\$}, r_{\mathrm{c}}^{€\$} - r_{\mathrm{c}}^{£\$}).$$

Covariances between assets and currencies transform under a change in numeraire in an analogous way:

$$\operatorname{cov}(r_i, r_{\mathrm{c}}^{¥£}) = \operatorname{cov}(r_i, r_{\mathrm{c}}^{¥\$} - r_{\mathrm{c}}^{£\$}),$$

where r_i is the local return to asset i.

The transformation of a covariance matrix from one currency perspective to another can be implemented by matrix multiplication. Suppose we have constructed the dollar-perspective covariance matrix $\boldsymbol{C}^{\$}$ to include the home currency and we want to switch to a pound perspective. Suppose further that the pound is the $(m+1)$st currency. Consider the two-block diagonal matrix $\boldsymbol{N}^{£}$ whose upper left block (corresponding to the asset factors) is the n-dimensional identity matrix and whose lower right block is an $(m+1)\times(m+1)$ dimensional matrix that transforms the currency factors:

$$\boldsymbol{N}^{£} = \begin{pmatrix} \mathbf{I} & \mathbf{0} \\ \mathbf{0} & \begin{pmatrix} 1 & 0 & 0 & \cdots & 0 & -1 \\ 0 & 1 & 0 & \cdots & 0 & -1 \\ & & & \vdots & & \\ 0 & 0 & 0 & \cdots & 1 & -1 \\ 0 & 0 & 0 & \cdots & 0 & 0 \end{pmatrix} \end{pmatrix}.$$

Then

$$\boldsymbol{C}^{£} = \boldsymbol{N}^{£\prime}\boldsymbol{C}^{\$}\boldsymbol{N}^{£}.$$

Note that the covariance matrix of the local asset returns $\boldsymbol{C}_{\text{a}}$ is the same for any numeraire. This is a very useful feature since it decouples cross-border risk modeling of underlying assets from risk modeling of currencies.

In theory, since riskless rates are known constants, we have

$$\operatorname{cov}(r_i^{¥} - r_0^{¥}, r_j^{€} - r_0^{€}) = \operatorname{cov}(r_i^{¥}, r_j^{€}). \tag{7.11}$$

In practice, riskless rates are constant for only one period ahead. When we apply time-series methods to measure covariances, the estimates for the two sides of (7.11) have different values. In the case of international covariances it is standard practice to use local excess returns in each market since time-varying differences in riskless rates may affect the estimated covariance. The use of local excess returns has a strong theoretical justification since it means that we are estimating the covariance of excess hedged returns from any perspective, as discussed in the previous section.

7.2 Optimal Currency Hedging

In an influential article, Perold and Shulman (1988) argue that currency hedging is a "free lunch" for the portfolio manager. Recall from (7.5) the negative symmetry between log currency returns. For example, the log currency return of British pounds from a U.S. dollar perspective equals exactly minus the log currency return to the U.S. dollar from a British pound perspective. This means that the "global average" currency return (considering all possible numeraire perspectives) is always zero, since each currency return can be paired with its reciprocal and their sum will be zero. From this global perspective, the average expected log return from holding foreign currencies is exactly zero. On the other hand, holding foreign currencies typically increases portfolio risk. So eliminating currency return from a portfolio by hedging tends to decrease portfolio risk without typically lowering the portfolio's expected return. This "free lunch" argument for currency hedging is important, but remains controversial. It does not show that the expected return to holding foreign currency is zero for any individual perspective, only that it is zero on average across all perspectives. It takes as given that foreign currencies increase portfolio risk, but if their covariance with the other components of the portfolio is sufficiently negative, they can actually decrease portfolio risk. It relies on log returns, and ignores the transaction costs associated with currency hedging.

The simplest currency hedge is one in which a unit of foreign currency is borrowed for each unit of foreign asset owned, or an equivalent short position is taken in currency forward contracts, as described in section 7.1.4. This type of hedge is called a *unit hedge*, and it completely eliminates all currency risk from the perspective of the approximate linear model. However, it is not the minimum-risk hedge. Let $(\boldsymbol{w}_{\mathrm{a}}, \boldsymbol{w}_{\mathrm{c}})$ denote the portfolio before hedging, written (as in the section 7.1.6) as an n-vector of assets weights and an m vector of currency weights (the sum of implicit and explicit currency positions). The unit-sum condition implies that the position in the domestic riskless asset is $1 - w_0 = \boldsymbol{w}_{\mathrm{a}}'\mathbf{1}^n + \boldsymbol{w}_{\mathrm{c}}'\mathbf{1}^m$. The minimum-variance currency hedge, $\boldsymbol{h}$, is the m vector that solves the problem

$$\min_{\boldsymbol{h}} (\boldsymbol{w}_{\mathrm{a}}, \boldsymbol{w}_{\mathrm{c}} + \boldsymbol{h})' \boldsymbol{C} (\boldsymbol{w}_{\mathrm{a}}, \boldsymbol{w}_{\mathrm{c}} + \boldsymbol{h}).$$

Using the partitioned form of $\boldsymbol{C}$ and dropping terms that do not depend upon $\boldsymbol{h}$, we obtain

$$\min_{\boldsymbol{h}} \boldsymbol{w}_{\mathrm{a}}' \boldsymbol{C}_{\mathrm{ac}} \boldsymbol{h} + \boldsymbol{w}_{\mathrm{c}}' \boldsymbol{C}_{\mathrm{c}} \boldsymbol{h} + \boldsymbol{h}' \boldsymbol{C}_{\mathrm{ac}}' \boldsymbol{w}_{\mathrm{a}} + \boldsymbol{h}' \boldsymbol{C}_{\mathrm{c}} \boldsymbol{w}_{\mathrm{c}} + \boldsymbol{h}' \boldsymbol{C}_{\mathrm{c}} \boldsymbol{h}.$$

Setting the vector derivative with respect to $\boldsymbol{h}$ equal to zero gives the formula for the minimum-variance hedge:

$$\boldsymbol{h}^* = -\boldsymbol{w}_{\mathrm{c}} - \boldsymbol{C}_{\mathrm{c}}^{-1} \boldsymbol{C}_{\mathrm{ac}}' \boldsymbol{w}_{\mathrm{a}}. \tag{7.12}$$

If $C_{\mathrm{ca}} = \mathbf{0}^{m\times n}$, then it follows from (7.12) that $\boldsymbol{h}^* = -\boldsymbol{w}_{\mathrm{c}}$, which is the unit hedge. Therefore, if there are no covariances between local asset returns and currency returns, the unit hedge is the minimum-risk hedge.

If $C_{\mathrm{ca}} \neq \mathbf{0}^{m\times n}$, then currencies can become a risk-reducing component of the portfolio rather than a source of increased risk. Kritzman (1993a) illustrates this in the case of a dollar-denominated investor with all his assets in U.S. markets. By currency "hedging," the investor can lower the risk of this portfolio, even though the initial portfolio has no currency exposure. A portfolio hedged to minimum currency risk has *negative* portfolio risk attributed to its currency positions—less portfolio variance than the same asset portfolio measured in local excess returns. This analysis relies on the elements of C_{ca} being reliably nonzero and estimable with good accuracy, which may be problematic.

Kritzman (1993b) notes that the minimum-variance hedge can be found by time-series regression. In the case of a single foreign currency, the minimum-variance hedge h^* from (7.12) is minus the beta of portfolio return r_w with respect to currency return:

$$h^* = \frac{-\operatorname{cov}(r_{\mathrm{c}}, r_w)}{\operatorname{var}(r_{\mathrm{c}})}. \tag{7.13}$$

Formula (7.13) shows that h^* is minus the slope obtained from an ordinary least-squares regression of the unhedged portfolio return on the foreign currency return. Suppose that in a multiple-currency environment we posit that the current portfolio is minimum-variance hedged with respect to all foreign currencies. Then a univariate regression of each currency return on the existing portfolio return should give, in each case, a regression coefficient of zero. This provides a simple and powerful test for whether the portfolio has been fully hedged.

7.2.1 The Expected Return from Currency Hedging

So far in the discussion of currency hedging, the expected returns from the hedge have been ignored in the determination of hedge positions. In the approximate linear model there are two components to the decrease in expected returns associated with currency hedges. These are the interest cost of hedging and the lost expected return from holding the currency. The net cost per unit of hedging in yen ¥ is

$$E[r_{\mathrm{c}}^{¥\$}] + (r_{0t}^{\$} - r_{0t}^{¥}).$$

From a multipolar perspective, the global average of each term is zero: for every currency ¥ with a positive expected return from numeraire € there is an exactly opposite negative expected return to currency € from numeraire ¥. The same identity holds across interest costs of hedging. However, for a particular numeraire, expected currency return and the interest costs of hedging can be positive or negative.

To study the relationship between expected currency return and hedging costs, we work with log returns rather than arithmetic returns. In the base-case scenario, the cost of hedging is zero:

$$E[r_{1c}^{¥€}] - (r_{10t}^{€} - r_{10t}^{¥}) = 0 \quad \text{for each } ¥, €. \tag{7.14}$$

That is, the expected log return from each currency is exactly offset by the interest cost of hedging it (in log units). This assertion is called *uncovered interest rate parity*, referring to its implication that the expected log return from holding the foreign riskless asset without hedging equals the domestic riskless log return. Bilson (1981), Fama (1984), Korajczyk (1985), and many others reject the null hypothesis that the uncovered interest rate parity relationship holds empirically. Combining the logarithmic version of covered interest rate parity with formula (7.14) for uncovered interest rate parity and expanding the term for exchange rate return gives

$$E[\log(p_t^{¥€}) - \log(p_{t-1}^{¥€})] = \log(F_{t-1}^{¥€}) - \log(p_{t-1}^{¥€}). \tag{7.15}$$

To evaluate the hypothesis of uncovered interest rate parity, the implied expected return relationship (7.15) is embedded in an unrestricted linear regression model:

$$\log(p_t^{¥€}) - \log(p_{t-1}^{¥€}) = \hat{a} + \hat{b}(\log(F_{t-1}^{¥€}) - \log(p_{t-1}^{¥€})) + \hat{c}Z_{t-1} + \hat{\varepsilon}_t,$$

where Z_{t-1} is a vector of variables in the time $t-1$ information set. Uncovered interest rate parity implies that $\hat{a} = 0$, $\hat{b} = 1$, and $\hat{c} = 0$. Fama shows that empirically $\hat{b}$ tends to be substantially less than one; for some pairs of currencies, the coefficient is even negative. Bekaert and Hodrick (1993, 2001) find that the empirical observation $\hat{b} < 1$ is robust to more general statistical assumptions. They show that the coefficient $\hat{b}$ has some time variation, related to changes in monetary and exchange rate policies. Baillie and Bollerslev (2000) show that accurate estimation of $\hat{b}$ requires long historical sample periods, due to the long-lived persistence in interest rate changes. This makes empirical analysis problematic since it is difficult to maintain the assumption that the relationship is stable over long time periods.

The failure of uncovered interest rate parity has consequences for currency hedging. It implies that investors should underhedge their positions in high-interest-rate currencies (where the net cost of hedging is positive) and over-hedge in low-interest-rate currencies (where the net cost is negative).

Given that currency hedging affects portfolio expected return, it makes sense to choose a hedge position by balancing expected return and risk, using, for example, the mean–variance objective discussed in chapter 1. In practice, currency hedging decisions are often made separately from the asset portfolio choice. This type of segmented management is called *overlay currency management*. This institutional feature probably reflects the impracticality of a single portfolio manager following both currency markets and asset markets simultaneously, while trying to generate superior risk-adjusted performance. Jorion (1994) compares overlay and integrated currency management to evaluate the lost utility from separate (overlay) management. He finds that overlay management does result in some lost value, but argues that this may be more than offset, at least for active portfolio management, by the informational advantage of having a separate manager dedicated to analyzing and forecasting currency market returns.

Burik and Ennis (1990) consider the disadvantages of currency hedging from the perspective of fixed-income investment. They argue empirically that hedged foreign bonds add very limited value to a diversified international portfolio. Once the currency risk of foreign bonds has been hedged away, little remains to differentiate them from domestic (U.S.) bonds. This means that the diversification benefit from holding hedged foreign bonds is near zero, at least from the perspective of a U.S. investor. Given the administrative costs of currency hedging, and the tax disadvantages of foreign bonds, they argue that currency-hedged foreign bonds provide little portfolio value. Unhedged bonds add value only if the investor has sufficient currency forecasting ability to offset the currency risk.

7.2.2 Second-Order Effects and the Currency Exchange Rate Paradox

The approximate linear model is a useful simplification but misses second-order effects. Consider the first-order approximation $r_{\mathrm{c}}^{¥€} = -r_{\mathrm{c}}^{€¥}$ and its implication that $E[r_{\mathrm{c}}^{¥€}] = -E[r_{\mathrm{c}}^{€¥}]$. The exact relationship is

$$E[r_{\mathrm{c}}^{¥€}] = E\left[\frac{1}{1 + r_{\mathrm{c}}^{€¥}}\right] - 1. \tag{7.16}$$

Applying Jensen's inequality to (7.16) and assuming that the currency return has nonzero variance gives that the product of the two reciprocal currency expected gross returns is strictly positive:

$$(1 + E[r_{\mathrm{c}}^{¥€}]) \times (1 + E[r_{\mathrm{c}}^{€¥}]) > 1.$$

Hence, the geometric average of any pair of reciprocal currency expected gross returns is strictly greater than one. Using this result, Black (1989,

1991) describes a global general equilibrium model in which hedging to zero currency risk is suboptimal. Instead, all worldwide investors hold a small residual position in all foreign currencies, in order to take advantage of this expected return gain.

7.2.3 Long-Horizon Currency Hedging

The use of a myopic one-period risk-management framework is particularly problematic for currency risk. As discussed in chapter 1, myopic portfolio management relies on the random walk behavior of asset returns; it breaks down when there are dynamic return patterns such as long-run mean reversion in asset prices. For currency returns, there are both theoretical and empirical grounds for positing strong mean reversion.

The variance ratio statistic provides a useful measure of mean reversion in returns. For a given asset or portfolio, the variance ratio is the return variance from holding the asset for T periods divided by T times the one-period return variance:

$$\mathrm{VR}(T) = \frac{\mathrm{var}(r_{1t-T,t})}{T\,\mathrm{var}(r_{1t})}.$$

If price follows a geometric random walk, then $\mathrm{VR}(T) = 1$ for all T. Note that it is necessary to use log returns for variance ratio tests, to eliminate compounding effects. Values of $\mathrm{VR}(T)$ less than one indicate mean reversion for risk horizon T. We discuss variance ratios in more detail in chapter 9. For currencies, there are theoretical grounds (based on long run purchasing power parity) for predicting values not only less than one for large T but actually approaching zero as T goes to infinity:

$$\lim_{T\to\infty} \mathrm{VR}(T) = 0. \tag{7.17}$$

This condition implies that foreign exchange rates are not (like most asset prices) a random walk, but instead are stationary in the long run. We call this condition (7.17) *stationary mean reversion*, to differentiate it from the more typical mean reversion in which $\mathrm{VR}(T)$ is less than one, but does not approach zero with T.

Most of the research on foreign exchange rate mean reversion uses real currency returns rather than nominal returns. This has the advantage that stationary mean reversion corresponds to the long-run tendency toward relative purchasing power parity between foreign exchange rates. Another advantage is that, when using real returns, currency returns are nonzero even when the nominal exchange rate is fixed. In the case of a fixed foreign exchange rate the real currency return just reflects the difference in the foreign and domestic inflation rates.

Froot and Rogoff (1995) survey the empirical literature and argue that stationary mean reversion (7.17) generally seems to hold for real currency returns. However, they note that the available evidence is weak and tentative. Reliable testing of (7.17) requires roughly a century of currency returns data to provide reliable inference. For most pairs of currencies, there are many currency regime changes over the course of a century. The statistical tests require that the mean reversion remains stable across several currency regimes. The more recent sample data after the publication of their study highlight the difficulty with this requirement. Some of the strongest evidence for stationary mean reversion cited in Froot and Rogoff relates to the collection of Western European currencies that no longer exist, having been absorbed into the euro.

Stationary mean reversion has an important consequence for portfolio risk management. It implies that for the very-long-horizon investor, currency risk is approximately zero. Froot and Rogoff suggest a mean-reversion half-life of four years. Consider a buy-and-hold position in a foreign currency (ignoring interest rate risk for simplicity). The per-period (say monthly) variance of the position held for four years is one-half its per-period variance if held for only one month. The per-period variance if held for eight years is one-quarter ($\frac{1}{4} = (\frac{1}{2})^2$) the per-period variance if held for one month.

Froot (1993) examines the performance of currency-hedged and unhedged portfolios of U.S. stock and bond indices from a British pound numeraire perspective over the period 1802–1990. The long time period allows him to test for long-horizon differences in the portfolio risk contribution of currency return. He finds that the risk contribution of currency declines substantially with the return horizon. The empirically estimated optimal hedge ratio declines from approximately 100% at a one-year horizon to 13% for an eight-year horizon. For an investor with a sufficiently long (eight-year) horizon, completely unhedged foreign assets have a lower risk than unit-hedged assets. Froot shows that this comes about because currency returns have strong, slow, mean reversion as well as long-run negative covariation with cumulative inflation and interest rate shocks. This second point means that at long horizons, foreign currencies serve as a natural hedge for the risks associated with foreign assets. In particular, they do not constitute additional sources of added risk.

Campbell et al. (2003) support this thesis in a different context. They consider a portfolio of domestic and foreign short-term default-free government bonds. These so-called riskless assets are, in fact, risk free for only one period. A long-term money market account is risky since there is reinvestment risk as the riskless rate varies unpredictably over time.

Campbell et al. use a vector autoregression model to describe the time-series interrelationships between exchange rates, short-term real interest rates, and inflation. Shocks to the domestic real interest rate are negatively correlated with currency returns, and so unhedged foreign cash investment has positive hedging value for long-horizon investors who hold domestic cash assets.

7.3 Currency Covariances with Stock and Bond Returns

The relationship between currency returns and asset returns is complicated by two issues. First, from the perspective of any single numeraire, the correlation between currency returns and the dominant "world" factor in a stock or bond market has a meaningful sign. However, the negative symmetry of currency returns, which is discussed in section 7.1.3, implies that the sign of this correlation cannot be consistent across numeraires. Second, the covariance between a home currency and the corresponding nation factor can be either positive or negative. It can confound the analysis of the relationship between currencies and assets if it is not accounted for. To remove the confounding influence of the global market factor with its indeterminate sign, it is common practice to work with active returns, defined as national index returns minus the global index return.

There is a substantial body of literature on the covariance between currency returns and industry factors. Griffin and Stulz (2001) estimate the currency sensitivities of industry portfolio returns. As suggested in the previous paragraph, their study relies on active returns on industries, which are given by the industry return minus the return to the national market index. They find that traded-goods industries tend to have more currency exposure than domestically focused industries. Japanese industries are the most currency sensitive of those in the six countries studied. However, even in the case of Japan, the explanatory power of currency returns is very limited. For example, for the Japanese auto industry, which is highly trade dependent, currency return explains only 2.4% of the active industry return. In most other industries and most other countries the explanatory power of currency return is even smaller.

Chow et al. (1997) show via bootstrap analysis that standard Student's t-tests overstate the statistical significance of currency return exposures for stocks and bonds. This is due to the positive excess kurtosis of currency returns. There are two effects: the usual degrees-of-freedom correction for unbiased standard errors is too modest, and the confidence interval (as a multiple of the true standard error) is too narrow. Their findings serve to further weaken the evidence for significant currency exposures of stock and bond factors, since most researchers use normality-based statistical tests. This kurtosis-related bias in Student's t-tests can be even more pronounced for F-tests or other multicoefficient tests. In modeling currency risk it is important to use testing methods that are robust to positive excess kurtosis.

If returns follow a geometric Brownian motion, then shrinking the return measurement interval increases the estimation precision of the covariance matrix. However, it is questionable whether this applies to vectors of asset and currency returns. Currency returns are endogenously determined with asset returns, and as discussed in the next section, there are macroeconomic feedbacks from cumulative asset returns to currency returns.

There is evidence that the currency exposures of equities are larger when returns are measured using a lower frequency. Like Griffin and Stulz (2001), Chow et al. (1997) find near-zero currency exposures for U.S. industry portfolios using monthly returns. However, currency exposures to annual returns are larger in magnitude, and they tend to be significantly positive. Chow et al. attribute this to a difference between the effect of a short-term interest rate shock (a positive shock to interest rates causes a negative shock to both stock returns and currency returns) and the effect of a longer-term shock to cash flows (a positive shock to long-term corporate cash flows causes a positive shock to stock returns and a negative shock to currency returns). Griffin and Stulz similarly find that the currency exposures of industry portfolios are larger in magnitude using annual returns than they are using monthly returns.

Bodnar and Gentry (1993) argue that the weak correlation between industry returns and currency returns stems from the confounding of several offsetting influences. A firm may be an importer of raw materials, a competitor against importers of foreign goods, a net exporter, or it may have foreign plants and investments whose values are set in units of foreign currency. All of these channels of influence have different, often conflicting, implications for currency exposure. Bodnar and Gentry use a structural system regression method to isolate the separate impact of each category using firm cost, revenue, and balance sheet data. They assume a linear relationship between their explanatory variables and firm currency exposures and find statistically significant linear coefficients.

7.4 Macroeconomic Influences on Currency Returns

7.4.1 The Meese–Rogoff Findings

In classic international trade theory, the exchange rate serves to equilibrate the flow of funds across nations. The change in the exchange rate is a function of the trade balance, relative inflation rates, relative monetary shocks, and differential productivity shocks. In an influential paper, Meese and Rogoff (1983) show that in fact, these macroeconomic variables have no ability to predict the exchange rate over short-to-medium forecast horizons of one, six, and twelve months. Even when they use the future realized values of the macroeconomic variables to artificially improve predictive performance, economic prediction models are outperformed by simple random walks. Mark (1995) shows that the economic models have nonnegligible predictive power for currency returns at longer horizons of three or four years. Therefore, it is only for short-horizon returns that these models fail entirely.

Roll (1979) makes the point that the absence of predictability in economic models of the exchange rate can be ascribed to the efficient-markets theory of capital market pricing. The efficient-markets theory asserts that asset prices are not predictable because profit-maximizing traders will impound all forecastable information into the current price. The efficient-markets theory combined with the limits to long-horizon arbitrage (see Shleifer and Vishny 1997) may explain the short-run unpredictability and long-run predictability of exchange rates in terms of economic fundamentals.

7.4.2 Exchange Rate Targets

The foreign exchange rate is both the market price of an investable asset and a key macroeconomic policy target. Through central bank intervention in foreign and domestic money markets, governments can influence foreign exchange rates, even to the extent of setting a particular nominal currency return variance equal to zero (at least temporarily). The interaction between the two aspects of foreign exchange rates leads to many open questions. While the focus of research in this area is not on portfolio management, the findings have considerable relevance nonetheless.

Krugman (1991) was the first to explicitly model the interaction between exchange rates as government targets and as freely traded asset prices. He considers a government imposing a fixed band on the foreign exchange rate, allowing the rate to move only between upper and

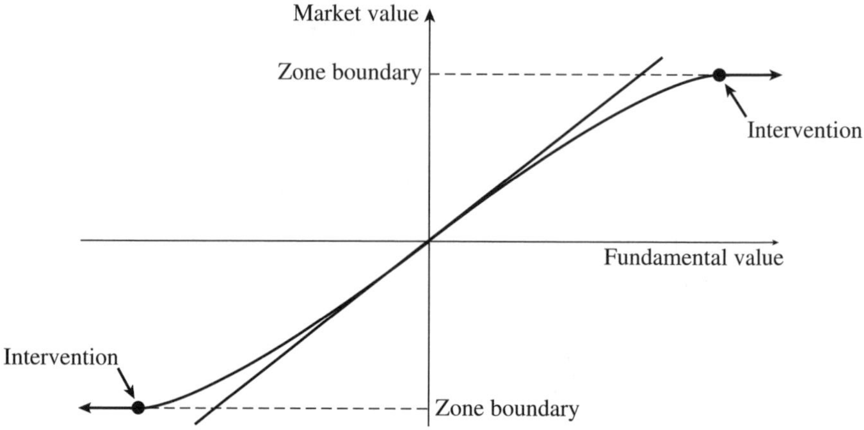

Figure 7.1. The relationship between the market exchange rate and its fundamental value given government intervention at the zone boundaries.

lower limits. When the exchange rate hits the upper limit of this target zone, the government intervenes, decreasing the domestic money supply (increasing the domestic interest rate) to force the exchange rate down. If the exchange rate hits the bottom of the target zone, the government increases the money supply to force the exchange rate up. Investors rationally anticipate the government's policies so that the exchange rate behavior is affected throughout the target zone not just at the boundaries. Krugman assumes that the fundamental value of the exchange rate (its value if the government has a policy never to intervene) follows a Brownian motion. The observed rate is a nonlinear function of its fundamental value due to the dampening effect of anticipated government intervention. Figure 7.1 gives a schematic description of the relationship between the market exchange rate and its fundamental value, given government intervention at the zone boundaries. The observed rate no longer follows Brownian motion: the return process has stationary mean reversion with time-varying currency return volatility. Volatility is highest in the middle of the target zone and lowest (going to zero) at the edges of the zone.

Krugman also considers the case in which the government's willingness to defend the target zone is uncertain. Investors posit a nonzero probability that the government will not defend the band. If the rate reaches the upper edge of the zone and is not defended, then it jumps to a new higher level, which is outside the zone, and then follows an unregulated Brownian motion. If the rate is defended, it remains inside the zone. The analogous mechanism applies if it hits the lower edge. Figure 7.2

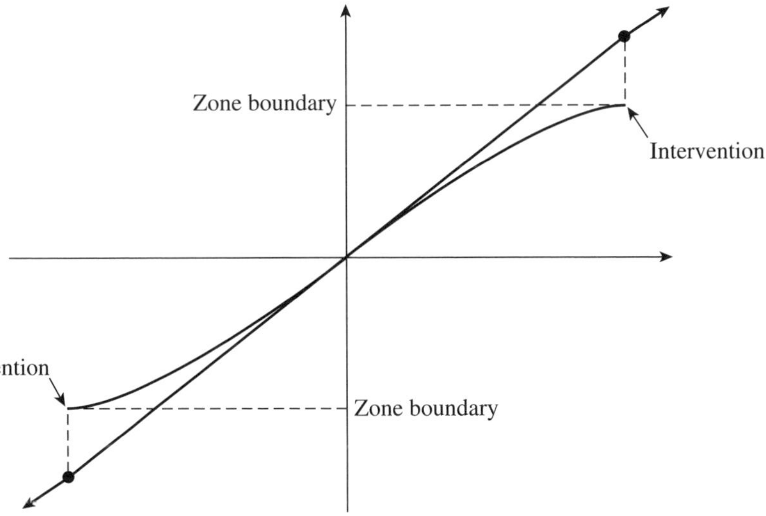

Figure 7.2. The relationship between the market exchange rate and its fundamental value given that the government's willingness to defend the target zone is uncertain.

illustrates how this affects the relationship between the fundamental value and the observed exchange rate.

Garber and Svensson (1995) extend Krugman's model to allow target zone realignments rather than simple abandonment of the target once the zone limit is breached. They also analyze the effects of central bank intervention inside the target zone rather than only at the edges. Target zones with occasional realignments are more descriptive of observed regimes than Krugman's assumption of a fixed zone that is replaced by a free floating currency. A targets-plus-realignments regime was adopted across many Western European currencies in the period 1971–99. Other common regimes include a dirty float (some attempt to dampen rate moves without an explicit target zone) and a rolling peg (a time series of fixed rates with episodic changes). Foreign exchange risk depends on both the existing currency regime and the probability of a switch to a different regime. See Hamilton (2008) for a review of estimation methods for regime-switching models.

7.4.3 Currency Crises

The nature of government exchange rate policies, using limited government monetary reserves to enforce fixed or bounded exchange rates, makes currency markets particularly prone to crises. When an exchange rate $p^{€¥}$ is at the limit of its target zone, or a pegged rate is subject to market pressure in one direction, investors perceive a "one-way bet" from borrowing the currency ¥ that is likely to fall in value and lending the strong currency, i.e., €. Unless the annualized interest rate differential $r_0^{¥} - r_0^{€}$ is extremely large, the very-short-term currency return $r_c^{€¥}$ more than compensates for the interest cost when there is a sudden jump in the exchange rate of the type illustrated in Figure 7.2. There are limits to the central bank's ability to use $r_0^{¥} - r_0^{€}$ to prevent speculation against the currency jump. The strong-currency interest rate $r_0^{€}$ cannot fall below zero. Increases in the weak-currency interest rate $r_0^{¥}$ can be counterproductive since too-high domestic interest rates can induce a national recession.

There is a game-theoretic aspect to central banks expending monetary reserves to manage the exchange rate. Central bank reserves are large enough to completely overwhelm the resources of any individual speculator. On the other hand, the combined capital flows from all potential speculators would overwhelm any central bank's ability to prevent a currency devaluation or revaluation. Speculators are in a coordination game, in which their optimal strategy is to mimic the chosen strategy of other speculators. Obstfeld (1986, 1994) argues that because of this game-theoretic feature, currency crises can arise endogenously from the interaction of speculators and need not correctly reflect fundamental valuation factors. Morris and Shin (1999) provide an alternative game-theoretic approach in which speculators have differing beliefs about the correct value of the currency; each speculator observes the actions of other speculators and uses it to infer others' beliefs about currency valuation fundamentals. In the Morris and Shin model, if many speculators attack a currency, then other speculators update their beliefs about the viability of the pegged exchange rate and join the speculative attack.

The contagious nature of currency crises is an important consideration in the risk modeling of currency returns. Currency crises are like city buses—for a long period there are none, and then several arrive together. Eichengreen et al. (1997) show that a currency crisis in one country tends to increase substantially the probability of a currency crisis in its trading partners. These contagion effects are difficult to estimate accurately in currency risk models since they reflect large, infrequent events, and hence are subject to the "peso problem." This contributes to the excess kurtosis of currency returns. Large infrequent jumps makes currency return variance and covariance estimates less reliable than for a same-length sample of normally distributed returns.

8
Integrated Risk Models

Previous chapters have discussed risk models for individual asset classes such as stocks, bonds, and foreign exchange. This chapter discusses the integration of asset-class risk models into models of aggregate portfolio risk, reaching across asset types and across national borders. The choice of architecture for a multicountry and/or multitype risk model depends crucially on the empirical structure of returns. If the common factors across asset types and countries are nearly the same, then the best architecture is a fully integrated approach. If, on the other hand, the markets are subject to very different factor risks, then a more segmented approach is preferable.

Section 8.1 defines international capital market integration and surveys the empirical evidence on the level and trends in international integration. Section 8.2 presents empirical evidence on integration across asset types. Section 8.3 discusses segmented risk models, in which the risk manager first analyzes the risk of the asset-class allocation and then the active risk of the subportfolio within each asset class. Section 8.4 discusses integrated risk models in which asset-class risk and security-selection risk are analyzed simultaneously.

8.1 Global and Regional Integration Trends

8.1.1 Definitions of International Capital Market Integration

There are at least three different definitions of international capital market integration. The most fundamental definition relates it to the presence of a common asset pricing model applying across national boundaries. We will call this *pricing integration*. For simplicity, consider the case of the capital asset pricing model:

$$E[x_i] = \alpha_i + \beta_i^m \pi, \qquad \alpha_i = 0 \quad \text{for all } i, \qquad \pi = E[x_{\mathrm{m}}],$$
$$\beta_i^m = \frac{\mathrm{cov}(x_i, x_{\mathrm{m}})}{\mathrm{var}(x_{\mathrm{m}})}. \tag{8.1}$$

Markets are pricing integrated if the asset pricing theory applies to all assets independently of their national location. So we test whether it is better to set x_m in (8.1) equal to the global market portfolio or to use a different national market portfolio for x_m for assets in each country. It is reasonably straightforward to extend this analysis to the multi-beta APT model and the intertemporal capital asset pricing model: see, for example, Harvey (1991) and Korajczyk and Viallet (1989) for empirical tests of pricing integration and Korajczyk (1996) for country-by-country measures of deviations from pricing integration.

Pricing integration is a cross-country restriction on expected returns, and expected returns have only a second-order effect on portfolio risk analysis. Although it is a central concern from the perspective of asset pricing theory, from the perspective of portfolio risk analysis the other definitions of market integration have more practical relevance.

A second definition of integration focuses on the absence of any barriers to cross-border investment. We will call this *capital flow integration*, since it relates to the free movement of capital across borders. Note that if investors are rational and perfectly informed, then capital flow integration should, in a frictionless market equilibrium, result in pricing integration through a demand–supply equilibrating process across markets. The well-documented presence of a strong home bias, which is the tendency for investors to overweight assets from their national markets in their portfolios, seems inconsistent with capital flow integration (see Lewis (1999) for a survey of research literature on the home bias).

A third definition ties market integration to the risk factors in asset returns. Capital markets are integrated if the common factors in security returns are global rather than nation specific. We call this *risk integration*. All three definitions have relevance, but the degree of risk integration is the primary concern in designing global portfolio risk models. We discuss the evidence for risk integration in section 8.1.2.

There are interesting relationships and dependencies among the three definitions of capital market integration. Capital flow integration should lead to pricing integration, through demand–supply equilibrium. Since a large proportion of the pervasive shocks to returns come from stochastic shocks to risk premia and discount rates, pricing integration should lead to a substantial degree of risk integration. However, even with full pricing integration and capital flow integration, some amount of risk segmentation will remain. For example, government taxation and spending policies can have a pervasive effect on domestic assets' after-tax cash flows, and therefore on domestic asset returns.

8.1.2 Measuring Global and Regional Risk Integration and Its Trend

A simple approach to detecting increased global risk integration is to test for changes in the covariance matrix of asset-class returns across countries. That is, using an international collection of asset-class index returns, test whether $\boldsymbol{C}$ is constant over time against the alternative hypothesis that the off-diagonal components increase with the secular increase in market integration. It is sensible to restate the alternative as a test for constant correlations, $\text{corr}_{ij} = C_{ij}/(C_{ii}C_{jj})^{1/2}$. Neither Kaplanis (1988) nor Ratner (1992) can reject the hypothesis that there is no increase in cross-border correlation of equity indices. Longin and Solnik (1995) find some evidence for increasing correlation of international equity indices, after adjusting for time variation in equity market volatilities. Solnik et al. (1996) argue that the evidence for increasing integration of global equity markets or global fixed-income markets during the 1980s and 1990s is not statistically strong. They emphasize the need to adjust for time-varying trends in volatility before testing for correlation trends. They find weak evidence for a slight increase in average correlation of bond markets during the 1980s, but this trend does not continue during the early 1990s. They find no positive trends in equity market integration. Figure 8.1 shows average correlations across ten country indices, using a rolling window of the previous forty-eight months of returns. Over this thirty-year period a positive (but unsteady) trend toward increased average correlation appears evident.

Chaumeton et al. (1996) look at the correlations of shift and twist factors in international bond markets over twelve-month subperiods. They find no evidence for an increase in average correlations, except for a weak positive trend within Western Europe. They perform similar tests using a five-factor model of equity markets and find no statistically significant trend toward increased correlations between national factors, neither within Western Europe nor globally.

The cross-national correlations of equity style and characteristic-based factor returns are low. Capaul et al. (1993) compute "style spread" return differences, by taking the difference between the monthly return of a low-price-to-book "value" portfolio and a high price to book "growth" portfolio. For the six developed equity markets in their study, these style spread returns have an average cross-market correlation of only 0.07. Sinquefield (1996) argues that the low correlation across equity style portfolio returns has substantive implications for international equity diversification strategies. For developed equity markets, the investor wishing to overweight small-size, high-value equities can substantially reduce risk by internationally diversifying.

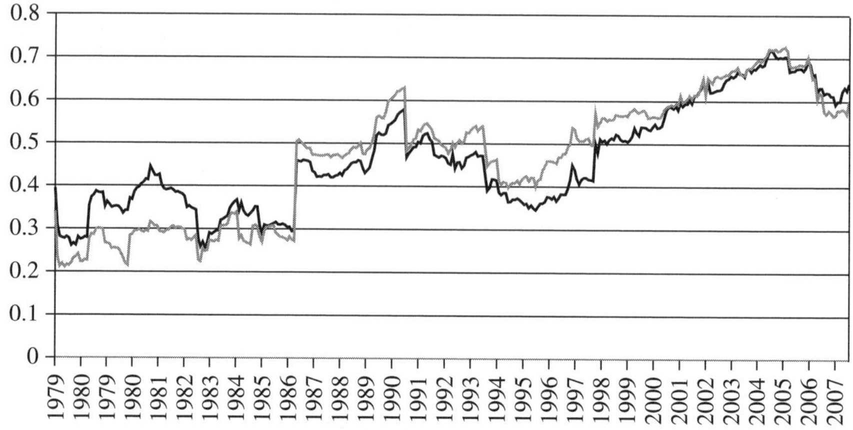

Figure 8.1. The time-series trend in the average correlations of national equity market indices. For each month, the figure shows the average of the correlations between the national index returns of Australia, France, Germany, Hong Kong, Italy, Japan, Spain, Switzerland, the United Kingdom, and the United States. At each date, correlations are measured over the previous forty-eight months. The black line relies on returns measured in U.S. dollars and the gray line on local-currency returns. The full sample period is January 1975 to December 2007; data courtesy of Ken French.

Griffin (2002) uses time-series regression to examine the global integration of the Fama–French three-factor model for four developed markets (the United States, the United Kingdom, Japan, and Canada). He compares Fama–French-type time-series regressions applied to individual equities using three specifications: (1) domestic market, size, and value factors; (2) international market, size, and value factors; and (3) both the domestic and international factors (a six-factor model). The domestic version vastly outperforms the international version in all four countries; the six-factor version with both domestic and international factors improves upon the domestic-only version by only a small amount in all cases. Hence, the Fama–French risk factors are mostly nation specific.

Note that in this section we are focusing on unconditional correlation: in particular, we are not conditioning on return sign or magnitude. In chapter 9 we will look at conditional correlations. We will see that there is strong evidence that global markets are more correlated during sharp market downturns than at other times.

8.2 Risk Integration across Asset Classes

Capital market integration is normally framed in terms of integration across national borders. Another important concern is the integration of returns across asset types, such as between corporate bond markets and equity markets, between long-maturity and short-maturity government bond markets, and across other asset types such as private equity and real estate. The same three definitions of integration apply. There is some evidence for less than perfect pricing integration and capital flow integration across asset types. For example, "the credit spread puzzle" refers to the anomalously high risk premia in corporate bond markets relative to equivalent risks in equities. There is also some anecdotal evidence for "preferred habitat" investment patterns, which mimic, for asset types, the home bias observed across national markets.

Fama and French (1993) test for risk integration of U.S. equity and fixed-income asset classes. They use the three stock market factors RMO, SMB, and HML discussed in chapter 6. For bonds they use two factors: the return difference between a long-term government bond portfolio and a one-month government bond, and the return difference between a long-term corporate and a long-term government bond portfolio. The two bond market factors have substantial explanatory power for the returns on a set of value- and size-sorted equity portfolios. On the other hand, the equity market factor has economically small, statistically insignificant explanatory power for bond portfolios (except low-grade bonds) in a regression that includes the two bond factors. The SMB factor has only limited explanatory power for a set of term and investment-grade-sorted bond portfolio returns, and the HML factor has almost none. In summary, they argue that U.S. stock and bond markets are not completely segmented, but most of the relationship seems to be unidirectional: bond factors explain stock returns, but stock factors do not explain bond returns once bond factors have been accounted for.

8.3 Segmented Asset Allocation and Security Selection

Many portfolio management decision processes proceed with an asset allocation step, choosing capital allocations across broad categories, followed by a security selection step, choosing individual securities within each category. The two-step approach to portfolio decision making evolved naturally as a way to simplify the complex full portfolio management problem across multiple countries and asset types. Portfolio risk models can be constructed to support this two-part decision structure.

A two-step risk model begins with an asset allocation risk model, based on covariances of asset-class indices. The individual assets are sorted into meaningful categories, usually with higher intra-class correlation and lower inter-class correlation. The chosen categories typically include a small set of domestic equity and fixed-income classes plus a collection of international asset classes (which may be country specific or regional, and typically cover either stocks or bonds or alternative asset classes such as real estate). Within each asset class the return on an investable index is used as the asset-class benchmark return.

In the first step the investor chooses a risk–return optimized allocation across the asset-class indices. This can use a mean–variance approach or an alternative such as a value-at-risk approach. Taking a linear mean–variance approach and letting $\boldsymbol{r}^{\mathrm{b}}$ denote the returns on the m asset-class benchmarks and $\boldsymbol{w}^{\mathrm{b}}$ the optimal allocation to these asset classes, we obtain

$$\boldsymbol{w}^{\mathrm{b}} = \underset{\boldsymbol{w}^{\mathrm{b}\prime}\mathbf{1}^m=1}{\arg\max}\, \boldsymbol{w}^{\mathrm{b}\prime}\boldsymbol{\mu}^{\mathrm{b}} - \tfrac{1}{2}\lambda \boldsymbol{w}^{\mathrm{b}\prime}\boldsymbol{C}^{\mathrm{b}}\boldsymbol{w}^{\mathrm{b}}.$$

In the second step the collection of portfolio managers each running subportfolios $h = 1, m$ select individual assets within each asset class, with investable funds equal to the asset-class allocation, w_h^{b}, from the first step. This individual security problem requires a separate, more detailed, risk model that describes the active risk characteristics of each security within the asset class. In this second step the various types of factor models described in chapters 3–6 are commonly employed.

The number of parameters in a two-step segmented risk model increases additively. If we use separate single-class risk models for m where asset class h depends on k_h factors, then the total number of parameters to estimate is

$$\tfrac{1}{2}m(m-1) + \sum_{h=1}^{m} \tfrac{1}{2}k_h(k_h - 1),$$

where the first term counts the parameters in the asset-class covariance matrix and the second term counts the parameters in the m separate factor covariance matrices. On the other hand, the number of estimable parameters in an unstructured factor covariance matrix increases quadratically with the number of factors included. If a single-factor covariance matrix were estimated for all factors simultaneously, this would require estimating

$$\tfrac{1}{2}k(k-1)$$

parameters, where $k = \sum_{h=1}^{m} k_h$, which typically is a much larger number of parameters.

Consider an integrated model for twenty asset classes, each consisting of twenty-five factors. The two-step, segmented approach requires an asset-class covariance matrix that depends on 190 parameters and twenty individual asset models that depend on 300 parameters each, giving a total of 6,190 parameters. By contrast, a one-step covariance matrix depends on simultaneous estimation of 124,750 parameters.

Suppose that the n_h assets in asset class h obey the following factor model:

$$\boldsymbol{r}^h = \boldsymbol{\mu}^h + \boldsymbol{B}^h f^h + \boldsymbol{\varepsilon}^h. \tag{8.2}$$

Subtracting the returns on the asset-class benchmark, $\boldsymbol{r}_h^{\mathrm{b}} = \mu_h^{\mathrm{b}} + \boldsymbol{B}_h^{\mathrm{b}} f^h + \varepsilon_h^{\mathrm{b}}$, from the vector of asset-class returns (8.2) gives a factor model expression for active returns:

$$\boldsymbol{r}_{\mathrm{a}}^h = \boldsymbol{\mu}_{\mathrm{a}}^h + \boldsymbol{B}_{\mathrm{a}}^h f^h + \boldsymbol{\varepsilon}_{\mathrm{a}}^h.$$

Each subportfolio manager maximizes a linear mean–variance problem in active returns relative to their asset-class index from the first step:

$$\begin{aligned}\boldsymbol{w}^h = {} & \underset{\boldsymbol{w}^{h\prime}1^n=1}{\arg\max}(\boldsymbol{w}^h - \boldsymbol{w}_b^h)'\boldsymbol{\mu}^h \\ & - \lambda^h[(\boldsymbol{w}^h - \boldsymbol{w}_b^h)'\boldsymbol{B}^{h\prime}\boldsymbol{C}_f^h\boldsymbol{B}^h(\boldsymbol{w}^h - \boldsymbol{w}_b^h) + (\boldsymbol{w}^h - \boldsymbol{w}_b^h)^{h\prime}\boldsymbol{C}_\varepsilon^h(\boldsymbol{w}^h - \boldsymbol{w}_b^h)].\end{aligned}$$

Active risk and return can be written equivalently using the active mean vector μ_{a}^h and active covariance matrix $\boldsymbol{C}_{\mathrm{a}}^h = \boldsymbol{C}_{\mathrm{fa}}^h + \boldsymbol{C}_{\varepsilon_{\mathrm{a}}}^h$:

$$\boldsymbol{w}^h = \underset{\boldsymbol{w}^{h\prime}1^n=1}{\arg\max}\, \boldsymbol{w}^{h\prime}\mu_{\mathrm{a}}^h - \lambda^h[\boldsymbol{w}^{h\prime}\boldsymbol{B}^{h\prime}\boldsymbol{C}_{\mathrm{fa}}^h\boldsymbol{B}^h\boldsymbol{w}^h + \boldsymbol{w}^{h\prime}\boldsymbol{C}_{\varepsilon_{\mathrm{a}}}^h\boldsymbol{w}^h].$$

The total portfolio return is the allocation-weighted sum of the component portfolio returns:

$$r_w = \sum_{h=1}^{m}(\boldsymbol{w}_h^{\mathrm{b}})(\boldsymbol{w}^{h\prime}\boldsymbol{r}^h).$$

If the active risks of each of the segmented subportfolios are independent of each other, and independent of all asset-class index returns, then the aggregate risk forecast from the two-step risk model correctly measures the overall risk of the total portfolio. That is, if

$$\operatorname{cov}((\boldsymbol{w}^{h\prime}\boldsymbol{r}^h - r_b^h), (\boldsymbol{w}^{j\prime}\boldsymbol{r}^j - r_b^j)) = 0 \quad \text{for all } i \neq j$$

and

$$\operatorname{cov}((\boldsymbol{w}^{h\prime}\boldsymbol{r}^h - r_b^h), r_j^{\mathrm{b}}) = 0 \quad \text{for all } i, j = 1, m,$$

then

$$\operatorname{var}(r_w) = \boldsymbol{w}^{\mathrm{b}\prime}\boldsymbol{C}^{\mathrm{b}}\boldsymbol{w}^{\mathrm{b}} + \sum_{h=1}^{m}(w_h^{\mathrm{b}})^2\operatorname{var}(\boldsymbol{w}^{h\prime}\boldsymbol{r}^h - r_b^h).$$

Hence the additive consistency of the risk forecasts from the two-step approach depends on the absence of correlation between active returns across asset classes, and between all active returns and all benchmark returns. These conditions for additive consistency are exceedingly strong and are unlikely to hold in practice. One motivation for integrated risk models is to relax these strong conditions and still have additively consistent risk forecasts.

8.4 Integrated Risk Models

An integrated risk model does not use different models for risk analysis of the asset allocation and security selection features of the portfolio. Although the distinction between these two steps in portfolio construction can still be supported by an integrated model, the same risk model applies to both steps.

8.4.1 An Integrated Equity Risk Model

A major innovation in risk integration was the creation of global single-class models. Grinold et al. (1989) develop a model that combines time-series estimation of market models within countries and cross-sectional estimation of extra-market global factors. The model has four global characteristic-based factors, thirty-six global industry factors, and a collection of twenty-four national equity market factors. Let x^h_{it} denote the excess return to asset i, located in country h, and let $x^h_{\mathrm{m}t}$ denote the excess return to the market index for country h. In a first estimation step, within each national market each individual equity is regressed on the national market index, giving an individual market factor beta and a nonmarket return:

$$x^h_{it} = \hat{\alpha}_i + \hat{\beta}_i x^h_{\mathrm{m}t} + \hat{\varepsilon}_{it} \quad \text{(TSR)},$$

where "TSR" indicates that this equation is estimated by time-series regression. The residuals from the first-step regressions $\hat{\varepsilon}_{it}$ are collated across all countries, creating an n^* vector of nonmarket returns at each time t. Here, n^* is the sum of the cross-sectional sample sizes from the twenty-four countries. These estimation residuals from the first step are used as nonmarket returns, $r^{\mathrm{nm}}_{it} = \hat{\varepsilon}_{it}$; this removes the dominant national market factor from the returns. In the second estimation step, a cross-sectional, characteristic-based model is used to identify thirty-six global industry factor returns and four global characteristic-based factor returns:

$$r_{it}^{\mathrm{nm}} = \left(\sum_{j=1}^{k_{\mathrm{I}}} \delta_{ij} \hat{f}_{jt}^{\mathrm{I}}\right) + \boldsymbol{B}_i \hat{\boldsymbol{f}}_t^{\mathrm{S}} + \varepsilon_{it}^* \quad \text{(CSR)},$$

where "CSR" denotes that this is estimated by cross-sectional regression and the $\boldsymbol{f}_t^{\mathrm{S}}$ are global style factors. The risk characteristics of each security are described by that security's national market beta, its global industry assignment, its exposures to the six global style factors, and its asset-specific variance. The factors in the model are the twenty-four national equity market factors, the four global style factors, and the thirty-six global industry factors. This gives a 64×64 covariance matrix of factor returns. The covariance matrix of asset-specific returns ε_{it}^* is assumed to be diagonal.

Consider the excess return to an asset i which is in country h and which is part of global industry j. Dropping the zero-exposure terms (that is, the other national market indices and global industry indices) gives a simple six-factor representation:

$$r_{it}^h = \alpha_i + \beta_i r_{\mathrm{m}t}^h + f_{jt}^{\mathrm{I}} + \boldsymbol{B}_i \boldsymbol{f}_t^{\mathrm{S}} + \varepsilon_{it}^*.$$

The covariance between two asset returns r_i^h and $r_{i*}^{h^*}$ depends upon their country and industry affiliations and their four global style factor exposures:

$$\operatorname{cov}(r_i^h, r_{i*}^{h^*}) = \operatorname{cov}(\beta_i r_{\mathrm{m}t}^h + f_{jt}^{\mathrm{I}} + \boldsymbol{B}_i \boldsymbol{f}_t^{\mathrm{S}}, \beta_{i*} r_{\mathrm{m}t}^{h*} + f_{j*t}^{\mathrm{I}} + \boldsymbol{B}_{i*} \boldsymbol{f}_t^{\mathrm{S}}),$$

which depends upon the covariances of at most eight factors. There are fewer than eight factors when the two assets are in the same industry or country.

The Grinold et al. architecture provides a risk decomposition with a balanced trade-off between parsimony and accuracy. It generates global equity portfolio risk forecasts using only sixty-four factors. One drawback of this architecture is its limited ability to address detailed structure in an individual market. Suppose, for example, that we want to examine the active and total risk of the Japan-only subportfolio. In the two-step method discussed in the previous section, subportfolio risk was measured using a model of the asset class alone. Here, the subportfolio risk analysis uses the submatrix of a global risk model. This is likely to be a substantially less detailed model than a single-country model. In particular, the model accounts only for global, not local, industry and characteristic-based factors. We know empirically that both industry factors and characteristic-based factors have strong local components, and these will be missed. So the two-step method in the last section has the advantage that it gives more accurate drill-down risk analysis for subportfolios.

An ad hoc solution is to use separate single-country risk models for drill-down analysis and the global model for aggregate portfolio analysis. This has the disadvantage that the risk manager now has two conflicting measures of the risk of the subportfolios: one coming from the global model and one from the single-country model.

8.4.2 A Two-Tier Multi-Asset-Class Model

Given the superiority of detailed risk models within asset classes, and the desire for consistency between aggregate risk forecasts and drill-down asset-class risk forecasts, there is an obvious benefit to combining the individual asset-class risk models into one large model. However, this generates a large increase in the number of factors in the model and a substantial loss in parsimony. Consider aggregating stock and bond models for thirty countries. If each country-based stock models has thirty-five industry factors and five style factors, and each bond model has five factors, the resulting global model has $30 \times 45 = 1{,}350$ factors. In this case, in the absence of additional structure, the factor covariance matrix depends on 910,575 parameters. The risk forecasts and marginal risk analysis from such a combined model will be unreliable and difficult, or impossible, to interpret, and mean–variance optimization would be, at best, unstable.

Puchkov et al. (2005) describe a two-tier factor model estimation methodology that produces a relatively parsimonious global model. The basic idea is to decompose each asset-class factor into one global and one purely local component, and then to impose zero cross-country correlations between the purely local components. By setting most correlations equal to zero the number of estimable parameters in the factor covariance matrix is substantially reduced.

The same technique can be applied to the term-structure factors in the set of local fixed-income models, and the equity/fixed-income models can be integrated, again with intuitive zero-correlation restrictions between purely local factors across countries.

The architecture developed in Puchkov et al. (2005) is a significant step forward but it does have drawbacks. First, it is extremely expensive to build such a model, since it requires building a complete collection of single-asset-class risk models. Second, it requires coordination of the different time-series data frequencies and return dynamics for different component single-asset-class models. So, for example, one may prefer a risk model based on daily data for U.S. equities and a risk model based on monthly data for the Turkish equity market due to its lower trading volumes and limited daily price liquidity. One might want to apply a generalized autoregressive conditional heteroskedasticity (GARCH; see chapter 9) model to some asset-class models and not to others, or use other dynamic adjustments on particular asset-class models. These disparate modeling strategies must be reconciled in the global model.

8.4.3 Drill-Down Consistency

A desirable feature linking a global risk model and a set of single-asset-class risk models is drill-down consistency, meaning that the pair of models (the global model and the single-asset-class model) give the same risk forecast when applied to the same single-asset-class portfolio. Anderson et al. (2005) derive general conditions on a global model to ensure that it is drill-down consistent with a set of single-class models. Consider n^* assets sorted into m asset classes, $h = 1, m$. Suppose that some of the asset classes have individual risk models with $n^h \times n^h$ covariance matrices, $\hat{\boldsymbol{C}}^h$, and that there is a global model with covariance matrix $\boldsymbol{C}^{\mathrm{G}}$. As discussed above, risk forecasts generated by the single-class models and the global model need not be consistent with each other. Anderson et al. (2005) pose the problem of finding a new global risk model $\boldsymbol{C}^*$ that is as close as possible to the initial global model $\boldsymbol{C}^{\mathrm{G}}$ and which is drill-down consistent with the individual asset-class risk models. In other words, the diagonal blocks of $\boldsymbol{C}^*$ must be identically equal to the single-class risk models $\hat{\boldsymbol{C}}^h$.

The naive approach of imposing drill-down consistency on $\boldsymbol{C}^*$ is to cut and paste the submatrices from $\hat{\boldsymbol{C}}^h$ into the diagonal blocks of $\boldsymbol{C}^{\mathrm{G}}$. This imposes drill-down consistency but typically results in a matrix that is not positive definite. Such a matrix implies negative variances for some portfolios. The drill-down consistency condition must be imposed in a way that produces a valid global covariance matrix.

Anderson et al. (2005) derive the general conditions for drill-down consistency between a global covariance matrix and a set of asset-class covariance matrices. Let $\boldsymbol{P}_h$, $h = 1, m$, denote any collection of m orthonormal matrices of dimensions $n^h \times n^h$ for $h = 1, m$. (An orthonormal matrix is defined by the condition $\boldsymbol{P}_h \boldsymbol{P}_h' = \boldsymbol{I}$.) Define the block diagonal matrix $\boldsymbol{D}$ composed from $\boldsymbol{P}_h$, $h = 1, m$, as follows.

$$\boldsymbol{D} = \bigoplus_{h=1}^{m} (\hat{\boldsymbol{C}}^h)^{1/2} \boldsymbol{P}_h (\boldsymbol{C}^{\mathrm{G}h})^{-1/2}, \tag{8.3}$$

where the operator $\bigoplus_{h=1}^{m}$ takes the m component matrices and connects them together as a block diagonal $n^* \times n^*$ matrix. Anderson et al. (2005)

prove that all possible drill-down consistent matrices can be expressed as

$$C^* = DC^{\mathrm{G}}D' \tag{8.4}$$

for some D obeying (8.3), and these two conditions (8.3) and (8.4) characterize the set of drill-down consistent positive-definite covariance matrices.

Next, Anderson et al. (2005) suggest an estimation methodology for modifying the initial global covariance matrix C^{G} to produce a drill-down consistent alternative. They suggest minimizing the Frobenius matrix norm

$$\min_{C^*} \|C^* - C^{\mathrm{G}}\| \tag{8.5}$$

over all possible consistent choices C^* obeying (8.3) and (8.4) for some P_h, $h = 1, m$. They offer an interpretation of this minimization problem as maximum-likelihood estimation of C^*. This minimization problem involves selecting the best-fitting collection of orthonormal matrices P_h, $h = 1, m$, using (8.3) and (8.4), using these matrices to construct D from (8.3), then C^* from (8.4), and minimizing the objective function (8.5). This is a high-dimensional, nonlinear estimation problem with an unusual structure. They coin the term "orthogonal double Procrustes problem," since (8.5) is an extension of the orthogonal Procrustes problem in linear algebra.

8.4.4 A Multitier, Multi-Asset-Class Model

Shepard (2008) develops an economically motivated framework for building multi-asset-class risk models that are parsimonious and consistent with detailed single-asset-class models. As above, the collection of single-asset-class factors are regressed onto a much smaller collection of global factors. However, the model architecture is different from that in Puchkov et al. (2005). In Shepard (2008), the set of model factors consists of global factors and purely local factors that are residual to the global factors. Shepard (2008) makes the assumption that the purely local factors are uncorrelated with the global factors. He then shows that this assumption can be satisfied by judiciously choosing the exposures of local-to-global factors, and that the choice results in integrated model risk forecasts that are consistent with single-asset-class risk forecasts. Shepard (2008) shows that it is possible to introduce nonzero correlations between purely local factors in different asset classes by introducing a third tier, consisting of purely local factors that have zero correlation with purely local factors in different asset classes. This construction does not disturb the consistency with single-asset-class forecasts, but rather affects covariances between assets in different asset classes.

9

Dynamic Volatilities and Correlations

The evidence for dynamic patterns in portfolio risk is very strong, with a variety of dynamic patterns clearly documented across a range of asset classes. The influence of these dynamic features on accurate portfolio risk analysis can be substantial. This chapter reviews some of the empirical evidence and discusses analytical refinements to portfolio risk analysis models to account for these dynamic patterns. Section 9.1 deals with generalized autoregressive conditional heteroskedasticity (GARCH) models and section 9.2 with stochastic volatility (SV) models. Section 9.3 discusses time aggregation of risk forecasts in the presence of risk dynamics. Section 9.4 examines the issue of asymmetry in asset return correlations, called asymmetric dependence. Section 9.5 discusses options-implied volatility and its use in portfolio risk management. Section 9.6 looks at portfolio risk for long return horizons and its dependence on expected return dynamics. Section 9.7 looks at dynamics in cross-sectional volatility.

9.1 GARCH Models

The research literature on GARCH is enormous. This section describes some key results that have particular relevance in portfolio risk analysis. Readers wanting a more detailed treatment of GARCH models can consult Christoffersen (2003), Engle (1995), or Taylor (2005).

In this section we assume that expected return is time constant and known, rather than estimated, in order to focus on the time variation in risk. In any case, most of the dynamic volatility effects discussed in this chapter are more powerful at high frequencies (with the exception of the long-horizon effects discussed in section 9.6). Recall from chapter 1 that for high-frequency portfolio returns the accurate estimation of expected returns is inconsequential to risk measurement. Consider the variance of log return for an asset or portfolio with constant per-period mean return μ and constant per-period variance σ^2. Consider the relationship between expected squared return and variance, for log return measured at frequency Δ,

$$E[r_{t,t+\Delta}^2] = \text{var}[r_{t,t+\Delta}] + (E[r_{t,t+\Delta}])^2 = \Delta\sigma^2 + \Delta^2\mu,$$

and note that with $\Delta \overset{\Delta}{\approx} 0$ the effect of the mean return is negligible, since $\Delta^2\mu$ is small relative to $\Delta\sigma^2$.

9.1.1 Univariate GARCH Models

First we consider the case of a single asset or portfolio. Letting μ denote the time-constant expected return, we remove it from total return and work in units of demeaned return:

$$r_t = \mu + \tilde{r}_t.$$

The demeaned returns are allowed to have time-varying volatility:

$$\tilde{r}_t = \sigma_t \eta_t, \tag{9.1}$$

where $\sigma_t = E_{t-1}[\tilde{r}_t^2]^{1/2}$ and it follows from the definition of σ_t that $E[\eta_t^2] = 1$. In the standard GARCH model, η_t is assumed to be independently and identically distributed over time. Sometimes, such as for likelihood inference, we add the assumption that η_t has a standard normal distribution, but this is not a necessary condition for a GARCH model.

The GARCH(1,1) model treats the variance at time t as a linear function of the last period's variance and the last period's squared demeaned return:

$$\sigma_t^2 = \alpha + \beta\sigma_{t-1}^2 + \gamma\tilde{r}_{t-1}^2, \tag{9.2}$$

where in order to ensure that variance remains nonnegative we impose $\alpha, \beta, \gamma \geqslant 0$. It is easy to show that time stationarity of returns requires that $\beta + \gamma < 1$; otherwise, return variance will tend to grow unboundedly over time. Given this stationarity condition, we can compute the unconditional variance as $\bar{\sigma}^2 = \alpha/(1 - \beta - \gamma)$ and rewrite (9.2) in a more intuitive form:

$$\sigma_t^2 = \bar{\sigma}^2 + \beta(\sigma_{t-1}^2 - \bar{\sigma}^2) + \gamma(\tilde{r}_{t-1}^2 - \bar{\sigma}^2). \tag{9.3}$$

Note that there is no error term in (9.2), so that given σ_{t-1}^2 and the parameters α, β, and γ, the value of σ_t^2 is known exactly after $\tilde{r}_{t-1}^2$ is observed.

The GARCH model can be estimated by maximum likelihood. Given normality of the innovations η_t the log-likelihood function of the parameters has a simple closed form:

$$\ln(L(\alpha, \beta, \gamma)) = -\frac{1}{2}\sum_{t=1}^{T-1}\left(\ln(\sigma_t^2) + \frac{\tilde{r}_t^2}{\sigma_t^2} + \ln(2\pi)\right) \tag{9.4}$$

where we can substitute from (9.2) using a starting value for σ_0^2. GARCH estimation amounts to nonlinear maximization of this function with respect to the parameter values. Engle and Sheppard (2001) suggest that it is preferable in practice to use the sample return variance for $\bar{\sigma}^2$ in (9.3), which provides a consistent estimate, and then estimate the other GARCH parameters β, γ using the likelihood function (9.4). This two-step procedure, called variance targeting, substantially improves the convergence reliability of the nonlinear estimator required to minimize (9.4).

Standard GARCH models provide simple formulas for variance forecasting. Suppose that after observing r_{t-1} the conditional variance for the next period is σ_t^2. Focusing on the GARCH(1, 1) model for notational simplicity, the conditional variance for the return in period $t+k$ is

$$\begin{aligned} E_{t-1}[\sigma_{t+k}^2] &= E_{t-1}[\tilde{r}_{t+k}^2] \\ &= \bar{\sigma}^2 + (\beta+\gamma)^k(\beta(\sigma_{t-1}^2 - \bar{\sigma}^2) + \gamma(\tilde{r}_{t-1}^2 - \bar{\sigma}^2)). \end{aligned} \tag{9.5}$$

Note that for $k = 0$, formula (9.5) reduces to formula (9.3). As k gets larger, the forecast for $E_{t-1}[\sigma_{t+k}^2]$ is dominated by the unconditional variance $\bar{\sigma}^2$.

The variance forecast of the cumulative return over the horizon from time $t-1$ to time $t+s$ is obtained by summing[1] the single-period variance forecasts for $k = 0, 1, \dots, s-1$ and is given by

$$\begin{aligned} \sigma_t^2(s) &= E_t\left[\sum_{k=0}^{s} \tilde{r}_{t+k}^2\right] \\ &= s\bar{\sigma}^2 + \frac{1-(\beta+\gamma)^s}{1-(\beta+\gamma)}(\beta(\sigma_{t-1}^2 - \bar{\sigma}^2) + \gamma(\tilde{r}_{t-1}^2 - \bar{\sigma}^2)). \end{aligned} \tag{9.6}$$

There are similarities between the time-t long-horizon variance forecast in formula (9.6) and the forecast of single-period variance at a time far in the future given in formula (9.5). For $s = 1$, formula (9.6) reduces to formula (9.3) as expected. As s increases, the forecast for $E_t[\sigma_{t+k}^2]$ is dominated by the unconditional variance $s\sigma^2$.

9.1.2 Asymmetric GARCH

The linear model (9.2) can be extended to allow asymmetries, for example to reflect the empirical pattern that negative returns seem to have a larger influence on volatility than positive returns of equal magnitude. An example of an asymmetric GARCH model is

$$\sigma_t^2 = \bar{\alpha}^2 + \beta(\sigma_{t-1}^2 - \bar{\sigma}^2) + \gamma_1(\tilde{r}_{t-1}^2 - \bar{\sigma}^2) + \gamma_2[\tilde{r}_{t-1}^2 - \bar{\sigma}^2]^-, \tag{9.7}$$

[1] Using log returns so that there is no additional term due to compounding.

where $[\tilde{r}_t^2 - \bar{\sigma}^2]^- = 0$ if $\tilde{r}_t > 0$ and otherwise it equals the value in brackets. The nonnegative coefficient γ_2 captures the larger effect of a negative return shock on variance.[2] The log-likelihood function (9.4) remains essentially the same (except for the change in the set of parameters), so estimation is straightforward.[3]

A useful tool for studying asymmetry in volatility models is the news impact curve suggested by Engle and Ng (1993). For a given volatility model, the news impact curve gives the nonlinear functional relationship between demeaned return at time $t-1$ and time-t variance, setting all other variables equal to their unconditional expected values:

$$\sigma_t^2 - \bar{\sigma}^2 = f(\tilde{r}_{t-1}).$$

The news impact curve can be generated from one or more preestimated GARCH models to visually identify the degree and type of asymmetry in the models. So, for example, computing the news impact curves for (9.3) and (9.7) gives

$$f(\tilde{r}_{t-1}) = \gamma(\tilde{r}_{t-1}^2 - \bar{\sigma}^2)$$

and

$$f(\tilde{r}_{t-1}) = \gamma_1(\tilde{r}_{t-1}^2 - \bar{\sigma}^2) + \gamma_2[\tilde{r}_{t-1}^2 - \bar{\sigma}^2]^-$$

respectively.

There are two potential causal mechanisms for the observed asymmetry in the relationship between realized returns and volatility; these two causal mechanisms are called the *leverage effect* and the *volatility feedback effect*. For both effects, the observed negative return and the volatility increase are simultaneous; the two causal mechanisms differ in which of the two simultaneous events is viewed as exogenous and which is viewed as endogenously caused by the other. The leverage effect posits that negative returns cause volatility increases. Suppose, for example, that the underlying source of a stock price decline is new publicly released information indicating that future earnings will be lower than previously anticipated. If the firm has outstanding debt, the decline in the stock price will increase the leverage ratio of the firm. This increased leverage ratio will increase the volatility of the stock price, since future shocks to firm value will be more amplified by the now-higher leverage

---

[2] There are many other specifications that have been proposed to capture this positive/negative return asymmetry: see Campbell et al. (1997) for an overview.

[3] Variates that are strictly exogenous to returns, such as interest rates or macroeconomic announcement dummy variables, can be added to the linear model (9.7) without changing the form of the likelihood function. An important restriction for logical consistency is that the variance-generating process (9.7) must be positive almost surely.

ratio. So as long as the volatility of overall firm value remains constant, the volatility of the stock price is increased by the price decline due to this leverage effect.

The other causal mechanism is volatility feedback, which posits that volatility increases cause negative returns. Suppose that an external event causes earnings volatility to be higher. This will directly cause the stock price to be more volatile. If the higher volatility of the stock price is all or partly market risk, then its increased volatility will cause the stock price to fall (a negative realized return) so that the expected (subsequent) return of the stock can move to risk–return equilibrium at a higher level of risk. Hence the equilibrium pricing response from a volatility increase causes a negative return realization.

It is difficult, but not impossible, to differentiate between the leverage effect and the volatility feedback effect. Bekaert and Wu (2000) and Bae et al. (2007) compare the two causal mechanisms empirically; Bae et al. (2007) show that the magnitude of the volatility feedback effect depends critically on the persistence of the volatility increase.

9.1.3 Weaknesses and Limitations of the GARCH Model

An important empirical finding is that daily and intra-daily asset returns have excess kurtosis.[4] The likelihood function (9.4) relies on normality of the innovations η_t in (9.1) and the parameter estimates are dependent upon this assumption. There are GARCH refinements that allow this limitation of the GARCH model to be overcome. Bollerslev (1987) derives the likelihood function for the case in which η_t follows a Student's t-distribution, and uses the parameter of the Student's t-distribution to set the amount of kurtosis in η_t. The Student's t-distribution parameter is estimated along with the standard GARCH parameters.

Another shortcoming of the standard GARCH model is its inability to explain volatility persistence. Volatility persistence can be understood by considering the autocorrelation function for squared returns:

$$\rho_k = \text{corr}(r_t^2, r_{t-k}^2). \tag{9.8}$$

It is straightforward to estimate ρ_k: simply compute the sample autocorrelations of squared returns. Empirical autocorrelations of squared daily returns only converge slowly—this is the empirical phenomenon known as *volatility persistence*. The implied autocorrelation function of a GARCH model can be derived by judicious rearrangement of the GARCH

[4]GARCH models directly induce a small amount of positive excess kurtosis, since normality of the innovations η_t does not imply normality of the demeaned returns $\tilde{r}_t$. However, this direct effect is insufficient to explain the large degree of kurtosis in returns.

equations (see Taylor (2005) for details). So, for example, in the case of GARCH(1, 1),

$$\rho_k = c(\beta + \gamma)^k, \tag{9.9}$$

where c is a positive constant.[5] Once a GARCH model has been estimated, one can use (9.9) and the estimated GARCH parameters to get a model-dependent estimate of ρ_k.

Note that the GARCH-based autocorrelations (9.9) converge to zero at rate $(\beta + \gamma)^k$, where k is the lag length. Unless $\beta + \gamma$ is very close to one, this converges quickly to zero. Figure 9.1 shows the sample autocorrelation coefficients of squared daily returns to the S&P 500 index and the implied autocorrelations from a GARCH(1, 1) model estimated using the same data. There is an obvious mismatch between the two estimated autocorrelation functions in the speed at which the autocorrelations converge toward zero for large lag lengths. This empirical mismatch is a weakness of the GARCH(1, 1) model as an adequate representation of observed volatility patterns.

There are a variety of ways to alter the standard GARCH model to make it consistent with observed volatility persistence. One approach is to drop the stationarity assumption $\beta + \gamma < 1$; this type of nonstationary GARCH model is called an integrated GARCH (IGARCH) model. There are drawbacks to the IGARCH model for portfolio risk analysis applications, since it implies that variance is not stationary over time and has no unconditional finite value.

Another method is to use higher-order GARCH models, but with restrictions imposed on the models so that the set of estimable parameters do not grow unduly. Two examples of this approach are the multiple-components GARCH model of Engle and Lee (1999) and the fractionally integrated GARCH model of Baillie et al. (1996).

Perhaps the most serious weakness of GARCH models is the lack of closure under time aggregation. If a GARCH model applies to daily returns, then that model does not apply to weekly returns, since the GARCH equation summed over periods is inconsistent with a GARCH equation for lower-frequency variances.[6]

---

[5] The constant c can be expressed in terms of the GARCH(1, 1) parameters:

$$c = \frac{\gamma(1 - \gamma\beta - \beta^2)}{(\gamma + \beta)(1 - 2\gamma\beta - \beta^2)}.$$

[6] There is a limited type of time aggregation of GARCH models; a true GARCH model for high-frequency returns gives rise to a "weak" GARCH model at lower frequencies (see Drost and Nijman 1993).

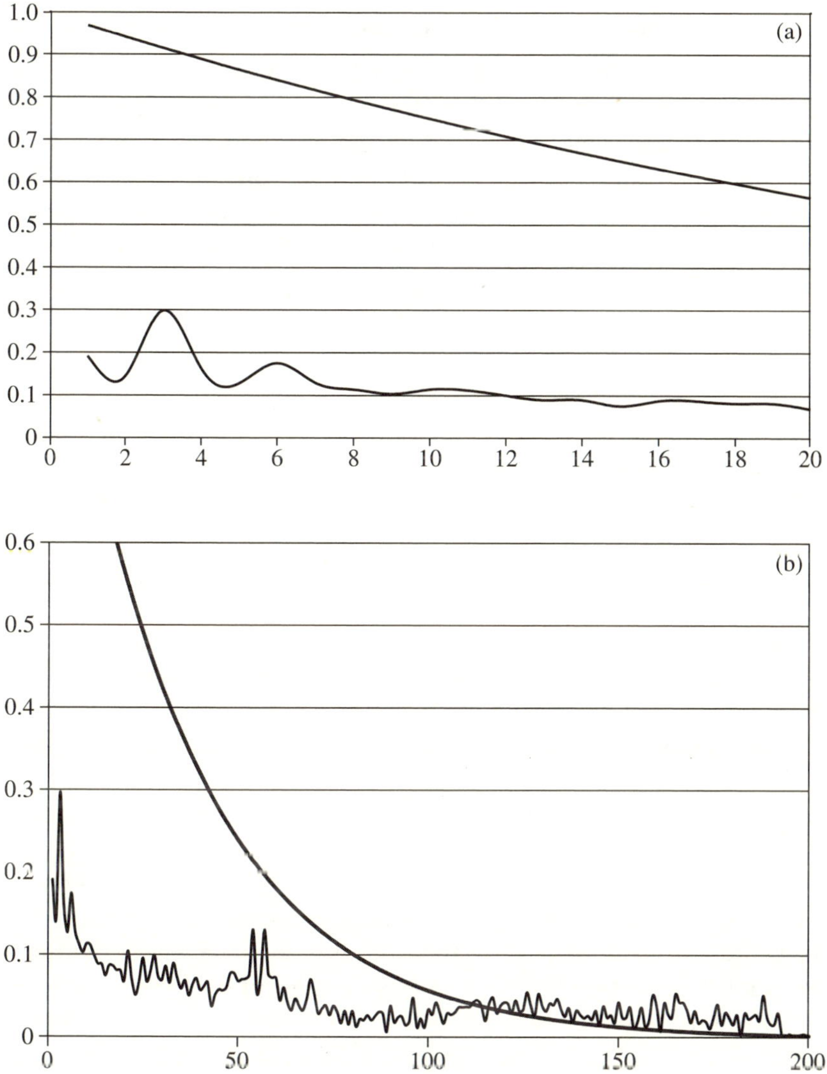

Figure 9.1. Sample versus GARCH(1, 1)-implied autocorrelations of squared returns to daily U.S. equity index returns, for (a) lags 1–20 and (b) all lags, truncated at 0.6.

GARCH models do not provide a consistent framework for continuous-time volatility modeling (however, we will see below that they can provide a useful approximation in this case). One reason for the growing popularity of SV models as an alternative to GARCH models is that SV models provide a consistent set of dynamic volatility models at all return frequencies, including continuous time.

9.1.4 GARCH Models as High-Frequency Approximations

It is informative to analyze GARCH models as approximation tools even when the models are not valid as true representations of the return-generating process. Nelson (1992) differentiates between estimation, filtering, and forecasting with a GARCH model. Consider a GARCH(1,1) model for simplicity. The *estimation problem* is determining the three parameters of the model by maximizing its likelihood function:

$$\begin{aligned}(\hat{\alpha},\hat{\beta},\hat{\gamma}) &= \arg\max L(\alpha,\beta,\gamma)\\ &= \arg\max -\frac{1}{2}\sum_{t=1}^{T-1}\ln(\sigma_t^2) + \frac{\tilde{r}_t^2}{\sigma_t^2} + \ln(2\pi).\end{aligned}$$

The *filtering problem* is the estimation of the time series of realized variances over the sample period:[7]

$$\hat{\sigma}_t^2 = \hat{\alpha} + \hat{\beta}\hat{\sigma}_{t-1}^2 + \hat{\gamma}\tilde{r}_{t-1}^2. \tag{9.10}$$

The *forecasting problem* summarized for GARCH(1,1) in formulas (9.5) and (9.6) is parallel to filtering, but is out of sample.

By iterated substitution of $\hat{\sigma}_{t-1}^2$ on the right-hand side of (9.10), using the left-hand side expression (lagged once), the GARCH(1,1) filtering equation (9.10) can be written equivalently as an infinite weighted sum of lagged squared returns:

$$\hat{\sigma}_t^2 = \kappa + \sum_{s=1}^{\infty} w_s \tilde{r}_{t-s}^2, \tag{9.11}$$

where $\kappa = \sigma_0^2(1-\beta-\gamma)\sum_{s=0}^{\infty}\beta^s$ and $w_s = \beta^{s-1}\gamma$. So, as a variance filter, the GARCH(1,1) model is equivalent to an infinite weighted sum of lagged squared returns. It is this infinite-moving-average feature of GARCH models that makes them robust and accurate variance filtering tools for high-frequency returns.

Suppose that we now drop the assumption that the GARCH model applies to returns. Instead we assume that a continuous-time price process p_t is observed at small, equally spaced intervals Δ. The return at time $t+\Delta$ is $r_{t+\Delta} = \log(p_{t+\Delta}) - \log(p_t)$ and its variance (per unit period) is $(1/\Delta)E_t[(r_{t+\Delta} - E_t[r_{t+\Delta}])^2]$. Applying a GARCH(1,1) model at frequency Δ and writing the model's filtering rule for variance as a weighted sum gives

$$\hat{\sigma}_t^2 = \frac{1}{\Delta}\left(\kappa + \sum_{s=1}^{\infty} w_s \tilde{r}_{t-s\Delta}^2\right). \tag{9.12}$$

[7] For simplicity we assume that the sample history is long enough that we can ignore the problem of setting starting values to begin the iterative definition of $\hat{\sigma}_t^2$.

Nelson (1992) shows that, as long as the continuous-time price process has sufficient regularity properties, then (9.12) provides consistent filtering estimates for the time series of true variances. So the GARCH(1, 1) model "works" (giving approximately correct variance estimates at high frequencies) even though it is not the correct model in the sense of exactly describing variance dynamics. Also, for regular variance processes, as the time interval shrinks, the term $\beta + \gamma$ in the GARCH(1, 1) model approaches one from below, so that the GARCH approximation is close to nonstationary when the return frequency is high. This also means that the constant term κ in (9.12) can be ignored for high-frequency returns.

Using a similar approach, Foster and Nelson (1996) examine moving-average-based variance filters for high-frequency returns. They consider the set of variance estimators or "filters" of the form

$$\hat{\sigma}_t^2 = \sum_{s=1}^{\infty} w_s \tilde{r}_{t-s}^2,$$

including the case of finite-lag averages by setting $w_s = 0$ for all s beyond an upper bound. They show that these models can provide consistent variance estimates as the return frequency goes to zero for a wide range of continuous-time price processes. They show that in most cases the asymptotically optimal filtering scheme is to use an exponentially weighted average variance

$$\hat{\sigma}_t^2 = c \sum_{s=1}^{\infty} (e^{-as}) \tilde{r}_{t-s}^2, \tag{9.13}$$

for some exponential smoothing parameter $a > 0$, where c is chosen so that the weights sum to one. They show that this result also applies in the multivariate case, where $\tilde{\boldsymbol{r}}_t$ is a vector of returns and we are estimating a dynamic covariance matrix rather than a scalar variance.

The exponential filter (9.13) is widely used by practitioners and is sometimes called the "RiskMetrics model" after the commercial organization that popularized its use. Note that the optimal value for a in (9.13) depends on the detailed specification of the true return generating process; there is no simple general rule for setting it.

It is important to distinguish between using (9.13) as a filter and using it as a variance-generating model. If we choose to use (9.13) as a variance-generating model by removing the hat from the left-hand side, then by simple backward substitution and rearrangement, it implies that

$$\sigma_t^2 = w\sigma_{t-1}^2 + (1 - w)\tilde{r}_{t-1}^2, \tag{9.14}$$

where $w = e^{-a}$. This is a version of the IGARCH model. In most contexts (9.14) is problematic as a variance-generating model, since it implies that in the long run variance collapses to zero (see Nelson (1990) for discussion on this). On the other hand, (9.13) is a very robust variance filter.

9.1.5 Multivariate GARCH Models

Let $\boldsymbol{C}_t$ denote the time-t covariance matrix of n assets, and let $\boldsymbol{Z}_{t-1} = \tilde{\boldsymbol{r}}_{t-1}\tilde{\boldsymbol{r}}'_{t-1}$ denote the $n \times n$ outer product of time-t demeaned returns. Define the function $\text{vech}(\boldsymbol{Z})$ as the function that takes a symmetric $n \times n$ matrix and write its nonredundant entries as a $\frac{1}{2}n(n-1)$ vector. The "simplest" model for covariance matrix dynamics is to mimic the GARCH$(1,1)$ approach in a vector form, writing $\text{vech}(\boldsymbol{C}_t)$ as a linear function of $\text{vech}(\boldsymbol{C}_{t-1})$ and $\text{vech}(\boldsymbol{Z}_{t-1})$:

$$\text{vech}(\boldsymbol{C}_t) = \boldsymbol{A} + \boldsymbol{B}\,\text{vech}(\boldsymbol{C}_{t-1}) + \boldsymbol{G}\,\text{vech}(\boldsymbol{Z}_{t-1}). \tag{9.15}$$

The problem with this "simple" approach is its extreme lack of parsimony. Note that both matrices B and $\boldsymbol{C}$ are $\frac{1}{2}n(n-1) \times \frac{1}{2}n(n-1)$ and so each has $\frac{1}{4}n^2(n-1)^2$ parameters—an unfeasibly large number to estimate even for modest values of n.

Another important concern is the need for positive definiteness of $\boldsymbol{C}_t$, if it is to represent a covariance matrix. Without tight restrictions on the matrices $\boldsymbol{B}$ and $\boldsymbol{G}$, there is no guarantee that (9.15) will preserve the positive definiteness of $\boldsymbol{C}_t$ through time.

9.1.6 Dynamic Scaling of the Correlation Matrix

The constant-correlation (CCOR) model (Bollerslev 1990) restricts the dynamics of the covariance matrix to the variance terms. Each of the n asset return variances follows a standard GARCH model:

$$\sigma_{it}^2 = \bar{\sigma}_i^2 + \beta_i(\sigma_{it-1}^2 - \bar{\sigma}_i^2) + \gamma_i(\tilde{r}_{it-1}^2 - \bar{\sigma}_i^2), \quad i = 1, n, \tag{9.16}$$

and for simplicity we assume GARCH$(1,1)$ but this is easily generalized to any member of the GARCH family. The correlation matrix of the pure innovations across firms η_{it}, $i = 1, n$, is assumed to be a constant matrix through time:

$$E[\boldsymbol{\eta}_t\boldsymbol{\eta}'_t] = \boldsymbol{C}_\eta. \tag{9.17}$$

Since η_{it} has unit variance by construction, the covariance matrix and the correlation matrix are the same. Combining (9.16) and (9.17) with the definition of demeaned return (9.1) gives

$$\text{cov}_{t-1}(\tilde{r}_{it}, \tilde{r}_{jt}) = \sigma_{it}\sigma_{jt}C_{\eta ij}.$$

Defining the diagonal matrix of time-t volatilities from the GARCH models, $\boldsymbol{D}_t = \text{Diag}[\sigma_{it},\ i = 1, n]$, gives the dynamic covariance matrix of returns:

$$\boldsymbol{C}_t = \boldsymbol{D}_t \boldsymbol{C}_\eta \boldsymbol{D}_t'. \tag{9.18}$$

To estimate the model we begin by estimating the set of n standard univariate GARCH models. Then, using the in-sample volatilities of the GARCH models, we construct the standardized outcomes, defined as the demeaned returns divided by the estimated volatilities:

$$\hat{\eta}_{it} = \frac{\tilde{r}_{it}}{\hat{\sigma}_{it}}.$$

We go on to estimate the sample correlation matrix of the standardized outcomes:

$$\hat{\boldsymbol{C}}_\eta = \text{corr}(\hat{\boldsymbol{\eta}}, \hat{\boldsymbol{\eta}}'),$$

where corr$(\cdot\,,\cdot)$ denotes the sample correlation matrix.

The dynamic conditional correlation (DCC) model described in Engle (2002) extends the CCOR model. It preserves the n univariate GARCH models for variances, but adds dynamics to the correlation matrix. The model assumes a simple linear GARCH framework for the quasi-covariance matrix of the innovations, $\boldsymbol{Q}_t$:

$$\boldsymbol{Q}_t = \boldsymbol{Q}_0 + \beta \boldsymbol{\eta}_{t-1} \boldsymbol{\eta}_{t-1}' + \gamma \boldsymbol{Q}_{t-1}, \tag{9.19}$$

where β and γ are nonnegative scalar coefficients and $\boldsymbol{Q}_0$ is a diagonal matrix of the unconditional variances from the univariate GARCH models (9.16). This is a quasi-covariance matrix not a true covariance matrix since the η have unit variance by definition. Engle uses the clever trick of reversing (9.18) to make a correlation matrix from the quasi-covariance matrix, by simply dividing the matrix by its diagonal entries. This gives the correlation matrix of innovations:

$$\boldsymbol{C}_{\eta t} = \text{Diag}[\boldsymbol{Q}_t]^{-1/2} \boldsymbol{Q}_t \, \text{Diag}[\boldsymbol{Q}_t]^{-1/2}. \tag{9.20}$$

The DCC model sacrifices the linearity of the standard GARCH model since (9.20) is a nonlinear transformation, but it provides a very parsimonious model of dynamic correlations. It is possible to extend (9.19) to higher order by adding more lagged terms and associated β, γ coefficients.

9.1.7 Dynamic Factor Volatilities

The CCOR and DCC models simplify the dynamic covariance matrix estimation problem by decomposing the covariance matrix into a correlation matrix and a vector of volatilities. An alternative way to simplify the problem is to decompose the covariance matrix using a factor model and then to build a dynamic model of the factor covariances. This is the essence of the Baba, Engle, Kraft, and Kroner (BEKK) model.

For simplicity we will treat the BEKK model in the case of one factor portfolio, which we assume equals the market portfolio. Note that the factor portfolio is a prespecified portfolio not a statistical factor portfolio estimated from the data. The random return of each asset is decomposed into a factor-related component and a nonfactor component:

$$\left.\begin{aligned} r_{it} &= c_i + \beta_i r_{\mathrm{m}t} + \varepsilon_{it}, \\ \beta_i &= \frac{\operatorname{cov}(r_i, r_{\mathrm{m}})}{\operatorname{var}(r_{\mathrm{m}})}. \end{aligned}\right\} \tag{9.21}$$

Note that the betas in (9.21) use unconditional variances and covariances. It is possible for nonfactor returns to be correlated across assets. However, it is assumed that the $n \times n$ covariance matrix of nonfactor returns is time constant,

$$\operatorname{cov}_{t-1}(\boldsymbol{\varepsilon}_t, \boldsymbol{\varepsilon}_t') = \boldsymbol{C}_{\varepsilon},$$

and that the observable market index return $r_{\mathrm{m}t}$ has dynamic volatility given by a univariate GARCH model. The dynamic covariance matrix of returns therefore has a simple structure combining the nonfactor covariance matrix with the GARCH-scaled factor covariance component:

$$\boldsymbol{C}_t = \sigma_t^2 \boldsymbol{\beta}\boldsymbol{\beta}' + \boldsymbol{C}_{\varepsilon}.$$

It is straightforward to generalize this from one market index to a collection of k observed factor portfolio indices; in that case it relies on a multivariate GARCH model of dimension k for the factor portfolios, with the nonfactor return covariances assumed constant.

9.2 Stochastic Volatility Models

The GARCH framework is elegant and concise but it relies on the direct observability of variance. A more intuitive approach is to treat variance as an unobservable state variable. This means that variance at time t is not fully determined by the preceding return history, so

$$\operatorname{var}[\sigma_t^2 \mid r_{t-1}, r_{t-2}, \dots] > 0. \tag{9.22}$$

Inequality (9.22) is the key property that distinguishes an SV model from a GARCH model. The simplest case is to impose a first-order autoregressive process for log variance:

$$\log(\sigma_t^2) = \alpha + \beta \log(\sigma_{t-1}^2) + \varepsilon_{t-1}, \tag{9.23}$$

where ε_{t-1} is the random innovation to variance.

A notable strength of SV models is their affinity with continuous-time pricing models. The models can be applied consistently to log returns at all frequencies, including continuous time. This makes SV models the preferred framework for high-frequency and/or continuous-time modeling of dynamic volatility.

A drawback of SV models is that they are difficult to estimate by maximum likelihood. For example, the process (9.23) provides no closed-form likelihood function for observed returns as a function of the model parameters. There is no obvious way to find a simple parallel to the likelihood function (9.4) that holds for the GARCH family of models. On the other hand, moving-average-based filters, although theoretically less efficient than maximum-likelihood estimates, provide a robust and reliable framework for estimation of SV models.

A commonly used moving-average-based estimator for SV models is realized variation. The *realized variation* of an asset over an interval t to $t+1$ is defined as the sum of its squared returns using a set of higher-frequency returns over the interval. If return variance is constant over the interval, then the realized variation is a good estimate of this constant variance. In high-frequency applications, demeaning returns before squaring is not necessary since the impact is negligible. (In fact demeaning returns before squaring can worsen the properties of the variance estimator for high-frequency returns because the true mean squared is approximately zero, whereas the sample mean squared is a nonnegligible source of estimation noise.)

To apply realized variation estimation to the case of nonconstant variance, it is necessary to subdivide the time-series sample using two return frequencies. Realized variation is estimated within each of a set of short intervals t to $t+\Delta$ divided into many (even shorter) return intervals Δ^*. So, for example, set the unit interval equal to a year and assume that there are 250 trading days in the year and that returns are observed for all of the 72 five-minute return intervals in each trading day. We treat $\Delta = \frac{1}{250}$ as "small" and $\Delta/\Delta^* = 72$ as "large," for the purposes of deriving approximations. Within each day, the realized variation using the five-minute returns provides an estimate of the integrated continuous-time variance during the day:

$$\hat{\sigma}^2_{t,t+\Delta} = \sum_{s=1}^{72} r^2_{t,t+s\Delta^*} \overset{*}{\approx} \int_t^{t+\Delta} \sigma_s^2 \, ds,$$

where the nature of the approximation and the conditions for convergence are quite technical.[8] This procedure generates a series of 250 daily

[8] See Taylor (2005, chapter 12) or Shephard (2005) and references therein.

variance estimates. If the true continuous-time variance process is sufficiently smooth, then σ_s^2 is approximately constant within each of the short intervals Δ. We can apply time-series analysis to the estimates $\hat{\sigma}^2_{t,t+\Delta}$ to learn about the true continuous-time variance process σ_s^2. See Shephard (2005) for a technical survey.

Two limitations of the realized-variation methodology are the infrequency of trades putting a lower bound on Δ^*, and market microstructure effects, which make high-frequency price changes differ in character from longer-run price changes. The realized variation approach works best in highly liquid markets with very frequent trades. Much of the empirical research on realized variation uses foreign exchange rate returns, where these asymptotic approximations are appropriate due to that market's high trading volume and low bid–ask spreads. Extending the analysis to account for market microstructure effects is a very active area of current theoretical and empirical research.

9.3 Time Aggregation

In many applications an analyst will use higher-frequency returns for empirical estimation than is the appropriate frequency for the firm's risk-management systems. So, for example, the analyst may estimate return variances and covariances with daily data and then perform monthly or annual portfolio risk analysis. This requires aggregation of the higher-frequency estimation results to risk measures at a lower frequency.

Let returns be measured over the unit period but let the analyst be concerned about risk measurement over a longer time frequency of m periods. Consider the covariance matrix of returns summed over m periods, assuming that expected returns are constant or zero:

$$\operatorname{cov}\left(\sum_{t=1}^{m} \boldsymbol{r}_t, \sum_{\tau=1}^{m} \boldsymbol{r}_\tau\right) = \sum_{t=1}^{m}\sum_{\tau=1}^{m} \operatorname{cov}(\boldsymbol{r}_t, \boldsymbol{r}_\tau). \tag{9.24}$$

There are three cases to consider. The first case is independently distributed returns through time, in which case $\operatorname{cov}(\boldsymbol{r}_t, \boldsymbol{r}_\tau) = \boldsymbol{0}$ for all $t \neq \tau$, and the covariance matrix of m-summed returns equals m times the covariance matrix of single-period returns. This gives rise to the *square-root-of-time rule*, which says that the volatility of a portfolio's return summed over m periods is $\sqrt{m}$ times its volatility over one period.

The second case is one in which return dynamics are governed by a time-series model such as a GARCH or SV model. In this case, the cross-covariance matrices in (9.24) can be inferred from the estimated dynamic model, by generalizing (9.6) to whatever dynamic model is used.

In the third case, the analyst allows for dependence between returns through time but does not invoke a specific model to capture this dependence, beyond requiring that the dependence is limited in its range. In this case a Newey–West estimator can be applied. The analyst assumes that the cross-covariances are nonzero up to a maximum lag length $m^* \leqslant m$ and the sample cross-covariance matrices $\text{cov}(\boldsymbol{r}_t, \boldsymbol{r}_{t+s})$ are estimated from the sample data for $s = -m^*, \dots, m^*$.

The analysis above ignores compounding effects and is therefore only truly valid in the case of log returns. Note also that it only deals with the time aggregation of covariance matrices. Time aggregation of tail-based risk measures such as VaR and ES is more complicated and there are no simple formulas. We will return to this briefly in the next chapter.

9.4 Downside Correlation

An important concern in portfolio risk analysis is determining whether correlations differ between up markets and down markets. This is called asymmetric dependence, or sometimes "downside correlation," since the chief concern is that correlations are higher, and therefore diversification is less effective, in down markets. Measuring asymmetric dependence is a delicate empirical problem. The appropriate definition is tricky since even under joint normality the correlation between two random variables conditioned on their realized magnitudes is not constant: see Longin and Solnik (2001) for a discussion.

Consider the standard definition of correlation between two returns:

$$\text{corr}_{ij} = \frac{\text{cov}(r_i, r_j)}{(\text{var}(r_i)\,\text{var}(r_j))^{1/2}}$$
$$= \frac{E[(r_i - E[r_i])(r_j - E[r_j])]}{(E[(r_i - E[r_i])^2]E[(r_j - E[r_j])^2])^{1/2}}. \tag{9.25}$$

Let E_0 denote the unconditional expectation and let E_S denote the expectation conditional of returns belonging to a set S: for example, $S = \{(r_i, r_j) \mid r_i > E[r_i],\ r_j < E[r_j]\}$. *Semicorrelation* is a modification of (9.25) that allows for conditioning on an event S. It uses conditional covariances and variances in (9.25) but taken with respect to unconditional means:

$$\text{semicorr}_{ij} = \frac{E_S[(r_i - E_0[r_i])(r_j - E_0[r_j])]}{(E_S[(r_i - E_0[r_i])^2]E_S[(r_j - E_0[r_j])^2])^{1/2}}.$$

Erb et al. (1994) examine the semicorrelation of monthly equity index returns of the G7 countries. They identify each equity return as "up" (positive demeaned return) or "down" (negative demeaned return). They then measure semicorrelation between the returns for each pair of markets using four subsets of the data: up–up, down–down, up–down, and down–up. It is a consequence of their sorting procedure that the semicorrelations for the sorted subsets S = up–down and S = down–up will be negative. They focus on the contrast between the semicorrelations in the up–up and down–down subsamples. If a pair of returns are time-invariant multivariate normal, then these up–up and down–down semicorrelations should be equal (this is easy to prove using the symmetry property of the normal distribution). In fact, Erb et al. find that for all pairs of countries, the semicorrelation measured over the down–down sorted subsample is substantially higher than (on average, almost double) the semicorrelation for the up–up subsample. Furthermore, they find that this difference in semicorrelation is related to business cycle phases: national equity markets tend to have higher semicorrelations when both national economies are in recessions and lower semicorrelations during in-phase expansions.

An extension of the semicorrelation model is the *exceedence correlation function*. Here the conditioning set S depends on a real parameter a. $S(a)$ is the set of return pairs such that r_i is greater than a *or* the set of return pairs for which r_i is less than a. By convention it is standard to use demeaned returns greater than a for a greater than zero and less than a for a less than zero; this gives

$$S(a) = \begin{cases} \{\tilde{r}_i \geqslant a\} & \text{if } a \geqslant 0, \\ \{\tilde{r}_i \leqslant a\} & \text{if } a \leqslant 0. \end{cases}$$

The function $S(a)$ has two different values at the jump point $a = 0$. In the definition of the exceedence correlation function, all expectations are conditioned on S:

$$\text{ecorr}_{ij}(a) = \frac{E_S[(r_i - E_S[r_i])(r_j - E_S[r_j])]}{(E_S[(r_i - E_S[r_i])^2]E_S[(r_j - E_S[r_j])^2])^{1/2}}.$$

To estimate $\text{ecorr}_{ij}(a)$ delete all observation pairs for which r_i is not in $S(a)$ and then compute the standard correlation coefficient on the truncated sample. Figure 9.2 shows the exceedence correlation function of the daily returns to the French and German equity indices, together with the theoretical exceedence correlation function for two joint normally distributed returns with the same unconditional mean, variance, and correlation as these two. Note that under joint normality, the true exceedence correlation function goes to zero for large-magnitude values of a, whereas this is not at all reflected in the sample data. If anything,

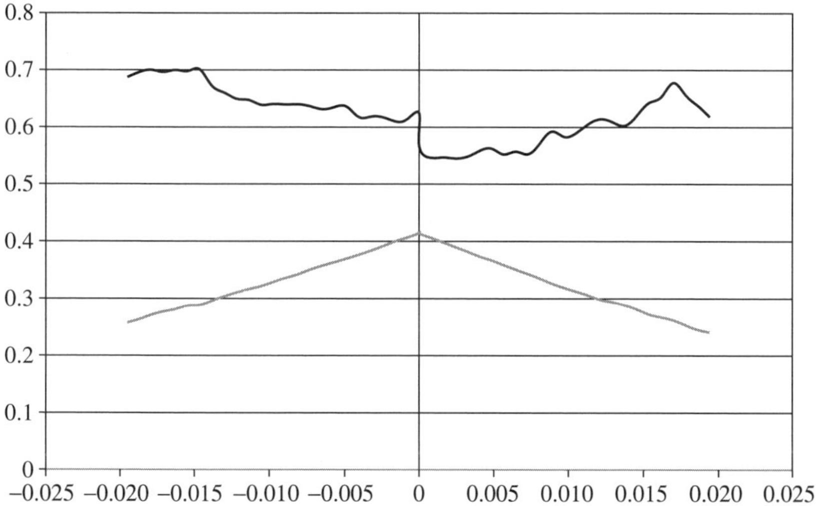

Figure 9.2. Empirical and theoretical exceedence correlations of daily returns to the French and German MSCI equity indices. The sample period is from January 2, 1995, to July 26, 2006. The black line shows the empirical exceedence correlations; the gray line shows the theoretical values given joint normality and using the sample volatilities and unconditional correlation between the two return series.

exceedence correlations tend to increase as a moves away from zero, particularly for negative a.

The exceedence correlation function can be applied to testing the notion that correlation, appropriately defined, is higher when realized return magnitudes are very large, particularly when the returns are negative in sign. Longin and Solnik (2001) model the asymptotic values $\text{ecorr}_{ij}(a)$ as $a \to \infty$ and $a \to -\infty$; see chapter 10 for a discussion of the asymptotic modeling of return tails. Longin and Solnick find empirical evidence for "fat-tailed" behavior when $a \to -\infty$ (the negative tail of returns) but not for $a \to \infty$. That is, when they fit a tail-index model to the exceedence correlation function, they reject $\text{ecorr}_{ij}(a) \to 0$ as $a \to -\infty$, indicating stronger tail dependency than if returns were bivariate normal.

Ang and Bekaert (1999) show that a dynamic regime-switching model provides an empirically credible alternative to the Longin–Solnick model of extreme-tail correlations. In the Ang and Bekeart model asset returns switch between a low-correlation/low-volatility regime and a high-correlation/high-volatility regime. When this regime-switching model is fitted to international equity indices it predicts exceedence correlation functions similar to those found in the Longin–Solnick empirical analysis.

Das and Uppal (2004) provide a different explanation for the empirical evidence: they argue that international equity market index prices can be modeled as following time-invariant continuous-time Brownian motions mixed with coordinated Poisson jumps, which give rise to simultaneous negative return shocks to all the index prices. Note that, like the Ang–Bekeart regime-switching model, this model explains the observed high exceedence correlations for large-magnitude negative values of the exceedence parameter a. In a related approach using a discrete-time setting, Lo (1999) suggests a phase-locking model, in which correlations between assets switch from moderate values to very high values when the market enters a crisis period.

9.5 Option-Implied Volatility

Options markets provide a fertile source of information on time variation in asset return volatilities and a valuable source of volatility forecasting data. The price of an option depends on the volatility of the underlying security or portfolio; an option pricing model can be inverted to infer the volatility of the underlying from the market prices of one or more options written on it. A volatility forecast obtained in this way is called *option-implied volatility*.

The concept of option-implied volatility can be illustrated using the Black–Scholes pricing model. If trading is continuous through time, there is a constant riskless return, and the underlying asset price follows a Brownian motion with constant mean and variance, then the nonarbitrage values of a European call and a European put with strike price K and maturity T on the underlying asset with price p are

$$\left.\begin{aligned} p_{\text{Call}} &= p\Phi(d_1) - K\mathrm{e}^{-r_0 T}\Phi(d_2), \\ p_{\text{Put}} &= K\mathrm{e}^{-r_0 T}\Phi(-d_2) - p\Phi(-d_1), \end{aligned}\right\} \tag{9.26}$$

where Φ is the standard Gaussian cumulative distribution function. The dependence of the option prices on stock volatility is encapsulated in expressions for d_1 and d_2:

$$d_1 = \frac{\log(p/K) + (r_0 + (\sigma^2/2))T}{\sigma\sqrt{T}}, \qquad d_2 = d_1 - \sigma\sqrt{T},$$

which also depend on the riskless rate r_0, the time to maturity T, and the exercise price K. It is not apparent at first glance, but the call and put formulas (9.26) can be inverted to express σ in terms of the option price and the other variables to give option-implied volatility.

Note that under the assumptions of the Black–Scholes model all options on a given asset will have the same option-implied volatility.

Empirically, the implied volatility from the Black–Scholes model differs substantially for different values of *moneyness*, K/p, and maturity, T. Thus, data from options markets are inconsistent with the hypothesis that volatility is constant, so the assumptions underlying the Black–Scholes model do not hold. It is possible to generate option-implied volatility forecasts using models adjusted for time-varying volatility, as discussed by Derman and Kani (1994), Dupire (1994), and Fouque et al. (2000).

9.5.1 Volatility Indices and Variance Swaps

In 1993, the Chicago Board of Options Exchange introduced the volatility index (VIX), which provides an important new source of market-based volatility forecasts for use in portfolio risk analysis. From 1993 until 2003, the VIX level was set each day to the average of the Black–Scholes implied volatility for eight near-the-money S&P 100 options. This calculation requires the prices of two calls and two puts at each of the two nearest maturities. The options are chosen so that their strike prices straddle the spot price and are as close to it as possible.

In 2003, the index methodology was revised and a new VIX was released in March 2004. At that time, the old VIX was renamed VXO. The VIX and the VXO differ in two important ways. First, the underlying index was changed from S&P 100 to S&P 500. Second, the new index level is set to the price of a portfolio of traded options as opposed to an average of option-implied volatilities. Thus, the index is independent of any model and in particular the Black–Scholes option pricing formula is not used. The new VIX is given by

$$\mathrm{VIX}^2 = \frac{2 \times 10^4}{T} \sum_{i=1}^{n} \frac{\Delta K_i}{K_i^2} Q(K_i) \mathrm{e}^{r_0 T} - \frac{1}{T}\left(\frac{F}{K_0} - 1\right)^2,$$

where T is the maturity,[9] F is the forward price of the index,[10] K_i is the strike price of the ith option,[11] ΔK_i is the interval between the strike prices on either side of K_i,[12] $Q(K_i)$ is the midpoint of the bid–ask spread for the ith option, K_0 is the highest strike price below F, and r_0 is the riskless interest rate. The new VIX represents market volatility in terms of a portfolio of traded securities and it facilitates a static volatility hedge, whereas a dynamic portfolio is required to hedge the VXO.

[9] The maturity is set at approximately thirty days.

[10] The implied forward price is derived from traded options prices.

[11] A put is used if $K_i > F$ and a call is used if $K_i < F$.

[12] The interval ΔK_i is set to $0.5(K_{i+1} - K_{i-1})$ for middle strikes and is set to $K_i - K_{i-1}$ and $K_{i+1} - K_i$ for the highest and lowest strikes.

The sensitivity of an asset or portfolio price to variance is known as its *variance gamma.* The new VIX methodology relies on the existence of an appropriately weighted portfolio of options and forward contracts whose variance gamma does not depend on the value of the portfolio. The VIX is used to set the strike price for variance swaps, which are derivative instruments used to hedge market volatility or to take a position on it.

Carr and Wu (2006) analyze the statistical properties of the two VIX indices and the consequences of the VIX methodology change. They find that two indices are very similar, although the VIX is slightly higher on average than the VXO.[13] There are significant discontinuities that translate into very high kurtosis, so that returns to the VIX index are highly nonnormal.

Variation in volatility is increasingly understood to be a significant source of portfolio risk. The VIX series can be used to represent this risk. It has a large impact on volatility and VaR forecasts, especially for portfolios with nontrivial concentrations in derivative securities. Blair et al. (2001) construct a VIX for the S&P 100 index based on traded options prices and compare its forecasting performance with that of a GARCH model. They find that the VIX forecast substantially outperforms the GARCH model.

In order to use VIX-based volatility forecasts it is necessary to remove the risk premium from the VIX. The risk premium associated with a stochastic volatility model is analyzed in Carr and Wu (2006) based on the observation that the square of the VIX is an estimator for expected variance:

$$\mathrm{VIX}_t^2 = E^*[R_{t,t+30}],$$

where $R_{t,t+30}$ is the realized variance of the S&P 500 over the thirty days subsequent to t and the expectation operator E^* is expectation with respect to the risk-neutral density.[14] As a consequence, they show that the variance risk premium λ_{V} can be estimated by

$$\lambda_{\mathrm{V}} = E[R_{t,t+30} - \mathrm{VIX}_t^2],$$

where the expectation is taken with respect to the true, not risk-neutral, density. Over the sample period beginning January 2, 1990, and ending October 18, 2005, the authors estimate a negative risk premium that has high statistical significance. Investors demand higher expected security

[13] The theoretical basis of this is Jensen's inequality, which comes into play since the VIX is the square root of a variance estimate while the VXO is a direct estimate of volatility.

[14] See chapter 1 for a brief discussion of the risk-neutral density, or Duffie (2001) for a more thorough and technical treatment.

returns in compensation for bearing return risk, and also demand lower expected variance in return for bearing variance risk. Thus, investors are averse not only to variance but also to increases in the time-series variance of return variance.

9.6 The Volatility Term Structure at Long Horizons

So far this chapter has focused on risk-management applications with fairly short horizons. This is appropriate since time-series variation in asset return variances and covariances is most evident at higher frequencies. Many investors can safely ignore these short-term patterns if their investment horizon is sufficiently long. For them, it is long-horizon patterns in portfolio risk that matter. For long-horizon investors, time variation in expected returns matters crucially to risk, so it is not possible to ignore expected returns in forecasting risk.

Campbell and Viceira (2002, 2004, 2005) explore the risk–return tradeoff and the term structure of volatility for long-horizon investors. Campbell and Viceira (2005) develop a vector autoregression model with six variates: the log of real returns on three-month Treasury bills and five-year maturity Treasury bonds, the value-weighted equity market index, the dividend yield on the equity index, and the nominal Treasury bill return. Note that the system indirectly includes quarterly inflation since log inflation equals the difference between the nominal and real Treasury bill rates (in units of log return). Let $\boldsymbol{y}_t$ denote the 6-vector of these variates. The first-order VAR system has the form

$$\boldsymbol{y}_t = \boldsymbol{\phi}_0 + \boldsymbol{\Phi}\boldsymbol{y}_{t-1} + \boldsymbol{\varepsilon}_t, \tag{9.27}$$

where $\boldsymbol{\phi}_0$ is a 6-vector of constant terms and $\boldsymbol{\Phi}$ is a 6×6 matrix of autoregressive coefficients. Campbell and Viceira assume that $\boldsymbol{\varepsilon}_t$, the 6-vector of innovations, is i.i.d. normal over time with covariance matrix $\boldsymbol{C}_\varepsilon$. Applying straightforward linear algebra to (9.27) it is not difficult to derive the unconditional mean vector and covariance matrix of $\sum_{s=1}^{k} \boldsymbol{y}_{t+s}$:

$$E\left[\sum_{s=1}^{k} \boldsymbol{y}_{t+s}\right] = \left[\sum_{s=0}^{k-1}(k-s)\boldsymbol{\Phi}^s\right]\boldsymbol{\phi}_0 + \left[\sum_{s=1}^{k}\boldsymbol{\Phi}^s\right]\boldsymbol{y}_t, \tag{9.28}$$

$$\begin{aligned} \operatorname{var}\left[\sum_{s=1}^{k} \boldsymbol{y}_{t+s}\right] &= \boldsymbol{C}_\varepsilon + (\boldsymbol{I}+\boldsymbol{\Phi})\boldsymbol{C}_\varepsilon(\boldsymbol{I}+\boldsymbol{\Phi})' + \cdots \\ &\quad + (\boldsymbol{I}+\boldsymbol{\Phi}+\boldsymbol{\Phi}^2+\cdots+\boldsymbol{\Phi}^{k-1})\boldsymbol{C}_\varepsilon(\boldsymbol{I}+\boldsymbol{\Phi}+\boldsymbol{\Phi}^2+\cdots+\boldsymbol{\Phi}^{k-1})'. \end{aligned} \tag{9.29}$$

We refer the reader to Campbell and Viceira (2004) for a clear and careful derivation of (9.28) and (9.29) from (9.27). These expressions (9.28) and

(9.29) are easily computed once the elements of the vector autoregression system (9.27) have been estimated by least-squares regression. Note that $\sum_{s=1}^{k} y_{t+s}$ includes among its components the k-period cumulative real log returns to the three assets. The mean vector and the covariance matrix also include cumulative sums of the dividend yield and nominal Treasury bill yields, but these two components can easily be deleted from the expressions.

The Campbell and Viceira model provides useful insights about long-horizon risk and its dependence upon conditional mean returns. First consider the diagonal (variance) components of (9.29) as functions of k. In their estimates the per-period stock market variance increases slightly from $k = 1$ to $k = 2$ (due to short-term momentum) and then shows a long steep decline over the range $k = 2$ to $k = 100$ (due to mean reversion). This provides a simple and robust demonstration of the well-documented empirical phenomenon of decreasing per-period risk from longer-horizon equity investment. Five-year Treasury bonds, rolled over each quarter so that they retain a five-year maturity, also show some mean reversion, but it is less substantial than for the equity index. Quarterly Treasury bills exhibit the opposite pattern. Their one-period real return is nearly riskless: the only risk is one-quarter-ahead inflation uncertainty. But the risk of holding quarterly Treasury bills increases steadily over time due to the risk of changing real yields as the short-term bills are rolled over; this reinvestment risk creates considerable long-horizon volatility.

The off-diagonal (covariance) terms of (9.29) also vary substantially with k. Campbell and Viceira compute mean–variance optimal combinations of the three assets and examine these optimal weights as functions of k. The simplest case is the global minimum-variance portfolio since this is unaffected by mean returns or risk preferences. For $k = 1$ the global minimum-variance portfolio consists 100% of the quarterly Treasury bill, but for $k = 100$ the proportion in Treasury bills has shrunk to 68%, with 20% in the five-year Treasury bond and 12% in the stock index. Allowing a mean–variance trade-off, moving away from strict variance minimization, gives even higher weights to stocks and long-term bonds for long-term investors. Note that for tractability this analysis relies on optimal linear combinations of log returns, which are not strictly equal to the log returns of optimally weighted portfolios.

9.7 Time-Varying Cross-Sectional Dispersion

In addition to the time-series volatility of assets and portfolios it is interesting to examine the cross-sectional dispersion of returns at a given point in time, and the patterns and trends in this dispersion. Let there be n assets with time-t excess returns vector $\boldsymbol{x}_t$, and define dispersion as the cross-sectional mean-square (or "cross-sectional variance") of these returns:

$$\mathrm{disp}_t = \frac{1}{n}\sum_{i=1}^{n}(x_{it} - \bar{x}_t)^2,$$

where

$$\bar{x}_t = \frac{1}{n}\sum_{i=1}^{n} x_{it}.$$

Suppose for simplicity that excess returns follow a strict factor model with one factor,

$$\boldsymbol{x}_t = \boldsymbol{b} f_t + \boldsymbol{\varepsilon}_t,$$

then ignoring cross-terms, which are small for large n, dispersion can be written

$$\mathrm{disp}_t = \frac{1}{n}\sum_{i=1}^{n}(b_i - \bar{b})^2 f_t^2 + \frac{1}{n}\sum_{i=1}^{n}\varepsilon_{it}^2,$$

so that it is the squared factor return at time t scaled by the cross-sectional dispersion of factor betas plus the average squared asset-specific return. It is straightforward to generalize this expression to multiple factors; the expression becomes slightly more cumbersome.

Jones (2001) shows that the asset-specific component of dispersion has substantial time-series variation. This result is at first surprising since, given that the asset-specific returns are cross-sectionally independent or only weakly dependent, the law of large numbers implies that the cross-sectional average squared asset-specific return should converge for large n to the average cross-sectional asset-specific variance. The average cross-sectional variance measures the amount of asset-specific "news" at time t. A naive view would be that this should stay constant over time, but empirically it is now clear that it varies substantially through time. Connor et al. (2006) build a factor model with dynamic variation in average asset-specific variance and show empirically that it has both short-term dynamic patterns related to the business cycle and longer-term secular trends.

Campbell et al. (2001) show a strong upward trend in dispersion across U.S. equity returns during the 1950–95 period. They decompose excess returns into market-related, industry-related, and asset-specific components:

$$x_{it} = x_{\mathrm{m}t} + x_{jt}^{\mathrm{I}} + \varepsilon_{it},$$

where $x_{\mathrm{m}t}$ is the excess return on the market portfolio and x_{jt}^{I} is the excess return on industry portfolio j; each asset $i = 1, n$ is assigned to an industry $j = 1, k$. Using daily returns within each month, Campbell et al. use a realized variance estimate to get capitalization-weighted market and industry portfolio variances. They then show that capitalization-weighted average variance across assets can be decomposed into market-, industry-, and asset-specific components, plus cross-terms giving the covariances between these components. Campbell et al. show that under fairly weak restrictions the cross-terms equal zero. Their most notable empirical finding is a strong upward trend in average asset-specific variance over the 1962–97 time period. Campbell et al. offer various possible explanations for the increase. They put particular weight on the possibility that more risky firms enter the sample of publicly traded securities over time, reflecting the deepening of the traded U.S. equity market over this sample period.

The upward trend in asset-specific variance has implications for the popular "twenty-stock rule" for portfolio diversification first proposed by Solnik (1991): the claim that a randomly selected portfolio of twenty stocks has almost complete diversification of asset-specific risk. Campbell et al. show that the same level of diversification achievable by a twenty-stock portfolio in the 1960s required fifty stocks during the 1990s, due to the large secular increase in asset-specific variance.

10
Portfolio Return Distributions

In previous chapters we have usually taken a narrow view of risk as the variance of return. In this chapter we take a broader view and consider the full distribution of portfolio return. All familiar risk measures, including variance, value-at-risk (VaR), and expected shortfall, can be derived from the return distribution. Although the approach to analyzing risk taken in this chapter is much broader, we will see that there are considerable costs in terms of the statistical reliability of the derived risk measures.

In section 10.1 we describe the main measures of a return distribution, including the cumulative distribution, the probability density, and return moments. In section 10.2 we discuss estimation procedures aimed at measuring the entire return distribution, and in section 10.3 we discuss the estimation procedures designed to measure only the tails of the return distribution (that is, large losses or gains).

In sections 10.1–10.3 we focus on the univariate case (the return distribution of a single asset or portfolio). In section 10.4 we discuss multivariable dependence structures that are generalizations of covariance, in order to facilitate multiple-asset analysis of distributions.

10.1 Characterizing Return Distributions

Throughout this section we consider a univariate return r, which we think of as the random return on some prespecified portfolio such as a stock or bond index.

10.1.1 The Poor Fit of the Normal Distribution for Return Tails

Recall from chapter 1 that if portfolio return is normally distributed, then its distribution is completely characterized by mean and variance. As a risk measure, portfolio variance has the attractive property that it can be expressed as a quadratic product of the portfolio weight vector

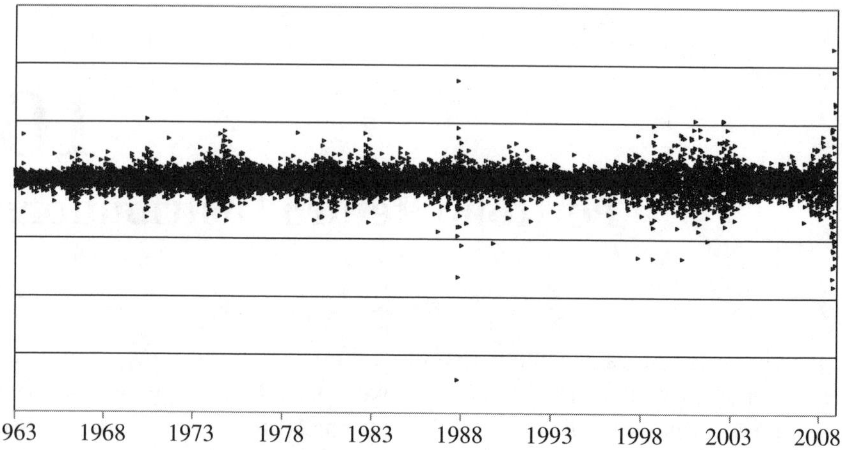

Figure 10.1. A time-series plot of daily returns of the Center for Research in Security Prices value-weighted U.S. equity market index from July 1, 1963, to November 28, 2008.

and the covariance matrix of asset returns. If we can tolerate the normal distribution as a reasonable approximation to the portfolio return distribution, we benefit in terms of analytical simplicity and tractability.

Figure 10.1 shows a history of daily returns to the value-weighted U.S. equity market index from July 1, 1963, to November 28, 2008. A notable feature is the 17% loss on October 19, 1987, which is known as Black Monday. The sample standard deviation is 0.95%. If we use sample mean and variance to fit a normal distribution, an event of this magnitude is absurdly unlikely—the probability of a daily loss greater than or equal to 17% being approximately 10^{-87}. This is not consonant with the 12% drop in the market on Black Tuesday, October 29, 1929, which preceded Black Monday by only about 20,000 days. According to the best-fit normal distribution using the sample mean and variance, the probability of a return of this magnitude or larger is less than 10^{-30}. Even after accounting for the fact that we have chosen the two lowest returns in this long sample period, two losses of this magnitude are absurdly unlikely for such a relatively short history if returns are normally distributed. This example illustrates a key empirical fact: the normal distribution does not adequately account for the relative magnitude of the largest events in many asset return samples.

10.1.2 Return Distribution, Density, and Moments

Recall from chapter 1 that the *cumulative distribution* of the return is the function $\text{cum}(a)$ defined over the interval $(-\infty, \infty)$, giving for each

a the probability that the return is less than or equal to a:

$$\text{cum}(a) = \Pr(r \leqslant a).$$

Since probabilities must be nonnegative and cannot exceed one, the distribution function must have the properties $\lim_{a\to-\infty} \text{cum}(a) = 0$, $\lim_{a\to\infty} \text{cum}(a) = 1$, and $\text{cum}(a + c) \geqslant \text{cum}(a)$ for any $c > 0$. If the return is arithmetic and the asset has limited liability, then $\text{cum}(a)$ can be restricted to the range $(-1, \infty)$. If $\text{cum}(a)$ is differentiable in the neighborhood of a point a, then $\text{den}(a) = \partial\,\text{cum}(a)/\partial a$ is called the probability density.

The jth moment of the random return r is the expected value of the return raised to the jth power, $E[(r)^j]$. Often it is more convenient to work with the central moments (subtracting the mean) or standardized moments (subtracting the mean and then dividing by the standard deviation). The third and fourth standardized moments are called skewness and kurtosis, respectively. The normal distribution has values of 0 and 3.0 for these two moments. Since the normal distribution serves as a useful benchmark, it is often convenient to subtract 3.0 from kurtosis to create *excess kurtosis*; positive/negative excess kurtosis corresponds to more/less kurtosis than a normally distributed return.

10.1.3 The Central Limit Theorem

The pervasiveness of the normal distribution can be explained by the central limit theorem: under very general conditions, the scaled average of independently distributed random variables becomes approximately normal as the number of terms in the average grows large. As a consequence, the normal distribution appears naturally in many contexts.

Consider a sequence r_t, $t = 1, \dots, T$, of independent observations of a random return r that has mean μ and standard deviation σ. The average return

$$\frac{1}{T}\sum_{t=1}^{n} r_t \tag{10.1}$$

converges to the true mean μ for large T by an application of the law of large numbers, with standard deviation $\sigma/\sqrt{T}$ approaching zero:

$$\frac{1}{T}\sum_{t=1}^{n} r_t \overset{\text{pr},T}{\approx} \mu.$$

If we "scale up" the average so as to hold its standard deviation constant, then the scaled average is approximately normal for large T by the central limit theorem:

$$\sqrt{T}\left(\frac{1}{T}\sum_{t=1}^{n} r_t - \mu\right) \overset{\mathrm{di},T}{\approx} N(0,\sigma^2). \tag{10.2}$$

Thus the normal distribution appears as an approximation whenever a random variable can be expressed as an average of a large collection of independent, finite variance random variables.

The rate of convergence to normality in (10.2) depends upon the circumstances, but in many applications, thirty observations is adequate to give approximate normality. If, for example, the underlying random variable has very high kurtosis, the convergence will be relatively slow.

The central limit theorem can be generalized in several important ways. It is not necessary that all the returns in (10.1) have the same distribution, nor that they are fully independent (as long as there are limits to the amount of dependence between them). It is not necessary that an equally weighted average of the underlying returns is taken. However, the individual weights do need to be at the same scale so that no small set of returns dominates the average.

If random variable z has a normal distribution, then its standardized moments are given by

$$E[(z)^k] = \begin{cases} \dfrac{k!}{2^{k/2}(k/2)!} & k \text{ even}, \\ 0 & k \text{ odd}. \end{cases} \tag{10.3}$$

Suppose that we can invoke the central limit theorem for a time-series average return where the underlying returns are not normal but have finite moments using a sample of T observations. The central limit theorem then guarantees that for large T the kth moment of the time-series average is well-approximated by the corresponding moments of the normal distribution in (10.3).

The normal approximation (10.2) is useful in a variety of contexts in portfolio risk analysis. One important application is in time aggregation. Suppose that one-period log returns are not normal but are i.i.d. (or, more generally, alpha-mixing) over time. Then, for a long enough aggregation interval, lower-frequency log returns will be approximately normal. Even if we cannot accept the normal approximation, we often find that the "degree" of nonnormality, captured for instance by the amount of skewness or excess kurtosis, declines for lower-frequency returns.

Daníelsson and Zigrand (2006) note that this time-aggregation effect has important, often underappreciated, implications for VaR calculations. Analysts and regulators often apply the square-root-of-time rule to calculate VaR over multiperiod horizons based on estimation obtained from high-frequency data. So, for example, if the 95% VaR for a daily horizon is 0.1, then the square-root-of-time rule says that the five-day 95% VaR is $0.1\sqrt{5} = 0.223$. This VaR application of the square-root-of-time rule is based implicitly on lognormal i.i.d. returns. However, if returns at high frequency have strong positive excess kurtosis, then this simple aggregation rule can vastly overstate five-day VaR since the multiperiod returns will typically have substantially less excess kurtosis.

Another important application of the central limit theorem is to portfolio asset-specific risk. Consider a well-spread portfolio $\boldsymbol{w}$ consisting of n assets, with $\boldsymbol{w}'\mathbf{1}^n = 1$ and $\boldsymbol{w}'\boldsymbol{w} \approx 0$. Although there is usually strong commonality in total asset returns, it is reasonable to treat asset-specific returns as uncorrelated, or weakly correlated and alpha-mixing. Therefore, the asset-specific return of a portfolio will be approximately normal, as $n \to \infty$ and $\boldsymbol{w}'\boldsymbol{w} \to 0$. The skewness and excess kurtosis in total portfolio returns is likely to be less of a problem for asset-specific returns, if the analyzed portfolios are reasonably well-diversified.

10.1.4 Quantiles and Value-at-Risk

The distribution function $\text{cum}(a)$ gives a value α between zero and one for the probability that return will be less than or equal to a. The quantile function, $Q(\alpha)$, is the left inverse of the distribution function, cum. If cum is continuous and strictly increasing, then $Q(\alpha) = a$ if and only if $\text{cum}(a) = \alpha$. For many useful return distributions, the higher moments and even the standard deviation may not be defined. However, it is always possible to describe a distribution in terms of its quantiles. Whether the distribution function or the quantile function is a more convenient characterization depends on the particular circumstances of the problem.

It is sometimes convenient to work on portfolio losses, which are negative returns: $\text{loss}_w = -r_w$. We can now correspondingly redefine the distribution function and the quantile function in terms of losses; in particular, $\text{cum}_{\text{loss}}(a) = \text{cum}(-a)$ and $Q_{\text{loss}}(\alpha) = \text{cum}_{\text{loss}}^{-1}(\alpha)$. An immediate benefit is a concise, straightforward expression for VaR. For confidence level $1 - \alpha$, VaR is the $(1 - \alpha)$th quantile of the loss distribution:

$$\text{VaR}(1 - \alpha) = Q_{\text{loss}}(1 - \alpha).$$

In practice, α is generally set to 5% or 1%, giving confidence levels of 95% and 99%, respectively. Investors concerned about extreme events sometimes quote VaR for higher confidence levels. However, as we discuss later, quantile estimates for α too close to zero have unacceptably low statistical accuracy.

10.1.5 Order Statistics

In risk analysis there is often a special focus on the worst outcome in a finite sample. Of course, the distribution of the *ex post* observed lowest return differs markedly from the unconditional return of a randomly selected observation. To facilitate the analysis of worst outcomes, we order a finite sample from lowest to highest and examine the distributions of the ordered returns. The ordered observations are called order statistics; the first order statistic is $\min\{r_1, \dots, r_T\}$ and the Tth order statistic is $\max\{r_1, \dots, r_T\}$. Given that the sample is i.i.d., the first order statistic, $r_{(1)}$, has a cumulative distribution with a simple relationship with that of the underlying returns:

$$\Pr(r_{(1)} \leqslant a) = 1 - [1 - \Pr(r \leqslant a)]^T.$$

Order statistics give a more appropriate statistical measure of the normality-based probability of the largest-magnitude loss in the daily S&P returns data discussed earlier. Using order statistics adjusts for the fact that we have chosen the largest loss *ex post*, based on its ranking in the observed sample of a given length. Recall that under normality a return this low has a cumulative probability of approximately 10^{-87}. Recalculating the cumulative probability, the probability of observing one return of -20% or lower in a 100-year sample of daily returns (260 daily returns per year) is $1 - [1 - 10^{-87}]^{26{,}000} < 10^{-30}$. So even with this sensible adjustment, the October 19, 1987, crash is wildly inconsistent with a normal distribution of daily returns.

10.2 Estimating Return Distributions

10.2.1 Estimating Return Moments

The simplest extension of variance-based risk analysis is to include estimates of skewness as a measure of distributional asymmetry, and kurtosis as a measure of the relative weight of the distribution tails. These can be estimated simply from the sample moments of the distribution.

Since estimated skewness and kurtosis depend on the third and fourth powers of returns, they are heavily influenced by any large-magnitude returns in a given sample period. The relative influence of the extreme observations in a sample is larger for variance estimation than for mean estimation, even larger for skewness estimation, and even larger again for kurtosis estimation. Bai and Ng (2005) show that this can be very important for finite-sample estimates of skewness and kurtosis. If the underlying distribution of portfolio return has a lot of weight in its tails—in other words, if it forecasts extreme events such as Black Monday and Black Tuesday with a high enough frequency—then estimated kurtosis based on finite data is unstable. A single observation can cause a big change in estimated kurtosis.

Bai and Ng find that the sample estimates of skewness and kurtosis are quite reliable if the underlying sample data are normally distributed. Related to this, they find that it is possible to test reliably for nonnormality using sample skewness and kurtosis estimates. However, if we accept that excess kurtosis is substantially positive, then accurately estimating its exact positive value with a finite sample becomes difficult. Also, we may choose a distribution model for return for which kurtosis does not have a finite value. Although sample kurtosis is always finite, we may choose to model the return distribution in a way that renders this sample estimate virtually meaningless.

The Bai and Ng findings for estimated skewness are less discouraging, although again there is a degree of instability associated with the large relative influence of one or a few observations in finite samples.

10.2.2 Estimation of a Parameterized Distribution

A parameterized distribution, such as the normal, exponential, Student's t, or Pareto distribution, belongs to a specific family indexed by a finite set of parameters, $\Theta = (\theta_1, \theta_2, \dots, \theta_q)$. For example, if we assume that r follows a normal distribution, then the vector of parameters consists of the mean and variance, $\Theta = (\mu, \sigma^2)$.

Two useful parameterized distributions for fitting return distributions are the Student's t-distribution and the binomial–normal mixture. The Student's t-distribution has a single parameter that is commonly known as the number of degrees of freedom. The term "degrees of freedom" comes from the original motivation for the Student's t-distribution: as a finite-sample test statistic based on a given (integer) number of observations. However, in applications to distribution fitting, the degrees of freedom parameter is allowed to take any real value, not just integer values. The parameter controls the amount of excess kurtosis in the distribution, with a lower value of the parameter corresponding to more kurtosis. As the parameter goes to infinity, the Student's t-distribution approaches the normal distribution, with excess kurtosis going to zero from above. The Student's t-distribution is symmetric for all values of the parameter, so it cannot be used to model return skewness. Since the Student's t-distribution has only one parameter it is standard to include additional parameters to fit the mean and variance. Letting z denote a

t-distributed random variable with degrees of freedom θ, this gives a three-parameter estimation problem:

$$r = \mu + \gamma z. \tag{10.4}$$

The mean, variance, skewness, and excess kurtosis of a t-distributed random variable with degrees of freedom parameter θ are 0, $\theta/(\theta - 2)$, 0, and $6/(\theta - 4)$. Using the sample mean, variance, and excess kurtosis, μ_s, σ_s^2, and κ_s, we can estimate the Student's t-distribution by applying the method of moments, giving $\hat{\mu} = \mu_s$, $\hat{\theta} = (6 + 4\kappa_s)/\kappa_s$, and $\hat{\gamma} = (\sigma_s(\theta - 2)/\theta)^{1/2}$. Alternatively, maximum-likelihood estimation can be applied, which involves numerically maximizing the likelihood function of the Student's t-distribution. It is also possible to extend the Student's t-distribution to include nonzero skewness (see Azzalini and Capitanio 2002).

Once the parameters have been estimated, VaR and expected shortfall (ES) can be computed from the cumulative Student's t-distribution. As a general rule, the Student's t-distribution is a superior choice to the normal distribution for parametric estimation of VaR and ES since it accounts for the excess kurtosis present in most portfolio returns.

A parametric model that can capture both skewness and excess kurtosis is the mixed binomial–normal distribution. In this model, random return is a convex combination of two normals with different means and variances, with a binomial variable selecting between them:

$$r = z_1\delta + z_2(1 - \delta), \tag{10.5}$$

where z_1, z_2 are univariate normals with means and variances μ_1, μ_2, σ_1^2, σ_2^2, and δ is an independent binomial equal to 1 (respectively 0) with probability α (respectively $1 - \alpha$). Using the method of moments, the five parameters can be fitted to the sample mean, the variance, the skewness, the kurtosis, and the sample fifth or sixth moment.[1] Alternatively, maximum-likelihood estimation can be applied (see Agha and Branker 1997).

Recall from chapter 9 that some of the nonnormality of returns can also be attributed to volatility dynamics. Note, for example, that if we replace the binomial variable δ in (10.5) with a zero/one Markov random process, we get a volatility regime-switching model similar to the Ang and Bekaert (1999) model discussed in chapter 9.

[1] If we set $\mu_1 = \mu_2$ so that we are imposing zero skewness, then the fifth moment is exactly zero for all parameter choices and we must use the sample sixth moment to fit the model.

10.2.3 Nonparametric Estimation of Return Densities

Nonparametric or *empirical* distributions are commonly used to describe portfolio risk. Essentially, these methodologies use the sample distribution as a measure of the true probability distribution.

The simplest nonparametric estimator is the histogram. A histogram gives the proportion of sample observations falling in each of a complete, nonoverlapping collection of intervals in $(-\infty, \infty)$. We divide the real line into a finite middle region (m_1, m_2) and two tail regions $(-\infty, m_1)$ and (m_2, ∞). Suppose that we have $k = (m_2 - m_1)/h$ intervals in the middle region, each of equal length h. Letting the sample size grow large and simultaneously shrinking the interval size h, it can be shown that the histogram approaches the true density function over the middle region (m_1, m_2) (see Li and Racine 2006). The length of the interval h is called the window size or bandwidth; note that the number of observations in each interval shrinks as the bandwidth shrinks. The choice of bandwidth is governed by the trade-off between a finer grid giving a more detailed picture of the distribution and a coarser grid giving a more accurate estimate within each interval.

The histogram estimates the return density at each point using the percentage of returns that fall in a fixed interval around the point. It is more statistically efficient to use a different weighted percentage for each value a, with weights declining with distance from a. This gives rise to a generalized version of the histogram called a kernel-based density estimate. Let $k(y)$ denote a nonnegative weighting function with weights declining as the magnitude of y increases, and such that the weights sum to one, $\int_{-\infty}^{\infty} k(y)\,\mathrm{d}y = 1$. For example, $k(y) = (1/\sqrt{2\pi})\exp(-y^2)$ is a popular kernel choice; it uses the normal density function as a weighting scheme and is essentially a two-sided exponential smoothing. Applying this weighting scheme to the distance between a sample point r_t and a using bandwidth h gives

$$k\left(\frac{r_t - a}{h}\right) = \frac{1}{\sqrt{2\pi}} \exp\left(-\left(\frac{r_t - a}{h}\right)^2\right).$$

For any a the nonparametric density estimate is the weighted percentage of returns near the value a:

$$\hat{f}(a) = \frac{1}{Th} \sum_{t=1}^{T} k\left(\frac{r_t - a}{h}\right).$$

Under fairly general conditions this gives consistent estimates of $f(a)$ as $T \to \infty$ and $h \to 0$, but only for a bounded inside the middle range (m_1, m_2). This is not an appropriate estimation methodology for the tail areas of the density, since the number of sample points in the tails is typically very small and the method relies on a large number of observations within the neighborhood of a. See Li and Racine (2006) for an introductory survey of these estimators, including alternative weighting schemes $k(\cdot)$, methods for choosing the bandwidth h, and related topics.

10.2.4 Historical Simulation

The return distribution estimates in section 10.2.3 rely on a time-series sample of returns. Suppose that we wish to estimate the return distribution of a newly implemented or untried portfolio strategy with a very short or nonexistent historical record. Suppose also that we have a reasonably long historical record for the asset returns used in the portfolio strategy. *Historical simulation* is the creation of a hypothetical portfolio return by applying a feasible investment rule to a historical record of asset returns. By applying the portfolio strategy retrospectively, we can replicate historically what the return distribution of the portfolio strategy would have been if we had implemented it over the observed sample period.

If the portfolio contains derivatives, we can historically simulate the portfolio's returns even if we do not have historical prices for the derivatives. To do this we infer the prices and payoffs on the derivatives by applying an option pricing model to the history of primary asset prices.

Historical simulation-based forecasts of portfolio risk and return are prone to data-snooping bias. A *data-snooping bias* in the historical measured return to a strategy is the upward bias in performance due to the selection by the analyst (from among many possible strategies that could be tested) of a strategy that has performed well historically, based on the analyst having the some prior knowledge about the data (see Sullivan et al. 1999). A portfolio manager will rarely suggest a strategy that, when applied retrospectively, has higher than predicted risk or lower than predicted average return. On the other hand, the analyst will often suggest a strategy that performed unexpectedly well on the historical data. This data-snooping bias can exert a strong upward (downward) bias on the mean return (risk) forecast from historical simulation.

10.2.5 Monte Carlo Simulation

Historical simulation has the weakness that it is limited by the length of the available asset return sample. Given a fully specified return-generating process for asset returns, it is possible to create a very long sample of artificial asset returns and then to apply a portfolio strategy to it. The risk–return properties of the strategy (contingent on the assumed properties of asset returns) can then be worked out exactly. Using a random number generator to produce an extremely long asset return sample, it is straightforward to mimic the historical simulation method and compute any distributional statistics for the strategy, such as variance, VaR, and ES.

There are three sources of estimation error in Monte Carlo based risk estimates. The first is the possible misspecification of the joint distribution used to create the artificial asset return histories. The second is the estimation error in the parameters of this joint distribution. The third is the use of a long but finite simulated sample, which makes the invocation of the law of large numbers inexact. This last source of error, called simulation noise, can be made negligible by using a suitably large simulated sample; given the power and speed of modern computing there is little excuse for nonnegligible simulation noise, except in the most complex financial engineering applications (see below).

In an influential article, Hendricks (1996) estimates twelve different VaR models and tests them on randomly generated portfolios of returns to eight currency exchange rates against the dollar. Eight of the models are parametric normal models: five are equally weighted moving-average models with different windows and three are exponentially weighted models with different weights. The remaining four models are nonparametric models that use different windows. The tests are a challenge to the normal models since currency return series are known to contain many extreme events. Hendricks methodically evaluates these models at the 95% and 99% confidence levels over a one-day horizon using a battery of statistical tests. He finds that at the 95% confidence level most of the models give reasonable forecasts. However, all models underforecast at the 99% confidence level, except the historical model with the longest (1,250-day) horizon. Hendricks concludes that there is no uniformly superior approach to estimating VaR and that further research combining the best features of the approaches may be worthwhile.

Monte Carlo methods for risk analysis are particularly important in financial engineering applications. For example, a financial engineering trading desk may sell, for a fee, a lookback option, which gives a client the right to purchase an equity or equity index at its lowest realized price over a chosen time interval. Measuring the VaR of a trading desk's entire portfolio, including many such option positions, is an extremely challenging problem. It requires Monte Carlo simulation of entire price paths for multiple assets, not just single-period returns. Because of the greatly increased complexity of simulating entire price paths, the risk analyst must ensure a careful balancing of computation speed, simulation noise, and accuracy of the assumed model of price dynamics. As mentioned in our introduction, we do not attempt to cover risk analysis for financial engineering in this book. See Glasserman (2003) for a sophisticated treatment of Monte Carlo simulation methods for financial engineering.

10.2.6 Scenario Modeling and Stress Testing

Scenario modeling is a simple variant of Monte Carlo simulation. The analyst specifies the space of possible outcomes as a discrete set of random events (such as high, average, and low outcomes for interest rates, stock market returns, and other key underlying variates determining portfolio value). The analyst must also specify the functional relationship between these key underlying variates and realized portfolio value, so that portfolio return can be calculated for each possible event. The analyst assigns a probability to each discrete event and from this the full (discrete) probability distribution of realized portfolio returns is easily derived. See Dowd (2005) for a detailed treatment.

Stress testing is an important variant of simulation modeling, particularly in large, complex trading desk environments. For stress testing, the analyst describes the discrete set of possible events for a finite set of key variates but does not assign probabilities to the individual event outcomes. Instead, the analyst searches across all events to find the joint event outcome of the underlying variates that generates the maximum implied loss on the portfolio. This serves as an estimate of portfolio worst outcome. Stress testing is particularly important for portfolios that include derivatives, since the worst outcome for such a portfolio need not correspond to the "worst" outcome of the key variates, depending on the nonlinear shape of the aggregate derivative position as a function of the key variates. See Dowd (2005) for a discussion and further references.

Drawdown analysis is a dynamic variant of stress testing. The *maximum drawdown* of a portfolio is its maximum decrease in value (including any cash outlays for margin calls on derivatives positions) between two dates. If a trading desk has a daily loss limit imposed upon it, then drawdown analysis of the trading desk's portfolio provides a guide to the likelihood that the loss limit might be breached. Liquidity modeling (see chapter 12) is crucial in drawdown analysis, since trading desks following similar investment strategies can hit their loss limits almost simultaneously.

10.3 Tail Risk

10.3.1 Nonparametric Estimation of Return Tails

Although nonparametric density estimates are not reliable for the tails of the distribution, it is possible to use nonparametric methods to estimate limited features of return tails.

Suppose that we have a sample of portfolio returns r_t, $t = 1, T$, and we wish to estimate the portfolio's VaR without imposing any parametric assumptions on returns. The historically estimated nonparametric VaR at 95% is just the 95% order statistic of the sample of losses. Estimating ES with this methodology is also easy: we simply find the average loss of the subset of the sample with losses greater than or equal to the 95% order statistic.

10.3.2 Statistical Accuracy of Nonparametric Tail Estimates

The merit of the nonparametric approach to estimating tail return features is clear: it does not rely on a priori assumptions about the return distribution. However, this approach has the undesirable consequence of assigning a probability of zero to any return that is greater in magnitude than the largest in the data set. Also, this approach provides only a point estimate of VaR and/or ES and does not give information about the confidence we can have in the statistical accuracy of the estimate. To derive a confidence interval for the estimate we need to make parametric assumptions, which we have specifically sought to avoid! It is not reasonable to use large-sample approximate confidence intervals, since estimates of tail features typically do not have large samples. For example, if we calculate ES with a confidence level of 0.99 we have an effective sample equal to only 1% of our total sample. Even if the original sample is very large, a sample one hundred times smaller may not be large enough to apply large-sample approximations to the confidence interval.

Lo (2001) notes that by suitably simplifying the problem we can generate a tail estimator with an exact known confidence interval while imposing no parametric restrictions on the return distribution. Consider the value-at-risk $a = Q_{\text{loss}}(1 - \alpha)$ for α close to zero and let $\hat{a}$ denote the nonparametric estimate. As noted above it is not feasible to nonparametrically estimate a confidence interval for $\hat{a}$ for a given α close to zero. Lo considers the simpler, inverse problem of estimating α given a for a small value of a. The advantage of this simplified problem relative to the VaR estimation problem is that it results in an exact distribution for the test statistic with no parametric restriction on the loss distribution.

In the absence of parametric restrictions, losses below a provide no information about the probability of losses above a, and the magnitude of the losses above a provides no information about the aggregate probability of losses above this threshold. Therefore, the number of losses n above a in the sample, denoted by (n, T), is a sufficient statistic for α. As long as losses are independently distributed over time, the likelihood of the observed sample information (n, T) given $\alpha = \hat{\alpha}$ has a binomial distribution with parameter $\hat{\alpha}$. So we have an exact binomial distribution for the observed sample, with no parametric restrictions on the underlying return distribution. This does not solve the nonparametric VaR problem, but it is illuminating in that it puts an upper bound on the amount of information available in the sample, in the absence of parametric restrictions.

Consider a historical sample of 21,500 daily returns of the U.S. market index. This corresponds to approximately eighty-five years of trading day observations. Suppose that there are two returns in the sample below -10% (as is the case for the U.S. market over the 1926–2007 period). Based on this large sample and without imposing distributional restrictions, what is the accuracy of the sample-estimated probability of a daily return less than -10%? That is, we wish to estimate $\alpha = \Pr(r < -0.1)$ and measure the reliability of our estimate. Using Lo (2001) we know that the likelihood function of the sample given α has a binomial distribution. Figure 10.2 shows the likelihood function for a range of values of α, and the 0.95 confidence interval. We can say with 0.95 confidence that the probability α is greater than 0.05 per 1,000 and less than 0.40 per 1,000, but this is a substantial range around its maximum-likelihood value of 0.22 per 1,000. Even with this truly enormous sample we can estimate the probability α only within an eightfold multiplicative range. This illustrates a basic limitation to the empirical analysis of return tails: in the absence of very strong (perhaps unreasonably strong) parametric assumptions, return tail estimation for α near zero gives poor estimation quality for typical sample sizes.

A typical trading desk will usually have sufficient capital reserves to weather a daily return loss that is ten or more times the historical standard deviation of return. We might ask what the probability of a percentage loss exceeding the capital reserves is. The answer is that, based on statistical analysis of the historical record alone and without imposing any distributional restrictions, we cannot know this probability within any reasonable degree of accuracy.

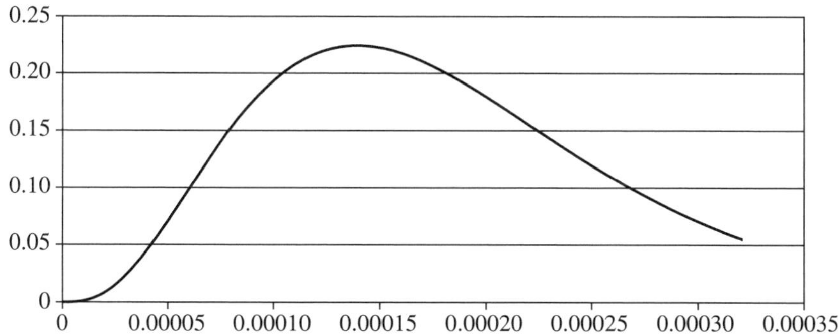

Figure 10.2. The likelihood function for the estimated probability of a 10% daily loss for a sample size of 21,500 using a nonparametric estimator.

10.3.3 Power Laws and the Tail Index

Suppose a one-day 0.95 VaR for a portfolio is 0.2, so portfolio loss exceeds 0.2 only 5% of the time. How often will portfolio loss exceed 0.4 (double the loss associated with a 0.95 cumulative probability) and how often will it exceed 10.0 (five times the loss associated with a 0.95 probability)?[2] The normal distribution assigns very low probabilities to such extreme losses. For notational simplicity, throughout this subsection we will assume that the expected loss equals zero. Under normality, the probability of a loss exceeding twice the 0.95 VaR is $\Pr_N(2(-1.6449)) = 0.000501458$; and the probability of exceeding five times the 0.95 VaR is $\Pr_N(5(-1.6449)) = 9.81932 \times 10^{-17}$ (which is a very, very small number). This rapid decline occurs because the normal distribution has exponential tails—once we have reached a cumulative probability moderately close to one, the residual probability declines extremely fast. This feature of the normal distribution is wildly inconsistent with financial market experience. It is clear that in most real-world trading or investment environments a loss five or more times the size of the one-in-twenty loss given by 0.95 VaR occurs with nonnegligible probability.

More realistic estimates of the probability of large losses can be obtained by replacing a normal distribution with a distribution based on a power law. A return distribution obeys a *power law* if one minus the cumulative probability for large losses is approximately proportional to the loss raised to a fixed power. More generally, the loss distribution $\text{cum}_{\text{loss}}(a)$ obeys a power law with *tail index* $\gamma \in (0, \infty)$ and height β if

$$1 - \text{cum}_{\text{loss}}(a) \overset{*}{\approx} \beta a^{-\gamma}, \tag{10.6}$$

[2]For a trading desk, portfolio loss can easily exceed initial value since liability is essentially unlimited (for example, through uncovered options writing).

where the approximation is accurate for all sufficiently large losses. The power law condition restricts only the lower tail of the return distribution (which is the upper tail of the loss distribution); the middle and upper ranges of the distribution are not restricted. Larger values of γ correspond to a distribution with a thinner tail. The normal, lognormal, and exponential distributions do not obey a power law since (10.6) does not hold for any finite value of the tail index γ. They are formally assigned a tail index of ∞.

The first step in estimating the height and tail index of a power law for a sample of losses is to order the sample of losses by size:

$$\text{loss}(1) \geqslant \text{loss}(2) \geqslant \cdots .$$

Let $n(u)$ denote the number of losses that exceed a fixed threshold u. A widely used estimator of the tail index is the Hill estimator $\hat{\gamma}$, which is given (in reciprocal form) by

$$\frac{1}{\hat{\gamma}} = \frac{1}{n(u)} \sum_{i=1}^{n(u)} \log\left(\frac{\text{loss}(i)}{u}\right).$$

Under reasonable assumptions, the Hill estimator $\hat{\gamma}$ is an asymptotically normal estimator of the tail index γ of a power law distribution (see, for example, Embrechts et al. 1997, theorem 6.4.6). In practice, it is desirable to choose u as large as possible in order to minimize the bias in the Hill estimator. On the other hand, for a given data set, larger values of u correspond to fewer usable observations $n(u)$, so the variance of the estimator increases with u. Thus, the optimal threshold u is determined by a bias–variance trade-off. Adopting the technical assumptions required for the Hill estimator to be asymptotically normal, Daníelsson and de Vries (1997) optimize the selection of the threshold u. Using a bootstrap method, they minimize the asymptotic mean square error of $1/\hat{\gamma}$ as a function of u. They show that for the critical value of u corresponding to the minimum, bias and variance are vanishing at the same rate.

It is important to be aware that tail estimates are necessarily very data intensive and have large standard errors. For example, Heyde and Kou (2004) show that 5,000 data points are inadequate to distinguish an exponential tail from a power law.

10.3.4 Excesses over a Threshold

The power function discussed in the last subsection concerns the tail of the distribution of all losses, where the tail is defined as consisting of all losses greater than a large upper bound u. A different perspective comes from analyzing the distribution of the *excesses*, defined as the set of positive differences, loss $- u$, for the set of realized losses greater than u. Note that the definition of the distribution differs from that used in the previous subsection, since for every fixed u we are analyzing the conditional distribution, given that a loss greater than u has occurred.

A powerful statistical theorem due to Pickands (1975) shows that under general conditions, excesses over a threshold approximately follow a generalized Pareto distribution as the threshold u and the sample size grow large. A generalized Pareto distribution with tail index γ and height β is given by

$$\mathrm{cum}_{\mathrm{loss},\gamma,\beta}(a) = \begin{cases} 1 - \left(1 + \dfrac{a}{\gamma\beta}\right)^{-\gamma} & \gamma < \infty, \\ 1 - \mathrm{e}^{-a/\beta} & \gamma = \infty. \end{cases}$$

The wide applicability of the generalized Pareto distribution in approximately describing excesses over thresholds parallels the generality of the normal distribution in describing scaled averages of weakly correlated random variables (the central limit theorem (see McNeil et al. 2005)).

The parameters of the generalized Pareto distribution can be found using maximum-likelihood estimation once a threshold u is selected. As is the case for the Hill estimator, it is challenging to find an optimal choice of u. Goldberg et al. (2008b) evaluate the fit of the conditional distribution of excesses using the Kuiper statistic and choose the smallest threshold for which the fit cannot be rejected at a 0.95 confidence level. Based on out-of-sample tests, Barbieri et al. (2008) conclude that tail risk forecasts based on the methodology in Goldberg et al. (2008b) are more accurate than forecasts made with a conditional normal model.

Excesses over a threshold can also be used to estimate the tail index of a power law model of the loss distribution. Let $n(u)$ denote the number of losses that exceed a fixed threshold u and define

$$\mathrm{ES}(u) = \frac{1}{n(u)} \sum_{i=1}^{n(u)} \mathrm{loss}(i) - u, \tag{10.7}$$

which is the average over the set of excesses as a function of u. For a power law with tail index $\gamma > 1$, the mean excess function (10.7) increases in u, with slope approximately equal to $\gamma/(\gamma - 1)$.

10.4 Nonlinear Dependence between Asset Returns

So far in this chapter we have analyzed the univariate return to a given portfolio. In this section we turn to multivariate distribution modeling.

10.4.1 Comoments of Returns

If an n-vector of returns is multivariate normal, then all the interdependencies of the returns are completely described by the $n \times n$ covariance matrix. However, this is not the case for nonnormal asset returns: we need more general measures of interdependencies. One obvious approach is to use higher comoments, just as we used the higher moments of a univariate return to describe its departures from normality.

The (p, q) comoment of two demeaned returns $\tilde{r}_1$ and $\tilde{r}_2$ is defined as $E[\tilde{r}_1^p \tilde{r}_2^q]$. The number of comoments for n assets is unmanageably large, even for a moderate number of assets and very small values of p and q. To make the analysis more manageable much of the attention in the finance literate has been focused only on market co-skewness, defined as the $(1, 2)$ comoment of each asset return with the market portfolio return:

$$\text{Co-skew}(r_i) = E[\tilde{r}_i \tilde{r}_{\text{m}}^2].$$

There is some empirical evidence that market co-skewness is a compensated source of risk: that is, assets with more positive market co-skewness receive higher average returns to compensate for this risk (see, for example, Harvey and Siddique 2000).

10.4.2 Copulas

Just as the correlation coefficient describes the linear dependence between two returns, irrespective of their variances, the *copula* function completely describes the dependence between two returns, irrespective of their univariate distributions. Given two random returns r_1 and r_2 the copula function $C(y_1, y_2)$ is defined over the range $y_1 \in (0, 1)$, $y_2 \in (0, 1)$ and gives the joint cumulative probability distribution as a bivariate function of the univariate cumulative probability distributions. The copula function $C(\cdot\,,\cdot)$ is therefore defined implicitly by setting the bivariate function of the univariate cumulative distributions equal to the joint cumulative distribution function:

$$C(\Pr(r_1 \leqslant a_1), \Pr(r_2 \leqslant a_2)) = \Pr(r_1 \leqslant a_1, r_2 \leqslant a_2), \tag{10.8}$$

so that the copula completely describes the probability dependency between r_1 and r_2. The entire joint probability function can be recovered from the copula function and the two univariate distribution functions, so the copula definition (10.8) imposes no restrictions on the joint distribution. Note that the copula function is equivalent to the distribution function if both marginal distributions are uniform on the unit interval. Note that if the returns r_1 and r_2 are completely independent, then $C(y_1, y_2) = y_1 y_2$.

To implement the copula approach empirically it is necessary to add enough structure to the problem such that the copula function can be estimated. Note that we only need to estimate three of the four functions in (10.8): the joint distribution, the two marginal distributions, and the bivariate copula function. This reflects the fact that knowing three of these functions gives the fourth function. It is straightforward to extend the copula definition to more than two returns but this makes the estimation problem correspondingly harder; the n-dimensional copula extends in an obvious way the bivariate case discussed above.

In order to use copulas as financial models, we need to specify functional forms for $C(\cdot,\cdot)$. There are a large number of potential choices for function form. The joint distribution of independent random variables generates the product copula, given by

$$C(u_1, u_2, \dots, u_n) = \prod_i^n u_i.$$

The Gaussian copula is the copula defined implicitly by two or more multivariate normal returns. There are four points worth noting about this choice of copula.

(1) It is fully determined by the correlation matrix of the underlying multivariate normal distribution (in the bivariate case, the correlation coefficient).

(2) As is true of the cumulative normal distribution that underlies it, the Gaussian copula does not have a simple closed-form expression.

(3) The Gaussian copula does not require that the univariate distributions are normal, only that the interdependencies between the returns mimic the multivariate normal case.

(4) Finally, and importantly, as discussed in the next subsection any jointly normal variables are asymptotically independent, no matter how highly correlated they are.

Thus, the Gaussian copula is not a suitable model for assets whose returns tend to experience common extreme losses or gains. Throughout the late 1990s and early 2000s, the Gaussian copula played a central role as a tool to price structured credit products such as credit default obligations. However, its modeling limitations have led researchers to consider alternatives, given its inconsistency with observed extreme-tail dependencies for large losses. Giesecke (2003) proposes the exponential copula for modeling commonality in default risk across credit instruments. See McNeil et al. (2005) and Patton (2009) for detailed discussions of copula applications and estimation techniques.

10.4.3 Tail Dependence

The risk-management consequences of extreme events occurring in tandem can be profound. Consider, for example, the effect of the collapse of Long Term Capital Management and the default of the Russian ruble that occurred in late summer of 1998, or the 2007–8 credit-liquidity crisis. In both cases, markets worldwide were thrown into turmoil that lasted months and a "flight to quality" resulting in a huge risk premium ensued. Asymptotic tail dependence studies the statistical dependency between large losses for two assets. Let $Q_{\text{loss},i}(1-\alpha)$, $Q_{\text{loss},j}(1-\alpha)$ denote the quantile functions for the loss probabilities for assets i and j. Poon et al. (2004) define the asymptotic dependence between loss_i and loss_j as the probability that asset i's loss will exceed $Q_{\text{loss},i}(1-\alpha)$ given that asset j has done so, for α close to zero:

$$\chi_{ij} = \lim_{\alpha\to 0} \Pr[\text{loss}_i > Q_{\text{loss},i}(1-\alpha) \mid \text{loss}_j > Q_{\text{loss},j}(1-\alpha)].$$

They note that χ_{ij} equals zero if the two loss distributions have a Gaussian copula and they use χ_{ij} as a measure of the asymptotic dependence between the loss distributions. Poon et al. (2004) study the asymptotic dependence in daily returns to five major market indices: the S&P in the United States, the FTSE in the United Kingdom, the DAX in Germany, the CAC in France, and the Nikeii in Japan. The study period beginning December 26, 1968, and ending November 12, 2001, consists of 8,577 returns. Roughly 2% of the observations are deemed "tail events" and thus appear in the estimation of asymptotic dependence. The study find no evidence of asymptotic dependence in the right tail, which corresponds to positive returns. However, there is statistically significant asymptotic dependence in the left tails, or losses, for United States–United Kingdom and for United Kingdom–Germany. Poon et al. note that the findings using daily returns across national securities markets can be influenced by the return-synchronization problem connected to differing market closing times (see chapter 2). In their analysis, they use the lagged daily value of the U.S. market viewed as synchronous (due to its late closing time) to the next-calendar-day market closes of the other four markets in their study.

Longin and Solnik (2001) examine the limiting behavior of exceedence correlations for monthly returns to five equity market indices: France,

Germany, Japan, the United Kingdom, and the United States. Recall the definition of the exceedence correlation from chapter 9, written here in terms of losses loss_1 and loss_2,

$$\text{ecorr}_{ij}(a) = \frac{E_S[(\text{loss}_i - E_S[\text{loss}_i])(\text{loss}_j - E_S[\text{loss}_j])]}{(E_S[(\text{loss}_i - E_S[\text{loss}_i])^2]E_S[(\text{loss}_j - E_S[\text{loss}_j])^2])^{1/2}},$$

where S denotes the conditioning set that both assets have losses greater than a:

$$E_S[\cdot] = E[\,\cdot \mid \text{loss}_i \geqslant a,\ \text{loss}_j \geqslant a].$$

Note that the exceedence correlation is just the linear correlation of the excesses over a common threshold, conditional on both assets having losses over the threshold. Hence the univariate tail theory of excesses over a threshold can be invoked in examining the limiting behavior of the exceedence correlation. Invoking the Pickands (1975) result mentioned above, each of the univariate excesses over threshold is assumed to have a generalized Pareto distribution. To analyze the asymptotic behavior of $\text{ecorr}_{ij}(a)$, Longin and Solnik need only to parameterize the dependency linking the two univariate distributions; based on earlier work by Ledford and Tawn (1997) they use a logistic function to model the dependency between the two generalized Pareto distributions. They find that exceedence correlations increase for large-magnitude loss exceedence levels. On the other hand, when they examine the positive tail of the return distributions (simultaneous large gains) there is no evidence for tail dependency.

11
Credit Risk

Credit risk refers to the uncertainty about whether a counterparty will honor a financial obligation. It is present to some degree in every financial asset and is therefore a central component of portfolio risk. Credit exposure is actively traded, giving rise to *indirect credit risk*. For example, a commercial bank owning home mortgages can package and sell the cash flows of these mortgages to insurance companies and other financial institutions. A homeowner defaulting on his mortgage obligation to the bank generates indirect credit risk for the insurance company, since the defaulted cash flow is passed through. Similarly, an investment bank can trade credit derivatives that are linked to the default of a corporation on its outstanding bonds. Even if the bank does not own bonds issued by the corporation, its positions in the credit derivatives market gives rise, indirectly, to credit risk. Opportunities for buying and selling indirect credit risk increase the "completeness" of the market by sharing credit risks more widely across investors. On the other hand, trading of indirect credit risk has the potential to exacerbate market failures associated with incomplete information and misaligned incentives.

In recent years there has been increasing attention on and more sophisticated modeling of the credit component of portfolio risk. While a significant fraction of credit risk is driven by market-wide factors, the linear factor modeling approach that dominates equity risk forecasting is not adequate. This is because the relationship between the return to a credit-sensitive instrument and market-wide risk factors is nonlinear. Also, credit-related return distributions tend to be far from normal. As a result, nonlinear models and nonstandard distributions are often used to analyze credit risk. Because of these differences, it remains a challenge to effectively integrate them with factor models and other standard portfolio risk models.

Section 11.1 discusses credit modeling of corporate bonds and describes factor models of spread risk based on agency ratings, sector, and issuer equity. In section 11.2 we look at credit risk models based on historical rating transitions. Section 11.3 sketches some of the most important credit instruments. In section 11.4 we consider several approaches to modeling the risk of single-name instruments (a *single-name* credit instrument is linked to the default of a single entity). In section 11.5 we briefly touch on the risk of loss given default. Section 11.6 discusses multiname credit instruments, also called portfolio credit instruments. Section 11.7 concludes with some thoughts on the credit-liquidity crisis of 2007–8, and the lessons that might be learned for portfolio risk analysis.

11.1 Agency Ratings and Factor Models of Spread Risk

Corporate bond issuance in the United States began in earnest early in the twentieth century and the two best-known credit rating agencies—Standard & Poor's and Moody's—started then.[1] Agencies rate both issuers and specific issues. Credit rating relies on a labor-intensive process that combines fundamental and quantitative analysis. Ratings are reviewed roughly once a year, so they are relatively unresponsive to market volatility.

Agency ratings affect the investment process in several ways. Investors use them as a guide to assessing both the relative value of securities and the creditworthiness of issuers. Corporate bond index construction rules involve agency ratings and a significant change in rating can lead to substantial index reconfiguration as well as market turmoil.

11.1.1 Corporate Bond Spreads

Structurally, a corporate bond is similar to a treasury bond. It is a contract for a loan from an investor to an issuer coupled with a stream of payments from the issuer to the investor. A basic contract consists of fixed interest payments at regular intervals over a specified horizon and a final principal payment at the horizon end. There are many variations on the basic contract and extra features such as embedded options, principal amortization schedules, sinking funds, payment-in-kind clauses, and stepped or floating interest rates.

Corporate bonds trade at a spread, defined as the extra yield relative to treasuries. Mathematically, the period-compounded spread of a corporate bond that pays coupons at regular intervals is the value "spr" for which the market price, p, of the bond satisfies

$$p = \sum_{j=1}^{T} \frac{\text{CF}_j}{(1 + y_j + \text{spr})^j},$$

[1] For a brief history of corporate bond markets see Crouhy et al. (2001, chapter 7).

where CF_j is the jth cash flow, T is the number of periods until the bond matures, and y_j is the yield on a default-free j-period pure-discount bond. A component of the spread compensates investors for the risk associated with issuer default. As for default-free interest rates, there are market-wide credit spread term structures that are estimated from pools of bonds. High-quality bonds trade at a spread of a few basis points while spreads of lower-quality issues can be hundreds or even thousands of basis points.

Credit spreads can be viewed as a coarse market assessment of creditworthiness; there is a strong relationship between agency ratings and spreads. An empirical study of this relationship in the United States and Europe is carried out by Kercheval et al. (2003). They develop a market-implied rating based on bond spreads and find that roughly 50% of the issues are rated differently by the market and by agencies. However, the implied ratings of most bonds are within a single notch of the agency ratings.

However, we have only an incomplete picture of the determinants of credit spreads. The *credit spread puzzle* refers to the fact that corporate bond spreads are many times wider than historical rates of default would indicate. Collin-Dufresne et al. (2001) consider numerous proxies for default and recovery risk and conclude that these factors explain roughly 25% of corporate bond spreads. Using principal-components analysis, the authors find that the residuals appear to be explained by a single common factor. However, they are unable to identify the factor. Tax effects, liquidity, risk premiums, and difficulty of diversification have been offered to explain the noncredit component of corporate bond spreads, but no firm conclusion has been reached.

11.1.2 Factor Models of Spread Variation

Investors are exposed to spread risk, which is the variation in spread over time, and linear factor models are commonly used to measure this risk. Below, we discuss several standard paradigms for model architecture and factor selection.

11.1.2.1 Choosing a Reference Curve

The credit spreads underlying the market-implied rating model in Kercheval et al. (2003) are estimated with respect to the treasury curve in the United States and with respect to the swap-LIBOR (London Interbank Offered Rate) curve, which represents interbank lending rates in Europe. The discrepancy between the U.S. and European benchmarks stems from standard issues: market convention and data availability.

Since the inception of the euro in 1999, the so-called European Currency Unit (ECU) countries have tended to operate as a single bond market and there is no natural choice for a riskless treasury curve. As a result, the swap curve, which incorporates some default risk, is the baseline for most models. By contrast, there is a highly liquid market for U.S. treasuries, which determine a riskless treasury curve. The treasury curve is the standard benchmark against which corporate spreads are measured. A detailed discussion of the effect of a reference curve on corporate bond pricing is in Duffie and Singleton (2003, section 7.2).

11.1.2.2 Sector Plus Rating Models

A parsimonious specification of a credit spread risk model includes a single factor for each sector and another for each (coarse) rating category. Thus, the number of credit spread factors is equal to the sum of the number of sectors and the number of rating categories.

On each date, factor returns are estimated by cross-sectional regression:

$$r_t^{\mathrm{C}} = \sum_{l=1}^{k_1} \beta_l^{\mathrm{IR}} f_{lt}^{\mathrm{IR}} + \sum_{j=1}^{k_2} \beta_j^{\mathrm{S}} f_{jt}^{\mathrm{S}} + \sum_{h=1}^{k_3} \beta_h^{\mathrm{R}} f_{ht}^{\mathrm{R}} + \varepsilon_t,$$

where β_l^{IR} is the prespecified sensitivity of the bond to the lth interest rate factor, β_j^{S} and β_h^{R} are the prespecified sensitivities of the bond return to the returns of the jth sector and the hth rating category, f_{lt}^{IR}, f_{jt}^{S}, and f_{ht}^{R} denote the corresponding factor returns to be estimated, and ε_t is the regression error. The factor covariance matrix can then be estimated from the time series of factor returns.

11.1.2.3 Sector Times Rating Models

A less parsimonious specification of a credit spread risk model includes a single factor for each sector by rating category. Here the number of credit spread factors is equal to the product of the number of sectors and the number of rating categories. This model gives a more detailed picture of market structure but requires more data in order to keep standard errors at an acceptable level.

On each date, factor returns are estimated by cross-sectional regression:

$$r_t^{\mathrm{C}} = \sum_{l=1}^{k_1} \beta_l^{\mathrm{IR}} f_{lt}^{\mathrm{IR}} + \sum_{j=1}^{k_2} \sum_{h=1}^{k_3} \beta_{jh}^{\mathrm{SR}} f_{jht}^{\mathrm{SR}} + \varepsilon_t,$$

where β_l^{IR} is sensitivity of the bond to the lth interest rate factor, β_{jh}^{SR} is the sensitivity to the factor for sector j and rating h, f_{jt}^{S} and f_{jht}^{SR} denote the corresponding factor returns to be estimated, and ε_t is the regression error. As in a sector plus rating model, the factor covariance matrix is estimated from the time series of factor returns.

11.1.2.4 Bond Spread Risk and Equity Factors

Cheyette and Postler (2006) develop a risk model for corporate bonds that relies on equity factors. The basis of the model is the return decomposition,

$$r_t^{\mathrm{C}} = \beta^{\mathrm{IR}} r_t^{\mathrm{G}} + \beta^{\mathrm{E}} r_t^{\mathrm{E}} + \varepsilon_t,$$

which describes the return, r_t^{C}, to a corporate bond in terms of the return to an equivalent government (default-free) bond, r_t^{G}, the return to the equity of the issuer, r_t^{E}, and an unexplained residual component, ε_t.[2] The exposures β^{IR} and β^{E} are functions of the corporate bond spread, spr, and the duration, dur:

$$\beta^{\mathrm{IR}} = 1 - (1 - \mathrm{e}^{-\alpha_1 \mathrm{spr}})^{\alpha_2}, \tag{11.1}$$

$$\beta^{\mathrm{E}} = \alpha_3((1 - \mathrm{e}^{-\alpha_4 \mathrm{spr}})(1 - \mathrm{e}^{-\alpha_6 \mathrm{dur}\cdot\mathrm{spr}}))^{\alpha_5}. \tag{11.2}$$

The Cheyette–Postler specifications take into account the positive relationship between credit quality and the explanatory power of interest rate factors, as well as the inverse relationship between credit quality and the explanatory power of equity returns. The parameters α_i in formulas (11.1) and (11.2) are calibrated using bond spreads pooled over time. For issues with a very low spread, β^{IR} is roughly equal to one and β^{E} is approximately zero, so interest rate risk dominates. The risk of a high spread issue has almost no dependence on interest rates and the value of β^{E} tends to α_3 as the spread increases.

Cheyette and Postler find that roughly 90% of the return variance of corporate bonds of very high quality is explained by interest rate factors. Bonds with spreads of roughly 200 basis points or more have significant equity exposure. Roughly 40% of the return variance of a bond of very low quality—one whose spread exceeds 800 basis points—is explained by equity factors. However, they find that neither interest rates nor issuer equity have strong explanatory power for issues in the intermediate spread range of 200–800 basis points, leaving open the question of what drives the risk for these securities.

[2] Their equivalent government bond is synthetic and its return is a duration-weighted sum of returns to actual government bonds.

11.2 Rating Transitions and Default

Agency ratings are used to define the factors in many of the risk models described above.[3] The possibility of a downgrade, which is a significant source of credit risk, is not specifically addressed by these models.

Both Standard & Poor's and Moody's publish the frequency of rating transitions and their estimates are conveniently displayed in matrix form. The entry in row i and column j is a historical estimate of the probability that an issuer with rating i will move to rating j within one year. The lowest state represents default, which is assumed to be an absorbing state. The overwhelming likelihood is that an issuer rating will remain where it is and that the likelihood of default increases as credit quality decreases. While these general features remain valid in different economic climates, the estimates of rating transitions and default vary substantially.

Jarrow et al. (1997) use rating transitions as the basis of a Markov model for forecasting credit spread risk. Their starting point is a Moody's historical rating transition matrix, which they use to estimate the average probability, $\Pr(i,j)$, that a firm will change from rating i to rating j over a fixed time horizon. In order to connect historical transition probabilities to security valuation, the probabilities must be adjusted for the market price of risk. Jarrow et al. introduce a family of time-dependent risk premium adjustments $\pi_i(t)$ to generate time-dependent risk-adjusted transition probabilities $\Pr^*_{ij}(t)$ satisfying

$$\Pr^*_{ij}(t) = \pi_i(t)\Pr(i,j).$$

Set

$$Q(t) = \begin{pmatrix} & \cdots & \\ \vdots & \Pr^*_{ij}(t) & \vdots \\ & \cdots & \end{pmatrix}.$$

From the Markov assumption, it follows that the entries of the T-fold matrix product

$$Q(t,T) = Q(0)\cdot Q(1)\cdot\cdots\cdot Q(T)$$

are T-period risk-adjusted transition probabilities. It follows that the probability of a bond in credit class i surviving for T periods is given by

$$S_i(t,T) = 1 - Q_i(t,T)$$

Finally, under the assumption that default risk is independent of interest rate risk, the time-t price $p_i(t,T)$ of a corporate pure-discount bond

[3] A market-implied approach to rating bonds can be found in Breger et al. (2003).

in class i that recovers a fraction δ of its value at default and matures in T periods is given by

$$p_i(t,T) = p_0(t,T)(\delta + (1-\delta)S_i(t,T)),$$

where $p_0(t,T)$ is the price of an analogous riskless pure-discount bond. It follows that the per-period model spread is given by

$$\mathrm{spr}_i(t,T) = -\frac{1}{T}\log(\delta + (1-\delta)S_i(t,T)). \tag{11.3}$$

The relative simplicity of formula (11.3) is the result of the many assumptions underlying the model, including temporal homogeneity of physical transition rates and independence of interest rates and defaults. The plausibility of these assumptions as well as their impact on the model are subjects of much debate. However, it is difficult to relax the assumptions while maintaining tractability.

11.3 Credit Instruments

Historically, corporate bonds and bonds issued by governments of uncertain financial stability were the main vehicles for trading credit risk. The development of collateralized mortgage obligations (CMOs) in the early 1980s led to a new paradigm for packaging privately contracted cash flows into tradeable securities. In their early forms, CMOs were mostly subject to prepayment risk and interest rate risk, so the credit risk contained in them was small. However, the concept of passing through cash flows from sets of original parties into a collection of market-traded securities was an important innovation. Over subsequent decades this innovation had a revolutionary effect on credit instruments. It led directly to collateralized debt obligations (CDOs), which applied the CMO technology to other types of debt (including debt instruments with substantial credit risk). It also inspired a wide range of other indirect credit instruments.

The term *credit instrument* refers to any security whose payoffs are linked to specified credit-related events such as a declaration of bankruptcy, a rating downgrade, a failure to make a payment, a restructuring, or a moratorium.[4] A credit event may involve one or more *reference entities*, and it may be determined by a collection of *reference obligations* issued by the reference entity. A credit instrument is essentially a contract between two parties where the cash flows of the contract

[4] A moratorium occurs when an obligor challenges the validity of a financial obligation.

depend on one or more default events of some observed debt instrument. The contracted party who pays cash when a default occurs is said to have the *default leg* of the contract; the party who receives cash when a default occurs has the *premium leg* of the contract.

The market for indirect credit instruments started in the late 1980s and experienced substantial growth at the turn of the twenty-first century as market participants recognized the need to manage and hedge credit risk. According to the British Bankers' Association and the International Swaps and Derivatives Association, the default swap market grew from roughly $180 billion in notional amount in 1997 to $34 trillion in 2006. The introduction of credit indices in the early 2000s led to market standardization and transparency, and therefore to increasingly reliable and transparent market data. The growth and standardization of credit markets made many credit instruments attractive and accessible to portfolio managers in the early 2000s. The 2007–8 credit crisis led to a precipitous decline in the use of some of these instruments, and the range of traded instruments is likely to evolve further in response to the lessons from this crisis. We will discuss the 2007–8 crisis in the final section of the chapter.

11.3.1 Default Swaps and Indices

Structurally, a default swap is an insurance policy. A protection buyer pays a premium or *spread* at regular intervals to a protection seller over a predetermined horizon on a fixed notional amount. In return, the protection seller compensates the protection buyer for his losses when a credit event occurs, at which time the contract is terminated. A typical default swap horizon is five years and spread payments are generally paid quarterly.

The default swap spread is similar to the spread of a corporate bond over a treasury or a LIBOR curve, and it is a determinant of discount factors for cash flows promised by the issuer of the reference instrument. A standard no-arbitrage argument shows that in the absence of liquidity, tax considerations, transactions costs, and other market frictions, the spreads on a bond and on a default swap referencing the same entity must be equal. In practice, the spreads do not agree and their difference, known as the *basis*, is maturity dependent and fluctuates over time. Further details about default swaps are in the survey article by Duffie (1999).

Default swap indices have helped to standardize credit markets. The two main families of these are CDX and iTraxx. Both include high-yield, investment-grade, and crossover indices in different geographical regions. Each index is composed of a fixed number of credits with equal notional value. The index composition is updated twice annually.

An index default swap affords an investor easy access to a broad market segment and it is structured just like a single-entity default swap. A protection buyer pays a premium at regular intervals to a protection seller in return for a guarantee of compensation if a credit event occurs for one of the names in the index. When a credit event occurs, the protection seller compensates the protection buyer for the loss, and the index notional, which is the sum of the notional amounts of the names in the index, is diminished. Thus, future protection payments are smaller since they are made on a lower notional amount.

The index spread is a weighted average of the spreads of the names in the index. Index default swaps are usually quite liquid and trade at a relatively small bid–ask spread.

11.3.2 Collateralized Debt Obligations and Structured Credit Products

Securitization of credit indices leads to the creation of securities with specified risk profiles. The result is a diverse class of structured credit products of which the most important and widely traded is perhaps a synthetic collateralized debt obligation (CDO), which is a "risk slice" or tranche, of a credit default swap index. A tranche is determined by an attachment point, $\underline{K}$, and a detachment point, $\overline{K}$. A schematic of a synthetic CDO with a standard decomposition into five tranches is given in figure 11.1. The slice that carries the highest risk and pays the highest spread is called the equity tranche. More information about default swap markets is in the survey article by Duffie and Gârleanu (2001).

There are more exotic and more complex credit instruments such as CDO-squareds, bespoke tranches, and nth-to-default baskets. These tend to be relatively illiquid.

11.4 Conceptual Approaches to Credit Risk

The linear factor models of corporate bond spreads are straightforward to estimate and integrate easily with equity risk models. However, they do not account for the nonlinear dependence of credit instruments on risk factors, nor do they effectively measure the asymmetry and heavy tails empirically observed in credit spread changes and returns. This has led researchers to look for alternative ways to model credit risk. We describe several below.

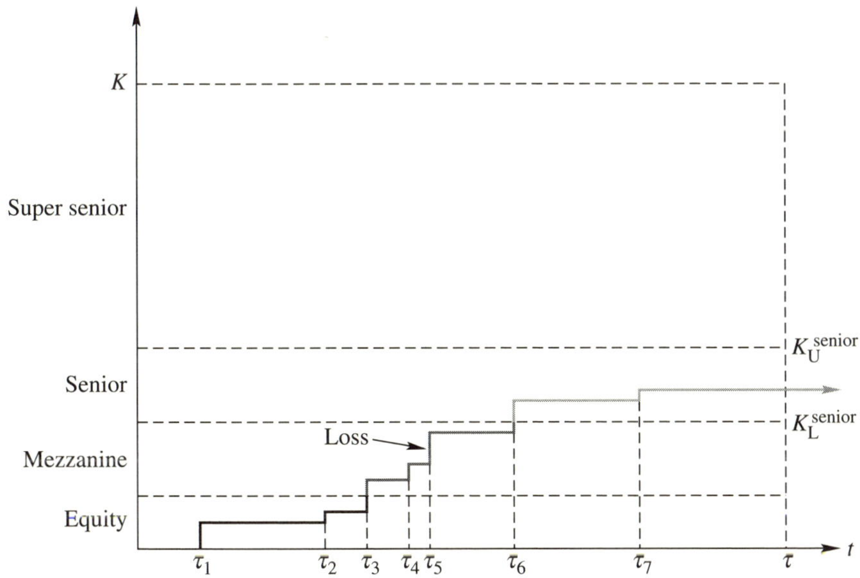

Figure 11.1. A schematic of a synthetic collateralized debt obligation.

11.4.1 Structural Models

A structural or cause-and-effect credit model is predicated on a specified definition of default. Structural models are intuitive and easy to calibrate and their powerful forecasting capabilities are empirically well-documented.

11.4.1.1 The Merton Model

In a seminal paper, Merton (1974) applies option theory to the pricing of corporate debt. Underlying the model are two assumptions. First, that the value of a firm is the sum of its equity and its debt:

$$V = E + B. \tag{11.4}$$

Second, that a firm's debt B is represented by a single pure-discount bond maturing at time T with a promised payment of D. Its value is

$$B = p_D(t, T).$$

Default occurs if a firm cannot pay what it owes at horizon T. If the firm value V_T at time T is less than the face value D of the debt, the bondholders take over the firm and equity holders receive nothing. Otherwise, their stake at horizon T is equal to the firm value less D. In other words, equity is a contingent claim on firm value whose payoff at time T has the profile of a European call option:

$$\max(V_T - D, 0).$$

Given a constant riskless interest rate r_0 and the assumption that firm value follows a geometric Brownian motion with volatility σ, the value of equity, E, can be computed from the Black–Scholes formula:

$$E = V\Phi(d_+) - De^{-r_0 T}\Phi(d_-), \tag{11.5}$$

where Φ is the cumulative normal distribution and

$$d_\pm = \frac{\log(V/D) + (r_0 \pm \sigma^2/2)T}{\sigma\sqrt{T}}.$$

Using $\Phi(-a) = 1 - \Phi(a)$, equations (11.4) and (11.5) lead to a simple, tractable formula for the value of the debt:

$$\begin{aligned} B &= V - E \\ &= V - (V\Phi(d_+) - De^{-r_0 T}\Phi(d_-)) \\ &= De^{-r_0 T} - (De^{-r_0 T}\Phi(-d_-) - V\Phi(-d_+)) \\ &= De^{-r_0 T} - p_{\text{put}}(r_0, T, D, V, \sigma), \end{aligned} \tag{11.6}$$

where

$$p_{\text{put}}(r_0, T, D, V, \sigma) = De^{-rT}\Phi(-d_-) - V\Phi(-d_+)$$

is the Black–Scholes value of a European put option on firm value with strike price and maturity equal to the face value and the maturity of the firm debt. This means that in the Merton model, corporate debt is equivalent to a portfolio that is long a riskless bond and short a European put option. Typically, the value of a creditworthy firm is far greater than the face value D of its debt. In this situation, the put option $p_{\text{put}}(r_0, T, V, D, \sigma)$ is out of the money and the value of firm debt is relatively close to the value of otherwise equivalent riskless debt.

Note that formula (11.6) can be rewritten

$$B = De^{-r_0 T}\Phi(d_-) + V\Phi(-d_+),$$

which is parallel to formula (11.5) for equity.

Firm leverage,

$$\ell = \frac{De^{-r_0 T}}{V},$$

which we define as the ratio of a firm's debt to its value,[5] plays a key role in the assessment of creditworthiness. A leverage near zero indicates

[5] There are many materially similar but technically different definitions of leverage used throughout the credit literature.

relatively high credit quality and a leverage near one indicates relatively poor credit quality. We can rewrite the formulas for the equity and the debt of a firm in terms of leverage:

$$E = V(\Phi(d_+) - \ell\Phi(d_-)), \tag{11.7}$$

$$B = V(\ell\Phi(d_-) + \Phi(-d_+)), \tag{11.8}$$

where

$$d_\pm = \frac{\pm\sigma^2 T/2 - \log\ell}{\sigma\sqrt{T}}.$$

It follows that if $p_0(t,T)$ denotes the value of a riskless pure-discount bond maturing at horizon T, the time-t model implied spread at T is given by

$$\begin{aligned} \operatorname{spr}(t,T) &= -\frac{1}{T}\log\left(\frac{p_D(t,T)}{p_0(t,T)}\right) \\ &= -\frac{1}{T}\log\left(\frac{B}{p_0(t,T)}\right) \\ &= -\frac{1}{T}\log\left(\Phi(d_-) + \frac{1}{\ell}\Phi(-d_+)\right). \end{aligned} \tag{11.9}$$

To be useful, the Merton model must be calibrated to market data. The required parameters are the riskless rate r_0, which can be sourced from public information, the default point, D, which is the face value of the pure-discount bond representing firm debt, and firm volatility, σ. There is no universally accepted way of calibrating D; a standard formulation sets it to the sum of long-term debt plus one-half short-term debt taken from a published data source.

Neither firm value nor firm volatility can be observed directly. One estimate relies on the formula

$$\sigma_{\mathrm{E}} = \sigma\Phi(d_+), \tag{11.10}$$

which expresses equity volatility in terms of firm volatility.[6] Together, equations (11.7) and (11.10) are a pair of nonlinear equations for equity value and volatility in two unknowns: firm value and firm volatility. For any observed (E, σ_{E}), there is a unique solution (V, σ) that can be used to generate model spread values using formula (11.9). An alternative calibration scheme based on the method of maximum likelihood can be found in Duan et al. (2003) and Ericsson and Reneby (2005).

In contrast to observed market data, model-predicted spreads tend to zero as maturity tends to zero. Also, the overall level of model-derived

[6] Formula (11.10) is a consequence of Ito's lemma, which is a standard in mathematical finance. See Hull (2002) for further details.

spreads is lower than in observed market data. This suggests that either the model is underforecasting credit risk or that bond spreads have a nontrivial component that is not attributable to credit risk. In an influential study, Jones et al. (1984) estimate the Merton model using secondary bond market prices over the period 1977–81. They corroborate the observation that, relative to empirical observation, forecast spreads are too low, or, equivalently, forecast bond prices are too high.

11.4.1.2 Extensions and Modifications of the Merton Model

Black and Cox (1976) remark that bond indentures typically include safety covenants that give bond holders the right to reorganize the firm if its value is sufficiently low. This leads them to introduce a first-passage model, in which default occurs when firm value crosses a fixed barrier. This definition of default is less restrictive than the one in Merton (1974) since default can occur at any time. If debt is modeled as a pure-discount bond with face value $K > D$, equity is a down-and-out call option, as opposed to a European option, in the case of the Merton model. Under the assumption that default follows a geometric Brownian motion with volatility σ,

$$E = p_{\text{call}}(r_0, T, D, V, \sigma) - V\left(\frac{D}{V}\right)^{(2r_0/\sigma^2)+1}\Phi(d'_+) + K\mathrm{e}^{-r_0T}\left(\frac{D}{V}\right)^{(2r_0/\sigma^2)-1}\Phi(d'_-), \tag{11.11}$$

where $p_{\text{call}}(\cdot)$ is the value of a European call and

$$d'_{\pm} = \frac{\log(D^2/(KV)) + (r_0 \pm \sigma^2/2)T}{\sigma\sqrt{T}}.$$

Since

$$B = p_D(t, T) = V - E, \tag{11.12}$$

as in the Merton model, a cumbersome but closed-form formula for the horizon T spread can be calculated by substitution using formulas (11.11) and (11.12) along with

$$\text{spr}(t, T) = -\frac{1}{T}\log\left(\frac{p_D(t, T)}{p_0(t, T)}\right).$$

Longstaff and Schwartz (1995) extend the Black and Cox (1976) model to handle stochastic interest rates. They use a one-factor mean-reverting Gaussian model for the short rate, which can be correlated with firm value. Leland (1994) and Leland and Toft (1996) develop a version of the Black and Cox model (1976) that has an endogenously defined default barrier chosen to maximize the value of firm equity. Collin-Dufresne and Goldstein (2001) modify the Black and Cox (1976) model so that the state variable is the leverage ratio instead of firm value. In a modification of Merton (1974), Geske (1977) allows debt to mature at multiple dates so that equity becomes a compound option.

11.4.1.3 Empirical Studies of Structural Pricing Models

Eom et al. (2004) compare five structural models of corporate bond spreads. Their study includes the models of Merton (1974), Leland and Toft (1996), Geske (1977), Longstaff and Schwartz (1995), and Collin-Dufresne and Goldstein (2001). It uses 182 noncallable bonds issued by firms with relatively simple capital structures over the period 1986–97. The study finds that all models underforecast spreads for very highly creditworthy bonds, which are issued by firms with low leverage and low volatility, and they overforecast spreads for very risky bonds, which are issued by high-leverage, high-volatility firms. All five models have substantial errors in spreads of bonds issued by firms that are at neither extreme, but the errors differ significantly in both sign and magnitude. The models of Merton and Geske underforecast bond spreads on average, while the model of Leland and Toft tends to overforecast spreads.

11.4.1.4 Structural Models and the Physical Probability of Default

Merton (1974) is concerned with the value of corporate securities. However, the most successful application of the model may be to forecasting default probability. Like interest rates and spreads, default probabilities form a term structure at any given time. We denote by $\Pr(t,T)$, the probability at time t that a firm or issue will default at horizon T.

In the Merton (1974) model, default occurs when the value of the firm is below the face value of a pure-discount bond maturing at horizon T that represents all the firm's debt liabilities. The *distance to default*, denoted by d_- in formula (11.5), which is the number of standard deviations between the firm value and the default point, is a key default risk factor. Recall from chapter 1 that the risk-neutral probability measure, $\Pr^*(\cdot,\cdot)$, is a transformation of the true (or "physical") probability measure such that the implied expected return on every asset equals the riskless return. Under the assumption that firm value is lognormal with volatility σ, the time-t risk-neutral probability of default at horizon T is given by

$$\Pr^*(t,T) = \Phi(-d_-). \tag{11.13}$$

The formula (11.13) cannot be used as a prediction equation for default probabilities since it relies on the risk-neutral probability measure rather than the physical probability measure. To apply it to default prediction we must reverse this transformation. In the Merton model, the reverse transformation, from risk-neutral to physical probabilities, is dependent upon an estimate of the true expected return of the firm's total assets (equal to the return to the firm's total liabilities of debt plus equity); this expected return is difficult to estimate.

A widely accepted approach to estimating physical default probabilities comes from the model of Moody's KMV (www.moodyskmv.com). Their methodology, documented in Crosbie and Bohn (2003), makes use of an extensive proprietary database of historical defaults. They use these data to estimate historical default rates and map the distance to default to an expected default rate, which is an estimate of the physical one-year rate of default. Expected default rates are used extensively by banks to manage loan portfolios.

A first-passage model, such as that in Black and Cox (1976), generates expected default rates that tend to be higher than Merton's probabilities because of a different model definition of default:

$$\Pr(t,T) = \Phi(-d_-) + \left(\frac{D}{V}\right)^{2(r_0-\sigma^2/2)/\sigma} \Phi(-d'_-). \tag{11.14}$$

Note that formula (11.14) for the Black and Cox default probability is equal to formula (11.13) for the Merton default probability incremented by a nonnegative term.

11.4.1.5 Event Forecasting

Properly calibrated, a structural credit model is an effective event-forecasting tool. Its forecasting power stems from the link to equity markets, which are highly liquid and rapidly incorporate new information. A typical application of a credit model is to rank firms on the basis of their probability of default. A ranking of this type can be used as a screening tool, as a trading signal, or as an ingredient to optimization.

The information content in a linear ranking can be assessed statistically with a *power curve*, also known as a receiver operating characteristic (ROC) curve, which takes account of the intrinsic tension between two kinds of mistakes. A type I forecasting error, or *false negative*, refers to an actual event that is not forecast by a model. A type II error, or *false positive*, is an unrealized forecast. To be of practical value, a forecasting model must be balanced to avoid both types of errors to the extent possible. This point is illustrated by a credit model that forecasts that all firms will default in the ensuing year. By construction, this model catches every default, but the model is useless due to the abundance of false positives—firms that survive in spite of the model forecasting that they would default.

Many studies, including Keenan et al. (2000), apply power curves to analyze default forecasting models. There is consistent evidence from many studies that well-calibrated structural models are more effective at default forecasting than agency ratings. However, it is important to emphasize that these studies evaluate only the rank ordering implied by a default-forecasting model, and not the levels of the forecasts.

11.4.2 Reduced-Form Models

The reduced-form approach to credit modeling has become the standard framework for quantitative valuation and hedging of credit instruments. This is because it provides tractable formulas for analyzing credit-sensitive instruments. In contrast to a structural model, the cause of default plays no role in the specification of a reduced-form model. Instead, the model is based on an exogenously specified conditional rate of default, or *intensity*. By definition, the intensity, λ_t, at time t is the local probability that a firm will default in the next instant, given that it has survived until time t. Mathematically,

$$\lambda_t = \lim_{\Delta \to 0} \left(\frac{1}{\Delta}\right) \frac{\Pr(t, t + \Delta)}{1 - \Pr(0, t)}.$$

The time-t probability of default over the horizon T is given in terms of the intensity λ by

$$\Pr(t, T) = 1 - E\left[\exp\left(-\int_t^{t+T} \lambda_s \, \mathrm{d}s\right)\right].$$

11.4.2.1 Reduced-Form Pricing

In a reduced-form model, credit-sensitive securities are priced as if they were default free, except that the riskless discount rate is augmented by a spread. We illustrate the idea with the simplest example: a constant-intensity Poisson model. In this setup, there is a security issuer whose time to default is exponentially distributed with intensity λ. This means that the time-t probability that the issuer will default over horizon T is given by

$$\Pr(t, T) = 1 - \mathrm{e}^{-\lambda T}.$$

Let $p(t, T)$ denote the time-t fair value of a pure-discount bond that pays one dollar at horizon T if the issuer has not defaulted. Suppose that the investor receives nothing if the issuer defaults. Then, if interest rate risk and default risk are independent, the fair value of the bond is given by

$$\begin{aligned} p(t,T) &= e^{-r_0 T} \cdot 1 \cdot (1 - \Pr(t,T)) + 0 \cdot \Pr(t,T) \\ &= e^{-(r_0+\lambda)T}. \end{aligned} \tag{11.15}$$

Consequently, the fair spread between the credit-risky pure-discount bond and an otherwise equivalent default-free pure-discount bond, p_0, is equal to the intensity λ:

$$\begin{aligned} \operatorname{spr}(t,T) &= -\frac{1}{T}\log\left(\frac{p(t,T)}{p_0(t,T)}\right) \\ &= \lambda. \end{aligned} \tag{11.16}$$

Formula (11.15) has a straightforward extension to a corporate bond, p_C, with a face value of 1 that pays a constant coupon C at horizons $t_1, t_2, \dots, t_n = T$:

$$\begin{aligned} p_C &= \sum_{\tau=1}^{n} e^{-r_0 t_\tau} C(1 - \Pr(t, t_\tau)) + e^{-r_0 t_n}(1 - \Pr(t, t_n)) \\ &= \sum_{\tau=1}^{n} e^{-(r_0+\lambda)} C + e^{-(r_0+\lambda)t_n}. \end{aligned} \tag{11.17}$$

While the Poisson model effectively illustrates the mechanics of the reduced-form approach, it does not reflect the dynamics of credit markets, which are influenced by market-wide factors such as interest rates and inflation, as well as the contagion and feedback effects that stem from significant events.

A straightforward generalization of the constant-intensity Poisson process is an inhomogeneous Poisson process, in which the intensity λ is allowed to depend on time. If both riskless interest rates and the default intensity depend on time, formula (11.15) for a credit-sensitive pure-discount bond generalizes to

$$p(t,T) = \exp\left(-\int_t^{t+T} (r_{0s} + \lambda_s)\,ds\right).$$

Similarly, formula (11.16) for the spread generalizes to

$$\operatorname{spr}(t,T) = -\frac{1}{T}\int_t^{t+T} \lambda_s\,ds.$$

The introduction of time dependence in a reduced-form model provides the flexibility required to accurately fit the spread curves corresponding to single names. However, greater flexibility is required to model credit markets. This is because, under weak assumptions, time-dependent Poisson processes are mutually independent. This is inconsistent with the empirical observation that there is strong dependence among firms due to common factors. This has led analysts to introduce reduced-form models in which the intensity is stochastic: it is allowed to depend on both state and time. This generalization provides the necessary flexibility—at the expense of substantial additional complexity.

In a stochastic intensity model,

$$p(t,T) = E\Big[\exp\Big(-\int_t^{t+T} (r_{0s} + \lambda_s)\,\mathrm{d}s\Big)\Big]. \tag{11.18}$$

Similarly, formula (11.16) for the spread generalizes to

$$\operatorname{spr}(t,T) = -\frac{1}{T}\log\Big(E\Big[\exp\Big(\int_t^{t+T} \lambda_s\,\mathrm{d}s\Big)\Big]\Big). \tag{11.19}$$

A very broad, tractable, and widely used class of stochastic intensity models are the affine models. Here, the intensity λ is an affine function of a vector of stochastic state variables whose conditional transform takes an affine exponential form. A survey article on affine processes is Duffie (2005) and technical details can be found in Duffie et al. (2000, 2003).

Formulas (11.16) and (11.19) highlight one of the strengths of reduced-form models relative to the structural models described above. For short horizons T, and even in the limit as T tends to zero, the Poisson model spread is positive. This is typical of reduced-form models, and it allows them to be calibrated accurately to fit empirical credit market observations.

11.4.2.2 Reduced-Form Models and the Physical Probability of Default

The probabilities and intensities in the last subsection are adjusted for the risk premium. They do not represent physical default rates and probabilities, but they can be used directly for the valuation of default-sensitive securities. A measure change from the risk-neutral to the physical probability measure results in a distinct specification for the intensity. There can be a substantial qualitative difference between equivalent physical and risk-adjusted intensities, as shown by Kusuoka (1999).

Berndt et al. (2005) use a reduced-form approach to estimate the credit risk premium. Their study begins with KMV's expected default frequencies (EDFs), which are estimates of the physical five-year probability of default. They use these data to back out implied five-year default (physical) intensities,[7] and compare these to risk-adjusted default intensities estimated from over 180,000 quotes from the default swap market. The authors find that over time, there is significant variation in the credit risk premium and that expected default frequencies explain roughly 74% of the variation in default swap spreads.

11.4.3 Hybrid Models and Incomplete Information

One component of credit risk stems from the difference between the information available to corporate insiders and that available to outside investors. This has led to the development of incomplete-information models, which account for the resolution of information available to investors.[8] In the context of credit, the assumption of incomplete information is very powerful: it leads to hybrid models that incorporate the strengths of structural and reduced-form models while avoiding some of their shortcomings (see Goldberg 2004).

In a seminal paper Duffie and Lando (2001) introduce the first incomplete-information model. In concept, it is a structural first-passage model analogous to that developed by Black and Cox (1976). It is augmented with the economically sound assumption that investors have access only to noisy accounting information. Mathematically, this assumption renders firm value unobservable, and it has the implicit effect of determining a model intensity (which may depend on state). In particular, the Duffie and Lando (2001) model is a structural/reduced-form hybrid that can be calibrated to both equity and credit markets. In contrast to the reduced-form models described above, the intensity in Duffie and Lando (2001) is endogenously specified.

Giesecke (2006) develops a class of incomplete-information models that generalizes Duffie and Lando (2001). A principal contribution of this article is to shift the focus from intensity λ to the cumulative intensity, defined as

$$A(t,T) = \int_t^{t+T} \lambda_s \, \mathrm{d}s. \tag{11.20}$$

Giesecke and Goldberg (2004) develop a first-passage incomplete-information model in which the default barrier is not observable by

[7] The results in this article are empirically interesting and valuable in spite of technical inconsistencies in the methodology. For example, the structural model used to generate the EDFs is technically incompatible with the reduced-form approach. The incompatibility between structural and reduced-form models can be resolved by considering incomplete information, as explained below.

[8] A stochastic volatility model is based on the same idea: the information required to precisely determine volatility cannot be observed by investors.

investors. Firm value follows a geometric Brownian motion, which retains the tractability of the implementation in Black and Cox (1976). Similar to Duffie and Lando's model, this model is consistent with the positive short spreads in credit markets. It is a hybrid structural/reduced-form model in the sense that it admits a cumulative intensity. Goldberg et al. (2008a) use this approach to generate model default swap spreads that are cross-calibrated to equity and default swap markets. In a companion article, Goldberg et al. (2009) test simple rich–cheap investment strategies based on the market-implied spreads and show that they generate positive returns even after adjusting for transaction costs.

In a brief overview, Jarrow and Protter (2004) compare the incomplete-information models described above and discuss the mathematical paradigm underlying their construction. The common feature of these models is that they have two underlying filtrations,[9] or information sets. The finer of the two filtrations includes all information that is relevant to portfolio valuation and risk measurement. The coarser of the two filtrations contains information observed by investors. In practice, observers have less information than they need, and the risk associated with that is captured by conditioning on the coarser of the two information sets.

11.4.3.1 Incomplete Information and the Physical Probability of Default

The risk premium in most structural credit models compensates investors for risk associated with fluctuation in firm value, which is modeled as a geometric Brownian motion. This specification neglects the risk that firm value will jump at default. This so-called *jump-to-default risk* has been empirically documented, for example, by Driessen (2005). Giesecke and Goldberg (2007) develop a two-factor model for the risk premium that is based on the incomplete-information model in Giesecke and Goldberg (2004). The first component is analogous to the risk premium in structural models: it compensates investors for risk due to change in firm value, and it is realized as an adjustment to the drift in the geometric Brownian motion that models firm value. The second component is less familiar: it compensates investors for jump risk, and it is realized as an adjustment to the distribution of the unobservable default barrier.

[9] A filtration is a time-dependent collection of sigma algebras that is typically associated with a stochastic process. The sigma algebra at time t quantifies the extent to which information can be discerned at that time. Further information is in Protter (2005).

11.5 Recovery at Default

In the event of default, an investor generally does not lose his entire stake. The magnitude of loss given default and the timing of recovery are both uncertain, and they affect the value and the risk profile of credit-sensitive securities. These uncertainties, collectively known as *recovery risk*, constitute an important component of credit risk. However, it is not possible to measure recovery risk accurately since there is no reliable source of data on post-default payments to bondholders. A standard proxy provided by Moody's is the market price of debt one month after default.

Credit models account for recovery risk in a variety of ways. One of the most common paradigms is to treat recovery as though it carried no risk at all. Some modelers use very crude recovery estimates, such as fifty cents on the dollar, and apply them uniformly to all securities. More typically, historical estimates based on sector, rating, and debt seniority are used to generate more narrowly defined estimates.

In credit markets, recovery is generally quoted as a fraction of par value, and these units are a natural basis for historical estimation. However, in a model that treats recovery as a risk factor, it can be more convenient to work in other units. For example, Jarrow and Turnbull (1995) express recovery in terms of the fraction of the value of a default-free bond that is otherwise equivalent to the default instrument. Duffie and Singleton (1999) express recovery in terms of the market value of the bond just prior to default and provide an approximate reduced-form formula that relates a credit spread, spr, to default intensity, λ, and recovery, R:

$$\text{spr} \overset{*}{\approx} \lambda(1 - R).$$

Altman et al. (2004) examine recovery rates on corporate bond defaults between 1982 and 2002. They document the inverse relationship between default rates and recovery rates, and they find that variation in default rate explains a significant portion of the variation in recovery rate at all seniority levels. This supports their thesis that recovery rates are a function of supply and demand, in which default rate plays an important role.

11.6 Portfolio Credit Models

A *portfolio credit instrument* is a security whose payoff stream is contingent on a credit event concerning a portfolio of firms. Index default swaps and CDOs are important examples. The value and risk of a

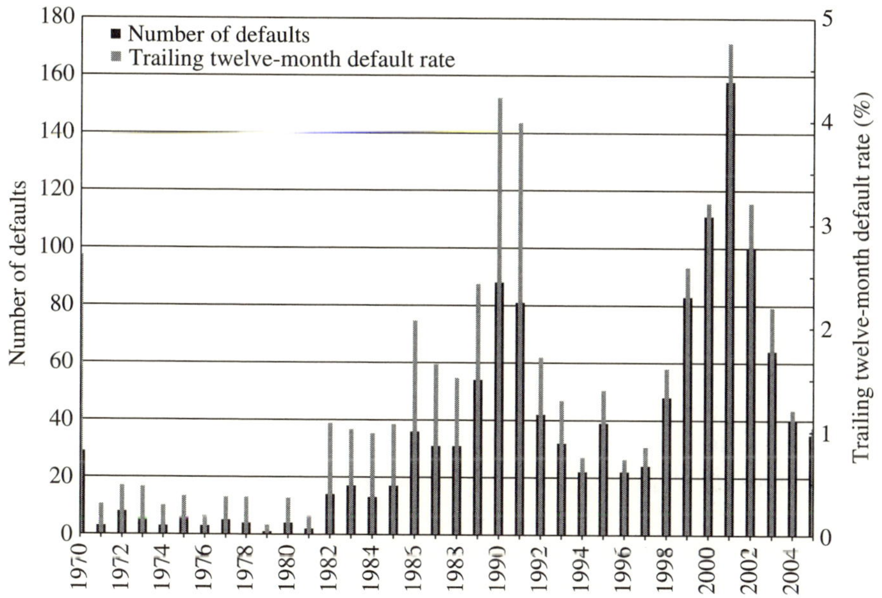

Figure 11.2. The number of defaults and default rates each year for all Moody's-rated U.S. firms.

portfolio credit instrument depend on the joint probability of default of the firms in the portfolio. If defaults were independent, then the joint default probability would be a product of the default probabilities of the portfolio's constituents. However, the empirical evidence indicates that this is not the case. Defaults tend to occur in clusters. This is illustrated in figure 11.2, which shows the number of defaults, by year, among Moody's-rated firms between 1970 and 2006. The distribution is irregular and there are prominent spikes in the early 1990s and the early 2000s corresponding to the collapse of the junk bond market and the internet bubble. The figure indicates a link between the state of the economy and default rates. It is also shaped, in part, by the contagion or feedback effects that stem from the complex web of counterparty relationships in the market. These contagion and feedback effects were a central component of the 2007–8 credit-liquidity crisis, as we discuss in the last section of this chapter.

Das et al. (2007) study default dependence among U.S. corporations between 1974 and 2004. They fit a Cox process to historical data and examine the goodness of fit. In a Cox process the intensity is stochastic, but it is conditionally independent. This means that the intensity does not incorporate feedback or market contagion. Using a battery of statistical tests, Das et al. reject the joint hypothesis of well-specified intensities and the doubly stochastic specification. This study and related ones have led analysts to investigate other paradigms.

There are two popular approaches to modeling portfolio credit instruments. The industry standard expresses the value of a portfolio instrument in terms of the values of its single-name constituents. This is a reasonable approach in light of the high degree of liquidity in single-name markets.

An alternative is to model the portfolio instrument directly and then to connect to the single-name constituents, for hedging and other purposes, in a subsequent step. The two approaches differ in conceptual and practical ways, and their strengths tend to be complementary. One of the most important distinctions concerns the input data. In the bottom-up approach, the identities of the defaulters are central, and there is a natural link to the copious data from the single-name default swap market. In the top-down approach the analysis depends only on the timing and magnitude of defaults. Defaulter identities need not enter the discussion. Top-down models naturally incorporate market risk factors as well as feedback effects that account for the clustering of defaults.

A comparison of the top-down and bottom-up approaches to credit modeling can be found in Giesecke (2008). Background on the top-down approach to credit modeling is given in Giesecke and Goldberg (2005), Sidenius et al. (2005), Brigo et al. (2006), Longstaff and Rajan (2006), Errais et al. (2007), Lopatin and Misirpashaev (2007), and elsewhere.

11.6.1 Credit Instruments from the Bottom Up

11.6.1.1 Bottom-Up Index Spread

A credit index is a portfolio of single-name default swaps with common payment dates and maturity and equal notional amounts. Let $t_1, t_2, \dots, t_m$ denote the lengths of time between current time t and future payment dates, and let α_τ denote the day count fraction of the τth period.[10] Suppose that there are n names in the index and that the index notional is I so that each name is allocated a notional amount of I/n. Let spr_j denote the time-t spread of firm j and let $\mathrm{Pr}_j(t,T)$ denote the time-t probability of firm j defaulting over horizon T. Then $(1 - \mathrm{Pr}_j(t,T))$ is the corresponding survival probability. For notational simplicity we will treat the riskless rate r_0 as constant over time. The premium from

[10] A day count fraction is an approximate time horizon that is given in units of years. It determines how interest accrues over time for fixed-income instruments.

holding a portfolio of single-name default swaps is

$$\begin{aligned}\operatorname{prem}(\operatorname{spr}_1, \operatorname{spr}_2, \dots, \operatorname{spr}_n) &= \sum_{\tau=1}^{m} \mathrm{e}^{-r_0 t_\tau} \frac{I}{n} \sum_{j=1}^{n} \alpha_\tau \operatorname{spr}_j (1 - \operatorname{Pr}_j(t, t_\tau)) \\ &= \frac{I}{n} \sum_{j=1}^{n} \left(\sum_{\tau=1}^{m} \mathrm{e}^{-r_0 t_\tau} \alpha_\tau (1 - \operatorname{Pr}_j(t, t_\tau)) \right) \operatorname{spr}_j \\ &= \frac{I}{n} \sum_{j=1}^{n} \mathrm{dv01}_j \operatorname{spr}_j, \end{aligned} \tag{11.21}$$

where

$$\mathrm{dv01}_j = \sum_{\tau=1}^{m} \mathrm{e}^{-r_0 t_\tau} \alpha_\tau (1 - \operatorname{Pr}_j(t, t_\tau))$$

is the price of a risky annuity called a dv01, which is a security that pays one unit times the appropriate daycount fraction at each payment day, as long as there is no default. This can be generalized to allow the riskless rate to vary by period, as long as interest rate risk is independent of default risk.

The premium leg of the index swap is the stream of regular payments equal to a spread, spr, times whatever notional amount has not defaulted at the payment date. Since the payment dates and the maturity of the index swap and the index constituents are perfectly aligned, we obtain

$$\begin{aligned}\operatorname{prem}(\operatorname{spr}) &= \sum_{\tau=1}^{m} \mathrm{e}^{-r_0 t_\tau} \frac{I}{n} \sum_{j=1}^{n} \alpha_\tau \operatorname{spr} (1 - \operatorname{Pr}_j(0, t_\tau)) \\ &= \operatorname{spr} \frac{I}{n} \sum_{j=1}^{n} \mathrm{dv01}_j . \end{aligned} \tag{11.22}$$

A no-arbitrage argument allows us to equate formulas (11.21) and (11.22), so that

$$\begin{aligned}\operatorname{spr} &= \frac{\sum_{j=1}^{n} \mathrm{dv01}_j \operatorname{spr}_j}{\sum_{j=1}^{n} \mathrm{dv01}_j} \\ &= \sum_{j=1}^{n} \omega_j \operatorname{spr}_j, \end{aligned} \tag{11.23}$$

where the jth weight is given by

$$\omega_j = \frac{\mathrm{dv01}_j}{\sum_{j=1}^{n} \mathrm{dv01}_j}.$$

Therefore, the index spread is a weighted average of spreads corresponding to single names.

11.6.1.2 Bottom-Up CDO Tranche Spread

As mentioned earlier, a CDO tranche is a "risk slice" of an index or portfolio of promised payments. A protection seller collects a premium, or CDO tranche spread, at regular intervals on whatever remains of the tranche's notional value. The fair value of the CDO tranche spread depends on the joint probability of the default times of the index constituents as well as on the timing and magnitude of recovery at default, interest rates, and many other factors.

The standard bottom-up approach to estimating CDO tranche spreads is based on a one-factor Gaussian copula model, which is described in Hull and White (2006). In this setting, the term structure of marginal default probabilities is estimated for each name in the index. The input data are riskless interest rates, market default swap spreads, and historical recovery estimates, which are usually broken down by sector and agency rating.[11] The joint dependence among firms is represented as a single average correlation. When this correlation is calibrated to a single tranche, it is called the "tranche implied correlation." A related value called a "base correlation" is used as a quoting convention for CDO tranches, much as implied volatility is used to quote index options. There is a large literature exploring the use of multifactor Gaussian copula models, as well as models based on more general copula functions. Further details can be found in Laurent and Gregory (2005).

11.6.2 Credit Instruments from the Top Down

The starting point in a top-down model is the cumulative loss process of a portfolio, or perhaps of the entire market. Consider a process L that keeps track of losses due to default for a portfolio of credit-sensitive securities. The process L is a pure jump process with a starting value of 0. Along each possible future path, L is constant between default events, which occur at unpredictable intervals. When a default occurs, the process L is incremented by a loss to the portfolio. As described by Errais et al. (2007) and others, many portfolio-sensitive securities can be described as derivatives on the loss process.

11.6.2.1 Top-Down Index Spread

We rely on the fact that the index spread is chosen so that the premium and default legs of the index swap are equal and, for simplicity, we assume that the riskless interest rate, r_0, is constant. The default leg

[11] Recovery is treated as a fixed value as opposed to a random variable.

of the index swap is given by

$$\begin{aligned}\text{default} &= E\bigg[\int_t^{t+T} \mathrm{e}^{-r_0 s}\,\mathrm{d}L_s\bigg] \\ &= \mathrm{e}^{-r_0 T}E[L_{t+T}] - L_t + r_0 \int_t^{t+T} \mathrm{e}^{-r_0 s}E[L_s]\,\mathrm{d}s, \qquad (11.24)\end{aligned}$$

where the second line follows from the first using integration by parts.

In the top-down approach, we take a slightly different perspective on the premium leg from the one in formula (11.22), where the single names play an explicit role. The key consideration is that the cash flow on a payment date depends on the spread and the nondefaulted principal but does not explicitly depend on any particular name. Therefore, we can express the present value of the premium leg without reference to issuer identities. To accomplish this, we introduce the random variable I that indicates the undefaulted notional at any horizon. In terms of this variable, and again assuming independence of interest rates and default rates,

$$\text{prem(spr)} = \sum_{\tau=1}^{m} \mathrm{e}^{-r_0 t_\tau}\text{spr}\,\alpha_\tau E[I_{t+t_\tau}]. \qquad (11.25)$$

Equating formulas (11.24) and (11.25) gives a top-down value for the index spread:

$$\text{spr} = \frac{\mathrm{e}^{-r_0 T}E[L_{t+T}] - L_t + r_0 \int_t^{t+T} \mathrm{e}^{-r_0 s}E[L_s]\,\mathrm{d}s}{\sum_{\tau=1}^{m} \mathrm{e}^{-r_0 t_\tau}\alpha_\tau E[I_{t+t_\tau}]}.$$

This form may not be tractable for a general loss process, but its general properties can be illustrated in a Poisson framework. Suppose that the defaults in a market follow a Poisson process N with intensity λ.[12] This means that at a time T in the future, the probability that there have been n defaults is given by

$$\Pr(N_T = k) = \mathrm{e}^{-\lambda T}\frac{(\lambda T)^k}{k!}$$

and the single model parameter λ is the expected number of defaults in one year. To keep the analysis simple and focused, we assume that recovery at default is zero so that the loss process L is equal to the product of the default process N and the notional I.

Then expected time-t notional is given by

$$\begin{aligned}E[I_t] &= I\Big(1 - \frac{1}{n}E[N_t]\Big) \\ &= I\Big(1 - \frac{\lambda t}{n}\Big). \qquad (11.26)\end{aligned}$$

[12] As we discuss below, this is not an economically reasonable assumption since the Poisson process does not reflect the clustering that is observed empirically.

Since

$$E[L_t] = E[N_t] = I\lambda t,$$

we get a top-down closed-form formula for the index spread at time $t = 0$:

$$\text{spr} = \frac{\mathrm{e}^{-r_0 T}\lambda T + \lambda(-T\mathrm{e}^{-r_0 T} - \mathrm{e}^{-r_0 T}/r_0 + 1/r_0)}{\sum_{\tau=1}^{m} \mathrm{e}^{-r_0 t_\tau}\alpha_\tau E[I_{t_\tau}]}.$$

11.6.2.2 Top-Down CDO Tranche Spread

There is an option-theoretic picture of the default leg of a CDO tranche that leads to a name-free assessment of its value. Let $\underline{K}$ and $\overline{K}$ denote the attachment and detachment points corresponding to a particular tranche. The protection seller is liable for losses to the index that exceed the product $\underline{K}I$ of the attachment point and the index notional, and that are no greater than the product $\overline{K}I$ of the detachment point and the index notional. In other words, the cumulative payments made by the protection seller to the protection buyer take the form of a call spread:

$$U_t = (L_t - \underline{K}I)^+ - (L_t - \overline{K}I)^+.$$

As shown in Errais et al. (2007), this leads to a straightforward expression for the fair value of the spread given by

$$\text{spr} = \frac{\mathrm{e}^{-r_0 T}E[U_{t+T}] - U_t + r_0\int_t^{t+T}\mathrm{e}^{-r_0 s}E[U_s]\,\mathrm{d}s}{\sum_{\tau=1}^{m}\mathrm{e}^{-r_0 t_\tau}((\overline{K} - \underline{K})I - E[U_{t+t_\tau}])}. \tag{11.27}$$

Even in the Poisson setting, formula (11.27) does not provide a closed-form formula for the tranche spread. However, it can be evaluated with transform and simulation methods. Further details can be found in Errais et al. (2007) and in Giesecke and Kim (2007).

11.7 The 2007–8 Credit-Liquidity Crisis

Starting in about August of 2007, global credit markets experienced a calamitous sequence of events sparked by illiquidity and price declines in the market for mortgage-backed securities. Panic selling, large upward jumps in credit risk premia, and frozen or illiquid trading in related markets led to numerous bank failures, massive losses in the financial services sector, and a global economic slowdown. See Brunnermeier (2008) for a detailed history of the episode. Credit market trading, which was the shining light of the financial services industry in the opening years of the twenty-first century, became the prime villain in the ensuing market collapse.

It is too soon for a definitive survey, but many of the early working papers on the poor performance of risk analysis models during the credit crisis argue that inadequate provision for the effects of information asymmetries and incentive misalignments played key roles.

A fundamental principle of capital markets is that increased opportunities to trade tend to improve economic welfare, since they allow individual risks to be distributed more widely. Credit risk trading has the potential to generate this type of economic welfare gain, since it allows individual credit events to be diversified more widely and evenly across investors. However, credit trading can also generate economic inefficiencies associated with asymmetric information and misaligned incentives.

We illustrate these potential inefficiencies using the influential Diamond (1984) model of a retail bank. In the Diamond model, a bank expends resources to learn about the credit quality of loan applicants and uses this information to differentiate between good and bad loan applications. The loan assets of the bank are backed by the bank's savings deposit liabilities. The bank's profitability depends on the difference between the realized revenues from its loan assets and the interest cost of its savings account liabilities.

Suppose that a bank can remove loan assets from its balance sheet by selling them. This is the *originate and distribute* approach to bank lending, which is now dominant in the U.S. banking market: the bank originating a loan distributes the credit risk of that loan to the broader investment community. Using the Diamond model as a base case, this has two effects. First, the bank's information about loan quality (which is specific to the bank and nontransferable in the Diamond model) is lost. Purchasers of the loan cannot differentiate between good and bad loans. This information asymmetry can lead to a "market for lemons" problem (see Akerlof 1970), in which the worst-quality loans are offered for sale. Second, it leads to an incentive misalignment. The bank no longer has a profit-making motive to expend resources in order to learn about lender quality, since the link between the bank's profits and the quality of its loan book is severed.

Coval et al. (2008) highlight the problem of undiversifiable model risk in the construction of high rated CMO tranches from mortgage pools. If the security rating agencies make small errors in the evaluation of mortgage default probabilities, and these errors are pervasively correlated across individual mortgages, then the safe-rated tranches of a CMO can have large errors in their estimated credit quality. It is clear, *ex post*, that the rating agencies did in fact systematically underestimate default rates for the 2007–8 period, missing a substantial decline in average loan quality.

Crouhy et al. (2008) cite a wide range of factors in the 2007–8 credit market failure, including lax risk-management and regulatory policies throughout the financial system, an explosive growth in very complex financial transactions, and a big increase in questionable lending policies by mortgage brokers that was not adequately reflected in banks' valuation models.

Franke and Krahnen (2008) identify misaligned incentives as the key source of the credit market failure; not only the misaligned incentives problem of mortgage originators and other securitized loan originators but also of traders and investment managers (including senior managers) throughout the financial system.

Brunnermeier (2008) provides a month-by-month account of the key events of the crisis, together with thoughtful analysis of its causes. He notes that it was both a credit and a *liquidity* crisis, since many of the feedback effects that led to the downward market spiral arose from market illiquidities rather than just from a tightening of the credit market. Brunnermeier stresses macroeconomic amplification effects, where relatively minor price declines or market illiquidities in particular submarkets can lead to panic selling and widespread losses throughout the capital market. He states, tellingly, that "the main disadvantage of securitization is that the transfer of credit risk distances the borrowers from the lenders." Indirect credit risk trading is particularly susceptible to liquidity problems due to this "distance" effect. Again, this links the crisis to information asymmetries and misaligned incentives, as mentioned above.

Notable by its absence in this recent literature on the credit crisis is much substantive discussion of the technical specifications of the credit risk models used by banks and other market participants. These technical credit risk models, with their underlying assumptions that markets will always function normally and prices will follow continuous time paths, seem largely irrelevant to understanding the crisis. There are many lessons to be learned from the credit crisis in the coming years. One important lesson is that portfolio risk analysis requires a balanced, multidisciplinary perspective, always skeptical of any one model, and avoiding too single minded a focus on technical details at the expense of the broader picture.

12
Transaction Costs and Liquidity Risk

Understanding and managing transaction costs is a critical component of portfolio risk analysis. Optimal rebalancing and hedging policies are heavily affected by consideration of transaction costs. Also, liquidity risk, which is the uncertainty connected to the ability to liquidate or rebalance a portfolio at a "fair price," is a very important component of portfolio risk, particularly during periods of market turmoil.

Section 12.1 provides some basic definitions. Section 12.2 discusses theoretical and econometric models of transaction costs. Section 12.3 looks at the time-series behavior of transaction costs and liquidity and their correlation with market movements. Section 12.4 considers optimal trading strategies in the presence of transaction costs and liquidity risk.

12.1 Some Basic Terminology

Markets for trading assets can take various forms: from decentralized search and negotiation (as for houses and used cars) to centralized electronic exchanges. Each market has its own set of rules that determine acceptable order types, priorities for order execution, and other attributes. We do not attempt to discuss all of these features in detail but instead characterize the main features that are common to most organized financial markets.[1]

So far in this book we have treated each asset price as having a unique value at each point in time. In fact, there are several definitions of an asset price at any time t. A trader may post a *limit order*, or *quote*, which is an order either to purchase or to sell a certain amount of an asset at the best price available, subject to a limit on the price. The quote specifies the direction of the trade (*buy* or *sell*), the *limit price*, the *size* of the trade, the *length of time* the order should be open, and other features of the order. For example, a limit buy order for 500 shares of XYZ Inc. at a limit price of $50.00 per share executes, or gets *filled*, if

[1] See Harris (2003) for a more detailed treatment of market structures.

there is ample inventory of XYZ at \$50.00 per share or less. A *partial fill* occurs if there is some inventory of XYZ at \$50.00 per share but not enough to fill a 500-share order. Note that both fills and partial fills may involve multiple trades and prices. The limit price is called a *bid price* for an order to buy and an *ask price* (or *offer price*) for an order to sell.

The menu of outstanding limit orders is called the *limit order book*. Ordering the quoted prices from highest to lowest, we first see orders to sell (ask prices) followed by orders to buy at lower prices. The total number of shares for which standing orders exist at a given price is called the *depth* of the limit order book at that price.

The *best bid and offer* (BBO) quotes are the highest bid price, p_t^{b}, and lowest ask price, p_t^{a}, in the limit order book. The difference between the best prices is called the *bid–ask spread*:

$$s_t = p_t^{\mathrm{a}} - p_t^{\mathrm{b}}.$$

Trades that are larger than the quote depth induce a less favorable price (a lower bid or a higher ask); the change in price in response to an order larger than the quote depth is called the *price impact*. Assuming no price impact, a round-trip purchase and immediate sale of an asset costs the trader the bid–ask spread. For a one-way trade, the relevant cost is half the spread. The average of the BBO quotes is called the *midpoint price*:

$$\mathrm{mid}_t = \frac{p_t^{\mathrm{a}} + p_t^{\mathrm{b}}}{2}.$$

The *proportional spread* is given by

$$s_t^{\mathrm{prop}} = \frac{p_t^{\mathrm{a}} - p_t^{\mathrm{b}}}{\mathrm{mid}_t}. \tag{12.1}$$

The proportional spread is a measure of the spread cost on a relative basis. The price at which an actual trade takes place is called the *transaction price*, which is denoted by p_t. In the simplest case, in which the market maker or another liquidity provider takes one side of each order and each trade is executed at the best bid price p_t^{b} or the best ask price p_t^{a}, we can view the historical record of transaction prices as a random sequence of bid and ask prices. It is important to note that this interpretation holds only in the simplest case when there is no price impact and all trades execute at the bid or ask prices. We discuss more general interpretations of the transaction price record below.

A *market order* is a directive to trade immediately at the best available price. For example, assume that there are limit orders to buy 400 shares of XYZ at \$50.00 and 600 shares of XYZ at \$49.98 and to sell 700 shares

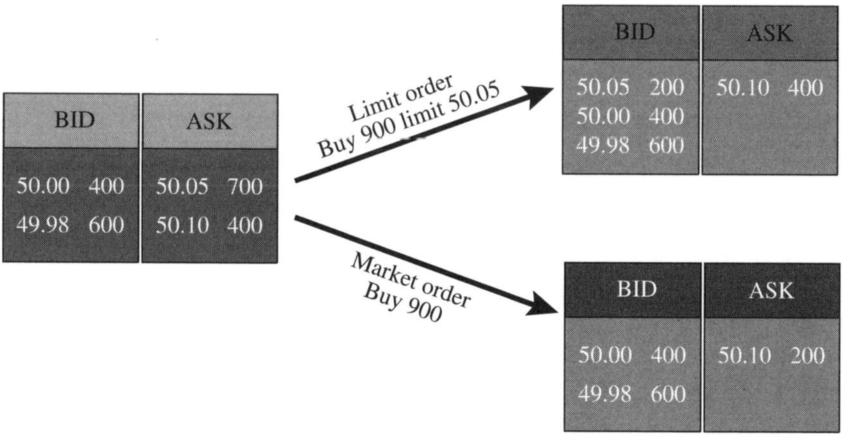

Figure 12.1. Changes in the limit order book due to different types of orders.

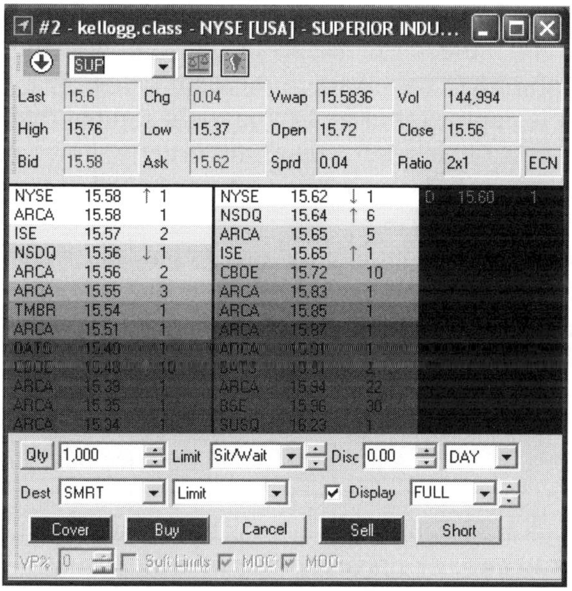

Figure 12.2. Limit order book for Superior Industries common stock.

of XYZ at \$50.05 and 400 shares at \$50.10, as shown in the left-hand side of figure 12.1. (There may be other limit orders further away from the best bid and offer quotes.) The quote midpoint is $\text{mid}_t = \$50.025$. A trader entering a market order to buy 900 shares would pay \$50.05 for the first 700 shares and \$50.10 for the next 200 shares, at an average price of \$50.0611, as illustrated in the lower right of figure 12.1. One measure of the cost of the trade is the difference between the transaction price and mid_t. For this hypothetical market order, the cost is

$$p_t - \text{mid}_t = \$50.0611 - \$50.025 = \$0.0361,$$

which is equal to half of the spread, $p_t^{\text{a}} - \text{mid}_t = \$0.025$, plus the additional price impact, equal to $p_t - p_t^{\text{a}} = \$0.0111$.

Some markets do not allow market orders. Nevertheless, a trader can effectively submit a market order in the form of a *marketable limit order*: that is, a limit order that crosses the order book. In the example above, a limit order to buy 900 shares at $50.10 is equivalent to a market order for 900 shares. However, a limit order to buy 900 shares at $50.05 is equivalent to a 700 share market order plus a 200 share limit order at $50.05: the first 700 shares would get filled by the standing limit order to sell at $50.05 and the remaining 200 shares will not be executed (since the next limit order to sell is at $50.10). The new best bid is $50.05 rather than $50.00, as illustrated in the upper right of figure 12.1. Figure 12.2 shows a snapshot of the limit order book for Superior Industries. Limit orders to buy are in the left panel, arranged from the best bid of $15.58 at the top. Limit orders to sell are in the right panel, arranged from the best ask of $15.62 at the top. The column to the right of the price column shows the number of shares for that limit order in units of 100 shares. The depth at the best bid is two round lots, or 200 shares, and the depth at the best ask is 100 shares.

The properties of limit and market orders tend to be complementary. For example, a standing limit order, which is one that does not execute immediately, supplies liquidity to the market since other traders have the option of taking the other side of the order at any time. In contrast, a market order diminishes liquidity by taking depth from the order book.

Similarly, the risks associated with limit orders and market orders complement one another. A limit order avoids price risk, since the order executes at the limit price or better. In exchange, it carries execution risk, since it is not known when, or even if, it will execute. In fact, a limit order generally fails to execute precisely when a trader would, *ex post*, have most liked it to execute, and it executes when a trader would, *ex post*, have least liked it to execute.

To illustrate, consider a trader placing a limit order to buy 500 shares of XYZ at the best bid price of $50.00. If good news about XYZ is released before the limit order is filled, the price rises and the limit order will not be filled, so the trader will have missed the chance to buy XYZ before the good news. Conversely, assume that after placing the limit order, bad news about XYZ is released. The price of XYZ drops and the order will be filled (assuming the trader did not cancel the order in time). Why, then, does a trader place a limit order? The advantage of a limit order is that, conditional on execution, it is filled at a lower price (for buys) than if the trader had placed a market order (and at higher prices for sales).

A trader who needs to execute immediately submits a market order or marketable limit order. The cost is paying a higher price (or receiving a lower price), relative to a limit order trader, in the form of a bid–ask spread and/or price impact. A market order carries price risk, since it is not guaranteed a set price. However, it avoids execution risk, since there is no uncertainty related to execution timing or execution failure.

For markets without organized exchanges, like over-the-counter (OTC) or negotiated markets, analogs to bid and ask prices and limit order books exist. In an OTC market different dealers may quote different prices for a given asset. An agent wishing to trade an asset will generally contact a number of dealers to obtain quotes. The lowest offer to sell and the highest bid to buy correspond to the observed best bid and offer. There may be undisplayed liquidity in the market if other dealers exist that have not been contacted by the agent. Thus, it is generally impossible to see the entire implicit limit order book in OTC markets.

A useful concept is the *shadow price*, p_t^*, which gives the fair-market valuation of the security, absent news about future trades. The shadow price is not directly observable and, in some cases, we use the midpoint price as a proxy. A *perfectly liquid* market is one in which the transaction price equals the shadow price at every time point.

Simulated or back-tested portfolio risk and performance measurement depend crucially on historical records of transaction prices. Implicit in many studies is the assumption that the portfolio manager can implement trades at the historically observed prices. Consider an analysis of the risk and expected return of a portfolio strategy. Typically, an artificial set of *paper portfolio returns* is generated by a historical simulation based on the record of transaction prices.

A common finding is that paper portfolios generated by historical simulation outperform actual portfolios, having both higher average returns and lower risk. This is true even in situations where the paper and actual portfolios are run simultaneously and therefore are not subject to in-sample overfitting. This difference in performance is called *implementation shortfall* (Perold 1988). Implementation shortfall is due to the fact that the paper portfolios typically assume zero transaction costs, no price impact, and infinite liquidity at the observed transaction prices.[2] In particular, the implementation shortfall is a measure of the disparity between the shadow price and the transaction price.

[2] Some exceptions that attempt to incorporate bid–ask spreads or price impact include Schultz (1983), Stoll and Whaley (1983), Ball et al. (1995), Knez and Ready (1996), Korajczyk and Sadka (2004), and Chen et al. (2005).

In addition to the transaction price, p_t, the transaction type (buy or sell) and volume play essential roles in the measurement of transaction costs and liquidity risk. An important quantity is *order imbalance*, which is the signed volume of a trade, $\mathrm{OI}_t = D_t \times V_t$, where V_t is the volume associated with trade t and D_t is an indicator variable equal to $+1$ for a buyer-initiated trade and -1 for a seller-initiated trade.

12.2 Measuring Transactions Cost

We consider two important facets of the cost of trading. The first is the *bid–ask spread*, which is the cost of an instantaneous round-trip purchase. Models of the bid–ask spread are generally based on a statistical analysis of transaction and quote data. The second is *price impact*, which is the effect of trading on price. We review several modeling approaches that depend on asymmetric information and adverse selection.

For both the bid–ask spread and price impact we discuss several measures that can be used when high-frequency data are available. We also consider measures that can be used in the more typical situation when only low-frequency data can be obtained.

The relationship between the bid–ask spread and market impact is complex and not completely understood. We provide some insight below in section 12.3.1, in connection with the analysis of the commonality of liquidity shocks to pools of assets.

12.2.1 Measuring the Bid–Ask Spread

12.2.1.1 Spread Measures Using High-Frequency Data

Quoted bid–ask spreads vary across stocks and over time. Figure 12.3 shows time series of the monthly average quoted spreads for stocks traded on the New York Stock Exchange (NYSE) over the period January 1983 to December 2000. For each month t, the quoted spread for firm i is defined by:

$$\mathrm{Qspread}_{it} = \frac{1}{n_{it}} \sum_{j=1}^{n_{it}} s_{jit}^{\mathrm{prop}},$$

where s_{jit}^{prop} is the proportional spread at the time of the jth trade of asset i in month t and n_{it} is the number of trades of asset i in month t.

For each month t, the market average (across firms) quoted spread is given by

$$\mathrm{Qspread}_t = \frac{1}{n_t} \sum_{i=1}^{n_t} \mathrm{Qspread}_{it},$$

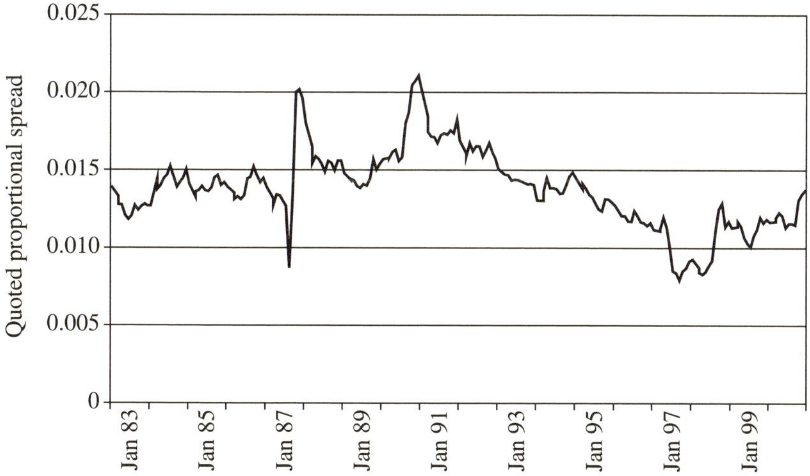

Figure 12.3. The time-series properties of the average proportional quoted spread, on a monthly basis, for stocks traded on the NYSE over the period January 1983–December 2000.

where n_t is the number of firms for which we have observations of Qspread_{it} in month t.

Over the period studied, the cross-sectional average quoted spread ranges between 0.7% and 2.1%, with a time-series mean of 1.4%. There are noticeable changes in quoted spread, particularly around the 1987 stock market crash: the months with the highest proportional quoted spreads are October and November 1987. There is a large increase in late 1990, and again in August and September of 1998 during the Russian ruble and Long Term Capital Management crises. There is a large decline in June and July of 1997 that coincides with the change in the minimum price increment for NYSE listed stocks from one-eighth of a dollar to one-sixteenth of a dollar. Between these periods of dramatic movement, there is a reasonable amount of persistence in the average quoted proportional spread.

While trades in many markets are executed at the quoted bid or ask prices, other markets have "hidden liquidity." This may be due to the fact that small limit orders are not displayed or because floor brokers may compete with market makers. In such instances, we may observe *price improvement* (see Petersen and Fialkowski 1994), which occurs when trades take place inside the quoted bid and ask prices. A measure of spread that takes price improvement into account is the *effective half spread*, defined as the absolute value of the difference between the transaction price and the midpoint price:

$$\text{es}_t = |p_t - \text{mid}_t|.$$

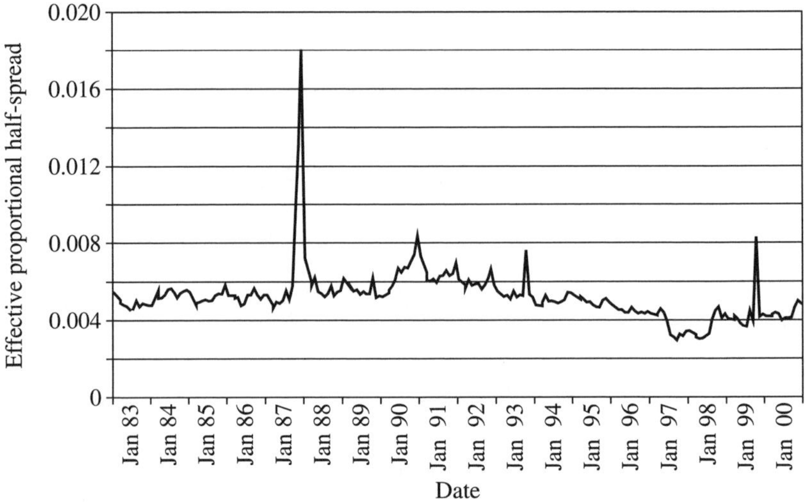

Figure 12.4. The time-series properties of the average proportional effective half spread.

The *proportional effective half spread* is defined as the *effective half spread* divided by the midpoint price:

$$\mathrm{es}_t^{\mathrm{prop}} = \frac{\mathrm{es}_t}{\mathrm{mid}_t}.$$

The effective half spread should be doubled before it is compared with a quoted spread. Figure 12.4 shows the time series of average proportional effective half spreads for NYSE firms.

For each month t, the effective half spread for firm i is the average effective spread associated with each trade of the asset within that month:

$$\mathrm{Espread}_{it} = \frac{1}{n_{it}} \sum_{j=1}^{n_{it}} \mathrm{es}_{jit}^{\mathrm{prop}},$$

where $\mathrm{es}_{jit}^{\mathrm{prop}}$ is the proportional effective spread for the jth trade of asset i in month t.

As above, we calculate the market average effective half spread by averaging cross-sectionally:

$$\mathrm{Espread}_t = \frac{1}{n_t} \sum_{i=1}^{n_t} \mathrm{Espread}_{it},$$

where n_t is the number of firms for which we have observations of $\mathrm{Espread}_{it}$ in month t.

Over the period studied, the market average proportional effective half spread varied between 0.3% and 1.8%, with a time-series mean of

0.5%. The average effective half spread is less than half of the average quoted spread, which is consistent with price improvement occurring on the NYSE. As for the quoted spread, there is a very large spike in the effective spread around the 1987 crash as well as an increase in late 1990 and in late 1998 and 1999. There is also a drop in June and July of 1997.

Schultz (2001) estimates effective spreads in the corporate bond market for a sample of 61,328 secondary market trades in investment-grade corporate bonds over the period January 1995–April 1997. Schultz regresses the difference between the trade price and an estimate of the prevailing bid price on an indicator variable, D_t, equal to $+1$ for a buyer-initiated trade and -1 for a seller-initiated trade. The regression coefficient yields an estimate of the effective spread. For this sample of bonds the estimated effective spread is 0.3%, which does not seem to be related to the credit rating of the bonds. The effective spreads are declining in trade size and are smaller for traders that are more active in the market. Note that an effective spread can be compared directly with a quoted spread, and it should be halved before it is compared with an effective half-spread.

12.2.1.2 Spread Measures Using Low-Frequency Data

The measures of liquidity discussed above rely on the availability of intraday prices and quotes. The estimators are data intensive and can be carried out only over the recent time period for which tick-by-tick intraday data are available.

There are a number of liquidity measures that are based on daily data. For example, Qspread and Espread can be estimated using daily closing bid–ask spreads. Liquidity measures that rely on low-frequency data may not be surrogates for trading cost estimates used by traders with access to intraday data. However, these measures are useful to those interested in back-testing strategies over periods or in markets for which intraday data are not available. In this section we discuss some additional measures that can be estimated with daily data.

Roll (1984) suggests a spread estimator that can be applied in situations for which direct spread data are not available, but for which transaction prices are available. Roll shows that when the chances of transacting at the bid and ask prices are each 50%, the covariance of successive price changes is determined by the spread, s,

$$\operatorname{cov}(p_t - p_{t-1}, p_{t-1} - p_{t-2}) = -\tfrac{1}{4}s^2,$$

so that the spread can be estimated from the first-order autocovariance of changes in price:

$$s = 2[-\operatorname{cov}(p_t - p_{t-1}, p_{t-1} - p_{t-2})]^{1/2}. \qquad (12.2)$$

Even though the population autocovariance should be negative in the Roll model, sample autocovariances may turn out to be positive. A common solution in this case is to estimate the spread using

$$\hat{s} = \begin{cases} 2[-\widehat{\operatorname{cov}}(p_t - p_{t-1}, p_{t-1} - p_{t-2})]^{1/2} & \text{if } \widehat{\operatorname{cov}} \leqslant 0, \\ 0 & \text{if } \widehat{\operatorname{cov}} > 0. \end{cases}$$

The Roll spread estimator can be applied to intraday data but it has typically been applied to daily data.

Bao et al. (2008) estimate the negative first-order autocovariance, $-\widehat{\operatorname{cov}}(p_t - p_{t-1}, p_{t-1} - p_{t-2})$, for a sample of 1,249 corporate bonds from April 2003 to December 2007, using both transaction data and daily data. They compare $\hat{s}$ with the actual bid–ask spread on the bonds and find that $\hat{s}$ is substantially larger. Thus, the autocovariance-based spread measure seems to be estimating not only the spread but the price impact induced by trades that are larger than the depth at the BBO. Bao et al. (2008) find that the covariance is smaller in absolute value for larger trades, and larger in absolute value when prices are declining.

Hasbrouck (2004, 2009) derives a Bayesian estimator of the Roll model that imposes the prior that the spread is positive. This addresses the problem caused by positive sample estimates of the autocovariance of price changes. The model is estimated using a Gibbs sampler. Hasbrouck evaluates the original Roll estimator and the Gibbs estimator by comparing their correlations with estimates of Espread using intraday data. The study runs from 1993 to 2005 and covers 300 stocks, half taken from the NYSE and AMEX and half taken from the NASDAQ. Hasbrouck finds that the correlation between the Roll estimator and Espread is 0.88, while the correlation between the Gibbs estimator and Espread is 0.97.[3] Thus, the Gibbs sampler estimate seems to be a better proxy than the moment-based $\hat{s}$.[4]

Holden (2009) extends the Roll model to accommodate data on days for which there is no trading. (Certain data vendors, such as the Center for Research in Security Prices, use the closing bid–ask midpoint.) He investigates versions of the Roll estimator that substitute alternative

[3] The Roll, Gibbs, and Espreads measures are estimated for each security over periods of one year. The correlation estimates are from a panel: they are based on a data set whose observations are indexed by company and year.

[4] Estimates are available from Joel Hasbrouck's Web site at http://pages.stern.nyu.edu/~jhasbrou/.

estimates of the spread when the serial covariance of price change is positive. Holden also derives a set of spread measures based on the frequency of closing prices at alternative price increments. These "effective tick" measures have high correlations with Espread.

Lesmond et al. (1999), hereafter referred to as LOT, develop a measure of effective spreads based on the insight that illiquidity impedes trading. It is often the case that on days when no trade has occurred, the reported closing price is the previous day's closing price. Thus, the frequency of days for which the closing price change is zero is a proxy for the number of days without trading. The measure of total cost (effective spread plus commission) in LOT is derived from a limited dependent variable estimator. They show that the LOT estimator is highly correlated with, but smaller than, the sum of the quoted spread and commissions.

Chen et al. (2007) study the relation between liquidity and credit spreads in the corporate bond market. Their sample includes over 4,000 noncallable corporate bonds over the period 1995–2003. They estimate three alternative measures of liquidity: the LOT estimator, an estimator based on the frequency of stock price changes equal to zero, and the proportional bid–ask spread of the bond. They find that credit spreads are significantly correlated with all the liquidity measures for both investment-grade and speculative-grade bonds, except for the "zeros" measure for speculative-grade bonds.

Goyenko et al. (2009) compare the performance of a number of low-frequency spread measures by studying their cross-sectional and time-series correlations with liquidity measures estimated using high-frequency data. The measures studied include the Roll estimator and its Bayesian extension by Hasbrouck (2004, 2009), the Holden estimator, and variants of the effective tick measure and the LOT estimator. They find that all of the low-frequency spread measures are highly correlated with the high-frequency measures. The low-frequency measures that have the highest correlation with the high-frequency measures are the Holden estimator, the effective tick model, and a variant of the LOT measure.

12.2.2 Measuring Price Impact

12.2.2.1 Price-Impact Measures Using High-Frequency Data

Price impact can have either a temporary or a permanent effect on transaction prices. The distinction depends on whether the trade changes the market's assessment of the underlying value of the asset or merely causes a temporary price movement. In the former case, the trade reveals value-relevant information held by the initiator of the trade. We now consider the effects of information asymmetry on the costs of trading.

We begin with the model of Glosten and Milgrom (1985), in which there are two types of traders: liquidity traders and informed traders. Only market orders are allowed and there is one trade per period. Every trade is of unit size and is mediated by the market maker. The shadow price, p_t^*, is the valuation by the market maker before the time-t trade is observed. An informed trader knows that it is misvalued, say by ω. The market maker cannot distinguish between orders submitted by an informed trader and those of a liquidity trader, whose trades contain no information about the true value of the security. The market maker knows only the proportion, $\Pr(I)$, of informed trades and the potential mispricing, ω. Note that $\Pr(I)$ is also the probability that any given trade is an informed trade.

For simplicity, and in order to highlight the relationship between information and liquidity, Glosten and Milgrom assume that the market maker's inventory and opportunity costs are zero. It follows that the only role of the bid–ask spread is to compensate the market maker for the adverse-selection effect that arises from the presence of informed traders. The market maker sets his bid–ask prices, p_t^{b} and p_t^{a}, so that, contingent on a buy or sell order, the quoted price equals the expected value of the security, given the probability of an informed trade:

$$p_t^{\mathrm{a}} = p_t^* + E[p_t - p_t^* \mid \text{buy}] = p_t^* + \Pr(I)\omega,$$
$$p_t^{\mathrm{b}} = p_t^* + E[p_t - p_t^* \mid \text{sell}] = p_t^* - \Pr(I)\omega.$$

The Glosten–Milgrom model has the property that in the absence of external information shocks, the market maker's new shadow price, p_{t+1}^*, equals the previous transaction price, p_t^{a} or p_t^{b}. This has two interesting consequences. First, since the new bid and ask prices are bracketed around the new shadow price, transaction price changes have zero autocovariance: there is no bid–ask bounce in this model. Second, the model makes clear that the Roll (1984) autocovariance estimate measures only a component of the bid–ask spread: the portion due to market making costs and dealer monopoly rents. The component due purely to adverse selection (the component captured by the Glosten–Milgrom model) does not induce negative autocorrelation.

Both the Roll and Glosten–Milgrom models contain fundamental insights about the components of transaction costs. However, the Roll model does not take account of the presence of informed traders and the Glosten–Milgrom model constrains informed traders to submit a single, unit-size buy or sell order. Kyle (1985) develops an alternative model of the adverse-selection component of the transaction costs, allowing for varying order size. In the Kyle model, as in the Glosten–Milgrom model, a competitive market maker sets a price schedule as a function of order imbalance, subject to a zero-profit condition and to the market maker's inability to distinguish between informed and liquidity traders. There is one informed trader and a collection of uninformed liquidity traders who submit orders simultaneously. The market maker accommodates the net order imbalance, which is the difference between total buy orders and total sell orders. In the Kyle model the market maker's bid–ask prices take the form of a price schedule, with higher ask prices and lower bid prices for larger absolute order imbalances. An informed trader chooses the optimal order size based on the market maker's price schedule and the quality of the information signal. The equilibrium in this model is a price schedule in which the change in transaction price is proportional to order imbalance OI:

$$p_t - p_{t-1} = \lambda \times \mathrm{OI}_t\,. \tag{12.3}$$

The price-impact coefficient, λ, is increasing in the precision of the informed trader's information and decreasing in the volatility of the noise trader's order flow.

A weakness of some of the models we have considered is the lack of a relationship between order flow and bid and ask prices. Consider, for example, the Roll model, in which the market maker sets a fixed bid–ask spread to compensate for the risk of holding inventory of the security. Suppose that, by chance, over a particular time period, there is a large excess of sell orders over buy orders. Then, over that period, the market maker's inventory will grow. It seems natural that the market maker's risk compensation should also grow with the size of his inventory. Madhavan and Smidt (1993) develop a model with a dynamic correction for the effect of order flow on bid and ask prices. In addition to the Kyle-type information-based spread, the market maker adjusts the bid–ask spread dynamically in order to control his inventory position.

Trading a block larger than the depth at the inside quotes moves the price adversely, pushing prices up with a purchase and down with a sale; recall that this movement in price is called the *price impact*. In the Kyle (1985) model, the only cost that the competitive market marker faces arises from the adverse selection inherent in trading against an informed trader. In reality the market maker needs to recover other costs such as inventory carrying costs, back-office costs, labor, and clearing fees. Additionally, if the market for market-maker services is not completely competitive, the market maker may earn monopoly profits. Glosten and Harris (1988) develop a model of the bid–ask spread that incorporates both the adverse-selection problem faced by a market maker trading with informed traders and the non-information-based costs of market making. The adverse-selection problem leads to permanent price impacts as in Kyle (1985). In contrast, market-maker transaction costs lead to transitory price impacts that generate negative serial correlation in transaction prices.

Glosten and Harris also develop an econometric model to estimate the adverse-selection and market-maker carrying-cost components. Their econometric technique estimates the trade direction, D_t, for each trade and incorporates discreteness of prices induced by a minimum price increment, or *tick size*. Variants of this model that rely on a separate trade classification algorithm (so that trade direction estimation is not part of the model) are commonplace.

Sadka (2006) develops an extension of the specification in Glosten and Harris. Consider the market maker's expected value of a security, mv_t, conditional on the information set available at the time of a trade, t:

$$\mathrm{mv}_t = E_t[\mathrm{mv}_{t+1} \mid D_t, V_t, y_t], \tag{12.4}$$

where V_t is the volume associated with trade t, D_t is an indicator variable equal to $+1$ for a buyer-initiated trade and -1 for a seller-initiated trade, and y_t is public, non-trade-related information.[5] To determine D_t, Sadka classifies a trade whose price is above the midpoint of the quoted bid and ask prices as being buyer initiated and a trade whose price is below the midpoint as being seller initiated. A trade whose price is at the midpoint is discarded from the estimation.

Glosten and Harris (1988) and Sadka (2006) assume that price impact has a linear functional form. Huberman and Stanzl (2004) show that the permanent component of the price-impact function must be linear in order to rule out quasi-arbitrage opportunities.[6] Sadka (2006) posits four components of price impact: permanent and transitory sensitivities to trade type (buy and sell), denoted by Ψ and $\bar{\Psi}$, and permanent and transitory sensitivities to order flow, denoted by λ and $\bar{\lambda}$.

To estimate the permanent price effects, Sadka follows the formulation proposed by Glosten and Harris and assumes that mv_t takes the linear form

$$\mathrm{mv}_t = \mathrm{mv}_{t-1} + D_t[\Psi + \lambda V_t] + y_t, \tag{12.5}$$

[5] In this case, the market maker's time-t price, mv_t, takes account of a trade that has just occurred at time t.

[6] Since traders do not know their execution prices with certainty, a pure arbitrage opportunity is not feasible. Instead, they search for quasi-arbitrage opportunities, which are unbounded price manipulations for which the limit of the Sharpe ratio is infinite.

where Ψ and λ are the trade-type and order-flow permanent price-impact costs, respectively. Equation (12.5) describes the innovation in the conditional expectation of the security value through new information that is trade related (D_t, V_t) or not trade related (y_t). Notice that new information has a permanent impact on expected value.

The (observed) transaction price, p_t, can be written as

$$p_t = \text{mv}_t + D_t[\bar{\Psi} + \bar{\lambda}V_t], \tag{12.6}$$

where $\bar{\Psi}$ and $\bar{\lambda}$ are transitory effects, since they affect p_t but not p_{t+1}. Taking first differences of p_t (equation (12.6)) and substituting $\text{mv}_t - \text{mv}_{t-1}$ from equation (12.5) we have

$$p_t - p_{t-1} = \Psi D_t + \lambda D_t V_t + \bar{\Psi}(D_t - D_{t-1}) + \bar{\lambda}(D_t V_t - D_{t-1}V_{t-1}) + y_t, \tag{12.7}$$

where y_t is the unobservable residual due to non-trade-related information.

Equation (12.7) allows us to interpret the model parameters Ψ and λ as the sensitivities of price to trade type and order flow. Similarly, the model parameters $\bar{\Psi}$ and $\bar{\lambda}$ are the sensitivities of price to *change* in trade type and *change* in order flow. Equation (12.7) assumes that the market maker revises expectations according to the total order flow observed at time t. However, there is documented predictability in order flow (Hasbrouck 1991a,b; Foster and Viswanathan 1993). For example, breaking large trades into smaller trades to reduce price impact creates autocorrelation in order flow. The value-relevant equation (12.7) is adjusted to account for the predictability in order flow. In particular, the market maker is assumed to revise the conditional expectation of the security value according to only the *unanticipated* order flow rather than the entire order flow at time t. The unanticipated order flow, denoted by $\varepsilon_{\lambda,t}$, is calculated as the fitted error term from a five-lag autoregression of order flow, $D_t \times V_t$ (after computing $\varepsilon_{\lambda,t}$, the unanticipated sign of the order flow, $\varepsilon_{\Psi,t}$, is calculated while imposing normality of the error term, $\varepsilon_{\lambda,t}$ (see Sadka (2006) for more details)). Therefore, equation (12.7) translates to

$$p_t - p_{t-1} = \Psi\varepsilon_{\Psi,t} + \lambda\varepsilon_{\lambda,t} + \bar{\Psi}(D_t - D_{t-1}) + \bar{\lambda}(D_t V_t - D_{t-1}V_{t-1}) + y_t. \tag{12.8}$$

Somewhat counterintuitively, the empirical literature documents an inverse relationship between the permanent order-flow sensitivity, λ, and the size of the order block. This is probably due to the fact that information about the block reaches the market in advance of the actual trade (Nelling 2003). Therefore, the block trade appears to have a small price impact when price change is measured relative to the previous trade. In

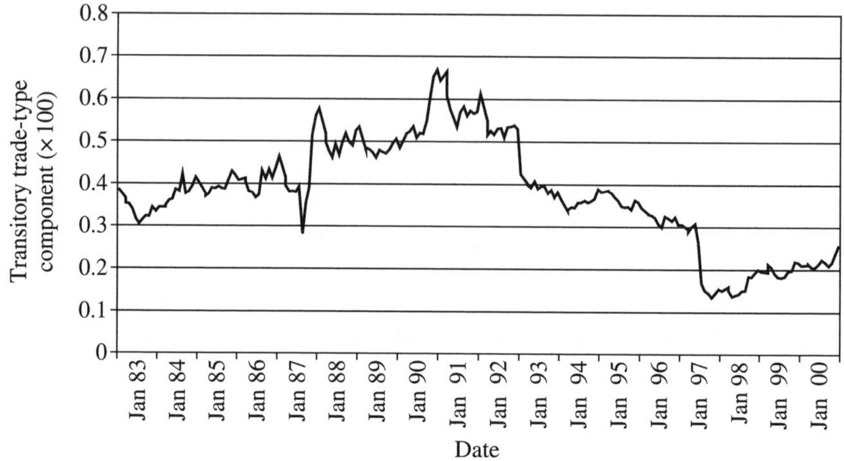

Figure 12.5. A plot of the monthly average of the transitory trade-type component of the bid–ask spread expressed as a percentage of the beginning-of-month price.

light of this, Sadka segregates block trades (trades above 10,000 shares) in the estimation. The model in equation (12.8) is estimated separately for each stock every month using ordinary least squares (including an intercept). In Glosten and Harris the primary parameters of the model are the transitory trade-type sensitivity and the permanent order-flow sensitivity. These are generally interpreted as the components of price change due to market-making costs and adverse selection. We focus on these two components of price impact here.

Figure 12.5 is a plot of the monthly average of the transitory component expressed as a percentage of the beginning-of-month price. From equation (12.6), this component is essentially half of the effective bid–ask spread. Because of this we would expect $\bar{\Psi}/p$ to behave much like the proportional spread measures discussed above. Indeed, the transitory sensitivity behaves very much like the quoted spread measure, except that it is, on average, smaller. This is to be expected since (a) $\bar{\Psi}/p$ is a half-spread measure while Qspread measures the full spread and (b) $\bar{\Psi}/p$ measures an effective spread while Qspread is a quoted spread. The transitory component, $\bar{\Psi}/p$, behaves like the effective spread measure, Espread, with the exception that Espread has a more pronounced peak during the crash of 1987.

Figure 12.6 is a plot of the monthly average of the permanent component expressed as a percentage of the beginning of month price. The quantity λ/p shows large jumps around the 1987 crash and the 1998 Long Term Capital Management and Russian ruble crisis. There are also

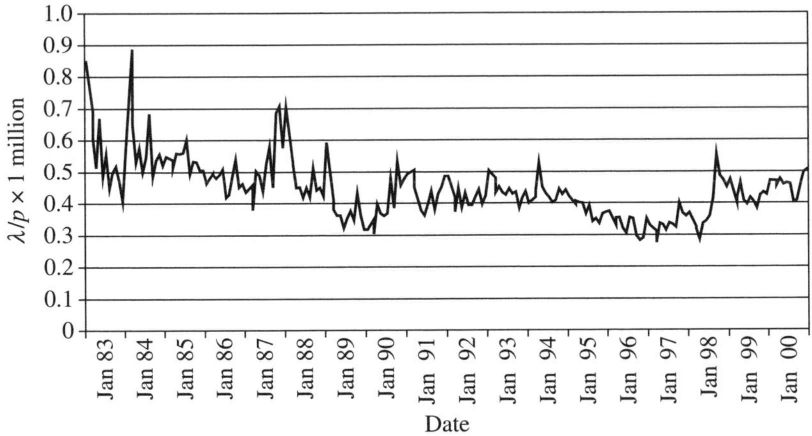

Figure 12.6. A plot of the monthly average of the permanent order-flow component of the bid–ask spread expressed as a percentage of the beginning-of-month price.

some large spikes in February 1983 and February 1984, which are more difficult to explain.

The Kyle (1985) and Glosten and Harris price-impact measures require transaction prices and a method of classifying trades as buyer initiated or seller initiated. Typically, trade classification algorithms use quote and transaction price data and do not require depth data. In markets for which it is possible to observe the limit order book, we can measure the price impact for a hypothetical trade by calculating the average price paid to fill the order by placing one market order and sweeping through the limit order book. Farmer et al. (2004) and Burghardt et al. (2006) calculate such "sweep-to-fill" price-impact measures for individual equities and E-mini S&P futures contracts, respectively.

12.2.2.2 *Price-Impact Measures Using Low Frequency Data*

Amihud (2002) considers the average daily ratio of the absolute value of stock return to dollar volume. Amihud argues that this measure "can be interpreted as the daily price response associated with one dollar of trading volume, thus serving as a rough measure of price impact." In a Kyle-type model, the average ratio of price change to order imbalance converges to the price-impact coefficient. Using the absolute return in the Amihud measure replaces the numerator and denominator with quantities that are upward biased. If the price change is due to information revealed by the order imbalance and to other news, then price changes are given by the Kyle model (12.3) plus non-trade-related news:

$$p_t - p_{t-1} = \lambda \times \mathrm{OI}_t + \varepsilon_t, \tag{12.9}$$

where ε_t represents the price reaction to non-order-related news. Thus, assuming that $E(\varepsilon_t)$ and $E(\mathrm{OI}_t)$ equal zero, the average ratio of the absolute price change to the absolute order imbalance converges to

$$\sqrt{\lambda^2 + \frac{\sigma_\epsilon^2}{\sigma_{\mathrm{OI}}^2}},$$

which is larger than λ unless the variance of ε is zero. However, the denominator in the Amihud measure is not the absolute value of OI but is instead the dollar volume. Since OI equals buyer-initiated volume minus seller-initiated volume while volume is the sum of the two, the Amihud measure has a denominator that is larger than the absolute value of OI. Since both the numerator and the denominator are upward biased, the net effect is indeterminate.

A positive feature of the Amihud measure is that it can be calculated using low-frequency data, whereas any measure using an estimate of the order imbalance requires intraday data. Figure 12.7 plots the monthly estimate of the Amihud measure, averaged across firms traded on the NYSE. For each firm the measure is estimated on a monthly basis by

$$A_{it} = \sum_{j=1}^{d_t} \frac{|r_{ij}|}{\mathrm{DV}_{ij}}, \tag{12.10}$$

where r_{ij} is the return on asset i on day j of month t, DV_{ij} is the dollar volume traded in asset i on day j of month t, and d_t is the number of trading days in month t. For inclusion in the month t sample we require asset i to have observations on $|r_{ij}|/\mathrm{DV}_i$ for at least fifteen days. The figure plots the cross-sectional average measure

$$\bar{A}_t = \sum_{i=1}^{n_t} \frac{A_{it}}{n_t},$$

where n_t is the number of firms for which data are available in month t. The Amihud measure has local peaks at many of the same times as the previous measures. However, the October 1987 crash stands out less prominently than it does for the other measures. In addition, the Amihud measure seems to have more month-to-month variability than the previous measures. Hasbrouck (2005) finds that A_{it} exhibits a large amount of kurtosis, so the high variability might be due to large outliers.

Downing et al. (2008) study the pricing of illiquidity in the corporate bond market using the Amihud measure and a variant that uses the

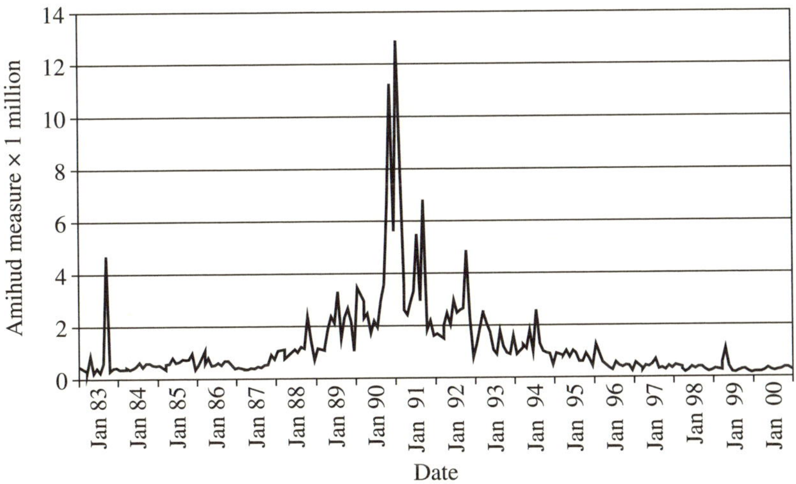

Figure 12.7. The monthly estimate of the Amihud liquidity measure, averaged across firms traded on the NYSE.

spread between the high and low prices over the observation interval instead of the period return in the numerator of (12.9). They find that the absolute level of bond liquidity as well as the covariance of bond returns with aggregate liquidity command a return premium in the corporate bond market.

Pástor and Stambaugh (2003) measure liquidity as the volume-related daily return reversal, γ, in the regression

$$r^a_{ij+1t} = \theta_{it} + \varphi_{it} r_{ijt} + \gamma_{it}\,\mathrm{sign}(r^a_{ijt})\,\mathrm{DV}_{ijt} + \varepsilon_{ij+1t},$$

where $r^a_{ijt} = r_{ijt} - r_{mjt}$, r_{ijt} and r_{mjt} are the returns on asset i and the market portfolio, m, respectively, on day j of month t, and DV_{ijt} is the dollar volume traded in asset i on day j of month t. The coefficient γ is expected to be negative since large volume on day j will lead to temporary price movements that will reverse themselves on day $j+1$. Pástor and Stambaugh (2003) scale the average values of the volume-related return reversals,

$$\hat{\gamma}_t = \frac{1}{n_t}\sum_{i=1}^{n_t} \hat{\gamma}_{it},$$

by the market capitalization of firms in month t relative to the market capitalization of firms in August 1962 (the beginning of their sample period). This yields an estimate

$$\hat{\gamma}^*_t = \hat{\gamma}_t \times \frac{\mathrm{mc}_t}{\mathrm{mc}_0},$$

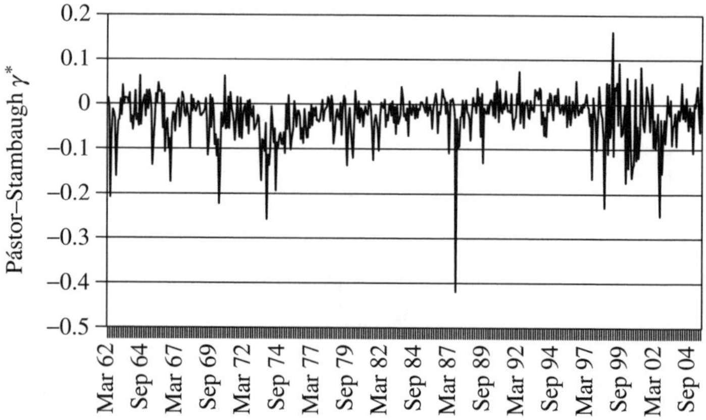

Figure 12.8. Pástor–Stambaugh γ^*.

where mc_t is the aggregate market capitalization of firms in their sample in month t. Their aggregate series, plotted in figure 12.8, shows pronounced declines in liquidity around the 1987 crash, the Long Term Capital Management and Russian ruble crises, and the 1973 oil embargo.

Goyenko et al. (2009) compare the performance of a number of low-frequency price-impact measures by studying their cross-sectional and time-series correlations with liquidity measures estimated using high-frequency data. The measures studied include A_{it}, the Amihud (2002) measure, γ from Pástor and Stambaugh (2003), and the Amivest liquidity ratio, which is constructed from $\text{DV}_{ij}/|r_{ij}|$, the inverse of the variable used in A_{it}. They find that A_{it} has significant correlation with the high-frequency price-impact measures. The Amivest measure and γ are not highly correlated with the high-frequency price-impact measures.

12.2.3 Other Variables Correlated with Liquidity

A number of variables are correlated with the level of an asset's liquidity. It is natural to expect liquid assets to have high turnover (volume divided by the number of units outstanding). For each stock i, turnover for month t is defined as

$$\text{Turnover}_{it} = \sum_{j=1}^{d_t} \frac{V_{ij}}{\text{SO}_{it}}, \tag{12.11}$$

where Turnover_{it} is the turnover in asset i for month t, V_{ij} is the trading volume in asset i for day j, d_t is the number of trading days in month t, and SO_{it} is the number of shares outstanding for asset i in month t. The cross-sectional average of Turnover_{it} gives us a measure of market-wide turnover. Figure 12.9 plots average monthly turnover for NYSE stocks.

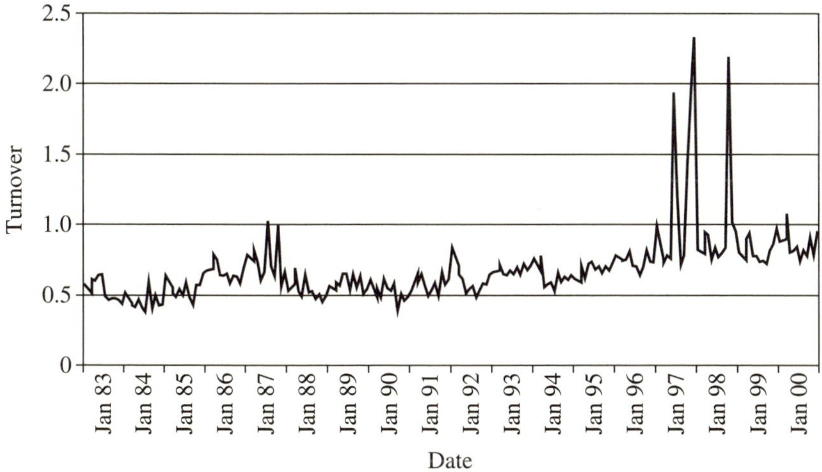

Figure 12.9. Plot of the average monthly turnover for NYSE stocks, defined as volume divided by shares outstanding.

While cross-sectional differences in average turnover are likely to be correlated with cross-sectional differences in liquidity, the time-series plot tends to show peaks in turnover when other metrics of liquidity are low. This occurred, for example, during the 1987 crash.

12.3 Statistical Properties of Liquidity

Many portfolio managers are subject to net investments that may be negatively correlated with both the portfolio return and the liquidity of the assets. In other words, they may experience redemptions when the assets in the portfolio are least liquid. Their portfolio positions and trading strategies should take into account the expected liquidity of assets as well as the risk associated with changes in assets' liquidity. The cost of liquidity in real portfolio trades is particularly large during market downturns, and this can be missed by risk estimates based on paper portfolio returns.

From a portfolio perspective, it is important to determine whether liquidity poses a systematic risk. An idiosyncratic shock to the liquidity of a single asset is less risky than a shock that affects a pool of assets. Additionally, it is important to determine the persistence of a liquidity shock. A shock that is transitory (relative to the flow of assets into and out of the portfolio) is of less concern than one that exhibits strong persistence.

12.3.1 Commonality of Liquidity Shocks

There are a number of papers that investigate whether liquidity shocks are common across assets. Chordia et al. (2000) find strong evidence of commonality across assets in liquidity, measured by quoted spreads, effective spreads, and depth. Their sample includes intraday transaction data for ordinary shares of NYSE firms over the year 1992. They require that firms be continuously listed over the year and that they have trading on at least ten days. They exclude firms who split their shares or have a stock dividend. There are 1,169 firms in the sample. They measure the common component by regressing daily changes in asset liquidity on changes in "market" liquidity, defined as the average liquidity across assets. While statistically significant, market-wide liquidity explains only a small fraction of the variability in liquidity across firms.

Eckbo and Norli (2002) take a similar approach at a monthly horizon, using turnover, spread, and price impact as measures of liquidity. They study NYSE, AMEX, and NASDAQ stocks over the period 1963–2000. Like Chordia et al., they find significant commonality in liquidity across assets.

Hasbrouck and Seppi (2001) study commonality in liquidity across the thirty stocks in the Dow Jones Industrial Average for the year 1994. Using high-frequency intraday data they find that liquidity measures, such as spreads, depth, and the "slope" of the supply curve, each have common systematic factors.

These studies and others provide clear evidence that most measures of liquidity have common components across assets. In addition there may be commonality across liquidity measures. This may be due to the fact that the measures are estimates of similar underlying quantities. For example, Qspread, Espread, and $\bar{\Psi}$ are all spread measures. Alternatively, the measures might estimate different aspects of liquidity that should, in theory, be correlated. For example, market-making costs reflected in $\bar{\Psi}$ should have an effect on the pool of informed traders, whose information precision is reflected in the permanent price-impact coefficient λ (see Glosten 1987). Korajczyk and Sadka (2008) estimate factor models for monthly observations on eight different measures of liquidity: the high-frequency measures of bid–ask spread, Qspread_{it} and Espread_{it}; the permanent and transitory components of price impact defined in Sadka (2006), Ψ_{it}, λ_{it}, $\bar{\Psi}_{it}$, and $\bar{\lambda}_{it}$; the lower-frequency Amihud (2002) ratio of absolute return to volume, A_{it}; along with Turnover_{it}. In addition to the factor models for each liquidity measure, they estimate a factor model pooled across the cross-sectional sample of stocks and liquidity measures. The sample consists of 4,055 NYSE traded stocks over the period January 1983–December 2000. For the eight liquidity measures, a one-factor model explains between 4% and 25% of the liquidity of individual assets, on average. A three-factor model explains between 12% and 55% of the liquidity of individual assets, on average. They find significant correlations between the factors extracted from the individual liquidity measures.

Liquidity is correlated with asset returns, as shown, for example, in Chordia et al. (2001) and Korajczyk and Sadka (2008). This implies that liquidity tends to dry up when asset returns are negative. This may be precisely when some portfolio strategies are forced to liquidate assets, thus exacerbating the liquidity problem.

12.3.2 Persistence of Liquidity Shocks

Monthly estimates of various liquidity measures generally show some time-series persistence, punctuated by occasional large jumps. We estimate first- and second-order autoregressive (AR(1) and AR(2)) models for several of the liquidity measures we study. The first-order autocorrelation of the measures ranges between 0.6 (for turnover) and 0.98 (for $\bar{\Psi}$) with the exception of the scaled Pástor–Stambaugh estimate $\hat{\gamma}_t^*$, whose first-order autocorrelation is 0.19. The same type of autocorrelation structure is evident in the factors extracted from the cross section of liquidity measures (see, for example, Korajczyk and Sadka 2008).

12.3.3 Jump and Event Risk

Figures 12.3–12.9 above show a high level of persistence in liquidity and also illustrate the striking fact that all of the liquidity measures exhibit evidence of large jumps. These jumps tend to occur during periods of market disruption. These disruptions include the 1987 stock market crash, the Russian financial crisis, and the period around the Gulf War in 1991. The Pástor–Stambaugh series also shows evidence of a shock to liquidity around the 1973 Arab–Israeli War.

It is clear that movements in liquidity can be correlated with asset returns. This is particularly evident during periods with downward jumps in liquidity, which are often associated with market downturns. If a portfolio is subject to redemption risk during such market disruptions, then there is additional risk induced by the correlation between portfolio flows and adverse changes in liquidity.

12.3.3.1 Headline-Generating Liquidity Crises

There is a large literature devoted to the analysis of headline-generating liquidity crises. Jorion (2000) chronicles the infamous disintegration of

Long Term Capital Management in the late summer and early autumn of 1998. This crisis, coupled with the contemporaneous ruble default, led to months of market decline and high volatility. Many believe that without the intervention of the Federal Reserve Bank of New York, the Long Term Capital Management crisis might have destroyed the world's financial systems. While spokespersons for Long Term Capital Management ascribe the fund's failure to events that were "beyond the fund's capacity to anticipate," Jorion asserts that the fund "severely underestimated its risk" and that "even if it had measured its risk correctly, the firm failed to manage its risk properly." Jorion explains how Long Term Capital Management failed to account for the dynamics of risk, described in chapter 9, using data from a lower-volatility regime to make forecasts in a higher-volatility regime. Furthermore, they ignored the asymmetric and heavy-tailed profiles of the loss distributions of their exotic, highly levered portfolio. These aspects of risk are described in chapter 10. Finally, when Long Term Capital Management encountered its first big losses in May 1998, it chose to sell off its most liquid positions because they were expected to be less profitable at the time. The firm retained only its less-liquid positions while holding inadequate capital reserves.

The causes, and even some of the effects, of the 2007–8 liquidity crisis remain obscure, despite extensive inquiry and analysis. This may be attributed to the secrecy surrounding hedge funds and to the complexity of global financial markets and securities. One of the most striking features of the crisis is the spike in interbank lending rates. On August 14, the LIBOR rate climbed to a high of over 200 basis points from its normal level of roughly 50 basis points. A contributing factor was the realization by market participants that the risk profile of exotic derivatives, such as the CDOs discussed in chapter 11, might be poorly understood. This resulted in a loss of confidence that constricted major banks and may account for at least part of the atypical risk premium associated with interbank lending rates in August 2007. Michaud and Upper (2008) decompose the risk premium[7] on interbank rates into a sum:

$$\text{rprem} = \text{credit} + \text{tprem} + \text{micro} + \text{mliq} + \text{bliq},$$

where credit, tprem, and micro are premia for the risk associated with default, term, and market microstructure, and mliq and bliq are liquidity premia. The measure mliq uses the Roll (1984) bid–ask spread estimator, which is given in equation (12.2). The term bliq is a measure of market impact obtained by regression of return onto order flow. The analysis

[7] Michaud and Upper (2008) model the interbank risk premium as the spread between LIBOR rates and rates on overnight index swaps.

in Michaud and Upper showed that both liquidity measures increased dramatically from norms of 1 or 2 basis points, during August 2007. The Roll measure mliq jumped to a high of 31 basis points, and the impact measure bliq jumped to a high of 15 basis points.

Many market-neutral hedge funds experienced substantial losses during August 2007, and quite a few went out of business. The opacity enjoyed by hedge funds precludes a careful analysis of what actually happened. However, Khandani and Lo (2007, 2008) attempt to reverse engineer the details using information from the Lipper–TASS hedge fund database and a simulation of a quantitative strategy. The authors posit that the turbulent market conditions generated margin calls that required many hedge funds to unwind their strategies simultaneously.

The events surrounding the financial market crisis beginning in 2007 were partly a credit problem and partly a liquidity problem. The housing downturn led to losses by holders of subprime mortgage obligations. However, as mentioned above, the opacity of the financial markets and the interlinkages present in them meant that it was difficult for any institution to assess the size of the risks to which any particular counterparty was exposed. This uncertainty led to the cessation of interbank lending due to the fact that it was nearly impossible to assess the credit condition of a given institution. The credit condition depended on the positions taken by that institution and on the soundness of all its counterparties, which, in turn, depended on the soundness of the counterparties' counterparties, and so on (see Gorton 2008, 2009).

The linkage between liquidity and opacity is evident in the comparison of equity and credit markets. The equity markets in 2007 and 2008 remained relatively liquid while the more opaque credit markets shut down in some instances.

12.3.3.2 Liquidity and Corporate Events

Liquidity can change around corporate events. It is often argued that stock splits increase the number of uninformed, retail investors holding the stock and, hence, increase liquidity. For some indirect measures of liquidity, there seems to be evidence to support this argument. Lamoureux and Poon (1987), Brennan and Hughes (1991), and Maloney and Mulherin (1992) document an increase in the number of shareholders, institutional ownership, the number of shares traded, dollar volume, and the number of trades following splits. Several authors find that more direct measures of liquidity decline after stock splits. Copeland (1979), Conroy et al. (1990), and Schultz (2000) find an increase in the proportional bid–ask spread after splits. Lakonishok and Lev (1987) and Gray et al. (2003) find reduced dollar market depth and dollar trading volume subsequent to splits. Goyenko et al. (2006) find that these declines in liquidity following splits are transitory and that liquidity increases in the long run for splitting firms.

There is also evidence that spreads and depth change in the period surrounding firms' earnings announcements. Lee et al. (1993) find that spreads widen and depth decreases in anticipation of earnings releases (see also Venkatesh and Chiang 1986; Libby et al. 2002).

The timing of some of these corporate events is forecastable and the anticipated changes in liquidity can be incorporated into the risk analysis of a trading strategy. Other events are unanticipated. The changes in liquidity due to these events must be dealt with after the fact. However, most event-driven liquidity shocks seem to be relatively short-lived, thus posing less of a problem for portfolios that can postpone trading.

12.4 Optimal Trading Strategies and Transaction Costs

Trading costs can be a significant source of portfolio risk and a substantial drag on portfolio performance. Schultz (1983) and Stoll and Whaley (1983) estimate the effects of commissions and spreads on size-based trading strategies. They find that transaction costs have a large effect on the profitability of small-capitalization trading strategies, particularly those with large turnover. Ball et al. (1995) show that microstructure effects, such as bid–ask spreads, significantly reduce the profitability of a contrarian strategy. Grundy and Martin (2001) calculate that at round-trip transaction costs of 1.5%, the profits on a long–short momentum strategy become statistically insignificant. At round-trip transaction costs of 1.77%, they find that the profits on the long–short momentum strategy are driven to zero.

The importance of incorporating nonproportional price impact into the analysis of trading strategies is increasingly apparent. Knez and Ready (1996) study the price-impact effects on the profitability of a trading strategy based on the autocorrelation and cross-autocorrelation of large-firm and small-firm portfolios. They find that the trading costs swamp the abnormal returns to the strategy. Mitchell and Pulvino (2001) incorporate commissions and price-impact costs into a merger arbitrage portfolio strategy. They find that the trading costs reduce the profits of the strategy by 300 basis points per year.

Lesmond et al. (2004) and Korajczyk and Sadka (2004) study the effects of illiquidity on momentum strategies, while Chen et al. (2005) study size, book-to-market, and momentum strategies. They find that trading costs have significant effects on the profits of the strategies they study. For example, while equal-weighted momentum trading strategies outperform value-weighted strategies before trading costs, value-weighted strategies dominate after taking account of the cost of the effective spread and price impact from a Glosten–Harris price-impact model (see Korajczyk and Sadka 2004). Korajczyk and Sadka (2004) also derive liquidity-tilted trading strategies. With a Kyle-type price-impact model and a number of simplifying assumptions, the optimal liquidity-tilted weights are proportional to value weights and are inversely proportional to the price-impact coefficient. Empirically, these liquidity-tilted portfolios provide superior performance after taking into account the cost of price impact.

A number of papers consider the problem of executing trades in a way that minimizes transaction costs. Bertsimas and Lo (1998) study the problem of minimizing the expected cost of executing an exogenously specified trade of size $\bar{S}$ over an exogenously given horizon. They obtain the best execution strategy as the solution to a dynamic optimization problem that is specified mathematically in terms of a transaction price process (that includes a random component and a price-impact term), an objective function, and constraints. The authors begin with a simple price process in which impact depends linearly on order imbalance and randomness is white noise. The change in price is given by equation (12.9). Bertsimas and Lo minimize the cost of buying $\bar{S}$ shares over the horizon $t = 1, 2, \dots, T$ as a sequence of orders. Their objective is represented mathematically as

$$\min_{\{\mathrm{OI}_t\}} E_t\left[\sum_{t=1}^{T} \mathrm{OI}_t\, p_t\right]$$

and it is subject to the constraint that

$$\sum_{t=1}^{T} \mathrm{OI}_t = \bar{S}.$$

Using iterated applications of the Bellman equation, the authors conclude that if prices follow the simple process specified in equation (12.9), then the optimal (lowest-impact) strategy is to trade an equal number of shares at every point in time.

Bertsimas and Lo consider price processes that are more economically plausible (and more complicated) than equation (12.9). For example, they consider an extension of equation (12.9) with a noisy, temporally dependent information term that changes the rate of trading. The linear price-impact term and price process are the same as in the equilibrium determined by the Kyle (1985) model. With the same price-impact models but with private information about the expected direction of future price changes, the optimal trading strategy can speed up or slow down trading relative to the strategy of trading equal numbers of shares each period. For example, we speed up purchases and slow down sales with a forecast of future price increases. Approaches to determining the optimal trading strategy corresponding to more general price dynamics and a nonlinear specification of market impact are derived and, in some cases, implemented. Bertsimas and Lo also consider optimal trading of multiple positions, taking into account the possibility that trades in one asset influence the prices of other assets. This is likely to be an issue for arbitrage positions in which some assets are hedges for others.

Bertsimas and Lo focus on minimizing the cost of the trade, given the exogenous constraints. Cost-minimizing strategies break orders into smaller components to reduce the effect of price impact. This exposes the trader to execution risk, primarily from two sources: (1) the equilibrium price of the asset may move adversely due to news that is unrelated to the trades being executed by the trader; and (2) the liquidity of the asset may deteriorate, making future trades more costly. The trade-off between execution costs and the first type of risk is studied by Almgren and Chriss (2000). Under assumptions very similar to those made by Bertsimas and Lo and using a price-impact function like that in Glosten and Harris (1988), Almgren and Chriss (2000) derive optimal trading strategies that explicitly trade off execution costs with the risk of adverse price movements when traders have mean–variance utility.[8] In their setting, the expected cost-minimizing strategy of Bertsimas and Lo is optimal for risk-neutral agents. Risk averse agents will liquidate the portfolios more rapidly initially, followed by slower trading. Similar results and a number of extensions are derived by Grinold and Kahn (2000), Huberman and Stanzl (2005), and Engle and Ferstenberg (2007).

In most of these analyses, the trading horizon is taken as exogenously given, but is unspecified. Huberman and Stanzl (2005) discuss the comparative statics of the determinants of the number of trades and the trading horizon. Empirically, most institutional orders are executed within a day. Breen et al. (2002) find that, in a sample of institutional orders, 92.5% are completed on the same day that trading is initiated. Thus, for most trades, the trader's horizon seems to be one trading day or less.

---

[8] The linear price-impact function allows for closed-form solutions, while numerical methods may be required for other functional forms.

With a one-day trading horizon, the trading strategy implied by quadratic utility, as used in Almgren and Chriss (2000), Grinold and Kahn (2000), Huberman and Stanzl (2005), and Engle and Ferstenberg (2007), implies a trading pattern different from the intraday pattern observed empirically (in Harris (1986) for example), where volume is high at the beginning and end of the trading day. It may be that the high volume at the beginning of the day is caused by traders following the optimal mean–variance trading strategy and that the high volume at the end of the day is due to some other type of trader (e.g., index funds that wish to trade at the closing price).

An alternative explanation for the observed pattern in trading volume is proposed in Hora (2006). Hora argues that mean–variance preferences over total execution costs induce a preference for early execution due, in part, to the manner in which the utility specification links risk aversion and the intertemporal elasticity of substitution (see, for example, Epstein and Zin 1989; Weil 1990). Hora specifies a cost function that depends on the implementation shortfall and its variance at each round of trading plus a term proportional to the squared unexecuted amount of the order. The optimal expected execution path is U-shaped, with high rates of execution at the beginning of trading and at the end of the trading horizon, similar to those observed empirically.

The papers discussed above analyze the appropriate trading strategy, given the order to execute a certain package of trades. Alternatively, one could consider the decision of what assets to trade, given a liquidity shock, such as a redemption by investors. Constantinides (1986) and Heaton and Lucas (1996) study portfolio decisions by a representative agent in which stocks are less liquid than bonds. The first-order effect is that investors concentrate trades in the most liquid assets, with infrequent rebalancing in the illiquid assets. Only when the agent's portfolio is sufficiently far from the optimum position (ignoring transaction costs) will the agent trade in the illiquid asset. This make sense from the standpoint of balancing trading costs with the utility loss of being far from the "optimum" position.

For institutional traders subject to asset withdrawals and financing risks, the strategy of responding to a liquidity shock by liquidating the liquid assets first has some associated risks, such as those discussed above regarding Long Term Capital Management. Selling the liquid assets first means that the remaining portfolio is less liquid. This might induce investors to "run" on the portfolio, lest they be the last investors left holding the least liquid of the assets. This problem is exacerbated if there are a number of portfolio managers holding similar positions and subject to correlated liquidity shocks. Their simultaneous trading may lead to large price disruptions (Khandani and Lo 2007, 2008) and a significant decrease in market liquidity (Persaud 2003).

Stress testing a portfolio under a variety of assumptions about correlations between trading costs, asset returns, and the trading induced by the strategy should give a better picture of the liquidity risk in the portfolio.

It seems plausible that many investment managers experience autocorrelated net flows into or out of the fund (e.g., a fund that has done well will tend to receive inflows while a fund that has done poorly is more likely to experience redemptions). Evidence of autocorrelated fund flows and institutional trading is found by Del Guercio and Tkac (2002), Campbell et al. (2009), Frazzini and Lamont (2008), and Lou (2008). With autocorrelated fund flows, following the optimal trading models in Almgren and Chriss (2000), Grinold and Kahn (2000), Huberman and Stanzl (2005), Hora (2006), and Engle and Ferstenberg (2007) may cause predictable price pressure for the assets held in the portfolio. For example, assume that Fund A receives a cash inflow and wants to buy shares of XYZ today using the trading strategy in Almgren and Chriss (2000). If Fund A also receives a fund inflow tomorrow, its traders are likely to want to buy more shares of XYZ, probably still using the Almgren and Chriss (2000) strategy. This implies that the fund will be buying XYZ more aggressively in the morning, both yesterday and today.

Heston et al. (2009) study the intraday patterns in stock returns by estimating cross-sectional regressions in which returns over each half-hour intraday period are regressed on half-hour returns j periods ago, where j runs from 1 to 520. The coefficient is negative for low lags, as one would expect given the fact that bid–ask bounce would induce a negative coefficient. However, at lags that are multiples of 13 (which corresponds to the same half-hour interval on different days) the coefficients are positive and statistically significant out to 520 lags (which corresponds to forty trading days). Thus, whether asset i had a high return in the 1:30 P.M.–2:00 P.M. time slot forty days ago has statistically significant explanatory power for its return in the 1:30 P.M.–2:00 P.M. time slot today. This periodicity does not provide an arbitrage opportunity, given the size of the bid–ask spreads. However, the periodicity might help traders time their trades. While there may be alternative explanations for this empirical regularity, persistence in order flows linked with trading algorithms might be the reason.

13
Alternative Asset Classes

Investments outside of the traditional mix of publicly traded equities, bonds, and money market instruments are generally referred to as alternative assets. These alternative investments include hedge funds, private equity, real estate, timberland, commodities, and collectibles. They pose interesting problems for portfolio risk analysis. While this is a diverse set of assets, two common features are low and unreliable levels of liquidity for the assets and limited information on transaction prices.[1] Some issues that are of primary interest in risk analysis of these assets are stale or smoothed valuations due to lack of current market pricing; style drift caused by the greater latitude given to some alternative asset managers; selection, survivorship, and backfill biases in available price records; and greater tail-area risk than is present in more traditional asset classes.

Section 13.1 discusses risk measurement for alternative assets with smoothed or stale price records. Section 13.2 discusses time-varying risk in alternative asset returns. Section 13.3 looks at return biases associated with incomplete records of transaction prices. Section 13.4 looks at measurement problems associated with infrequent repeat sales or large quality differences associated with different transactions—problems that plague collectibles.

13.1 Nonsynchronous Pricing and Smoothed Returns

Measuring the true risk of a portfolio consisting of positions in illiquid assets poses considerable difficulties. One problem is that the observed prices of various assets might be determined at different times. This is a variant of the nonsynchronous pricing problem discussed in chapter 2. A related issue is that the prices themselves may not be transaction prices but rather estimates of what a transaction price would have been if a

[1] Commodities can be an exception. One way to gain exposure to commodities is through exchange-traded futures contracts rather than through ownership of physical commodities. Exchange-traded commodity futures are often very liquid and therefore exhibit few of the measurement problems associated with other alternative investments.

transaction had occurred (when, in fact, a transaction has not occurred). In this case, the prices to which assets are "marked" may be appraisals, or interpolations between adjacent transaction prices. It is well-known that appraisal prices tend to be smoother than transaction prices (see Gyourko and Keim 1992, 1993). Most forms of price interpolation also lead to observed price series that are smoother than price series based on transaction prices. For example, a private equity manager may carry an illiquid position "marked" at the value implied by the last liquidity event until the next liquidity event occurs for that position (Woodward 2005). Thus, the imputed value of the asset might not change for months or even years.

This price smoothing leads to downward biases in estimates of contemporaneous covariances and betas and in the estimated variance of asset returns. It also leads to an upward bias in estimated risk-adjusted portfolio performance, measured either by Jensen's alpha, $\hat{\alpha}_w$, or the Sharpe measure, $\hat{S}_w$:

$$\hat{\alpha}_w = \bar{x}_w - \hat{\beta}_w(\bar{x}_m),$$

$$\hat{S}_w = \frac{\bar{x}_w}{\hat{\sigma}_w},$$

where $\bar{x}_w$ is the average excess return on portfolio w, $\bar{x}_m$ is the average excess return on the market benchmark portfolio, and $\hat{\sigma}_w$ is the sample standard deviation of the return on portfolio $\boldsymbol{w}$. Smoothing of prices does not lead to biases in average returns in the long run, so the standard estimates $\hat{\alpha}_w$ and $\hat{S}_w$ are upward biased due to the downward bias in $\hat{\beta}_w$ (assuming a positive market benchmark premium, $\bar{x}_m$) and $\hat{\sigma}_w$.

For most portfolios, the bias imparted by smoothing is likely to be an artifact of the propensity to overweight past observations when one is unsure of the correct valuation model. However, the incentive effects of biases induced in measuring performance by using contemporaneous moments of smoothed prices have not gone unnoticed. Weisman and Abernathy (2000) discuss the possibility of managers engaging in "marketing supportive" accounting practices by smoothing price changes, thereby increasing measured risk-adjusted performance.

Clearly, the issues of nonsynchronous pricing and smoothing lead to an underestimate of the risk and an overestimate of the risk-adjusted performance of a portfolio. When used naively, these measures will lead to over-allocation, in the overall portfolio, to these illiquid subportfolios. This would result in the overall portfolio having greater risk and lower liquidity than is optimal.

It has long been recognized that, even for exchange-traded assets, nonsynchronous observation of prices can lead to important biases in estimating the risk of an asset. Assume that we have daily pricing of assets at the reported closing price. For most data sources, the closing price is the last transaction price of the day. This transaction might have happened at the closing time or much earlier in the day. Assume that true asset returns are not serially correlated and that p_{it} and p_{jt} represent the (potentially unobservable) prices of two assets if they were traded at the closing time. Let p^s_{it} and p^s_{jt} be the recorded closing prices. Similarly, let

$$r_{it} = \frac{p_{it}}{p_{it-1}} - 1 \quad \text{and} \quad r^s_{it} = \frac{p^s_{it}}{p^s_{it-1}} - 1$$

be the returns calculated from the "true" and "observed" price series. We might consider estimating the covariance between the assets, $\operatorname{cov}(r_i, r_j)$, by calculating the sample covariance between the observable returns:

$$\widehat{\operatorname{cov}}(r^s_i, r^s_j) = \frac{1}{T}\sum_{t=1}^{T}(r^s_{it} - \bar{r}^s_i)(r^s_{jt} - \bar{r}^s_j).$$

The problem with this estimate is illustrated in figure 13.1. One asset, say i, is heavily traded and for this asset the last trade of the day is always close to the closing time. The measured return on asset i on day t, r^s_{it}, reflects the value-relevant news since the close of trading on day $t-1$. For asset j, which is much less heavily traded than i, the last trade tends to be much earlier in the day. The measured return on asset j on day t, r^s_{jt}, reflects only some of the value-relevant news on day t since the close on day $t-1$ (plus some news from day $t-1$). We would get a consistent estimate of the covariance between the returns on assets i and j from the sample covariance between r_{it} and r_{jt}, were it observable. However, the sample covariance between r^s_{it} and r^s_{jt} is downward biased (in absolute value) since this sample covariance picks up only the common movements over the overlapping time intervals. This implies that variances and systematic risk measures, or betas, which do not account for the nonsynchronous trading, will also be biased. The remainder of the common movement between the assets will manifest itself as cross-correlation between the measured return of asset i on day t and the measured return of asset j on day $t+1$. This suggests using autocovariances to correct the bias in estimates of covariances and betas that arises from using only contemporaneous returns.

Scholes and Williams (1977), Dimson (1979), and Cohen et al. (1983) propose methods for estimating systematic risk that account for the biases in the simple contemporaneous moment estimators. Scholes and

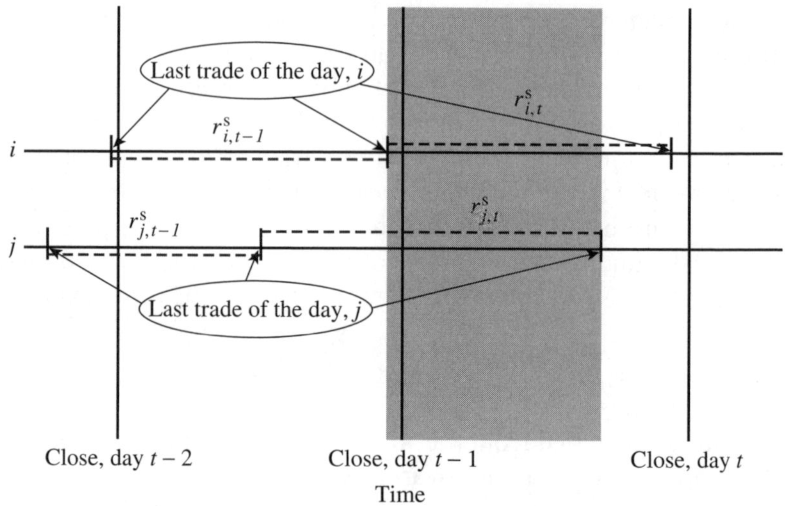

Figure 13.1. Schematic of nonsynchronous trading prices across two contiguous trading days.

Williams (1977) assume that assets trade each day, with last trades possibly at different times of the day. They derive a consistent estimator of an asset's beta relative to an index, m. Let b_i^s, b_i^{s-}, and b_i^{s+} denote the ordinary least-squares estimates of the slope coefficient in the regression of r_{it}^s on r_{mt}^s, r_{mt-1}^s, and r_{mt+1}^s, respectively. That is,

$$b_i^s = \frac{\widehat{\text{cov}}(r_{it}^s, r_{mt}^s)}{\widehat{\text{var}}(r_{mt}^s)},$$

$$b_i^{s-} = \frac{\widehat{\text{cov}}(r_{it}^s, r_{mt-1}^s)}{\widehat{\text{var}}(r_{mt-1}^s)},$$

$$b_i^{s+} = \frac{\widehat{\text{cov}}(r_{it}^s, r_{mt+1}^s)}{\widehat{\text{var}}(r_{mt+1}^s)}.$$

Let $\hat{\rho}_m^s$ denote the first-order sample autocorrelation of the return on the market index portfolio, m. The Scholes and Williams (1977) consistent estimator of the beta of asset i, relative to the market index m, is

$$\hat{\beta}_i = \frac{b_i^{s-} + b_i^s + b_i^{s+}}{1 + 2\hat{\rho}_m^s}. \tag{13.1}$$

The estimator incorporates not only the contemporaneous covariance between measured returns but also lead and lagged covariances induced by the nonsynchronous timing of the last trade of the day. Scholes and Williams show that the estimator (13.1) is asymptotically equivalent to an instrumental variables estimator (Greene 2008, chapter 12) of the regression of r_{it}^s on r_{mt}^s, where the instrument is a three-period moving average of r_m^s.

Even among exchange-traded equities, there are many assets that do not trade every day. This implies that nonsynchronous price observations may lead to cross-correlations at longer leads and lags. Cohen et al. (1983) extend the Scholes–Williams result to include N leads and lags. They show that if $N-1$ is the longest period over which an asset might not trade, leading to autocorrelation at N lags, then their modified estimator is consistent. Shanken (1987) applies the Cohen et al. (1983) model to the study of the covariance structure of asset returns, which is a primary input into a portfolio optimization process. The covariance between r_i and r_j is estimated using N leads and lags:

$$\widehat{\text{cov}}(r_{it}, r_{jt}) = \sum_{k=-N}^{k=N} \widehat{\text{cov}}(r^s_{it}, r^s_{jt-k}).$$

Shanken (1987) finds that the estimated covariance structure of equity returns is significantly altered by accounting for stale pricing. Shanken does not adjust the standard variance estimate since a pure nonsynchronous trading problem does not induce a large bias (see Scholes and Williams 1977, equation (6)).

A related beta estimator is proposed by Dimson (1979). Rather than estimating $2N+1$ simple ordinary least-squares equations and summing the coefficients, Dimson (1979) proposes estimating one multiple regression with $2N+1$ independent variables and summing the slope coefficients. Using observed excess returns $x^s_{it} = r^s_{it} - r_0$ and $x^s_{mt} = r^s_{mt} - r_0$ gives

$$\left.\begin{aligned} x^s_{it} &= \alpha_i + \sum_{k=-N}^{N} \beta_{i,k} x^s_{mt-k} + \varepsilon^s_{it}, \\ \hat{\beta}^{\text{Dimson}}_i &= \sum_{k=-N}^{N} \hat{\beta}_{ik}. \end{aligned}\right\} \tag{13.2}$$

While the Dimson (1979) estimate is inconsistent for fixed N (Fowler and Rorke 1983); the inconsistency seems to be empirically small and vanishes as N increases (Dimson 1985).

A variant of the Dimson approach used, for example, in Fama and French (1992) is to include only the contemporaneous and lagged market returns as independent variables. That is,

$$\left.\begin{aligned} x^s_{it} &= \alpha_i + \sum_{k=0}^{N} \beta_{ik} x^s_{mt-k} + \varepsilon^s_{it}, \\ \hat{\beta}^{\text{Fama-French}}_i &= \sum_{k=0}^{N} \hat{\beta}_{ik}. \end{aligned}\right\} \tag{13.3}$$

The Fama–French approach is useful in cases where asset i is likely to be much less liquid than the average asset in the index, m. This is likely to be the case if the asset is in the alternative investment class and the index consists of traded assets. In this case, including the future market returns is likely to merely add noise without any improvement in bias.

Smoothed asset returns and nonsynchronous trading affect estimates based on observed asset returns in different ways. Both induce cross-autocorrelations between individual asset returns and between asset returns and the benchmark portfolio returns. Both induce a downward bias in beta estimates for illiquid assets relative to more liquid benchmark portfolios. However, while nonsynchronous pricing leads to a small upward bias in standard variance estimates (see Scholes and Williams 1977, equation (6)), smoothing leads to a downward bias. Getmansky et al. (2004) present a model of smoothed returns in which observed returns are a convex combination of contemporaneous and lagged "true" returns:

$$r_{it}^s = \theta_0 r_{it} + \theta_1 r_{it-1} + \theta_2 r_{it-2} + \cdots + \theta_N r_{it-N},$$

with

$$\theta_0 + \theta_1 + \theta_2 + \cdots + \theta_N = 1$$

and $\theta_k \in [0, 1]$, $k = 1, 2, \dots, N$. If we denote the variance of the "true" return on asset i by σ_i^2, the variance of observed returns is equal to $c_\sigma^2 \sigma_i^2$, with

$$c_\sigma^2 = \theta_0^2 + \theta_1^2 + \theta_2^2 + \cdots + \theta_N^2 \leqslant 1.$$

Similarly, if r_{mt} is the return on a liquid benchmark portfolio (whose assets are not smoothed), then

$$\frac{\operatorname{cov}(r_{it}^s, r_{mt-k})}{\operatorname{var}(r_{mt-k})} = \theta_k \beta,$$

where

$$\beta = \frac{\operatorname{cov}(r_{it}, r_{mt})}{\operatorname{var}(r_{mt})}$$

for $k = 1, 2, \dots, N$. Hence, the Sharpe ratio is upward biased by a multiplicative factor $1/c_\sigma > 1$. Getmansky et al. (2004) propose maximum-likelihood and regression-based methods for estimating the smoothing parameters $\theta_k \in [0, 1]$, $k = 1, 2, \dots, N$, and β. The regression estimates of β are equivalent to the Fama–French estimates in (13.3).

For publicly traded assets, with nonsynchronous trading, the lead–lag horizon may be measured in days. For traded but illiquid assets, or for nontraded assets, the lead–lag horizon may be months or quarters. As noted in Woodward (2005), carrying private equity investments at historical cost between liquidity events implies that the horizon may be quite long.

Carrying assets at historical cost will lead to price behavior similar to that implied by the nonsynchronous trading literature, while the use of appraisal pricing will lead to price behavior similar to that implied by the smoothing models. Many real estate indices are based on a combination of transaction and appraisal pricing. These exhibit the characteristics of smoothed series (see, for example, Geltner 1991; Gyourko and Keim 1992, 1993; Healey et al. 2005).

Illiquid securities that are not carried at cost, but for which observable transactions are infrequent, are often priced by representative quotes from dealers. These quotes will tend to have the same characteristics as appraisal-based returns, particularly if the dealer knows that the quote is for valuation purposes rather than for trading. In these cases, the dealer has no incentive to devote large resources to ensuring that the quotes are based on the most up-to-date market information.

Another approach to risk estimation with stale pricing is to increase the observation interval, L, over which returns are calculated. For example, instead of calculating returns for a daily or monthly observation interval, calculate returns on a quarterly, semiannual, or annual basis. Let $r^s_{it,t+L}$ denote the observed return on asset i from t to $t+L$. As L increases the effect of nonsynchronous trading and smoothing will decline. Cohen et al. (1983) show that, for nonoverlapping intervals of length L,

$$b_i^{s,L} = \frac{\widehat{\text{cov}}(r^s_{it,t+L}, r^s_{mt,t+L})}{\widehat{\text{var}}(r^s_{mt,t+L})}$$

is a consistent estimator of β as $L \to \infty$. Some increase in precision can be obtained by using overlapping intervals in estimating β. In this case, consistent standard errors can be obtained using an autocorrelation-consistent estimator, such as that in Newey and West (1987).

Asness et al. (2001) apply the types of techniques discussed here to investigate the risk of the Credit Suisse/Tremont hedge fund indices. There is an aggregate hedge fund index and nine subindices (convertible arbitrage, event driven, equity market neutral, fixed-income arbitrage, long/short equity, emerging markets, global macro, managed futures, and dedicated short bias). Using monthly data over the period January 1994–September 2000, the funds exhibit correlations with the S&P 500 index between −76% and 60%, with the aggregate index having a correlation of 52% with the S&P 500. Annualized standard deviation ranges from 3.5% for the equity market neutral index to 20.8% for the emerging markets index. Using the standard contemporaneously observed returns to estimate b_i^s, they get beta estimates that range from −0.99 (dedicated short bias) to 0.74 (emerging markets), with the aggregate index having an estimated beta of 0.37. The standard approach also leads to (annualized) estimates $\hat{\alpha}_i$ that range from −8.38% (emerging markets) to 7.34% (dedicated short bias), with the aggregate index having an $\hat{\alpha}_i$ of 2.63%.

Asness et al. (2001) first study how estimated standard deviations and correlations with the S&P 500 index change as we move from $L = 1$ month to $L = 3$ months. For some funds, such as global macro, managed futures, and dedicated short bias, there is little increase in standard deviation. However, some indices show very large percentage increases in estimated standard deviation: convertible arbitrage, a 41.5% change from 5.1% to 7.2%; event driven, 28.3%; equity market neutral, 22.9%; and emerging markets, 28%. The standard deviation of the aggregate index does not change much.

The correlation with the S&P 500 index also increases. For example, the convertible arbitrage index's correlation with the S&P 500 increases by 77%, from 0.13 to 0.23. For every index except one, the correlation increases in absolute value. The aggregate index's correlation with the S&P 500 increases by 23%, from 0.52 to 0.64.

The authors go on to estimate $\hat{\beta}_i^{\text{Fama-French}}$ for the hedge fund indices using $N = 3$. The estimated betas increase in absolute value for all of the indices. The changes for selected indices are: dedicated short bias, 28% (from −0.99 to −1.27); global macro, 165% (from 0.37 to 0.98); long/short equity, 80% (from 0.55 to 0.99); event driven, 114% (from 0.28 to 0.60); and, for the aggregate index, 127% (from 0.37 to 0.84). It is clear that the smoothing in asset valuations leads to a downward bias in risk estimates obtained from the estimators using contemporaneous moments. This increase in estimated systematic risk implies a decline in estimated abnormal return, α. Using contemporaneous moments to estimate β, seven of the nine indices have positive estimates of α. Using the $\hat{\beta}_i^{\text{Fama-French}}$ estimator, only three of the nine indices have positive estimates of α. The estimated α for the aggregate index falls from 2.63% per year to −4.45% per year. It is clear from Asness et al. (2001) that the smoothing in asset valuations leads to large upward biases in performance estimates obtained from the estimators using contemporaneous moments only.

We have replicated the results of Asness et al. (2001) on an updated set of Credit Suisse/Tremont indices. The data are from January 1994 through June 2009. In table 13.1 we show annualized mean returns (monthly mean returns multiplied by twelve), as well as annualized standard deviations estimated using $L = 1, 3, 6$, and 12 months. The last four columns show the percentage increase in estimated standard deviation when moving from monthly to quarterly, quarterly to semiannual, semiannual to annual, and monthly to annual horizons, respectively. For two of the indices (dedicated short bias and managed futures) the estimated standard deviation actually declines as we move from monthly to annual observation intervals. This is similar to the negative or small positive changes found by Asness et al. For the remaining eleven indices, standard deviations increase as we move from monthly to annual observation intervals, although not always monotonically. The percentage increases for these indices range from 11% to 58%.

We also compare beta and alpha estimates using the traditional estimators and the Fama–French estimators. Since none of the beta estimates are significant for the third lag, we use $\hat{\beta}_i^{\text{Fama-French}}$ with $N = 2$, rather than $N = 3$, which is used by Asness et al. The results are shown in table 13.2. The first three columns show the α, β, and R^2 estimates using only contemporaneous observed returns. As in Asness et al. (2001), the estimated Fama–French betas are larger, in absolute value, than the standard estimates for all of the indices except one. The changes for selected indices are: global macro, 69% (from 0.16 to 0.22); market neutral, 155% (from 0.18 to 0.45); event driven, 69% (from 0.23 to 0.39); multistrategy, 71% (from 0.22 to 0.37); and, for the aggregate index, 63% (from 0.27 to 0.44). While the percentage changes are a bit lower in our sample, nine of the thirteen changes are statistically significant.

We find that measured performance declines for eleven of the thirteen indices. However, only one of the αs changes sign in our sample. This may be due to the fact that the average return of the S&P 500 index is larger in Asness et al. (2001) sample (1.73% per month) than in ours (0.63% per month). The change in alpha is equal to the change in beta times the mean excess return on the market index. Thus, a given change in estimated beta will lead to a smaller change in alpha over our sample period.

In summary, the updated data are consistent with the original results in Asness et al. Traditional estimates of beta are biased toward zero and traditional estimates of alpha and the Sharpe measure are upward biased due to smoothing in the return series.

We have also replicated the analysis of Asness et al. on another alternative asset class: venture capital (VC). We use the VC indices from Sand Hill Econometrics (see Woodward and Hall 2003; Hwang et al. 2005). These indices are constructed to minimize the smoothing behavior of pricing in VC funds. The indices use valuations of portfolio companies at adjacent liquidity events and interpolate value between those events using an index of traded assets. Therefore, we expect the smoothing

Table 13.1. Annualized mean returns (monthly mean returns times twelve) and annualized standard deviations estimated using lags of $L = 1$, 3, 6, and 12 months for the Credit Suisse/Tremont hedge fund indices.

	Mean (annualized)	Monthly annualized standard deviation	Quarterly annualized standard deviation	Six-monthly annualized standard deviation	Annual standard deviation	Percentage increase monthly to quarterly	Percentage increase quarterly to semiannual	Percentage increase semiannual to annual	Percentage increase monthly to annual
Aggregate hedge fund	5.28	7.82	8.93	9.32	9.88	14.1	4.5	5.9	26.3
Convertible arbitrage	3.19	7.06	9.45	10.30	10.55	33.8	9.1	2.5	49.5
Dedicated short bias	−3.70	16.94	17.43	15.80	13.99	2.9	−9.3	−11.4	−17.4
Emerging markets	4.74	15.76	18.94	19.37	20.16	20.1	2.3	4.1	27.9
Equity market neutral	2.53	10.90	11.42	12.12	10.72	4.8	6.2	−11.6	−1.6
Event driven	5.90	6.05	7.68	8.59	9.13	27.0	11.7	6.4	51.0
Event driven: distressed	6.79	6.69	8.65	9.87	10.57	29.4	14.0	7.1	58.1

Table 13.1. (*Cont.*)

	Mean (annualized)	Monthly annualized standard deviation	Quarterly annualized standard deviation	Six-monthly annualized standard deviation	Annual standard deviation	Percentage increase monthly to quarterly	Percentage increase quarterly to semiannual	Percentage increase semiannual to annual	Percentage increase monthly to annual
Event driven: multistrategy	5.52	6.44	7.93	8.72	9.36	23.2	9.9	7.3	45.4
Event driven: risk arbitrage	3.49	4.20	4.89	4.76	4.65	16.5	−2.7	−2.2	10.8
Fixed-income arbitrage	0.60	5.97	7.65	8.05	7.97	28.1	5.1	−0.9	33.5
Global macro	8.57	10.36	10.88	11.69	12.49	5.0	7.5	6.8	20.6
Long/short equity	6.42	10.10	11.89	11.94	12.71	17.7	0.4	6.5	25.9
Managed futures	3.34	11.82	12.09	10.94	10.16	2.3	−9.5	−7.1	−14.1

Table 13.2. Comparison of β and α estimates using the traditional estimators and the Fama–French estimators for the Credit Suisse/Tremont hedge fund indices.

	Contemporaneous			Fama–French							Percentage change	Percentage change
	α	β	$\bar{R}^2$	α	β_0	β_1	β_2	$\bar{R}^2$	Sum	$\beta_1 + \beta_2$	β to sum	α
Aggregate hedge fund	4.23 (2.50)	0.27 (8.52)	0.28	3.90 (2.41)	0.26 (8.65)	0.07 (2.27)	0.11 (3.52)	0.34	0.44 (8.92)	0.18 (4.38)	62.8	−7.9
Convertible arbitrage	2.61 (1.53)	0.15 (4.68)	0.10	2.07 (1.26)	0.14 (4.41)	0.13 (4.14)	0.04 (1.33)	0.19	0.30 (6.11)	0.17 (4.13)	104.7	−20.8
Dedicated short bias	−0.54 (−0.19)	−0.81 (−15.00)	0.55	−0.76 (−0.26)	−0.80 (−14.66)	−0.04 (−0.76)	0.09 (1.69)	0.55	−0.75 (−8.48)	0.05 (0.70)	−7.2	−40.5
Emerging markets	2.67 (0.78)	0.53 (8.33)	0.27	1.57 (0.46)	0.51 (8.05)	0.13 (1.99)	0.04 (0.70)	0.28	0.68 (6.64)	0.17 (2.03)	28.5	−41.2
Equity market neutral	1.84 (0.68)	0.18 (3.49)	0.06	0.93 (0.36)	0.16 (3.23)	0.20 (4.15)	0.09 (1.81)	0.15	0.45 (5.69)	0.29 (4.51)	154.3	−49.7
Event driven	5.00 (4.02)	0.23 (9.96)	0.35	4.28 (3.76)	0.22 (10.23)	0.12 (5.52)	0.06 (2.59)	0.46	0.39 (11.34)	0.17 (6.12)	68.9	−14.4
Event driven: distressed	5.80 (4.22)	0.26 (9.97)	0.35	5.01 (3.98)	0.24 (10.27)	0.13 (5.32)	0.07 (2.91)	0.46	0.44 (11.44)	0.19 (6.22)	70.4	−13.7

t-statistics in parentheses.

Table 13.2. (*Cont.*)

	Contemporaneous			Fama–French							Percentage change	Percentage change
	α	β	$\bar{R}^2$	α	β_0	β_1	β_2	$\bar{R}^2$	Sum	$\beta_1 + \beta_2$	β to sum	α
Event driven:	4.68	0.22	0.27	3.96	0.20	0.12	0.05	0.36	0.37	0.17	70.6	−15.3
multistrategy	(3.33)	(8.31)		(3.00)	(8.26)	(4.75)	(2.00)		(9.28)	(5.10)		
Event driven:	2.99	0.13	0.22	2.92	0.12	0.05	−0.01	0.24	0.16	0.04	27.0	−2.4
risk arbitrage	(3.16)	(7.29)		(3.09)	(6.93)	(2.69)	(−0.39)		(5.71)	(1.74)		
Fixed-income	0.12	0.12	0.10	−0.37	0.11	0.09	0.07	0.20	0.28	0.17	128.7	−403.9
arbitrage	(0.09)	(4.58)		(−0.27)	(4.39)	(3.67)	(2.89)		(6.77)	(4.95)		
Global macro	7.96	0.16	0.05	8.05	0.16	−0.01	0.12	0.07	0.27	0.11	69.3	1.1
	(3.10)	(3.27)		(3.16)	(3.33)	(−0.24)	(2.48)		(3.44)	(1.69)		
Long/short	4.84	0.41	0.38	4.51	0.40	0.05	0.09	0.41	0.55	0.15	34.9	−7.0
equity	(2.40)	(10.79)		(2.25)	1(0.75)	(1.35)	(2.52)		(9.03)	(2.92)		
Managed	3.81	−0.12	0.02	4.01	−0.11	−0.09	0.02	0.02	−0.18	−0.07	49.0	5.2
futures	(1.28)	(−2.19)		(1.33)	(−1.94)	(−1.63)	(0.36)		(−1.99)	(−0.96)		

t-statistics in parentheses.

effects to be much smaller than in the return series using valuations reported by the VC funds themselves.

The sample period used here is from January 1989 through September 2008. There are subindices for health, information technology, retail, other, as well as an aggregate VC index. Table 13.3 gives the results for estimating the standard deviation over various return horizons. Estimates of annualized standard deviation increase for all funds as the return horizon is increased from one month to one year. The smallest increase is 24% for the subindex labeled other, and the largest is 183% for retail. Table 13.4 reports the differences between estimating α and β with contemporaneous moments and estimating them with the Fama–French approach with a quarterly horizon ($N = 3$ months). The Fama–French estimates of β are 2%–29% higher than the standard ordinary least-squares estimates. Similarly, estimates of α decline by between 2% and 94%. Since the Sand Hill Econometrics indices are constructed to minimize the staleness in prices and thereby to minimize smoothing, it is likely that other indices in the venture capital/private equity asset class will have larger understatement of systematic and total risk and the attendant larger overstatement of risk-adjusted returns as measured either by α or by the Sharpe ratio.

Kat and Oomen (2007a,b) study the properties of the return distributions of investments in commodity futures. They find volatility and kurtosis similar to that found in U.S. large-capitalization equities. There is little evidence of skewness in the commodity futures returns. Kat and Oomen find mild autocorrelation in returns on commodity futures at daily frequencies, but none at monthly frequencies. Therefore, commodity futures do not exhibit the levels of staleness and smoothing apparent in private equity, real estate, and hedge funds.

13.2 Time-Varying Risk, Nonlinear Payoff, and Style Drift

Among the advantages claimed for alternative assets, particularly hedge funds, is the ability to use vehicles not typically available to traditional money managers (short positions, derivatives, leverage, etc.) and the ability to quickly switch the allocation across strategies. These advantages imply that risk is time varying and nonlinear. As a simple example of time-varying systematic risks, suppose a fund follows a momentum strategy. If the return on the market is high over the ranking period, the winning portfolio will tend to include high market beta assets, and if the return on the market is low over the ranking period, the winning portfolio will tend to include low market beta assets. Grundy and Martin (2001) derive a model in which momentum-based portfolios have conditional factor risk exposures that are linear functions of the ranking-period factor portfolio returns. Korajczyk and Sadka (2004, figure 3) show that, empirically, the beta of a winner's momentum portfolio varies between 0.80 and 1.45 and is closely related to lagged market returns.

The appropriate manner in which to model the time variation in risk for an alternative asset portfolio depends on the strategy characteristics of the portfolio. Therefore, a one-size-fits-all approach to modeling time variation in risk may not be possible.

Ferson and Schadt (1996) and Ferson and Warther (1996) derive performance evaluation measures when conditional betas and alphas are linear functions of observed predetermined variables, $\boldsymbol{z}_{t-1}$. With conditional betas and a constant alpha, the data-generating process for excess returns becomes

$$x_{w,t} = \alpha_w + \beta_w(x_{m,t}) + \boldsymbol{b}'_w \boldsymbol{z}_{t-1}(x_{m,t}) + \eta_{w,t}. \tag{13.4}$$

With conditional alphas and betas, the data-generating process becomes

$$x_{w,t} = \alpha_{0,w} + \boldsymbol{\alpha}'_{1,w} \boldsymbol{z}_{t-1} + \beta_w(x_{m,t}) + \boldsymbol{b}'_w \boldsymbol{z}_{t-1}(x_{m,t}) + \eta_{w,t}. \tag{13.5}$$

One can test for time variation in betas and alphas by testing whether $\boldsymbol{b}_w$ and $\boldsymbol{\alpha}_{1,w}$ are zero vectors.

Kat and Miffre (2002) estimate equation (13.5) for a set of hedge funds and test for time variation in performance (i.e., whether $\boldsymbol{\alpha}_{1,w} = \mathbf{0}$) and in risk exposure (i.e., whether $\boldsymbol{b}_w = \mathbf{0}$). They estimate conditional factor models with one, three, and six factors. They reject constant performance (at the 5% significance level) for 43%–49% of the hedge funds, depending on the number of factors included. They also reject constant risk exposures (at the 5% significance level) for 64%–100% of the hedge funds, depending on the number of factors included.

In addition to simple time variation in systematic risk, many hedge funds invest in assets or have portfolio strategies that induce nonlinear relations between fund returns and aggregate market indices. As a simple example of nonlinear payoffs, consider a fund with a strategy of writing covered calls on the market index. The sensitivity, or beta, of the fund to market down movements is much larger than the sensitivity to up movements. The traditional estimators, which assume a linear relationship between fund returns and factor portfolio returns (discussed in the last section), would estimate a beta between the up-market and down-market betas, underestimating the fund's down-market beta and overestimating its up-market beta.

The issue of evaluating portfolio risk and performance with nonlinear payoffs was first addressed in the context of measuring market-timing

Table 13.3. Comparative results from estimating the standard deviation over various return horizons for the Sand Hill Econometrics venture capital indices.

	Mean (annualized)	Monthly annualized standard deviation	Quarterly annualized standard deviation	Six-monthly annualized standard deviation	Annual standard deviation	Percentage increase monthly to quarterly	Percentage increase quarterly to semiannual	Percentage increase semiannual to annual	Percentage increase monthly to annual
All	9.61	13.10	16.68	21.69	31.04	27.3	30.0	43.1	136.9
Health	13.24	12.47	13.76	15.88	20.23	10.4	15.4	27.4	62.2
IT	10.72	13.95	18.85	25.60	38.15	35.2	35.8	49.0	173.6
Retail	3.96	14.31	19.65	26.68	40.54	37.4	35.7	52.0	183.4
Other	1.28	10.86	11.23	11.75	13.52	3.4	4.6	15.1	24.5

Table 13.4. The differences between estimating alpha and beta with contemporaneous returns versus estimating them with the Fama–French approach with a quarterly horizon ($N = 3$ months) for the Sand Hill Econometrics VC indices.

	Contemporaneous			Fama–French								Percentage change	Percentage change
	α	β	$\bar{R}^2$	α	β_0	β_1	β_2	β_3	$\bar{R}^2$	Sum	$\beta_1 + \beta_2 + \beta_3$	β to Sum	α
All	4.34	0.80	0.72	3.60	0.81	0.05	0.06	0.07	0.75	1.00	0.18	24.2	−17.2
	(2.78)	(24.86)		(2.32)	(26.21)	(1.56)	(1.99)	(2.33)		(15.72)	(3.32)		
Health	7.82	0.83	0.85	7.63	0.84	0.02	0.02	0.03	0.86	0.91	0.08	10.1	−2.4
	(7.03)	(35.97)		(6.82)	(37.14)	(0.91)	(0.93)	(1.54)		(19.83)	(1.91)		
IT	5.44	0.81	0.64	4.50	0.82	0.06	0.08	0.09	0.67	1.05	0.23	29.3	−17.2
	(2.87)	(20.65)		(2.40)	(21.74)	(1.49)	(2.01)	(2.43)		(13.56)	(3.35)		
Retail	−1.23	0.79	0.59	−2.40	0.80	0.07	0.08	0.06	0.61	1.02	0.22	28.7	−94.5
	(−0.59)	(18.47)		(−1.13)	(18.81)	(1.70)	(1.93)	(1.48)		(11.71)	(2.88)		
Other	−3.43	0.72	0.84	−3.13	0.73	0.01	−0.01	0.01	0.86	0.74	0.01	2.1	8.8
	(−3.52)	(35.70)		(−3.24)	(37.50)	(0.43)	(−0.36)	(0.30)		(18.52)	(0.21)		

t-statistics in parentheses.

ability (see Treynor and Mazuy 1966; Henriksson and Merton 1981). (See chapter 14 for a general discussion of performance measurement.) In this section we highlight some performance issues of particular relevance to hedge funds. Henriksson and Merton (1981) model the market-timing manager as moving between being fully invested in the market and being fully invested in cash, depending on the timer's expectations of market returns. Their parametric model is one where up-market and down-market betas are allowed to be different:

$$x_{w,t} = \alpha_w^{\text{selection}} + \beta_w^{\text{up}}(x_{m,t}) + \beta_w^{\text{diff}} y_t + \eta_{w,t}, \tag{13.6}$$

where $y_t = \max[0, -x_{m,t}]$. In this model, $\alpha_w^{\text{selection}}$ is the abnormal return generated through pure security selection, β_w^{up} is the up-market systematic risk, and β_w^{diff} is the difference between the up-market and down-market betas of the fund and a measure of market-timing ability. Henriksson and Merton (1981) show that true market-timing ability in their model is equivalent to receiving free put options on the market index. In their model, β_w^{diff} is the number of free put options on the index that are due to the manager's timing ability. A manager could generate pseudo-timing ability by buying put options rather than by generating free put-option-like payoffs through true timing ability. Jagannathan and Korajczyk (1986) show that this pseudo-timing strategy would lead to a positive β_w^{diff} and a negative $\alpha_w^{\text{selection}}$ due to the cost of purchasing the put options. For a strategy that mimics the Henriksson and Merton (1981) timing ability, Jagannathan and Korajczyk (1986) show that total performance can be measured by

$$\frac{\alpha_w^{\text{selection}}}{1 + r_0} + \beta_w^{\text{diff}} \times p_{\text{put}},$$

where p_{put} is the price of a one-period put on the market index with current value normalized to one and a strike price of $1 + r_0$. They show that, for a pseudo-timer who holds the index and one-period protective puts, total performance is zero. However, more complicated derivative strategies could lead to nonzero measurement of total performance. Glosten and Jagannathan (1994) suggest using a series of index options to measure the risk and total performance of a portfolio with nonlinear payoff structures:

$$x_{w,t} = \alpha_w^{\text{selection}} + \beta_{w,m}(x_{m,t}) + \sum_{j=1}^{k} \delta_{w,j} \max(x_{m,t} - \mathrm{EX}_j, 0) + \eta_{w,t},$$

where EX_j is the exercise price of the jth index option.

Hedge funds may exhibit nonlinear payoffs for multiple reasons. They may be explicit market timers, as in the Henriksson and Merton (1981)

Table 13.5. Estimates of the Henriksson–Merton model for the Credit Suisse/Tremont hedge fund indices.

	α	β	β^{diff}	R^2
Aggregate hedge fund	8.07 (2.97)	0.17 (2.52)	−0.18 (−1.80)	0.29
Convertible arbitrage	6.23 (2.27)	0.05 (0.78)	−0.17 (−1.68)	0.11
Dedicated short bias	1.80 (0.38)	−0.87 (−7.72)	−0.11 (−0.63)	0.55
Emerging markets	11.52 (2.09)	0.29 (2.22)	−0.42 (−2.05)	0.28
Equity market neutral	5.14 (1.18)	0.09 (0.82)	−0.16 (−0.96)	0.06
Event driven	10.44 (5.35)	0.08 (1.80)	−0.26 (−3.54)	0.39
Event driven: distressed	11.99 (5.57)	0.09 (1.71)	−0.29 (−3.66)	0.39
Event driven: multistrategy	9.80 (4.41)	0.08 (1.48)	−0.24 (−2.93)	0.30
Event driven: risk arbitrage	4.90 (3.22)	0.08 (2.10)	−0.09 (−1.60)	0.23
Fixed income arbitrage	6.49 (2.87)	−0.05 (−0.88)	−0.30 (−3.58)	0.15
Global macro	11.05 (2.66)	0.07 (0.73)	−0.15 (−0.95)	0.05
Long/short equity	7.09 (2.17)	0.35 (4.39)	−0.11 (−0.88)	0.38
Managed futures	−3.30 (−0.69)	0.07 (0.60)	0.34 (1.89)	0.03

t-statistics in parentheses.

model (e.g., the Hedge Fund Research indices include a market-timing-style category). Funds may also have positions in options explicitly or through assets with embedded options. Certain fund strategies, such as merger arbitrage, can exhibit nonlinear payoff structures that look very much like option positions (see, for example, Mitchell and Pulvino 2001).

Table 13.5 shows the estimates of equation (13.6) for the Credit Suisse/Tremont hedge fund indices. Five of thirteen indices have statistically significant nonlinearities, as measured by $\hat{\beta}_w^{\text{diff}}$. All of the indices that have a significant difference between up-market and down-market betas have larger betas in down markets (as evidenced by the negative values of β_w^{diff}). These indices include event driven, fixed-income arbitrage, multistrategy, and distressed. They exhibit a risk profile similar to writing put options, much like the event-driven strategy studied in Mitchell and

Pulvino (2001). Thus, many funds seem to be short volatility. Only the managed futures index has a nearly significant positive value of $\hat{\beta}_w^{\text{diff}}$, which corresponds to long volatility, with a t-statistic of 1.89.

Fung and Hsieh (1997, 2001) analyze the risk and performance of funds in the Lipper TASS commodity trading advisor (CTA) database. They find important nonlinearities in hedge fund returns. In Fung and Hsieh (2001) they apply versions of the Glosten and Jagannathan (1994) technique to measure the risk of trend-following hedge funds. They use straddles of regular options and straddles of lookback options in addition to linear benchmark returns. They find that linear factor models provide little evidence of systematic risk for these hedge funds. The linear models have adjusted R^2 values between −3.2% and 7.5%, depending on the set of asset classes included. A model with five lookback straddle portfolio returns has an adjusted R^2 value of 47.9%. Over the sample period the straddle portfolios and the trend-following hedge funds exhibited positive skewness and positive returns during periods of large movements in equity markets. Thus, it seems that the funds analyzed in Fung and Hsieh (2001) are long volatility, which the standard linear factor models are unable to detect. Since these funds are CTAs, this evidence is consistent with our finding of a positive value of $\hat{\beta}_w^{\text{diff}}$ for the Credit Suisse/Tremont managed futures index.

Bondarenko (2004) investigates a wider array of hedge fund styles and also finds that linear factor models miss the large nonlinear exposure of hedge funds to variance risk. For most hedge fund style categories, Bondarenko (2004) finds that the funds are short volatility. An exception is the "market-timing" category, which he equates in style to the trend following funds studies by Fung and Hsieh (2001). The results in Bondarenko (2004) are consistent with our findings using the Credit Suisse/Tremont hedge fund indices. Similar results are reported in table 8 of Lo (2001).

In addition to allowing for nonlinearity, Bondarenko (2004) also adjusts for nonsynchronous and stale pricing when estimating risk exposures. This is done along the lines proposed in Getmansky et al. (2004). The adjustment for nonsynchronous and stale pricing has a significant effect on the risk estimates. Bondarenko (2004) finds that funds appear to have positive alphas when their exposure to variance risk is ignored. However, alphas tend to become negative, or insignificantly positive, when one accounts for funds' exposures to variance risk and stale pricing.

While the higher betas of hedge funds in down markets is consistent with funds holding certain derivative positions, it is also consistent with asymmetric movements in correlations. That is, the correlations between funds and factor portfolios may increase in periods of market stress. For example, during the Russian crisis of 1998 there appeared to be a "flight to quality," when the correlations across many assets increased dramatically (Scholes 2000). The same phenomenon was evident during the 2007–8 credit-liquidity crisis. Various terms have been used to describe the phenomenon of increased correlation in volatile and bad times, such as "herding," "informational cascades," and "phase locking." Longin and Solnik (2001) use extreme value theory to study movements in the correlation structure of various national equity indices. They find a significant increase in correlation across markets when markets are declining but do not find an increase in correlation for large upward movements. One practical implication is that unconditional correlations overestimate the diversification potential across assets precisely when one wishes for the benefits of diversification the most: when asset values are falling. Lo (2001) provides a "phase-locking" model in which unconditional correlations can be low across assets but can approach unity during a phase-locking period. Dynamic and tail-related risk analysis methods (see chapters 9 and 10) are particularly important in the risk analysis of hedge funds.

13.3 Selection and Survivorship Biases

Various types of biases can be induced by the manner in which financial data sets are constructed. While these issues are not specific to alternative assets, the nature of most of these investments makes some of the biases more severe. Since many alternative asset managers are prohibited from advertising (at least in the United States), obtaining performance data is generally difficult. There are a number of data providers who collect valuations from the managers and sell historical data to subscribers. The release of data to these data vendors by the managers of these alternative assets is voluntary.

13.3.1 Self-Selection Biases

We distinguish between two types of self-selection biases based on managers choosing whether or not to report: start-up/backfill biases and termination biases. Consider two hedge fund managers who start operations at the same time. Assume that they do not wish to report performance to a data vendor until they have a sufficient track record. After a year of operation, Fund A posts a 100% return and Fund B posts a −90% return. Clearly, Fund A has a greater incentive to report its performance to data vendors than does Fund B, especially since Fund B is likely to go out of business. Therefore, funds that, *ex post*, chose to enter the data set are likely to have had good performance prior to entering. This would not cause particular concern if databases included only performance for the period after a fund is added to the data set since, on average, future performance should be related to past performance only through persistence in skill and not persistence in luck. However, since subscribers to a database generally wish to see performance over a number of periods, it is often the case that added funds' data are backfilled. Thus, Fund A's full history (or possibly a shorter history if that looks more favorable) is provided to the vendor and entered into the database. For example, if Fund A's annual 100% return came in the first six months, with a zero return over the second six months, the fund would wish to report the full twelve-month back history. However, if the return over the first six months is zero and the return over the second six months is 100%, they have an incentive to report only the last six months.

The voluntary nature of reporting, combined with backfilling, obviously leads to an upward bias in the average performance of funds and a downward bias in the average volatility of funds since the "unlucky" Fund B chooses not to report. This leads to an impression of higher average alphas and Sharpe ratios than would be the case if either (a) only Fund A's data after the initiation of reporting are included or (b) both Fund A's and Fund B's full history are included. This can be illustrated by considering the relationship between the mean and variance of a distribution truncated from below and the original distribution. For simplicity, assume that uncensored returns are normally distributed, with a mean of μ and a standard deviation of σ. However, assume that funds with returns below a do not report their returns. The distribution of the reported returns is a truncated normal with a mean of μ_{Trunc} and a standard deviation of σ_{Trunc}:

$$\begin{aligned}\mu_{\text{Trunc}} &= \mu + M_a\sigma,\\ \sigma_{\text{Trunc}} &= [M_a(M_a - a)]^{1/2}\sigma,\end{aligned}$$

where M_a is the inverse Mills ratio

$$M_a = \frac{\phi((a-\mu)/\sigma)}{1-\Phi((a-\mu)/\sigma)}.$$

Here ϕ and Φ are the normal density and cumulative distribution functions, respectively (see Johnson and Kotz 1970, pp. 81–83; Greene 2008, p. 866). Since $M_a > 0$ and $0 < M_a(M_a - a) < 1$, this gives $\mu_{\text{Trunc}} > \mu$ and $\sigma_{\text{Trunc}} < \sigma$. This backfill bias is sometimes referred to as "instant history bias." For hedge funds, the backfill bias is most severe in data for the early 1990s since many data vendors were building their databases at that time (see Fung and Hsieh 2002; Lo 2008). Thus, most data for periods prior to 1994 are backfilled.

Some data vendors do not indicate when the fund was added to the data set. Therefore, it is difficult to determine how much of the data are backfilled. This makes it impossible to completely purge the data of backfill self-selection bias. One approximate approach is to discard the initial observations, say the first n months, for all funds. Fung and Hsieh (2000) and Barry (2003) compare the average fund returns in the TASS database using (a) the complete data for each fund and (b) discarding the first twelve months of returns for each fund (over the 1994–98 and 1994–2001 periods, respectively). Both papers find a return difference of 1.4% per year. However, Barry (2003) argues that much of that return difference is due to the change in the style mix of the average fund when the backfill period is eliminated.

Self-selection is also an issue when firms leave the data set. Given the large amounts of leverage and the concentrated positions in many funds, it is often the case that they will perform well for a long period of time followed by a rapid demise. Examples are Long Term Capital Management in 1998, Bayou Funds in 2005, Amaranth in 2006, and some Bear Stearns funds in 2007 (see, for example, Lowenstein 2001; Till 2006). Since the fund managers in such situations have much more pressing issues than reporting performance to data vendors, and since they are going out of business, they have no incentive to report the final and very negative performance figures. Again this imparts an upward bias in reported returns and a downward bias in volatility.[2] For example, Bayou Funds closed in August 2005 with investors losing most of their money due to fraud on the part of the fund's management. However, the data for Bayou Funds available in the hedge fund/CTA database of the Center for International Securities and Derivatives Markets[3] stop in February 2005 and show positive returns in thirty-four of the last thirty-six months of available data. An analyst taking the voluntarily reported data at face value will drastically overestimate the returns experienced by Bayou's investors.

13.3.2 Survivorship Biases

Whether it is data for traded equities, corporate bonds, private equity funds, or hedge funds, the customers of most commercial databases generally use them to make decisions about securities of existing companies or existing funds. Therefore, they have little interest in data on

[2] Similar issues even arise with publicly traded equity (see Shumway 1997).

[3] The data were downloaded from Wharton Research Data Services on July 24, 2007.

firms or funds that no longer exist since there is no way to invest in them. For this reason some data vendors purge their data sets of defunct firms or funds. Some data vendors offer a separate product for defunct entities and some include data on all entities, both alive and defunct. For individual equity pricing data, a data set suffering from survivorship biases excludes both bankrupt firms (which are poor performers) and firms that have been acquired (which may be a combination of poor and good performers). For hedge funds and private equity funds, leaving the data set might be due to the fund being shut down because of poor performance. A fund might also leave the data set due to the fund closing to new investments and deciding to cease reporting performance to the data vendor. This latter cause is likely to be associated with good performance. While the net effect is ambiguous, the evidence seems to indicate that the poor performers have a larger effect than the funds that disappear due to good performance.

Fung and Hsieh (2000) study funds in the TASS hedge fund database, which includes defunct funds, over the period 1994–98. To measure survivorship bias, Fung and Hsieh (2000) compare the average annual return of a portfolio including all TASS hedge funds to the average annual return of a portfolio including only those funds still reporting data at the end of 1998. They find that the difference in returns is 3% per annum. Barry (2003) also studies the TASS data, but over the period 1994–2001. His estimate of the survivorship bias is 3.8% per annum. This way of estimating survivorship bias gives results that are dependent on the length of the sample period (since that length determines the survival period required) and market conditions over the sample period. Although most data vendors retain data for defunct funds, this practice is not uniform.[4] The results of Fung and Hsieh (2000) and Barry (2003) should give a useful sense of the possible magnitude of the bias for those databases that eliminate defunct funds. Fung and Hsieh (2000) study the average annual returns for defunct funds as a function of the reason for exit. All of the average returns for defunct funds are lower than the full observed sample (average return of 10.2%), ranging from average returns of −0.4% for liquidated funds to 7.2% for merged funds and 8.0% for funds that simply stop reporting returns. This, of course, is only over the period before the funds cease reporting and it might mask some very negative returns, like those of Bayou Funds discussed above.

[4] For example, Lhabitant (2004) indicates that www.hedgefund.net removes funds that have ceased operations from its database.

13.3.3 Biases and Performance Persistence

As described above, data sources that are subject to self-selection or survivor biases generally give an upward-biased estimate of performance and a downward-biased estimate of volatility. In addition, these biases can give an upward-biased estimate of performance persistence. Brown et al. (1992) show that a performance-based survival rule, when combined with heterogeneous fund volatility, can lead to the appearance of performance persistence when none actually exists. Conditional on survival, a high-variance fund is more likely to outperform a low-variance fund, because high-variance funds with very low returns are likely to be censored from the sample.

Brown et al. (1992) discuss a number of adjustments to standard test statistics that make them more robust to the censoring problem caused by survival: (a) standardizing a fund's risk-adjusted performance by the fund's residual standard deviation (known as the appraisal ratio); and (b) adjusting the performance by an estimate of the bias induced by censoring. Given the evidence of high exit rates in the hedge fund industry (see Ackermann et al. 1999; Brown et al. 1999; Amin and Kat 2003), standard tests of performance persistence should be viewed with caution.

13.4 Collectibles: Measuring Return and Risk with Infrequent and Error-Prone Observations

The discussion above focused on the properties of hedge funds, private equity, and, to a lesser extent, real estate and timberland. While these all have issues of liquidity and stale pricing, collectible assets have similar, but more extreme, issues. Collectibles are usually unique, making comparables valuation difficult. In addition, collectibles are generally illiquid and infrequently traded, making observations of repeat sales rare.

There is also an unobservable service yield associated with owning a collectible. For example, the owner of a rare antique or artwork receives nonpecuniary utility from viewing it or displaying it for others. This service yield is not conventionally included in the measured return of a collectible asset, even though, from an economic perspective, it is the underlying source of the collectible's market value. Note that the service yield of a collectible will often vary dramatically across potential owners. In a competitive market, the traded price of the collectible should be dependent upon the service yield received by the highest bidder.[5] The

[5] Unless the highest bidder is a speculator hoping to sell it for a profit to a subsequent owner with a high service yield.

expected future service yield can affect the current trade price. Variation in the imputed future service yield is a large, unpredictable, and difficult-to-measure component of the risk of owning a collectible.[6]

Goetzmann (1993) analyzes auction transactions for repeat sales of paintings for 3,329 price pairs of 2,809 paintings over the period 1715–1986. He discusses a number of selection biases that might plague the auction data for the repeat sales. These include self-selection on the part of data source and on the part of the painting owners, who choose which pieces of art to bring to auction. For example, a painting that becomes worthless does not appear in the data set, thereby imparting an upward bias in the observed returns. However, Goetzmann (1993) notes that the data set also excludes priceless masterpieces that are donated to museums, whose deletion imparts a downward bias in the observed returns. These two truncations will probably lead to an underestimation of the volatility of investing in paintings, since the very-low-return and very-high-return paintings are excluded. The data set also includes instances where the auction price was below the seller's reservation price, and hence the painting was not sold. In these cases, the reservation price is recorded as a transaction price, which imparts an upward bias to returns. McAndrew and Thompson (2007) estimate the effect of this form of censoring on calculating value-at-risk (VaR) in the art market. Adjusting for the censoring significantly increases VaR.

Goetzmann (1993) uses a repeat-sales regression to construct annual returns (excluding the service yield of owning art) to holding paintings. The model is one in which the (unobserved) annual log return to holding painting i, $r_{\mathrm{l}it}$, is given by

$$r_{\mathrm{l}it} = \mu_t + \epsilon_{it},$$

where μ_t is the common component to the return on holding paintings in period t. If painting i is bought at time t_i^{b} and sold at time t_i^{s} at prices $p_{it_i^{\mathrm{b}}}$ and $p_{it_i^{\mathrm{s}}}$, then the multiperiod return is given by

$$r_{\mathrm{l}i} = \ln\left(\frac{p_{it_i^{\mathrm{s}}}}{p_{it_i^{\mathrm{b}}}}\right) = \sum_{t=t_i^{\mathrm{b}}}^{t_i^{\mathrm{s}}} \mu_t + \sum_{t=t_i^{\mathrm{b}}}^{t_i^{\mathrm{s}}} \epsilon_{it}. \tag{13.7}$$

Let $\boldsymbol{r}_{\mathrm{l}}$ be the n-vector of multiperiod log returns for the n repeated sales and let $\boldsymbol{A}$ be an $n \times T$ matrix of dummy variables where $A_{it} = 1$ if $t_i^{\mathrm{b}} <$

[6] An amusing example comes from the auction market for the rare and unpublished works of the Irish writer James Joyce. There is a bookdealer's anecdote recounted in Bookride (2007) that the market prices for these collectible works used to vary with the severity of the North American winter, since the highest bidder was frequently a U.S. glove manufacturer!

$t \leqslant t_i^{\mathrm{s}}$. The time series of estimated returns to holding paintings, $\hat{\boldsymbol{\mu}}$, can be estimated from the regression

$$\hat{\boldsymbol{\mu}} = (\boldsymbol{A}'\boldsymbol{\Omega}^{-1}\boldsymbol{A})\boldsymbol{A}'\boldsymbol{\Omega}^{-1}\boldsymbol{r}_1. \tag{13.8}$$

Under the assumptions that ϵ_{it} is i.i.d. through time for all i, and that ϵ_{it} and ϵ_{jt} are independent for $i \neq j$, the covariance matrix, $\boldsymbol{\Omega}$, has diagonal elements proportional to $t_i^{\mathrm{s}} - t_i^{\mathrm{b}}$ and has off-diagonal elements equal to zero. Goetzmann (1993) discusses several alternative estimators.

Goetzmann's estimated returns to holding paintings (exclusive of service yield) are below the return on Bank of England bonds over the full period. The low returns to art are driven by the early part of the observation period (1715–1849), which is also the period with the fewest cross-sectional observations. Over the more recent periods (1850–1986 or 1900–1986), the returns to art are above the Bank of England bond rate, and are even higher than the returns to stocks trading on the London Stock Exchange. The returns to art exhibit high volatility (more than twice that of a London Stock Exchange index) and are highly correlated with stock returns. Those correlations range from 0.67 to 0.79. These large correlations lead Goetzmann (1993) to conclude that there is substantial market risk in artwork. In addition, the high volatility indicates that there is substantial asset-specific risk in artwork investment.

Taylor (1983, 1992) studies a different collectible, postage stamps, for which data on repeat sales are not available. There are, however, data on the transaction prices for the same issue of stamps. The observed prices are determined by the underlying average value of that particular issue of stamp as well as the difference between the quality of the specific auctioned stamp and the average quality of stamps in the issue. Taylor (1983) finds that the log auction prices follow a first-order integrated moving average (IMA(1, 1)) process. This is consistent with a random walk in a constant-quality series plus independent noise due to quality variations. Empirically, the variance of the stamp-specific quality variation is large, relative to the variability in the constant-quality series. Taylor (1983) estimates the average annual return on a constant-quality stamp to be 12% over the period 1963–76. Over the same period, the average return on NYSE stocks was 8.7%. The beta of the quality-adjusted series, estimated using annual returns, is 0.11, so the implied alpha of stamps is economically large (8.7%) but statistically insignificant.

The signal extraction problem solved in Taylor (1983) estimates the constant-quality return series from a forward and backward exponentially weighted average of observed returns. Thus, the smoothed series may understate the estimated beta and the volatility of returns. However, the paper uses long-horizon returns, which should partially solve this problem.

Sanning et al. (2006) use the Fama and French (1993) three-factor model to study the risk and risk-adjusted return on wine using repeat sales of wine from Bordeaux.[7] They find very little sensitivity of wine returns to the movements in the stock market or the Fama–French value/growth and large-/small-capitalization hedge portfolios. There is no correction for stale prices in the paper. Most, but not all, auctions are close to the end of the month, so stale prices may not be much of an issue.

13.5 Summary

Alternative asset classes often suffer from illiquidity and a lack of current market quotes. Use of historical prices, appraisals, or other pricing methods in the absence of transaction prices for a deep market can lead to significant underestimation of the risk of these asset classes. This also leads to overestimation of the risk-adjusted performance of these assets. Some alternative assets also exhibit nonlinear payoff structures that may be due to holding derivative securities or employing dynamic trading strategies. Additionally, many common sources of data for alternative asset classes have potential survival and reporting biases that could lead to upward bias in estimated performance. We discuss a number of risk measurement paradigms that are designed to lead to unbiased risk estimates and to accommodate nonlinear payoff structures. Empirically, the adjusted levels of risk for these asset classes is significantly higher than those from standard methods that do not account for stale pricing.

[7] Some data are available at www.tcwc.com/pauct.htm.

14
Performance Measurement

The purpose of portfolio performance measurement is to monitor, motivate, and reward portfolio managers. Although not strictly part of portfolio risk analysis, performance measurement is closely linked to it, since one of its fundamental objectives is to assess the balance between portfolio risk and realized return. Also, performance measurement is intimately linked with manager compensation, and compensation has powerful effects on portfolio risk through its influence on manager behavior.

In this chapter we also consider the evaluation of portfolio risk-forecasting accuracy. This is essentially performance evaluation applied to the risk-modeling system, and it is a topic that straddles traditional performance measurement and risk analysis.

Section 14.1 considers performance measurement when only returns (and not asset holdings) are available to the analyst. Section 14.2 considers the case in which asset holdings are also observed. Section 14.3 looks at the evaluation of portfolio volatility forecasts. Section 14.4 looks at the evaluation of value-at-risk forecasts. Section 14.5 does the same for density forecasts.

14.1 Return-Based Performance Measurement

In the first two sections of this chapter we focus on performance measurement of portfolio risk and return. In this section we consider the case in which the returns to the portfolio are known to the risk manager while the individual holdings are not. This is the relevant perspective in the case of hedge funds and other nontransparent investment vehicles.

14.1.1 The Jensen Model

A classic and influential performance-measurement framework is developed in Jensen (1968). Suppose that the capital asset pricing model

(CAPM) holds for uninformed investors, who dominate the security market and set prices. A small set of informed investors select securities based on their superior information about returns, and thereby generate portfolio return streams equal to a beta-adjusted return plus a positive premium and an asset-specific return uncorrelated with the market return. Their portfolio excess returns are assumed to follow a linear regression form:

$$x_w = \alpha_w + \beta_w x_{\mathrm{m}} + \varepsilon_w, \tag{14.1}$$

where $E[\varepsilon_w] = 0$ and the intercept $\alpha_w > 0$ is a measure of outperformance. The Jensen model (14.1) can be estimated by time-series ordinary least-squares regression of the managed-portfolio excess returns onto the market portfolio excess returns, relying on the strengthened assumption that $E[\varepsilon_w \mid x_{\mathrm{m}}] = 0$. The regression generates estimates of the market exposure $\hat{\beta}_w$ and the average excess return over the market, $\hat{\alpha}_w$. The latter can be used to test for superior performance. If $\hat{\alpha}_w$ is positive and statistically distinct from zero, then the information ratio $\hat{\alpha}_w / \hat{\sigma}_{\varepsilon_w}$ measures the return outperformance per unit of portfolio nonmarket risk. A statistically significant $\alpha_w < 0$ indicates "below-market" risk-adjusted returns on the managed portfolio, where the underperformance may be due to excessive transaction costs.

Dybvig and Ross (1985) explore restrictions on information and preferences under which the Jensen model provides a legitimate measure of outperformance. They show that the Jensen model is not valid if the portfolio manager's superior information is related to the return on the market portfolio; it relies implicitly on the assumption that the investment information concerns asset-specific returns only. In particular, if the investor's superior information is correlated with the return on the market portfolio, then his optimal mean–variance portfolio can have a negative average premium α_w when written in the unconditional linear form (14.1). Furthermore, the manager's market exposure β_w will vary with the information signal, which thereby invalidates the linear regression formulation, which treats β_w as a constant coefficient.

Connor and Korajczyk (1986) embed the Jensen model in the factor modeling framework of the arbitrage pricing theory (APT). Let the exact form of the APT hold for uninformed investors, so that excess returns are linear in factor returns:

$$\boldsymbol{x} = \boldsymbol{B}\boldsymbol{f} + \boldsymbol{\varepsilon}.$$

Suppose that an informed investor observes a vector of signals $\boldsymbol{s}$ that is partially revealing about $\boldsymbol{\varepsilon}$ in the sense that $\boldsymbol{\varepsilon} = \boldsymbol{s} + \boldsymbol{\eta}$, where $\boldsymbol{s}$ is independent of $\boldsymbol{\eta}$ and $\boldsymbol{f}$. Connor and Korajczyk show that the investor will

Table 14.1. An illustration of the incorrect use of the CAPM for performance measurement of portfolios with derivatives exposures causing abnormal returns to the market insurance provision portfolio.

	Abnormal return	Market β	Variance	Skewness	Excess kurtosis
Market index	0	1	0.0056	0	0
Portfolio insurance provision	0.0016	1	0.0335	−7.9300	76.9200
β-hedged market insurance provision	0.0078	0	0.6979	−6.8000	67.2000

choose a portfolio that overweights securities with positive signals and underweights those with negative signals. The result is an unconditional return decomposition:

$$x_w = \alpha_w + \boldsymbol{b}'_w \boldsymbol{f} + \varepsilon_w,$$

where $\alpha_w > 0$. They also show that under additional restrictive conditions (normally distributed asset-specific returns and constant absolute risk-averse preferences) it is valid to treat the information ratio $\hat{\alpha}_w / \hat{\sigma}_{\varepsilon_w}$ as an ordered measure of the informational superiority of the manager.

Jensen-based performance measurement is generally invalid in portfolios that include options, since it relies on the CAPM or a multibeta variant such as the APT. Recall the artificial economy constructed in chapter 1, in which investors have constant absolute risk aversion and the CAPM holds for equities. Note that in this economy the CAPM is, by construction, the correct pricing model for equities. Investors can also trade options, including a put option on the equity market index. Table 14.1 uses this artificial economy to illustrate the bias in Jensen-style performance measurement for portfolios including options. The stock market index is calibrated to have an annualized volatility of 20% and an expected annualized return of 8%; the annualized riskless return is set at 4%. One period (the economy is a static one-period economy) is calibrated to equal one quarter of a year. Using the Jensen model (which correctly applies to all equity portfolios in this economy since the CAPM holds by construction) the table shows the substantial "outperformance" of the market insurance provision portfolio (a written put option on market index, financed with a cash account). A portfolio manager can "outperform" without having any security selection skill or market-timing ability simply by writing equity market put options.

14.1.2 Market-Timing Performance Measurement

The measurement and attribution problem becomes more difficult if the manager engages in market-timing strategies. As noted above, dynamic variation in the market exposure β_w violates the assumptions of the standard time-series regression used to estimate the Jensen model (14.1). As discussed in chapter 13, Henriksson and Merton (1981) develop an alternative model in which an informed investor receives a binary signal $s = 0, 1$ about the return to the market portfolio. The signal provides conditional probabilities that the market return will exceed the riskless return:

$$\Pr(r_{\mathrm{m}} \lessgtr r_0 \mid s = 0, 1) = \begin{pmatrix} p_{11} & p_{12} \\ p_{21} & p_{22} \end{pmatrix},$$

where the first and second columns of the matrix refer to the signal realizations 0, 1, respectively, and the first and second rows refer to the return outcomes $r_{\mathrm{m}} \leqslant r_0$, $r_{\mathrm{m}} > r_0$, respectively. An informative signal is determined by the condition $p_{11} + p_{22} > 1$. Suppose that an investor holds a portfolio consisting of the riskless asset with weight $1 - \beta(s)$ and the market portfolio with weight $\beta(s)$. Under mild conditions on return distributions and preferences, it follows from a second-order stochastic dominance argument that $\beta(1) > \beta(0)$.

Suppose that we normalize the current price of the market portfolio to one and consider a free put option on the market portfolio with exercise price equal to $(1 + r_0)$:

$$y(r_{\mathrm{m}}) = \begin{cases} r_0 - r_{\mathrm{m}} & \text{if } r_{\mathrm{m}} < r_0, \\ 0 & \text{otherwise.} \end{cases}$$

Henriksson and Merton consider the regression of portfolio excess return on the excess return to the market portfolio and on the payoff to the free put option:

$$x_w = \beta x_{\mathrm{m}} + \gamma y + \eta,$$

where $\beta = \beta(1)$, $\gamma = p_{22}(\beta(1) - \beta(0))$. The coefficient β is the chosen market exposure of the investor when he receives the "good-news" signal and the coefficient γ captures the manager's *free insurance*, which is his ability to anticipate negative excess returns to the market portfolio and decrease his market exposure prior to their occurrence. The mean-zero residuals η are realizations of *market-timing noise*, which reflect the manager's imperfect information about the direction of the market.

Henriksson and Merton add the possibility of superior asset-specific selection ability by including an alpha intercept as in (14.1), giving

$$x_w = \alpha_w + \beta_w^{\mathrm{h}} x_{\mathrm{m}} + \gamma y + \varepsilon_w. \tag{14.2}$$

Henriksson (1984) applies the model to a panel data set of monthly mutual fund returns. His results are discouraging regarding the empirical reliability of this approach to timing and selection measurement. Henriksson finds that the measured market-timing performance of funds, which is captured by positive γ, is more often significantly *negative.* This outcome is not covered by the Henriksson–Merton theory. A negative γ would require that the fund manager has an informative signal about future market performance, but uses it to deliberately *lower* his return by *increasing* his market beta when the market is likely to fall. The empirical anomaly of negative timing ability is sometimes called *perverse timing.* Jagannathan and Korajczyk (1986) posit that the anomalous evidence for perverse timing comes from a dynamic trading bias. If a manager alters his portfolio during a return interval rather than at its beginning or end, then the Henriksson–Merton model can mismeasure timing effects. This can occur, for example, if a manager increases his market exposure in a month when the early-month return has been positive. It can also occur if the manager's investment strategy includes options, since an option return is equivalent to the return on a dynamically changing portfolio of the underlying asset and riskless borrowing and lending. The Henriksson–Merton timing model is applied to hedge fund indices in chapter 13. The hedge fund indices often exhibit significant nonlinearities.

Treynor and Mazuy (1966) develop a measure of market-timing performance that is similar to the Henriksson–Merton measure. The main distinction is that Treynor and Mazuy use a quadratic function of market excess return in place of the option-based nonlinear function in (14.2). The Treynor–Mazuy model is given by

$$x_w = \alpha_w + \beta_w^{\mathrm{h}} x_{\mathrm{m}} + \gamma x_{\mathrm{m}}^2 + \varepsilon_w,$$

where $\gamma \neq 0$ is taken as evidence of market-timing ability.

14.2 Holdings-Based Performance Measurement and Attribution

In the previous section we relied only on observation of the returns of the managed portfolio. The accuracy and reliability of performance measurement is greatly enhanced by observation of period-by-period portfolio holdings. In this section we assume that in addition to returns over the performance-measurement period, we also have the individual portfolio weights of all assets in the portfolio at each time point, $\boldsymbol{w}_t$, $t = 1, T$.

To begin, we consider the special case in which data on holdings does not provide any additional information for performance measurement. Suppose that the manager chooses fixed portfolio weights throughout the observation period, $\boldsymbol{w}_t = \bar{\boldsymbol{w}}$, $t = 1, T$. Suppose that we estimate the Jensen equation (14.1) on each of the individual assets:

$$x_{it} = \alpha_i + \beta_i x_{\mathrm{m}t} + \varepsilon_{it}. \tag{14.3}$$

Collating across n assets, we obtain n-vector estimates $\hat{\boldsymbol{\alpha}}$, $\hat{\boldsymbol{\beta}}$ and an $n \times T$ matrix of estimated nonmarket returns $\hat{\boldsymbol{\varepsilon}} = \varepsilon_{it}$, $i = 1, n$, $t = 1, T$. We can replicate the Jensen regression (14.1) for the portfolio by taking portfolio-weighted sums of the individual-asset estimates:

$$\left.\begin{aligned} \hat{\alpha}_w &= \boldsymbol{w}'\hat{\boldsymbol{\alpha}}, \\ \hat{\beta}_w &= \boldsymbol{w}'\hat{\boldsymbol{\beta}}, \\ \hat{\varepsilon}_w &= \boldsymbol{w}'\hat{\boldsymbol{\varepsilon}}. \end{aligned}\right\} \tag{14.4}$$

Under these conditions the ordinary least-squares estimates from (14.1) will be algebraically identical to those from (14.3), (14.4).

Next consider the more interesting case in which the manager has time-varying portfolio weights. The portfolio-based return regression (14.1) is no longer valid since the true regression coefficient $\beta_{wt} = \boldsymbol{w}_t'\boldsymbol{\beta}$ may be time varying. However, we can still estimate (14.4) from the collated regression estimates (14.3) under the assumption that each individual asset has time-constant coefficients in this linear model (14.3). For simplicity we begin with the case $E[w_t'\varepsilon_t] = 0$; this will be generalized below. Portfolio excess returns can be decomposed as follows:

$$x_{wt} = \alpha_w + (\beta_{wt} - \bar{\beta}_w)x_{\mathrm{m}t} + \bar{\beta}_w x_{\mathrm{m}t} + \varepsilon_{wt}, \tag{14.5}$$

$$\beta_{wt} = \boldsymbol{w}_t'\boldsymbol{\beta}, \tag{14.6}$$

where

$$\bar{\beta}_w = \frac{1}{T}\sum_{t=1}^{T}\beta_{wt},$$

$$\alpha_w = \frac{1}{T}\sum_{t=1}^{T}\boldsymbol{w}_t'\boldsymbol{\alpha} = \bar{\boldsymbol{w}}'\boldsymbol{\alpha}.$$

All the terms can be efficiently estimated using the collated regression estimates from (14.3) together with the time series of holdings. The term $(\beta_{wt} - \bar{\beta}_w)x_{\mathrm{m}t}$ in (14.5) captures period-by-period market-timing performance. Taking a time average over the observation period gives a measure of market-timing performance:

$$\phi_w = \frac{1}{T}\sum_{t=1}^{T}(\beta_{wt} - \bar{\beta}_w)x_{\mathrm{m}t}. \tag{14.7}$$

The coefficient $\bar{\beta}_w$ captures the average market exposure of the portfolio. This decomposition allows (14.5) to be written as

$$x_{wt} = \alpha_w + \phi_w + \bar{\beta}_w x_{\mathrm{mt}} + \eta_{wt}, \tag{14.8}$$

where the residual term includes both nonmarket returns and timing noise:

$$\eta_{wt} = \varepsilon_{wt} + [(\beta_{wt} - \bar{\beta}_w)x_{\mathrm{mt}} - \phi_w].$$

It is straightforward to extend the model to include dynamic stock selection ability by defining

$$\alpha_w = \bar{\boldsymbol{w}}'\boldsymbol{\alpha} + E[\boldsymbol{w}_t'\boldsymbol{\varepsilon}_t]. \tag{14.9}$$

The second additive component of (14.9) is easily estimated from the collated regression results using

$$\frac{1}{T}\sum_{t=1}^{T} \boldsymbol{w}_t'\hat{\boldsymbol{\varepsilon}}_t.$$

As a general rule, a holdings-based measure of market timing such as (14.8) is more accurate than a returns-only measure such as (14.2), since the former uses substantially more information about the underlying portfolio than the latter does. Disadvantages of the holdings-based approach include a substantial data requirement and a reliance on time-constancy of individual-asset risk exposures.

Holdings-based performance measurement is particularly valuable in the case of characteristic-based return decompositions. Suppose that individual asset returns follow a characteristic-based factor model with observed $n \times k$ exposure matrix $\boldsymbol{B}$:

$$\boldsymbol{x} = \boldsymbol{B}\boldsymbol{f} + \boldsymbol{\varepsilon}.$$

Using holdings data and applying multifactor versions of (14.7), (14.8),

$$x_{wt} = \alpha_w + \sum_{j=1}^{k} \phi_{wj} + \bar{\boldsymbol{b}}_w \boldsymbol{f} + \eta_{wt}, \tag{14.10}$$

where

$$\begin{aligned}
\alpha_w &= E[\boldsymbol{w}_t'\boldsymbol{\varepsilon}_t], \\
b_{wt} &= \boldsymbol{w}_t'\boldsymbol{B}, \\
\bar{\boldsymbol{b}}_w &= \frac{1}{T}\sum_{t=1}^{T} \boldsymbol{b}_{wt}, \\
\phi_{wj} &= \frac{1}{T}\sum_{t=1}^{T} (b_{wjt} - \bar{b}_{wj}) f_{jt}.
\end{aligned}$$

In (14.10), portfolio excess return is decomposed into asset-selection performance α_w, factor timing performance ϕ_{wj}, average factor exposures $\bar{\boldsymbol{b}}_w$, and residual return η_{wt}, which includes both unpredicted asset-specific return and factor-timing noise.

Jiang et al. (2007) show that holdings-based performance measurement can be used to recast and improve the empirical reliability of the Henriksson–Merton and Treynor–Mazuy models. After estimating market betas of individual securities using rolling-window time-series regressions up to time t, they use (14.6) to estimate the time-t portfolio beta. They then regress these dynamic portfolio betas on subsequent excess returns to measure timing ability. Jiang et al. (2007) provide two possible specifications:

$$\hat{\beta}_t = a + \gamma x_{\text{m}t+1} + \eta_{t+1} \tag{14.11}$$

and

$$\hat{\beta}_t = a + \gamma \operatorname{Ind}[r_{\text{m}t+1} \geqslant r_0] + \eta_{t+1}, \tag{14.12}$$

where $\operatorname{Ind}[r_{\text{m}t+1} \geqslant r_0]$ is an indicator function: it equals 1 if the condition in brackets is met and zero otherwise. They call these two regression specifications the holdings-based Treynor–Mazuy (14.11) and holdings-based Henriksson–Merton (14.12) models. Note that this holdings-based variant eliminates the Jagannathan–Korajczyk dynamic trading bias.

14.2.1 The Grinblatt–Titman Model

Grinblatt and Titman (1989, 1993) and Daniel et al. (1997) extend holdings-based measurement to capture more detailed static and dynamic components of performance by matching the characteristic exposures of the managed portfolio to equivalent benchmarks. The approach relies on the assumption that the characteristics of individual securities stay constant while the components of the portfolio change with the changing information set of the portfolio manager.

The GT measure (from Grinblatt and Titman 1989) is the difference between the excess return on the current portfolio and the excess return on a hypothetical portfolio using current asset excess returns and weights lagged by thirteen months:

$$\text{GT}_t = \sum_{i=1}^{n} (w_{it} - w_{it-13}) x_{it}. \tag{14.13}$$

The time-series average of GT_t measures the manager's ability to shift the portfolio profitably in response to information about returns. The notion behind the GT measure is that the lagged portfolio weights provide a comparison portfolio with the same risk profile but without the new information set of the investor. The difference between the return on this comparison portfolio and the return on the actual portfolio measures investment performance.

Daniel et al. (1997) extend the GT model to separately measure components of performance. Using data on holdings and a database of security characteristics for assets in the investment universe (publicly traded U.S. equities), they decompose managed-portfolio excess returns into characteristic-selection (CS), average-style (AS), and characteristic-timing (CT) components. They follow the GT model in using lagged portfolio weights to create information-free comparison portfolios. In addition they create for each asset i at each date t the excess return on a benchmark portfolio with the same characteristics as asset i. So $\boldsymbol{w}'_{t-1}\boldsymbol{x}_t^{\mathrm{b},t-1}$ is the vector of time-t returns on a collection of benchmark portfolios designed to capture the characteristics of each of the n assets; similarly, $\boldsymbol{w}'_{t-13}\boldsymbol{x}_t^{\mathrm{b},t-13}$ is the excess return at time t on a collection of benchmark portfolios designed to capture the characteristics of the securities at time $t-13$.

CS measures the return to asset-selection ability, which is equal to the return on the managed portfolio minus the return on a benchmark portfolio with the same characteristic exposures as the managed portfolio. Given that the characteristics fully describe the common components of asset returns, any difference in these two returns can be attributed to the manager's ability to select assets based on his information about asset-specific returns:

$$\mathrm{CS} = \boldsymbol{w}'_{t-1}(\boldsymbol{x}_t - \boldsymbol{x}_t^{\mathrm{b},t-1}).$$

AS measures the excess return on the portfolio due to its average characteristic exposures. It is constructed so that it does not account for the manager's ability (if he has any) to successfully "time" these exposures by varying them dynamically. It does this by using lagged characteristics rather than current characteristics, but applied to current excess returns:

$$\mathrm{AS} = \boldsymbol{w}'_{t-13}\boldsymbol{x}_t^{\mathrm{b},t-13}.$$

The CT measure captures the ability of the manager to dynamically vary his characteristic-based exposures in response to information about characteristic-based returns. CT relies on the difference in excess return between a portfolio using current characteristic exposures and a calculation of what the excess return would have been if the characteristic exposures lagged by thirteen months were applied to current excess returns:

$$\mathrm{CT} = \boldsymbol{w}'_{t-1}\boldsymbol{x}_t^{\mathrm{b},t-1} - \boldsymbol{w}'_{t-13}\boldsymbol{x}_t^{\mathrm{b},t-13}.$$

The three measures have an additive consistency property that their sum equals the excess return to the managed portfolio.

14.2.2 Static and Dynamic Components of Return

Treating portfolio weights as random variables leads to a different decomposition of portfolio return. Recall that if a and b are any covariance-stationary random variables, then $E[ab] = E[a]E[b] + \operatorname{cov}(a, b)$. Following a suggestion in Grinold and Kahn (2000, p. 504), Lo (2008) uses this to decompose expected portfolio return into static and dynamic components:

$$\begin{aligned} E[r_w] &= \sum_{i=1}^{n} E[w_i r_i] \\ &= \sum_{i=1}^{n} \operatorname{cov}(w_i, r_i) + E[w_i]E[r_i]. \end{aligned} \tag{14.14}$$

Lo calls the first term in (14.14) the *active component*; it measures the dynamic comovement of the portfolio weights chosen at the beginning of the period and the security returns observed at the end of the period. This is similar in spirit to the GT measure (14.13), but the statistical analysis is slightly different. Lo calls the second additive term in (14.14) the *passive component*. Lo (2008) defines a *passive investment* as one with an active component of zero. Under this definition, value-weighted portfolios such as indices are passive investments, so long as subsequent security returns are serially independent of any variation in index weights.

14.2.3 The Brinson Model

Consider a portfolio $\boldsymbol{w}$ that is actively or passively managed against a broad benchmark. It is standard practice to allocate funds to portfolio managers, each with expertise in a particular asset class. Recall from chapter 1 that active return is the difference between portfolio return r_w and the return r_{B} to a benchmark. Recall also that we can also describe any portfolio return as a weighted combination of subportfolio returns. Suppose that the universe of securities is divided into m distinct asset classes such as stocks, bonds, real estate, or fixed-income maturity classes, or industry sectors, or any other useful asset-class categories.

Brinson et al. (1986) decompose active return as follows:

$$
\begin{aligned}
r_w - r_{\mathrm{B}} &= \sum_{h=1}^{m} w_h r_h - \sum_{h=1}^{m} w_{\mathrm{B}h} r_{\mathrm{B}h} \\
&= \sum_{h=1}^{m} (w_h - w_{\mathrm{B}h})(r_{\mathrm{B}h} - r_{\mathrm{B}}) + \sum_{h=1}^{m} w_h (r_h - r_{\mathrm{B}h}),
\end{aligned} \tag{14.15}
$$

where r_h and $r_{\mathrm{B}h}$ are the returns of the subportfolio and subbenchmark within asset class h, and w_h and $w_{\mathrm{B}h}$ are the proportions of the total value of the aggregate portfolio and aggregate benchmark that are invested within asset class h. The first summand in (14.15) is the *allocation effect*. This measures the portfolio's active return due to relative overweighting or underweighting of asset classes. The second summand is the *selection effect*; it measures active performance due to within-asset-class active return. The sum of the two components exactly equals active return for the total portfolio. Due to compounding effects, the Brinson model (as it is often called) does not apply exactly to compound arithmetic returns. Analysts have suggested various procedures for attributing the "cross-terms" that arise when the model is applied to multiperiod returns (see Davies and Laker (2001) for a good treatment).

In the context of institutional portfolio management, investment clients often prefer to see performance attribution using a simple asset-class breakdown in the style of the Brinson model. Portfolio managers and risk managers often prefer a more detailed factor-model-based analysis, using the types of models discussed in chapters 4–6. Menchero and Poduri (2008) discuss the problem of integrating a performance attribution model like (14.15) with a more detailed factor-based risk model.

14.3 Volatility Forecast Evaluation

The previous two sections of this chapter considered the risk–return performance of a portfolio. In the remaining sections we focus on the performance of the portfolio risk model.

14.3.1 The Bias Test

The *bias test* is a risk forecast evaluation procedure that is popular among practitioners. Let $\hat{\sigma}_{wt}$ denote the volatility forecast for portfolio return r_{wt}. The standardized outcome SO_t is the ratio of demeaned portfolio return to forecast volatility:

$$\mathrm{SO}_t = \frac{\tilde{r}_{wt}}{\hat{\sigma}_{wt}};$$

if the volatility forecast is correct, $\hat{\sigma}_{wt} = \sigma_{wt}$, then the variance of SO_t equals one. Given that returns are uncorrelated through time, it follows immediately that the expected value of the time-series standard deviation of SO_t equals one. The bias statistic is defined as the standard deviation of standardized outcomes:

$$b = \left(\frac{1}{T}\sum_{t=1}^{T} \text{SO}_t^2\right)^{1/2}. \tag{14.16}$$

Under the alternative hypothesis that forecast volatility equals true volatility multiplied by a positive constant,

$$\hat{\sigma}_{wt} = a\sigma_{wt}, \tag{14.17}$$

the bias statistic has an expected value of $1/a$, so (under this restrictive alternative hypothesis) $b < 1$ indicates an overforecast and $b > 1$ indicates an underforecast of portfolio volatility.

Exact and approximate confidence intervals for the bias test can be derived in closed form under the assumption that portfolio return is normally and independently distributed. Note using (14.16) that under the assumption of return normality, Tb^2 has a chi-squared distribution with T degrees of freedom, denoted by $\chi^2(T)$:

$$Tb^2 \sim \chi^2(T). \tag{14.18}$$

Recall also that, by the properties of the chi-squared distribution,

$$\sqrt{T}\frac{1}{\sqrt{2}}\left(\frac{1}{T}\chi^2(T) - 1\right)$$

is approximately standard normal for large T; for notational convenience we will call this random variable x:

$$\left.\begin{aligned} x &= \frac{1}{\sqrt{2}}\left(\frac{1}{T}\chi^2(T) - 1\right), \\ \sqrt{T}x &\overset{\text{di},T}{\approx} N(0,1). \end{aligned}\right\} \tag{14.19}$$

It follows from (14.18) and (14.19) that b is a smooth function of an approximately normal random variable and is therefore also approximately normal. In particular, $\sqrt{T}b = \sqrt{T}f(x)$, where

$$f(x) = \sqrt{2}(x+1)^{1/2}.$$

Applying the delta rule[1] to $b = f(x)$ gives

$$\sqrt{T}b \overset{\text{di},T}{\approx} N\left(1, \frac{1}{\sqrt{2}}\right).$$

---

[1] The delta rule is that if $\sqrt{T}x$ is asymptotically standard normal and f is a smooth function, then $(\sqrt{T}/f'(0))(f(x) - f(0))$ is also asymptotically standard normal.

Problems with the bias test arise if the volatility forecast contains estimation error. Suppose, for example, that the forecast is unbiased but noisy:

$$\ddot{\sigma}_{wt} = \sigma_{wt} + \eta_t, \tag{14.20}$$

where the noise term is independent of return. Then it follows from the Jensen inequality that $\text{SO}_t / \hat{\sigma}_{wt}$ has variance strictly less than one, and the bias statistic gives an incorrect indication that the volatility forecasts are too low. Related to this, the bias test is problematic when used to compare the relative accuracy of two or more competing forecasts. Such a comparison relies on the restrictive assumption that both risk forecasts are proportional to true risk but that they differ in the proportional bias, as in (14.17) above. If the two forecasts differ in the amount of forecasting noise, as in (14.20), then no valid comparison can be made between them based on the bias test.

14.3.2 Variance Forecasting Errors

The bias test provides an indication of average overprediction or underprediction of volatility during the assessment period. In other words, it examines the forecasts for directional bias, but it does not allow the analyst to gauge period-by-period accuracy of the risk forecasts,

In order to measure the accuracy of volatility forecasts, it is necessary to measure the difference between forecast and realized volatility. However, the "true" level of volatility is not observable *ex post* so the analyst must rely on *ex post* proxies. The simplest proxy is squared demeaned return at time t, which is an unbiased (but noisy) proxy for true variance at time t. Recent research shows that, when available, a superior choice is realized variation of higher-frequency returns over the time-t interval (see, for example, Andersen et al. 2004). So, for example, a good *ex post* proxy for true daily return variance is the sum of squared five-minute returns over the course of the day; a good proxy for true monthly return variance is the sum of squared daily returns over the course of the month. We will use RV_t^{Δ} to denote the realized variation during period t using returns at frequency Δ. A third choice of *ex post* proxy, advocated by Parkinson (1980), is the scaled range between the high and low price over the course of the return period:

$$\text{SR}_t = \frac{1}{4 \log 2} \left(\frac{p_t^{\text{h}}}{p_t^{\text{l}}} \right)^2,$$

where p_t^{h} and p_t^{l} are the high and low logarithmic prices during the interval. If prices follow a (continuous-time) Brownian motion, this is an unbiased, and surprisingly accurate, proxy for the true time-t variance of log return.

The range estimator is generalized in Dobrev (2007). While the standardized range is based on the maximum price difference, the generalized range is based on the maximum of the sum of multiple price differences:

$$\mathrm{GR}_{k,t} = \max_{t-1 \leqslant t_1 \leqslant \cdots \leqslant t_{2k} \leqslant t} \sum_{i=1}^{k} |p_{t_{2i}} - p_{t_{2i-1}}|. \tag{14.21}$$

Since most of the performance analysis in this section does not depend upon which *ex post* proxy is used, we allow $\tilde{\sigma}_t^2$ to denote any one of them:

$$\tilde{\sigma}_t^2 = \tilde{r}_t^2,\ \mathrm{RV}_t^{\Delta},\ \mathrm{SR}_t,\ \text{or } GR_{k,t}.$$

Let $\hat{\sigma}_t^2$ denote the *ex ante* variance forecast to be evaluated over the assessment period $t = 1, T$. The simplest performance metric is the mean-squared forecasting error:

$$\mathrm{MSE} = \frac{1}{T} \sum_{t=1}^{T} (\tilde{\sigma}_t^2 - \hat{\sigma}_t^2)^2. \tag{14.22}$$

Note that MSE does not equal zero when $\hat{\sigma}_t^2 = \sigma_t^2$, due to the noise in the *ex post* proxy $\tilde{\sigma}_t^2$. However, the MSE criteria does have the crucial property that the minimum expected value of MSE is attained when $\hat{\sigma}_t^2 = \sigma_t^2$. To see this note that

$$\begin{aligned} E\left[\frac{1}{T}\sum(\tilde{\sigma}_t^2 - \hat{\sigma}_t^2)^2\right] &= E\left[\frac{1}{T}\sum((\tilde{\sigma}_t^2 - \sigma_t^2) - (\hat{\sigma}_t^2 - \sigma_t^2))^2\right] \\ &\geqslant E\left[\frac{1}{T}\sum(\tilde{\sigma}_t^2 - \sigma_t^2)^2\right] \end{aligned}$$

under the weak assumption that $(\tilde{\sigma}_t^2 - \sigma_t^2)^2$ and $(\hat{\sigma}_t^2 - \sigma_t^2)^2$ are uncorrelated.

A significant drawback of MSE applied to variance forecasts is its reliance on the fourth power (squares of squares) of realized return. Given the empirically evident fat-tailed distributions of portfolio return, this creates a very high dependence of MSE on the small number of large-magnitude returns in typical samples, and thereby lowers its reliability in finite samples. The variance of MSE as a statistic, $E[(\mathrm{MSE} - E[\mathrm{MSE}])^2]$, depends on the eighth moment of portfolio return.

MSE provides an evaluation metric and also serves as the foundation of an alternative to the bias test. Consider a linear time-series regression of the *ex post* variance proxy on an intercept and the variance forecast.

If the variance forecast is an unbiased estimate of the *ex post* variance proxy, then we expect an intercept of zero and a slope coefficient of one. This is an application of the forecast evaluation method suggested by Mincer and Zarnowitz (1969):

$$\tilde{\sigma}_t^2 = a + b\hat{\sigma}_t^2 + \eta_t. \qquad (14.23)$$

Given $\hat{\sigma}_t^2 = \sigma_t^2$, it can be shown that $E[\hat{a}] = 0$ and $E[\hat{b}] = 1$ and the null hypotheses $a = 0$ and $b = 1$ are easily testable. It is also possible to add predetermined explanatory variables and test that they are not related to variance forecast errors. For example, we could posit that

$$\tilde{\sigma}_t^2 = a + b\hat{\sigma}_t^2 + cx_{t-1} + \eta_t$$

and test that $c = 0$. The Mincer–Zarnowitz regression applied to variance forecasts has heteroskedastic error terms, and the standard errors of the coefficients rely on the eighth power of realized returns.

Some analysts suggest replacing the mean-squared criterion with a criterion that is less dependent on extreme returns, such as the mean absolute error (see, for example, Hansen and Lunde (2005) for a variety of alternative metrics and their comparative performances). However, Patton (2007) shows that using an *ex post* variance proxy in combination with some non-MSE metrics can create a logical inconsistency. Many reasonable-looking forecasting error metrics will not be minimized at the true variance σ_t^2 due to measurement error in the *ex post* proxy $\tilde{\sigma}_t^2$. This makes it difficult to interpret and use the resulting performance metric, given that the "best-performing" variance forecast will outperform true variance. One popular metric that passes Patton's consistency test is a log-likelihood measure:

$$Q(\hat{\sigma}_t^2) = \frac{1}{T}\sum\left[\frac{\tilde{\sigma}_t^2}{\hat{\sigma}_t^2} - 1\right] + \log(\hat{\sigma}_t^2).$$

Note that this is analogous to the log-likelihood criterion used to estimate a GARCH model; it provides a reasonable alternative to MSE.

14.3.3 Diebold–Mariano Forecast Comparison

Diebold and Mariano (1995) develop a general framework for the comparative evaluation of two or more forecasts of an economic variable. Their framework assumes that the forecast variable is observed *ex post*, which is not in general true for portfolio risk forecasts, but the framework still provides useful tools and insights. Diebold and Mariano note that the analyst will use the forecast of the economic variable to make an investment or management decision. In the case of portfolio risk forecast, the decision might concern the allocation of capital across a collection of subportfolios. Let $d(\hat{\sigma})$ denote the decision as a function of the forecast variable, which we take to be portfolio volatility. Let $u(d(\hat{\sigma}), y)$ denote the realized utility given the decision; this is a function of other random variates y including realized return. The loss function of the forecast is defined as minus the *ex post* realized utility of the decision as a function of the forecast:

$$\text{Lossutil}(\hat{\sigma}, y) = -u(d(\hat{\sigma}), y). \tag{14.24}$$

It is crucial that the decision rule $d(\cdot)$ maximizes expected utility, so that the expected loss function is minimized when $\hat{\sigma} = \sigma$. Note that realized utility must be observable for the method to be implementable.

To decide whether one forecasting model is superior to another, the analyst can test whether

$$E[\text{Lossutil}(\hat{\sigma}, y)] = E[\text{Lossutil}(\hat{\sigma}^*, y)].$$

This can be implemented by testing whether average difference in mean loss over the assessment period,

$$\frac{1}{T}\sum_{t=1}^{T}(\text{Lossutil}_t - \text{Lossutil}_t^*),$$

is significantly different from zero using a Student's t-test. In most cases, the difference $\text{Lossutil}_t - \text{Lossutil}_t^*$ is both heteroskedastic and autocorrelated through time so it is important to adjust the standard errors for both effects.

14.3.4 Indirect Tests

As Patton and Sheppard (2009) note, an alternative to creating a loss function from the expected utility of forecast-based decisions as in (14.24) is to use an indirect comparison. In an indirect comparison, two or more competing risk-forecasting models are simulated to make optimal risk-based investment decisions, and then the *ex post* outcomes associated with these decisions are compared. This approach is implemented in, for example, Chan et al. (1999). Chan et al. compare the performance of various covariance matrix forecasting models using three criteria: minimum-variance portfolios, minimum-tracking-error portfolios subject to constraints, and predicted pairwise covariances of stocks. For the first two applications, the superior risk-forecasting model is the one whose realized risk is lowest in the assessment period, since each model seeks to minimize this risk. For the pairwise covariances,

Chan et al. use various mean-squared-type assessment criteria analogous to (14.22) and (14.23) above.

In order to focus on assessing risk-forecasting performance, Chan et al. use minimum-risk objectives in their optimization. This prevents the expected return forecasts from influencing the comparison of the risk-forecasting models, as might be the case using a mean–variance objective. However, Engle and Colacito (2006) show that it is possible to use full mean–variance optimization, as long as the mean–variance optimization problem is stated in the dual form of minimizing variance subject to a fixed target portfolio expected return, and the competing forecasts rely on the same vector of asset expected returns. Engle and Colacito show that under these conditions, the superior risk-forecasting model will always have the lower expected *ex post* variance, for any chosen expected return constraint.

Engle et al. (1993, 1996) propose and implement an interesting indirect test. An option straddle, consisting of a long position in a call option and a long position in a put option, is a bet on volatility. Engle et al. assess the relative performance of variance forecasts by having competing variance forecasting models trade a synthetically created straddle on the asset. The superior variance forecasting model will have a positive expected profit at the expense of the inferior one.

Engle et al. use a straddle on the S&P 500 index with one day to expiration. Each day, for the purpose of determining the options payoffs, the index price is renormalized to \$1; this daily renormalization ensures that random price drift in the index does not affect the magnitude of trading profits over time. The exercise price of the one-day put and call options is equal to $\$1e^{r_0}$, where r_0 is the one-day Treasury bill rate. This choice of exercise price has the advantage that the interest rate cancels out of the Black–Scholes pricing formula for the straddle. In particular, the Black–Scholes price of the straddle is

$$\text{Price(long call + long put)} = 2 - 4\Phi(-\tfrac{1}{2}\sigma), \tag{14.25}$$

where $\Phi(-\frac{1}{2}\sigma)$ is the value of the cumulative standard normal distribution evaluated at $-\frac{1}{2}\sigma$. The model having the higher valuation (i.e., the higher one-day variance forecast) goes long one unit of the straddle, while the other model goes short. The trade price is the average of their two valuations from (14.25). Testing whether one variance forecasting model is significantly better than the other amounts to testing whether the time series of profits from this trade has a mean significantly greater than zero, using a Student's t-test.

A limitation of the Engle et al. test is that it compares only one-day-ahead variance forecasting accuracy. In many applications the analyst is concerned with the forecast accuracy at longer horizons. Engle et al. (1996) address this concern by extending the technique to allow longer-horizon option straddles (they use straddles with expiration dates of up to one year). This requires two modifications to the analysis above. First, the Black–Scholes formula for the straddle price (14.25) is no longer a reasonable choice since it assumes time-constant volatility over the life of the option. To account for this, Engle et al. implement the Hull and White (1987) adjustment to Black–Scholes pricing to account for time-varying volatility. Second, the series of realized daily trading profits have induced time-series correlation, since the variance forecasting intervals overlap. The authors implement the autocorrelation adjustments of both Hansen and Hodrick (1980) and Richardson and Stock (1989) to account for this.

14.4 Value-at-Risk Hit Rates

The absence of parametric structure in the VaR measure makes performance measurement of VaR forecasts very straightforward. The VaR forecast is set so that $\Pr(-r \geqslant VaR) = \alpha$, where $1 - \alpha$ is the predefined confidence level (usually either 0.95 or 0.99). The *ex post hit rate* of a VaR forecast is the percentage of portfolio return observations during the sample period that are below $-$VaR:

$$h = \frac{1}{T}\#(r_t \leqslant -\mathrm{VaR}),$$

where $\#(\cdot)$ denotes the number of occurrences in the sample. If we assume that the VaR forecast is correct and that returns are independent over time, the hit rate is the average of T Bernoulli random variables with parameter α, and so T times h has a binomial distribution:

$$\mathrm{Prob}(Th = a) = \frac{T!}{a!(T-a)!}\alpha^a(1-\alpha)^{T-a}. \tag{14.26}$$

This binomial distribution for the hit rate of a VaR forecast holds with complete generality; this requires no parametric structure on returns. A realized return loss that exceeds VaR by a large multiple is given the same $1/T$ weighting as a realized loss that just barely exceeds the loss boundary, so the underlying distribution of returns has no impact. In real-time forecasting applications where sample sizes are limited, the hit rate can be weak in detecting an incorrectly specified risk model. The hit rate test can be useful in the context of historical simulations of risk forecasts since simulations produce very large sample sizes.

If VaR is calculated repeatedly over time, and the VaR forecasts are updated at each date to take account of new information (including r_{t-1}), then the Bernoulli random variable (1 if $r_t < -\text{VaR}$, 0 otherwise) is independently distributed through time. This provides an additional set of testable hypotheses based on the sequence of 0, 1 realizations having no correlation patterns.

If αT is reasonably large, the binomial distribution for the hit rate is well approximated by a normal distribution. This provides a simple shortcut to computing binomial probabilities for large αT. In particular,

$$\sqrt{T}(h - \alpha) \overset{\text{di},T}{\approx} N(0, \sqrt{\alpha(1 - \alpha)}),$$

which gives a simple approximation to the true binomial distribution (14.26). In real-time applications one drawback is that using this simple formula adds approximation error to what is already a weak statistical test.

14.5 Forecast and Realized Return Densities

In this section we consider the case in which we have forecasts of the entire return distribution over a performance-measurement period. Let $\text{cum}_{t-1}(\cdot)$ denote the true cumulative distribution function for r_t based on the observable information set at $t - 1$ (the information set must include r_{t-1}). Applying a classic result from Rosenblatt (1952), by a simple transformation of distributions, without any loss of generality the realized return r_t evaluated at the cumulative distribution must have a uniform distribution on the interval [0, 1]:

$$\text{cum}_{t-1}(r_t) \sim U[0, 1]. \tag{14.27}$$

This transformation provides the foundation for many density forecast evaluation methods. Diebold et al. (1998) propose treating the cumulative distribution as a "primitive input" (that is, the estimated cumulative distribution equals the true distribution without estimation error) and then examining the sample distribution of the realized cumulative distribution outcomes:

$$\{\text{cum}_{t-1}(r_t)\}_{t=1,T}, \tag{14.28}$$

which should consist of T i.i.d. realizations from a uniform distribution. Diebold et al. suggest creating histograms of the sample of values (14.28) and examining the histograms for evidence that they do not follow a uniform distribution. This graphical exercise can be combined with formal statistical tests to examine the uniform distribution of the sample realizations (14.28).

Berkowitz (2001) suggests that for the purpose of evaluating risk forecasts, it is convenient to transform the uniformly distributed variables

$\{\text{cum}_{t-1}(r_t)\}_{t=1,T}$ to variables that are normally distributed. The transformation is in terms of the standard normal distribution function $\Phi(\cdot)$:

$$z(r_t) = \Phi^{-1}(\text{cum}_{t-1}(r_t)).$$

Tests for standard normality can be applied to $z(r_t)$.

Recall the low power of the VaR nonparametric hit-rate test discussed in the last section. Berkowitz (2001) advocates using a truncated density forecast to test the reliability of large-loss predictions. This allows the use of density forecast evaluation methods focusing exclusively on the tail density. Letting VaR denote the forecast α-level value-at-risk, Berkowitz defines a truncated density forecast as follows:

$$\text{cum}^*(r_t) = \begin{cases} \text{cum}(r_t) & \text{for } r_t < -\text{VaR}, \\ 1-\alpha & \text{for } r_t > -\text{VaR}, \end{cases} \tag{14.29}$$

such that the return distribution is truncated at $-$VaR. Forecast evaluation procedures applied to (14.29) have the advantage that the predicted return density above $-$VaR has no effect on the forecast performance evaluation. In the context of tail risk forecasting, this provides a more powerful alternative to the hit-rate test of the previous section. It requires the additional parametric structure required to forecast $\text{cum}^*(r_t)$ in addition to VaR.

Evaluating the entire return density forecast $\widehat{\text{cum}}(\cdot)$ can be data intensive. An alternative is to aggregate forecast quality via a scalar metric using a loss function. Diebold et al. (1998) suggest a variant of the approach of Diebold and Mariano (1995). The analyst can define the loss function over the space of forecast return densities rather than over the scalar space of point forecasts:

$$\text{Lossutil}(\widehat{\text{cum}}(\cdot), y) = -u(d(\widehat{\text{cum}}(\cdot)), y), \tag{14.30}$$

where $u(\cdot)$ and $d(\cdot)$ are analogous to those in (14.24). It is likely to prove difficult to specify (14.30) exactly in most applications, so the loss function typically only approximates the functional relationship between density forecast and realized utility. Nonetheless, the framework is useful for analyzing how the accuracy of the density forecast impacts the investor's underlying decision-making objective. For example, suppose that the only decision that depends on the return density forecast $\widehat{\text{cum}}(\cdot)$ is whether to cut risk capital to the portfolio (e.g., in the case of a trading desk's portfolio), and this decision is contemplated only if the cumulative probability of return below some risk limit $-$VaR is greater than α. It is then clear from (14.30) that the truncated density performance measures, like those in (14.29), can be fully optimal, since only the truncated part of the density function enters into the loss function.

15
Conclusion

This book provides an overview of quantitative portfolio risk analysis, concentrating mainly on primary asset classes such as stocks, bonds, real estate, and foreign exchange. Our approach relies on statistical modeling of asset returns, framed by economic theory and cognizant of the institutional settings of contemporary capital markets.

15.1 Some Key Messages

One key message that emerges from empirical research over the last forty years is that risk regimes change, often suddenly and in unexpected ways. This emphasizes the importance of a solid understanding of the statistical modeling used for risk analysis and risk management. To prepare adequately for sudden shifts, and to adjust quickly to them, a risk analyst needs a deep understanding of the assumptions and vulnerabilities of his modeling approach.

We stress the need for a multidisciplinary perspective. There is no single framework for portfolio risk analysis that works in all situations. A risk analyst must be able to take a purely statistical modeling approach, a microeconomic or macroeconomic perspective, or an institutional-behavioral perspective, carefully balancing the contributions of each of these points of view, in order to properly analyze portfolio risk in the ever-changing environment of global capital markets.

Two competing yardsticks in portfolio risk analysis are return variance and worst-case losses; the latter is usually measured by value-at-risk or expected shortfall. The advantage of variance-based modeling is its statistical reliability and analytical elegance. The drawback is that return variance completely characterizes the portfolio return distribution only in the unrealistic case in which returns follow a normal distribution. More generally, two portfolios with very different loss profiles can have the same return variance. It is imperative to note that although variance–covariance analysis can be very informative about return dispersion and return commonalities, portfolio variance on its own is insufficient to fully describe portfolio risk. There are clear empirical violations of the normal distribution assumption for most asset classes.

Risk measurement based on worst outcomes has the advantage that it looks exclusively at the far-left-hand tail of the return distribution, which corresponds to large losses. It is less tractable than variance-based risk measurement, particularly in the case of many-asset portfolios, but it still makes a critical contribution to portfolio risk analysis. We argue that these two measures of portfolio risk, variance and worst outcome, are complementary; the risk analyst should be familiar with both of them and combine them to maximum advantage.

15.2 Questions for Future Research

We conclude by mentioning some unresolved research questions related to portfolio risk analysis.

15.2.1 Risk of Extremes

Quantitative analysis of extremes and worst outcomes is necessarily based on relatively small data sets. Consequently, estimates of worst-outcome risk measures have large standard errors, which affects their applicability to real-life investment problems. Despite their unreliable empirical properties, worst-outcome risk measures play an increasingly central role in portfolio risk analysis.

- How can we obtain estimates of worst-outcome risk that are sufficiently stable and accurate to be useful in the investment process?
- What is a useful, estimable measure of comovement of extreme returns?
- How can one construct a robust portfolio optimization framework using extreme risk criteria?
- How should the square-root-of-time rule (for adjusting risk measures to different time horizons) be modified to account for nonnormal return distributions and intertemporally dependent returns?

15.2.2 Liquidity

The evaporation of liquidity in turbulent times is tremendously damaging to individuals, communities, and institutions. Yet this important issue tends to be overshadowed by other considerations when markets are calm, and our understanding of how to measure and manage liquidity risk remains primitive. Ironically, most of the research to date concerns equities, which comprise the most liquid asset classes.

- What are the liquidity properties of bonds, default swaps, and alternative asset classes?
- What are the drivers of market impact?
- Can appropriate government regulation of leverage help to dampen the severity and frequency of liquidity crises?
- What is the relationship between securitization and liquidity?

15.2.3 The Dynamics of Asset Price Comovements

The bulk of existing research on return comovements relies on a static modeling framework. Yet there is also conclusive evidence for dynamic features in return comovements. There are many unanswered questions about the dynamics of return comovements.

- Can we statistically identify ephemeral factors that temporarily affect return comovements and then disappear?
- What is the relationship between return comovements in market-crisis periods and full-sample return comovements?
- The degree of segmentation of factor structures across national markets and across asset classes is surprising. What explains this high degree of segmentation in what seems an efficient, globalized capital market? How does the degree of market segmentation differ between normal market conditions and turbulent markets? Will the degree of market segmentation trend downward over time?
- The research on return comovements is overwhelmingly empirical. Can researchers provide a better theoretical understanding of these strong empirical patterns and their dynamics?
- What is the best technique for extracting information about return comovements from high-frequency transaction data, given the presence of short-term microstructure noise in transaction prices?

References

Ackermann, C., R. McEnally, and D. Ravenscraft. 1999. The performance of hedge funds: risk, return, and incentives. *Journal of Finance* 54:833–74.

Adler, M., and B. Dumas. 1984. Exposure to currency risk: definition and measurement. *Financial Management* 13(2):41–50.

Agha, M., and D. S. Branker. 1997. Algorithms AS 317: maximum likelihood estimation and goodness-of-fit tests for mixtures of distributions. *Journal of the Royal Statistical Society: Series C (Applied Statistics)* 46:399–407.

Akerlof, G. 1970. The market for lemons: quality uncertainty and the market mechanism. *Quarterly Journal of Economics* 84:409–14.

Alford, A. W., J. J. Jones, and M. E. Zmijewski. 1994. Extensions and violations of the statutory SEC for 10-K filing requirements. *Journal of Accounting and Economics* 17:229–54.

Almgren, R., and N. Chriss. 2000. Optimal execution of portfolio transactions. *Journal of Risk* 3(2):5–39.

Altman, E., A. Resti, and A. Sironi. 2004. Default recovery rates in credit modelling: a review of the literature and empirical evidence. *Economic Notes* 33: 183–208.

Amihud, Y. 2002. Illiquidity and stock returns: cross-section and time-series effects. *Journal of Financial Markets* 5:31–56.

Amihud, Y., and H. Mendelson. 1986. Asset pricing and the bid–ask spread. *Journal of Financial Economics* 17:223–49.

Amin, G. S., and H. M. Kat. 2003. Welcome to the dark side: hedge fund attrition and survivorship bias over the period 1994–2001. *Journal of Alternative Investments* 6(1):57–73.

Andersen, T. G., T. Bollerslev, and N. Meddahi. 2004. Analytic evaluation of volatility forecasts. *International Economic Review* 45:1079–110.

Anderson, G., L. R. Goldberg, A. N. Kercheval, G. Miller, and K. Sorge. 2005. On the aggregation of local risk models for global risk management. *Journal of Risk* 8(1):25–40.

Ang, A., and G. Bekaert. 1999. International asset allocation with time-varying correlations. NBER Working Paper 7056 (available at http://ssrn.com/abstract=156048).

Ang, A., R. J. Hodrick, Y. Xing, and X. Zhang. 2006. The cross-section of volatility and expected returns. *Journal of Finance* 61(1):259–99.

Ariely, D. 2008. *Predictably Irrational*. New York: Harper-Collins.

Asness, C., R. Krail, and J. Liew. 2001. Do hedge funds hedge? *Journal of Portfolio Management* 28(1):6–19.

Azzalini, A., and A. Capitanio. 2002. Distributions generated by perturbation of symmetry with emphasis on a multivariate skew T-distribution. Working Paper, Università di Padova.

Bae, J., C. Kim, and C. R. Nelson. 2007. Why are stock returns and volatility negatively correlated? *Journal of Empirical Finance* 14:41–58.

Bai, J., and S. Ng. 2002. Determining the number of factors in approximate factor models. *Econometrica* 70:191–221.

——. 2005. Tests for skewness, kurtosis, and normality for time series data. *Journal of Business & Economic Statistics* 23:49–60.

Baillie, R., and T. Bollerslev. 2000. The forward premium anomaly is not as bad as you think. *Journal of International Money and Finance* 19:471–88.

Baillie, R. T., T. Bollerslev, and H. O. Mikkelson. 1996. Fractionally integrated generalized autoregressive conditional heteroskedasticity. *Journal of Econometrics* 74:3–30.

Ball, R., S. P. Kothari, and J. Shanken. 1995. Problems in measuring portfolio performance: an application to contrarian investment strategies. *Journal of Financial Economics* 38:79–107.

Ball, R., G. Sadka, and R. Sadka. 2009. Aggregate earnings and asset prices. *Journal of Accounting Research* 47(5):1097–133.

Baltagi, B. H. 1995. *Economic Analysis of Panel Data.* John Wiley.

Banz, R. W. 1981. The relationship between return and market value of common stocks. *Journal of Financial Economics* 9(1):3–18.

Bao, J., J. Pan, and J. Wang. 2008. Liquidity of corporate bonds. Working Paper, MIT (available at http://ssrn.com/abstract=1106852).

Barbieri, A., V. Dubikovsky, A. Gladkevick, L. R. Goldberg, and M. Y. Hayes. 2008. Evaluating risk forecasts with central limits. Working Paper, MSCI Barra, Berkeley, CA (available at http://ssrn.com/abstract=1114216).

Barry, R. 2003. Hedge funds: a walk through the graveyard. Working Paper 25, Applied Finance Centre, Macquarie University (available at http://ssrn.com/abstract=333180).

Beckers, S., G. Connor, and R. Curds. 1996. National versus global influences on equity returns. *Financial Analysts Journal* 52(2):31–38.

Bekaert, G., and R. Hodrick. 1993. On biases in the measurement of foreign exchange risk premiums. *Journal of International Money and Finance* 12:115–38.

——. 2001. Expectations hypotheses tests. *Journal of Finance* 56:1357–94.

Bekaert, G., and G. Wu. 2000. Asymmetric volatility and risk in equity markets. *Review of Financial Studies* 13:1–42.

Ben-David, I. 2008. The manipulation of collateral value by borrowers and intermediaries. Working Paper, University of Chicago.

Berkowitz, J. 2001. Testing density forecasts, with applications to risk management. *Journal of Business and Economic Statistics* 19:465–74.

Berndt, A., R. Douglas, D. Duffie, M. Ferguson, and D. Schranz. 2005. Measuring default risk premia from default swap rates. Working Paper, Stanford University (available at http://ssrn.com/abstract=556080).

Berry, M. A., E. Burmeister, and M. B. McElroy. 1988. Sorting out risks using known APT factors. *Financial Analysts Journal* 44(2):29–42.

Bertsimas, D., and A. W. Lo. 1998. Optimal control of execution costs. *Journal of Financial Markets* 1:1–50.

Bhandari, L. C. 1988. Debt/equity ratio and expected common stock returns: empirical evidence. *Journal of Finance* 43(2):507–28.

Bilson, J. F. O. 1981. The speculative efficiency hypothesis. *Journal of Business* 54:435–51.

Black, F. 1989. Universal hedging: optimizing currency risk and reward in international equity portfolios. *Financial Analysts Journal* 45(4):6–22.

——. 1991. Equilibrium exchange rate hedging. *Journal of Finance* 45:899–907.

Black, F., and J. C. Cox. 1976. Valuing corporate securities: some effects of bond indenture provisions. *Journal of Finance* 31:351–67.

Black, F., and R. Litterman. 1990. Asset allocation: combining investors' views with market equilibrium. *Fixed Income Research*, Goldman Sachs.

——. 1992. Global portfolio optimization. *Financial Analysts Journal* 48:28–43.

Blair, B. J., S. Poon, and S. J. Taylor. 2001. Forecasting S&P 100 volatility: the incremental information content of implied volatilities and high-frequency index returns. *Journal of Econometrics* 105:5–26.

Bodie, Z., A. Kane, and A. J. Marcus. 2009. *Investments*, 8th edn. New York: McGraw-Hill Irwin.

Bodnar, G. M., and W. M. Gentry. 1993. Exchange rate exposure and industry characteristics: evidence from Canada, Japan and the U.S.A. *Journal of International Money and Finance* 12:29–45.

Bollerslev, T. 1987. A conditionally heteroskedastic time series model for speculative prices and rates of return. *Review of Economics and Statistics* 69: 542–47.

——. 1990. Modelling the coherence in short-run nominal exchange rates: a multivariate generalized ARCH approach. *Review of Economic and Statistics* 72:498–505.

Bondarenko, O. 2004. Market price of variance risk and performance of hedge funds. Working Paper, University of Illinois at Chicago (available at http://ssrn.com/abstract=542182).

Bookride. 2007. Et Tu Healy? James Joyce, 1891. www.bookride.com, March 25, 2007.

Boyd, J. H., J. Hu, and R. Jagannathan. 2005. The stock market's reaction to unemployment news: why bad news is usually good for stocks. *Journal of Finance* 60:649–72.

Breeden, D. 1979. An intertemporal asset pricing model with stochastic consumption and investment opportunities. *Journal of Financial Economics* 7: 265–96.

Breen, W. L., S. Hodrick, and R. A. Korajczyk. 2002. Predicting equity liquidity. *Management Science* 48:470–83.

Breger, L., O. Cheyette, and L. R. Goldberg. 2003. Model-implied ratings. *Risk Magazine* 16(7):85–89.

Brennan, M. J., and P. J. Hughes. 1991. Stock prices and the supply of information. *Journal of Finance* 46:1665–91.

Brennan, M. J., T. Chordia, and A. Subrahmanyam. 1998. Alternative factor specifications, security characteristics, and the cross-section of expected stock returns. *Journal of Financial Economics* 49:345–73.

Brigo, D., A. Pallavicini, and R. Torresetti. 2006. Calibration of CDO tranches with the dynamical generalized Poisson loss model. Working Paper, Banca IMI (available at http://ssrn.com/abstract=900549).

Briner, B., and G. Connor. 2008. How much structure is best: a comparison of market model, factor model and unstructured equity covariance matrices. *Journal of Risk* 10:3–30.

Brinson, G. P., L. R. Hood, and G. L. Beebower. 1986. Determinants of portfolio performance. *Financial Analysts Journal* 42(4):52–58.

Brooks, R., and M. Del Negro. 2004. The rise in co-movement across national stock markets: market integration or IT bubble? *Journal of Empirical Finance* 11:659–80.

Brown, S. J. 1989. The number of factors in security returns. *Journal of Finance* 44:1247–62.

Brown, S. J., W. Goetzmann, R. G. Ibbotson, and S. A. Ross. 1992. Survivorship bias in performance studies. *Review of Financial Studies* 5:553–80.

Brown, S. J., W. Goetzmann, and R. G. Ibbotson. 1999. Offshore hedge funds: survival and performance, 1989–95. *Journal of Business* 72:91–117.

Brunnermeier, M. K. 2009. Deciphering the 2007–8 liquidity and credit crisis. in *Journal of Economic Perspectives* 23:77–100.

Burghardt, G., J. Hanweck, and L. Lei. 2006. Measuring market impact and liquidity. *Journal of Trading* 1(4):70–84.

Burik, P., and R. M. Ennis. 1990. Foreign bonds in diversified portfolios: a limited advantage. *Financial Analysts Journal* 46(2):31–40.

Campbell, J. Y. 1991. A variance decomposition for stock returns. *Economic Journal* 101:157–79.

Campbell, J. Y., and R. J. Schiller. 1989. The dividend–price ratio and expectations of future dividends and discount factors. *Review of Financial Studies* 1: 195–228.

Campbell, J. Y., and L. M. Viceira. 1999. Consumption and portfolio decisions when expected returns are time varying. *Quarterly Journal of Economics* 114: 433–95.

——. 2001. Who should buy long-term bonds? *American Economic Review* 91: 99–127.

——. 2002. *Strategic Asset Allocation: Portfolio Choice for Long-Term Investors.* Oxford University Press.

——. 2004. Long-horizon mean-variance analysis: a user guide. Working Paper, Department of Economics, Harvard University.

——. 2005. The term structure of the risk–return trade-off. Discussion Paper, Centre for Economic Policy Research, London (available at http://ssrn.com/abstract=666003).

Campbell, J. Y., and T. Vuolteenaho. 2004. Bad beta, good beta. *American Economic Review* 94(5):1249–75.

Campbell, J. Y., A. W. Lo, and A. C. MacKinlay. 1997. *The Econometrics of Financial Markets.* Princeton University Press.

Campbell, J. Y., M. Lettau, B. G. Malkiel, and Y. Xu. 2001. Have individual stocks become more volatile? An empirical exploration of idiosyncratic risk. *Journal of Finance* 56:1–43.

Campbell, J. Y., Y. L. Chan, and L. M. Viceira. 2003. A multivariate model of strategic asset allocation. *Journal of Financial Economics* 67:41–80.

Campbell, J. Y., T. Ramadorai, and A. Schwartz. 2009. Caught on tape: institutional trading, stock returns, and earnings announcements. *Journal of Financial Economics* 92:66–91.

Capaul, C., I. Rowley, and W. F. Sharpe. 1993. International value and growth stock returns. *Financial Analysts Journal* 49(1):27–36.

Carhart, M. M. 1997. On persistence in mutual fund performance. *Journal of Finance* 52:57–82.

Carr, P., and L. Wu. 2006. A tale of two indices. *Journal of Derivatives* 13(3):3–29.

Cavaglia, S., C. Brightman, and M. Aked. 2000. The increasing importance of industry factors. *Financial Analysts Journal* 56(5):41–53.

Chamberlain, G., and M. Rothschild. 1983. Arbitrage, factor structure, and mean-variance analysis on large asset markets. *Econometrica* 51:1281–304.

Chan, K. C., N. Chen, and D. A. Hsieh. 1985. An exploratory investigation of the firm size effect. *Journal of Financial Economics* 14:451–71.

Chan, L. K. C., J. Karceski, and J. Lakonishok. 1998. The risk and return from factors. *Journal of Financial and Quantitative Analysis* 33:159–188.

——. 1999. On portfolio optimization: forecasting covariances and choosing the risk model. *Review of Financial Studies* 12:937–74.

Chaumeton, L., G. Connor, and R. Curds. 1996. A global stock and bond model. *Financial Analysts Journal* 52(6):65–74.

Chen, L., D. A. Lesmond, and J. Wei. 2007. Corporate yield spreads and bond liquidity. *Journal of Finance* 62:119–49.

Chen, N. 1991. Financial investment opportunities and the macroeconomy. *Journal of Finance* 46(2):529–54.

Chen, N., R. Roll, and S. A. Ross. 1986. Economic forces and the stock market. *Journal of Business* 59:383–403.

Chen, Z., W. Stanzl, and M. Watanabe. 2005. Price impact costs and the limit of arbitrage. Working Paper, Yale School of Management (available at http://ssrn.com/abstract=302065).

Cheyette, O., and B. Postler. 2006. Empirical credit risk. *Journal of Portfolio Management* 32(4):1–14.

Chinn, M. A. 2006. Partial rehabilitation of interest rate parity: longer horizons, alternative expectations and emerging markets. *Journal of International Money and Finance* 25:7–21.

Chordia, T., R. Roll, and A. Subrahmanyam. 2000. Commonality in liquidity. *Journal of Financial Economics* 56:3–28.

——. 2001. Market liquidity and trading activity. *Journal of Finance* 56(2):501–30.

Chow, E. H., W. Y. Lee, and M. E. Solt. 1997. The exchange rate risk exposure of asset returns. *Journal of Business* 70:107–23.

Christoffersen, P. F. 2003. *Elements of Financial Risk Management.* Academic Press.

Clarida, R., and D. Waldman. 2007. Is bad news about inflation good news for the exchange rate? Working Paper, Columbia University.

Cochrane, J. H. 2005. *Asset Pricing Theory,* revised edn. Princeton University Press.

Cohen, K. J., G. A. Hawawini, S. F. Maier, R. A. Schwartz, and D. K. Whitcomb. 1983. Friction in the trading process and the estimation of systematic risk. *Journal of Financial Economics* 12:263–78.

Collin-Dufresne, P., and R. Goldstein. 2001. Do credit spreads reflect stationary leverage ratios? Reconciling structural and reduced form frameworks. *Journal of Finance* 56:1929–58.

Collin-Dufresne, P., R. Goldstein, and J. S. Martin. 2001. The determinants of credit spread change. *Journal of Finance* 56:2177–207.

Connor, G. 1995. The three types of factor models: a comparison of their explanatory power. *Financial Analysts Journal* 51(3):42–46.

Connor, G., and R. A. Korajczyk. 1986. Performance measurement with the arbitrage pricing theory: a new framework for analysis. *Journal of Financial Economics* 15:373–94.

——. 1987. Estimating pervasive economic factors with missing observations. Working Paper, Northwestern University (available at http://ssrn.com/abstract=1268954).

——. 1991. The attributes, behavior, and performance of U.S. mutual funds. *Review of Quantitative Finance and Accounting* 1:5–26.

——. 1993. A test for the number of factors in approximate factor model. *Journal of Finance* 48:1263–91.

Connor, G., and O. Linton. 2007. Semiparametric estimation of a characteristic-based factor model of common stock returns. *Journal of Empirical Finance* 14:694–717.

Connor, G., R. A. Korajczyk, and O. Linton. 2006. The common and specific components of dynamic volatility. *Journal of Econometrics* 132:231–55.

Conroy, R., R. Harris, and B. Benet. 1990. The effects of stock splits on bid–ask spreads. *Journal of Finance* 45:1285–95.

Constantinides, G. M. 1986. Capital market equilibrium with transaction costs. *Journal of Political Economy* 94:842–62.

Conway, D. A., and M. R. Reinganum. 1988. Stable factors in security returns: identification using cross-validation. *Journal of Business and Economic Statistics* 6:24–88.

Copeland, T. E. 1979. Liquidity changes following stock splits. *Journal of Finance* 34:115–41.

Coval, J., J. Jurek, and E. Stafford. 2008. The economics of structured credit. Working Paper 09-060, Harvard Business School.

Crosbie, P., and J. Bohn. 2003. Modelling default risk. Working Paper, Moody's KMV.

Crouhy, M., D. Galai, and R. Mark. 2001. *Risk Management.* New York: McGraw-Hill.

Crouhy, M., R. A. Jarrow, and S. M. Turnbull. 2008. The sub-prime credit crisis of 2007. Working Paper, Johnson Graduate School of Management, Cornell University.

Curds, R. M. 2004. Concentrating on concentration: forecasting risk in a top-heavy equity market. *Journal of Portfolio Management* (European Edition) 30: 150–59.

Cutler, D. M., J. M. Poterba, and L. H. Summers. 1989. What moves stock prices. NBER Working Paper 2538.

Daniel, K., M. Grinblatt, S. Titman, and R. Wermers. 1997. Measuring mutual fund performance with characteristic-based benchmarks. *Journal of Finance* 52:1035–58.

Daníelsson, J., and C. G. de Vries. 1997. Tail index and quantile estimation with very high frequency data. *Journal of Empirical Finance* 4:241–57.

Daníelsson, J., and J. P. Zigrand. 2006. On time-scaling of risk and the square-root-of-time rule. *Journal of Banking and Finance* 30:2701–13.

Das, S. R., and R. Uppal. 2004. Systemic risk and international portfolio choice. *Journal of Finance* 59:2809–34.

Das, S. R., D. Duffie, N. Kapadia, and L. Saito. 2007. Common failings: how corporate defaults are correlated. *Journal of Finance* 62:93–118.

Davies, O., and D. Laker. 2001. Multiple-period performance attribution using the Brinson model. *Journal of Performance Measurement* 6(1):12–22.

Del Guercio, D. and P. A. Tkac. 2002. The determinants of the flow of funds of managed portfolios: mutual funds vs. pension funds. *Journal of Financial and Quantitative Analysis* 37:523–57.

Dempster, A. P., N. M. Laird, and D. B. Rubin. 1977. Maximum likelihood from incomplete data via the EM algorithm. *Journal of the Royal Statistical Society* B 39:1–38.

Derman, E., and I. Kani. 1994. The volatility smile and its implied tree. Goldman Sachs Quantitative Strategies Research Notes.

Dhrymes, P. J., I. Friend, and N. B. Gultekin. 1984. A critical re-examination of the empirical evidence on the arbitrage pricing theory. *Journal of Finance* 39: 323–46.

Diamond, D. W. 1984. Financial intermediation and delegated monitoring. *Review of Economic Studies* 51:393–414.

Diebold, F. X., and R. S. Mariano. 1995. Comparing predictive accuracy. *Journal of Business and Economic Statistics* 13:253–63.

Diebold, F. X., T. A. Gunther, and A. S. Tay. 1998. Evaluating density forecast with applications to financial risk management. *International Economic Review* 39: 863–83.

Dimson, E. 1979. Risk measurement when shares are subject to infrequent trading. *Journal of Financial Economics* 7:197–226.

——. 1985. Friction in the trading process and risk measurement. *Economic Letters* 18:251–54.

Dobrev, D. 2007. Capturing volatility from large price moves: generalized range theory and applications. Working Paper, Northwestern University.

Dowd, K. 2005. *Measuring Market Risk*, 2nd edn. John Wiley.

Dowen, R. J., and W. S. Bauman. 1986. A fundamental multifactor asset pricing model. *Financial Analysts Journal* 42(4):45–51.

Downing, C., S. Underwood, and Y. Xing. 2008. Is liquidity priced in the corporate bond market? Working Paper, Rice University.

Driessen, J. 2005. Is default event risk priced in corporate bonds? *Review of Financial Studies* 81:165–95.

Drost, F. C., and T. E. Nijman. 1993. Temporal aggregation of GARCH processes. *Econometrica* 61:909–27.

Drummen, M., and H. Zimmerman. 1992. The structure of European stock returns. *Financial Analysts Journal* 48(4):15–26.

Duan, J. C., G. Gauthier, J. G. Simonato, and S. Zaanoun. 2003. Estimating Merton's model by maximum likelihood with survivorship consideration. Working Paper, Rotman School of Management.

Duffie, D. 1999. Credit swap valuation. *Financial Analysts Journal* 55(1):73–87.

——. 2001. *Dynamic Asset Pricing Theory*, 3rd edn. Princeton University Press.

——. 2005. Credit risk modelling with affine processes. *Journal of Banking and Finance* 29:2751–802.

Duffie, D., and N. Gârleanu. 2001. Risk and valuation of collateralized debt obligations. *Financial Analysts Journal* 57(1):41–59.

Duffie, D., and D. Lando. 2001. Term structures of credit spreads with incomplete accounting information. *Econometrica* 69:633–64.

Duffie, D., and K. J. Singleton. 1999. Modelling term structures of defaultable bonds. *Review of Financial Studies* 12:687–720.

——. 2003. *Credit Risk.* Princeton University Press.

Duffie, D., J. Pan, and K. Singleton. 2000. Transform analysis and asset pricing for affine jump diffusions. *Econometrica* 68:1343–76.

Duffie, D., D. Filipovich, and W. Schachermayer. 2003. Affine processes and applications in finance. *Annals of Applied Probability* 13:984–1053.

Dupire, B. 1994. Pricing with a smile. *Risk* 7:18–20.

Dybvig, P. H., and S. A. Ross. 1985. Differential information and performance using a security market line. *Journal of Finance* 40:393–99.

Eckbo, B. E., and Ø. Norli. 2002. Pervasive liquidity risk. Working Paper, Dartmouth College (available at http://ssrn.com/abstract=996069).

Eichengreen, B., A. Rose, and C. Wyplosz. 1997. Contagious currency crises. NBER Working Paper 5681.

Elton, E. J., M. J. Gruber, S. J. Brown, and W. N. Goetzmann. 2010. *Modern Portfolio Theory and Investment Analysis*, 8th edn. John Wiley.

Embrechts, P., C. Klúppelberg, and T. Mikosch. 1997. *Modelling Extremal Events.* Springer.

Engle, R. F. (ed.). 1995. *ARCH: Selected Readings.* Oxford University Press.

Engle, R. F. 2002. Dynamic conditional correlation: a simple class of multivariate generalized autoregressive conditional heteroskedasticity models. *Journal of Business and Economic Statistics* 20:339–50.

Engle, R. F., and R. Colacito. 2006. Testing and evaluating dynamic correlations for asset allocation. *Journal of Business and Economic Statistics* 24:238–53.

Engle, R. F., and R. Ferstenberg. 2007. Execution risk: it's the same as investment risk. *Journal of Trading* 2(2):10–20.

Engle, R. F., and G. G. J. Lee. 1999. A long-run and short-run model of stock return volatility. In *Cointegration, Causality and Forecasting: A Festschrift in Honour of Clive Granger*, pp. 475–87. Oxford University Press.

Engle, R. F., and V. K. Ng. 1993. Measuring and testing the impact of news on volatility. *Journal of Finance* 48:1749–78.

Engle, R. F., and K. Sheppard. 2001. Theoretical and empirical properties of dynamic conditional correlation MVGARCH. Working Paper, University of California, San Diego.

Engle, R. F., C. H. Hong, A. Kane, and J. Noh. 1993. Arbitrage valuation of variance forecasts with simulated options. In *Advances in Futures and Options Research* (ed. D. M. Chance and R. Tripp), volume 6. Greenwich, CT: JAI Press.

Engle, R. F., A. Kane, and J. Noh. 1996. Index-option pricing with stochastic volatility and the value of accurate variance forecasts. *Review of Derivatives Research* 1:39–157.

Eom, Y., H. J. Helwege, and J. Huang. 2004. Structural models of corporate bond pricing. *Review of Financial Studies* 17:499–544.

Epstein, L. G., and S. E. Zin. 1989. Substitution, risk aversion, and the temporal behaviour of consumption and asset returns: a theoretical framework. *Econometrica* 57:937–69.

Erb, C. B., C. R. Harvey, and T. E. Viskanta. 1994. Forecasting international equity correlations. *Financial Analysts Journal* 50(6):32–45.

Ericsson, J., and J. Reneby. 2005. Estimating structural bond pricing models. *Journal of Business* 78:707–35.

Errais, E., K. Giesecke, and L. R. Goldberg. 2007. Pricing credit from the top down with affine point processes. Working Paper, Stanford University (available at http://ssrn.com/abstract=908045).

Evans, M., and P. Wachtel. 1992. Interpreting the movements in short-term interest rates. *Journal of Business* 65(3):395–429.

——. 1993. Were price changes during the great depression anticipated? Evidence from nominal interest rates. *Journal of Monetary Economics* 32:3–34.

Fama, E. F. 1975. Short-term interest rates as predictors of inflation. *American Economic Review* 65:269–82.

——. 1976. *Foundations of Finance*. New York: Basic Books.

——. 1981. Stock returns, real activity, inflation, and money. *American Economic Review* 71:545–65.

——. 1984. Forward and spot exchange rates. *Journal of Monetary Economics* 14:319–38.

Fama, E. F., and K. R. French. 1989. Business conditions and expected returns on stocks and bonds. *Journal of Financial Economics* 25:23–49.

——. 1992. The cross-section of expected stock returns. *Journal of Finance* 47: 427–65.

——. 1993. Common risk factors in the returns on stocks and bonds. *Journal of Financial Economics* 33:3–56.

Fama, E. F., and M. R. Gibbons. 1982. Inflation real returns and capital investment. *Journal of Monetary Economics* 9:297–323.

——. 1984. A comparison of inflation forecasts. *Journal of Monetary Economics* 13:327–48.

Fama, E. F., and J. D. MacBeth. 1973. Risk, return, and equilibrium: empirical tests. *Journal of Political Economy* 81:607–36.

Fama, E. F., and M. H. Miller. 1972. *The Theory of Finance*. New York: Rhinehart and Winston.

Farmer, J. D., L. Gillemot, F. Lillo, S. Mike, and A. Sen. 2004. What really causes large price changes? *Quantitative Finance* 4:383–97.

Ferson, W. E., and R. W. Schadt. 1996. Measuring fund strategy and performance in changing economic conditions. *Journal of Finance* 51:425–62.

Ferson, W. E., and V. A. Warther. 1996. Evaluating performance in a dynamic market. *Finance Analysts Journal* 52(6):20–28.

Foster, D. P., and D. B. Nelson. 1996. Continuous record asymptotics for rolling sample variance estimators. *Econometrica* 64:139–74.

Foster, F. D., and S. Viswanathan. 1993. Variations in trading volume, return volatility, and trading costs: evidence on recent price formation models. *Journal of Finance* 48:187–211.

Fouque, J. P., G. Papanicolaou, and R. Sircar. 2000. *Derivatives in Financial Markets with Stochastic Volatility*. Cambridge University Press.

Fowler, D. J., and C. H. Rorke. 1983. Risk measurement when shares are subject to infrequent trading. *Journal of Financial Economics* 12:279–83.

Franke, G. and J. P. Krahnen. 2008. The future of securitization. Working Paper 2008/31, Center for Financial Studies, Goethe University, Frankfurt.

Frazzini, A., and O. A. Lamont. 2008. Dumb money: mutual fund flows and the cross-section of stock returns. *Journal of Financial Economics* 88:299–322.

Friedman, M. 1953. *Essays in Positive Economics.* University of Chicago Press.

Froot, K. A. 1993. Currency hedging over long horizons. NBER Working Paper 4355 (available at http://ssrn.com/abstract=253996).

Froot, K. A., and K. Rogoff. 1995. Perspectives on PPP and long-run real exchange rates. In *Handbook of International Economics* (ed. G. M. Grossman and K. Rogoff). Amsterdam: Elsevier Science.

Fung, W., and D. A. Hsieh. 1997. Empirical characteristics of dynamic trading strategies: the case of hedge funds. *Review of Financial Studies* 10(2):275–302.

——. 2000. Performance characteristics of hedge funds and commodity funds: natural vs. spurious biases. *Journal of Financial and Quantitative Analysis* 35: 291–307.

——. 2001. The risk in hedge fund strategies: theory and evidence from trend followers. *Review of Financial Studies* 14:313–41.

——. 2002. Hedge-fund benchmarks: information content and biases. *Financial Analysts Journal* 58(1):22–34.

Garber, P., and L. Svensson. 1995. The operation and collapse of fixed exchange rates. In *Handbook of International Economics* (ed. G. M. Grossman and K. Rogoff). Amsterdam: Elsevier Science.

Geltner, D. M. 1991. Smoothing in appraisal-based returns. *Journal of Real Estate Finance and Economics* 4:327–45.

Geske, R. 1977. The valuation of corporate liabilities as compound options. *Journal of Financial and Quantitative Analysis* 12:541–52.

Getmansky, M., A. W. Lo, and I. Makarov. 2004. An econometric model of serial correlation and illiquidity in hedge fund returns. *Journal of Financial Economics* 74:529–609.

Giesecke, K. 2003. A simple exponential model of dependent defaults. *Journal of Fixed Income* 13(3):74–83.

——. 2006. Default and information. *Journal of Economic Dynamics and Control* 30:2281–303.

——. 2008. Portfolio credit risk: top down vs. bottom up approaches. In *Frontiers in Quantitative Finance: Credit Risk and Volatility Modeling* (ed. R. Cont). John Wiley.

Giesecke, K., and L. R. Goldberg. 2004. Forecasting default in the face of uncertainty. *Journal of Derivatives* 12(1):11–25.

——. 2005. A top down approach to multi-name credit. Working Paper, Stanford University.

——. 2007. The market price of credit risk. Working Paper, Stanford University (available at http://ssrn.com/abstract=450120).

Giesecke, K., and B. Kim. 2007. Estimating tranche spreads by loss process simulation. In *Proceedings of the 2007 Winter Simulation Conference* (ed. S. G. Henderson, B. Biller, M. H. Hsieh, J. Shortle, J. D. Tew, and R. R. Barton). Society for Computer Simulation International.

Gilbert, T. 2007. Dispersed macroeconomic information: announcements, revisions and stock returns. Working Paper, University of California, Berkeley.

Glasserman, P. 2003. *Monte Carlo Methods in Financial Engineering.* Springer.

Glosten, L. R. 1987. Components of the bid–ask spread and the statistical properties of transaction prices. *Journal of Finance* 42:1293–307.

Glosten, L. R., and L. E. Harris. 1988. Estimating the components of the bid/ask spread. *Journal of Financial Economics* 21:123–42.

Glosten, L. R., and R. Jagannathan. 1994. A contingent claim approach to performance evaluation. *Journal of Empirical Finance* 1:133–60.

Glosten, L. R., and P. Milgrom. 1985. Bid, ask and transaction prices in a specialist market with heterogeneously informed traders. *Journal of Financial Economics* 14:71–100.

Goetzmann, W. N. 1993. Accounting for taste: art and the financial markets over three centuries. *American Economic Review* 83:1370–76.

Goetzmann, W. N., K. G. Rouwenhorst, and L. Li. 2005. Long term global market correlations. *Journal of Business* 78:1–38.

Goldberg, L. R. 2004. Investing in credit: how good is your information? *Risk* 17: 16–18.

Goldberg, L. R., R. Kamat, and V. Poduri. 2008a. A structural analysis of the default swap market: part 1 (calibration). *Journal of Investment Management* 6(3):48–72.

Goldberg, L. R., G. Miller, and J. Weinstein. 2008b. Beyond value-at-risk: forecasting portfolio loss at multiple horizons. *Journal of Investment Management* 6(2):73–98.

Goldberg, L. R., R. Kamat, and J. Kremer. 2009. A structural analysis of the default swap market: part 2 (relative value). *Journal of Investment Management* 7(2):4–22.

Gorton, G. 2008. The panic of 2007. Working Paper, MIT (available at http://ssrn.com/abstract=1106852).

——. 2009. Information, liquidity, and the (ongoing) panic of 2007. Working Paper, Yale University (available at http://ssrn.com/abstract=1324195).

Goyenko, R., C. W. Holden, and A. D. Ukhov. 2006. Do stock splits improve liquidity? Working Paper, Indiana University (available at http://ssrn.com/abstract=675923).

Goyenko, R., C. W. Holden, and C. A. Trzcinka. 2009. Do liquidity measures measure liquidity? *Journal of Financial Economics* 92:153–81.

Gray, S. F., T. Smith, and R. E. Whaley. 2003. Stock splits: implications for models of the bid/ask spread. *Journal of Empirical Finance* 10:271–303.

Greene, W. H. 2008. *Econometric Analysis*, 6th edn. Upper Saddle River, NJ: Prentice Hall.

Griffin, J. M. 2002. Are the Fama and French factors global or country specific. *Review of Financial Studies* 15:783–803.

Griffin, J. M., and G. A. Karolyi. 1998. Another look at the role of the industrial structure of markets for international diversification strategies. *Journal of Financial Economics* 50:351–73.

Griffin, J. M., and R. M. Stulz. 2001. International competition and exchange rate shocks: a cross country industry analysis of stock returns. *Review of Financial Studies* 14:215–41.

Grinblatt, M., and S. Titman. 1989. Mutual fund performance: an analysis of quarterly portfolio holdings. *Journal of Business* 62:393–416.

——. 1993. Performance measurement without benchmarks: an examination of mutual fund returns. *Journal of Business* 66:47–68.

Grinold, R. C. 1994. Alpha equals IC times volatility times score. *Journal of Portfolio Management* 20(4):9–16.

Grinold, R. C., and R. N. Kahn. 2000. *Active Portfolio Management: A Quantitative Approach for Producing Superior Returns and Selecting Superior Returns and Controlling Risk*, 2nd edn. New York: McGraw-Hill.

Grinold, R., A. Rudd, and D. Stefek. 1989. Global factors: fact or fiction. *Journal of Portfolio Management* 16(1):79–88.

Grundy, B. D., and J. S. Martin. 2001. Understanding the nature of the risks and the source of the rewards to momentum investing. *Review of Financial Studies* 14:29–78.

Gyourko, J., and D. B. Keim. 1992. What does the stock market tell us about real estate returns? *Journal of the American Real Estate and Urban Economics Association* 20:457–85.

——. 1993. Risk and return in real estate: evidence from a real estate stock index? *Financial Analysts Journal* 49(5):39–46.

Hamilton, J. D. 2008. Regime-switching models. In *New Palgrave Dictionary of Economics* (ed. S. Durlauf and L. Blume), 2nd edn. Houndmills, U.K.: Palgrave Macmillan.

Hansen, L. P., and R. J. Hodrick. 1980. Forward exchange rates as optimal predictors of future spot rates: an econometric analysis. *Journal of Political Economy* 88:829–53.

Hansen, P. R., and A. Lunde. 2005. A forecast comparison of volatility models: does anything beat a GARCH(1, 1)? *Journal of Applied Econometrics* 20:873–89.

Harris, L. 1986. A transaction data study of weekly and intradaily patterns in stock returns. *Journal of Financial Economics* 16:99–117.

——. 2003. *Trading and Exchanges: Market Microstructure for Practitioners.* Oxford University Press.

Harvey, C. R. 1991. The world price of covariance risk. *Journal of Finance* 46: 111–57.

Harvey, C. R., and A. Siddique. 2000. Conditional skewness in asset pricing tests. *Journal of Finance* 55:1263–95.

Hasbrouck, J. 1991a. Measuring the information content of stock trades. *Journal of Finance* 66:179–207.

——. 1991b. The summary informativeness of stock trades: an econometric analysis. *Review of Financial Studies* 4(3):571–95.

——. 2004. Liquidity in the futures pits: inferring market dynamics from incomplete data. *Journal of Financial and Quantitative Analysis* 39:305–26.

——. 2005. Trading costs and returns for us equities: the evidence from daily data. Working Paper, New York University.

——. 2009. Trading costs and returns for us equities: estimating effective costs from daily data. *Journal of Finance* 64:1445–77.

Hasbrouck, J., and D. J. Seppi. 2001. Common factors in prices, order flows, and liquidity. *Journal of Financial Economics* 59:383–411.

Healey, T., T. Corriero, and R. Rozenov. 2005. Timber as an institutional investment. *Journal of Alternative Investments* 8(3):60–74.

Heaton, J., and D. J. Lucas. 1996. Evaluating the effects of incomplete markets on risk sharing and asset pricing. *Journal of Political Economy* 104:443–87.

Heckman, L., S. R. Narayanan, and S. A. Patel. 2001. Country and industry importance in European returns. *Journal of Investing* 10(1):27–34.

Hendricks, D. 1996. Evaluation of value-at-risk models using historical data. *FRBNY Economic Policy Review* 2:39–70.

Henriksson, R. D. 1984. Market timing and mutual fund performance: an empirical investigation. *Journal of Business* 57:73–96.

Henriksson, R. D., and R. C. Merton. 1981. On market timing and investment performance. II. Statistical procedures for evaluating forecasting skills. *Journal of Business* 54:513–33.

Heston, S. L., and K. G. Rouwenhorst. 1994. Does industrial structure explain the benefits of international diversification? *Journal of Financial Economics* 36:3–28.

Heston, S. L., R. A. Korajczyk, and R. Sadka. 2009. Intraday patterns in the cross-section of stock returns. Working Paper (available at http://ssrn.com/abstract=1107590; also to appear in *Journal of Finance*).

Heyde, C. C., and S. G. Kou. 2004. On the controversy over tailweight of distributions. *Operations Research Letters* 32:399–408.

Hodder, J. E. 1982. Exposure to exchange-rate movements. *Journal of International Economics* 13(3):375–86.

Holden, C. W. 2009. New low-frequency spread measures. *Journal of Financial Markets* 12:778–813.

Holmström, B., and J. Tirole. 2001. LAPM: a liquidity-based asset pricing model. *Journal of Finance* 56(5):1837–67.

Hopkins, P. J. B., and C. H. Miller. 2001. *Country, Sector and Company Factors in Global Equity Models.* Charlottesvile, VA: The Research Foundation of AIMR and the Blackwell Series in Finance.

Hora, M. 2006. Tactical liquidity trading and intraday. Working Paper, Credit Suisse.

Hsiao, C., and M. H. Pesaran. 2004. Random coefficient panel data models. Discussion Paper 1236, Institute for the Study of Labour (IZA), Bonn.

Huberman, G., and W. Stanzl. 2004. Price manipuation and quasi-arbitrage. *Econometrica* 72:1247–75.

——. 2005. Optimal liquidity trading. *Review of Finance* 9:165–200.

Hull, J. C. 2002. *Options, Futures and Other Derivatives*, 5th edn. Upper Saddle River, NJ: Prentice Hall.

Hull, J. C., and A. White. 1987. The pricing of options on assets with stochastic volatility. *Journal of Finance* 42:281–300.

——. 2006. Valuing credit derivatives using an implied copula approach. *Journal of Derivatives* 14(2):8–28.

Hwang, M., J. M. Quigley, and S. E. Woodward. 2005. An index for venture capital, 1987–2003. *Contributions to Economic Analysis & Policy* 4:1–43.

Jacobs, B. I., and K. N. Levy. 2007. Twenty myths about enhanced active 120–20 strategies. *Financial Analysts Journal* 63(4):19–26.

Jegadeesh, N., and S. Titman. 1993. Returns to buying winners and selling losers: implications for stock market efficiency. *Journal of Finance* 48:65–91.

——. 2001. Profitability of momentum strategies: an evaluation of alternative explanations. *Journal of Finance* 56:699–720.

Jagannathan, R., and R. A. Korajczyk. 1986. Assessing the market timing performance of managed portfolios. *Journal of Business* 59:217–35.

Jagannathan, R., and T. Ma. 2003. Risk reduction in large portfolios: why imposing the wrong constraints helps. *Journal of Finance* 43:1651–83.

Jagannathan, R., and Z. Wang. 1996. The conditional CAPM and the cross-section of expected returns. *Journal of Finance* 51:3–53.

——. 1998, An asymptotic theory for estimating beta-pricing models using cross-sectional regression. *Journal of Finance* 53(4):1285–309.

Jarrow, R. A., and P. Protter. 2004. Structural versus reduced form models: a new information based perspective. *Journal of Investment Management* 2(2): 1–10.

Jarrow, R. A., and S. M. Turnbull. 1995. Pricing derivatives on financial securities subject to credit risk. *Journal of Finance* 50:53–86.

Jarrow, R. A., D. Lando, and S. M. Turnbull. 1997. A Markov model for the term structure of credit risk spreads. *Review of Financial Studies* 10:481–523.

Jegadeesh, N., and S. Titman. 1993. Returns to buying winners and selling losers: implications for stock market efficiency. *Journal of Finance* 48:65–91.

Jensen, M. C. 1968. The performance of mutual funds in the period 1945–1964. *Journal of Finance* 23:389–416.

Jiang, G. J., T. Yao, and T. Yu. 2007. Do mutual funds time the market? Evidence from portfolio holdings. *Journal of Financial Economics* 86:724–58.

Johnson, N. L., and S. Kotz. 1970. *Distributions in Statistics: Continuous Univariate Distribitions*, volume 1. John Wiley.

Jones, C. S. 2001. Extracting factors from heteroskedastic asset returns. *Journal of Financial Economics* 62:293–325.

Jones, E. P., S. Mason, and E. Rosenfeld. 1984. Contingent claims analysis of corporate capital structures. *Journal of Finance* 39:1–14.

Jorion, P. 1985. International portfolio diversification with estimation risk. *Journal of Business* 58:259–78.

——. 1990. The exchange-rate exposure of U.S. multinationals. *Journal of Business* 63(3):331–45.

——. 1994. A mean/variance analysis of currency overlays. *Financial Analysts Journal* 50(3):48–56.

——. 2000. Risk management lessons from long-term capital management. *European Financial Management* 6:277–300.

——. 2007. *Value at Risk: The New Benchmark for Managing Financial Risk*, 3rd edn. New York: McGraw-Hill.

Kan, R., and C. Zhang. 1999. Two-pass tests of asset pricing models with useless factors. *Journal of Finance* 54(1):203–35.

Kan, R., C. Robotti, and J. Shanken. 2009. Pricing model performance and the two-pass cross-sectional regression methodology. Working Paper, University of Toronto (available at http://ssrn.com/abstract=1342538).

Kandel, S., and R. Stambaugh. 1996. On the predictability of asset returns: an asset allocation perspective. *Journal of Finance* 51:385–424.

Kaplanis, E. C. 1988. Stability and forecasting of the co-movement measures of international stock market return. *Journal of International Money and Finance* 8:63–75.

Kat, H. M., and J. Miffre. 2002. Performance evaluation and conditioning information: the case of hedge funds. Working Paper 0006, Alternative Investment, Research Centre, City University London.

Kat, H. M., and R. C. A. Oomen. 2007a. What every investor should know about commodities. Part I. Univariate return analysis. *Journal of Investment Management* 5(1):4–28.

——. 2007b. What every investor should know about commodities. Part II. Multivariate return analysis. *Journal of Investment Management* 5(3):40–64.

Keenan, S. C., J. R. Sobehart, and R. Stein. 2000. Validation methodologies for default risk models. *Credit Magazine* May:51–56.

Keim, D. B. 1985. Dividend yields and stock returns: implications of abnormal January returns. *Journal of Financial Economics* 14(3):473–89.

Keim, D. B., and R. F. Stambaugh. 1986. Predicting returns in the stock and bond markets. *Journal of Financial Economics* 17:357–90.

Kercheval, A. N., L. R. Goldberg, and L. Breger. 2002. Examining market influence on credit risk. *Risk Magazine* 15(6):S21–S22.

——. 2003. Modeling credit risk. *Journal of Portfolio Management* 29(2):90–100.

Khandani, A. E., and A. W. Lo. 2007. What happened to the quants in August 2007? *Journal of Investment Management* 5(4):29–78.

——. 2008. What happened to the quants in august 2007? Evidence from factors and transactions data. Working Paper, MIT (available at http://ssrn.com/abstract=1288988).

Knez, P. J., and M. J. Ready. 1996. Estimating the profits from trading strategies. *Review of Financial Studies* 9:1121–63.

Korajczyk, R. A. 1985. The pricing of forward contracts for foreign exchange. *Journal of Political Economy* 93:346–68.

——. 1996. A measure of stock market integration for developed and emerging markets. *World Bank Economic Review* 10:265–89.

Korajczyk, R. A., and R. Sadka. 2004. Are momentum profits robust to trading costs? *Journal of Finance* 59(3):45–72.

——. 2008. Pricing the commonality across alternative measures of liquidity. *Journal of Financial Economics* 87:45–72.

Korajczyk, R. A., and C. J. Viallet. 1989. An empirical investigation of asset pricing. *Review of Financial Studies* 2:553–85.

Kritzman, M. 1993a. About hedging. *Financial Analysts Journal* 49(5):22–26.

——. 1993b. The minimum risk currency hedge ratio and foreign asset exposure. *Financial Analysts Journal* 49(5):77–78.

Krugman, P. 1991. Target zones and exchange rate dynamics. *Quarterly Journal of Economics* 56:669–82.

Kusuoka, S. 1999. A remark on default risk models. *Advances in Mathematical Economics* 1:69–82.

Kyle, A. S. 1985. Continuous auctions and insider trading. *Econometrica* 53:1315–35.

Lakonishok, J., and B. Lev. 1987. Stock splits and stock dividends: why, who, and when. *Journal of Finance* 42:913–32.

Lamoureux, C., and P. Poon. 1987. The market reaction to stock splits. *Journal of Finance* 42:1347–70.

Laurent, J. P., and J. Gregory. 2005. Basket default swaps, CDOs and factor copulas. *Journal of Risk* 7(4):103–22.

Ledford, A. W., and J. A. Tawn. 1997. Modelling dependence within joint tail regions. *Journal of the Royal Statistical Society* 59:475–99.

Ledoit, O. 1996. A well-conditioned estimator for large dimensional covariance matrices. Working Paper 24-95, John E. Anderson Graduate School of Management, University of California.

Ledoit, O., and M. Wolf. 2003. Improved estimation of the covariance matrix of stock returns with an application to portfolio selection. *Journal of Empirical Finance* 10:603–21.

——. 2004. Honey, I shrunk the sample covariance matrix. *Journal of Portfolio Management* 30(4):110–19.

Lee, C. M. C., B. Mucklow, and M. J. Ready. 1993. Spreads, depths, and the impact of earnings information: an intraday analysis. *Review of Financial Studies* 6: 345–74.

Lehmann, B. N., and D. M. Modest. 2005. Diversification and the optimal construction of basis portfolios. *Management Science* 51:581–98.

Leland, H. 1994. Corporate debt value, bond covenants, and optimal capital structure. *Journal of Finance* 49:1213–52.

Leland, H., and K. Toft. 1996. Optimal capital structure, endogenous bankruptcy, and the term structure of credit spreads. *Journal of Finance* 51:987–1019.

Leroy, S. F., and R. D. Porter. 1981. The present value relation: tests based on implied variance bounds. *Econometrica* 49:555–74.

Lesmond, D. A., J. P. Ogden, and C. A. Trzcinka. 1999. A new estimate of transaction costs. *Review of Financial Studies* 12:1113–41.

Lesmond, D. A., M. J. Schill, and C. Zhou. 2004. The illusory nature of momentum profits. *Journal of Financial Economics* 71:349–80.

Lessard, D. R. 1974. World, national and industry factors in equity returns. *Journal of Finance* 29:379–91.

——. 1976. World, country, and industry relationships in equity returns: implications for risk reduction through international diversification. *Financial Analysts Journal* 32(1):32–38.

Lewis, K. K. 1999. Trying to explain home bias in equities and consumption. *Journal of Economic Literature* 37:571–608.

——. 1995. Puzzles in international financial markets. In *Handbook of International Economics* (ed. G. M. Grossman and K. Rogoff). Amsterdam: Elsevier Science.

Lhabitant, F.-S. 2004. *Hedge Funds: Quantitative Insights*. John Wiley.

L'Her, J. F., O. Sy, and M. Y. Tnani. 2002. Country, industry, and risk factor loadings in portfolio management. *Journal of Portfolio Management* 28(4): 70–79.

Li, Q., and J. S. Racine. 2006. *Nonparametric Econometrics: Theory and Practice*. Princeton University Press.

Libby, T., R. Mathieu, and S. Robb. 2002. Earnings announcements and information asymmetry: an intra-day analysis. *Contemporary Accounting Research* 19:449–72.

Litterman, R. 1996. Hotspots and hedges. Risk Management Series, Goldman Sachs.

Litterman, R., and J. Scheinkman. 1991. Common factors affecting bond returns. *Journal of Fixed Income* 1(1):54–61.

Litzenberger, R. H., and K. Ramaswamy. 1979. The effect of personal taxes and dividends on capital asset prices: theory and empirical evidence. *Journal of Financial Economics* 7(2):163–95.

Lo, A. W. 1999. The three p's of total risk management. *Financial Analysts Journal* 55(1):13–26.

——. 2001. Risk management for hedge funds: introduction and overview. *Financial Analysts Journal* 57(6):16–33.

——. 2008. *Hedge Funds: An Analytic Perspective*. Princeton University Press.

Lo, A. W., and A. C. MacKinlay. 1990. When are contrarian profits due to stock market overreaction? *Review of Financial Studies* 3:175–205.

——. 1999. *A Non-Random Walk Down Wall Street*. Princeton University Press.

Longin, F., and B. Solnik. 1995. Is the correlation in international equity returns constant: 1960–1990? *Journal of International Money and Finance* 14:3–26.

——. 2001. Extreme correlation of international equity markets. *Journal of Finance* 56:649–76.

Longstaff, F., and A. Rajan. 2006. An empirical analysis of collateralized debt obligations. Working Paper, UCLA (available at http://ssrn.com/abstract=902562).

Longstaff, F., and E. Schwartz. 1995. A simple approach to valuing risky fixed and floating rate debt. *Journal of Finance* 50:789–819.

Lopatin, A., and T. Misirpashaev. 2007. Two-dimensional Markovian model for dynamics of aggregate credit loss. Working Paper, Numerix.

Lou, D. 2008. A flow-based explanation for return predictability. Working Paper, Yale University.

Lowenstein, R. 2001. *When Genius Failed: The Rise and Fall of Long-Term Capital Management.* New York: Random House.

——. 2008. Triple-A failure. *New York Times Magazine*, April 23.

Lucas, R. E. 1976. Econometric policy evaluation: a critique. *Carnegie-Rochester Conference Series on Public Policy* 1:19–46.

——. 1978. Asset prices in an exchange economy. *Econometrica* 46:1429–45.

Madhavan, A., and S. Smidt. 1993. An analysis of changes in specialist inventories and quotations. *Journal of Finance* 48:1595–628.

Maloney, M. T., and H. H. Mulherin. 1992. The effects of splitting on the ex: a microstructure reconciliation. *Financial Management* 21:10.

Mark, N. 1995. Exchange rates and fundamentals: evidence on long-horizon predictability. *American Economic Review* 85:201–18.

Martens, M., and S. Poon. 2001. Returns synchronization and daily correlation dynamics between international stock markets. *Journal of Banking and Finance* 25:1805–27.

McAndrew, C., and R. Thompson. 2007. The collateral value of fine art. *Journal of Banking & Finance* 31:589–607.

McCulloch, R., and P. E. Rossi. 1990. Posterior, predictive, and utility-based approaches to testing the arbitrage pricing theory. *Journal of Financial Economics* 28:7–38.

——. 1991. A Bayesian approach to testing the arbitrage pricing theory. *Journal of Econometrics* 49:141–68.

McNeil, A. J., R. Frey, and P. Embrechts. 2005. *Quantitative Risk Management.* Princeton University Press.

McQueen, G., and V. V. Roley. 1993. Stock prices, news, and business conditions. *Review of Financial Studies* 6:683–707.

Meese, R., and K. Rogoff. 1983. Empirical exchange rate models of the seventies: do they fit out of sample? *Journal of International Economics* 14:3–24.

Mehra, R., and E. C. Prescott. 1985. The equity premium: a puzzle. *Journal of Monetary Economics* 15:145–61.

Menchero, J., and V. Poduri. 2008. Custom factor attribution. *Financial Analysts Journal* 64(2):81–92.

Merton, R. C. 1971. Optimum consumption and portfolio rules in a continuous time model. *Journal of Economic Theory* 3:373–413.

——. 1974. On the pricing of corporate debt: the risk structure of interest rates. *Journal of Finance* 29:449–70.

Michaud, F.-L., and C. Upper. 2008. What drives interbank rates? Evidence from the Libor panel. *BIS Quarterly Review* March:47–58.

Michaud, R. O. 1998. *Efficient Asset Management.* Cambridge, MA: Harvard Business School Press.

Miller, G. 2006. Needles, haystacks, and hidden factors. *Journal of Portfolio Management* 32(2):25–32.

Miller, M. H., and M. Scholes. 1978. Dividends and taxes. *Journal of Financial Economics* 6(4):333–64.

Mincer, J., and Zarnowitz, V. 1969. The evaluation of economic forecasts. In *Economic Forecasts and Expectations* (ed. J. Zarnowitz). New York: NBER.

Mitchell, M., and T. Pulvino. 2001. Characteristics of risk and return in risk arbitrage. *Journal of Finance* 56:2135–75.

Morris, S., and H. Shin. 1999. Unique equilibrium in a model of self-fulfilling currency attacks. *American Economic Review* 88:587–97.

Nelling, E. 2003. The price effects of "shopping the block." Working Paper, Drexel University.

Nelson, D. B. 1990. Stationarity and persistence in the GARCH(1,1) model. *Econometric Theory* 6:318–34.

——. 1992. Filtering and forecasting with misspecified ARCH models. 1. Getting the right variance with the wrong model. *Journal of Econometrics* 25:61–90.

Newey, W. K., and K. D. West. 1987. A simple, positive semi-definite, heteroskedasticity and autocorrelation consistent covariance matrix. *Econometrica* 55:703–8.

Obstfeld, M. 1986. Rational and self-fulfilling balance of payments crises. *American Economic Review* 76:72–81.

——. 1994. The logic of currency crises. NBER Working Paper 4640.

Parkinson, M. 1980. The extreme value method for estimating the variance of the rate of return. *Journal of Business* 53:61–65.

Pástor, Ľ., and R. F. Stambaugh. 2000. Comparing asset pricing models: an investment perspective. *Journal of Financial Economics* 56:335–81.

——. 2003. Liquidity risk and expected stock returns. *Journal of Political Economy* 111:642–85.

Patton, A. J. 2007. Volatility forecast comparison using imperfect volatility proxies. Working Paper, Oxford University.

——. 2009. Copula-based models for financial time series. In *Handbook of Financial Time Series* (ed. T. G. Andersen, R. A. Davis, P. Kreiss, and T. Mikosch), pp. 767–86. Springer.

Patton, A. J., and K. Sheppard. 2009. Evaluating volatility and correlation forecasts. In *Handbook of Financial Time Series* (ed. T. G. Andersen, R. A. Davis, J. P. Kreiss, and T. Mikosch), pp. 801–38. Springer.

Perez-Quiros, G., and A. Timmermann. 2000. Firm size and cyclical variations in stock returns. *Journal of Finance* 55(2):1229–62.

Perold, A. F. 1988. The implementation shortfall: paper versus reality. *Journal of Portfolio Management* 14(3):4–9.

Perold, A. F., and E. C. Shulman. 1988. The free lunch in currency hedging: implications for investment policy and performance standards. *Financial Analysts Journal* 44(3):45–52.

Persaud, A. D. 2003. Liquidity black holes. In *Liquidity Black Holes: Understanding, Quantifying, and Managing Financial Liquidity Risk* (ed. A. D. Persaud). London: Risk Books.

Petersen, M. A., and D. Fialkowski. 1994. Posted versus effective spreads: good prices or bad quotes? *Journal of Financial Economics* 35:269–92.

Pickands, J. 1975. Statistical inference using extreme order statistics. *Annals of Statistics* 3:119–31.

Poon, S., M. Rockinger, and J. A. Tawn. 2004. Extreme value dependence in financial markets: diagnostics, models and financial implications. *Review of Financial Studies* 17:581–610.

Protter, P. 2005. *Stochastic Integration and Differential Equations*, 2nd edn. Springer.

Puchkov, A. V., D. Stefek, and M. Davis. 2005. Sources of return in global investing. *Journal of Portfolio Management* 31(2):12–21.

Ratner, M. 1992. Portfolio diversification and the inter-temporal stability of international indices. *Global Finance Journal* 3:67–78.

Rebonato, R. 2007. *Plight of the Fortune Tellers: Why We Need to Manage Risk Differently*. Princeton University Press.

Reinganum, M. R. 1981. Misspecification of capital asset pricing: empirical anomalies based on earnings' yields and market values. *Journal of Financial Economics* 9(1):19–46.

Richardson, M., and J. H. Stock. 1989. Drawing inferences from statistics based on multiyear asset returns. *Journal of Financial Economics* 25:323–48.

Rigobon, R., and B. Sack. 2003. Measuring the reaction of monetary policy to the stock market. *Quarterly Journal of Economics* 118:639–69.

——. 2006. Noisy macroeconomic announcements, monetary policy, and asset prices. NBER Working Paper 12420 (available at http://ssrn.com/abstract=913307).

Roll, R. 1979. Violations of purchasing power parity and their implications for efficient international commodity markets. In *International Finance and Trade* (ed. M. S. Sarnat and G. P. Szego). Cambridge: Ballinger Press.

——. 1984. A simple implicit measure of the effective bid ask spread in an efficient market. *Journal of Finance* 39:1127–39.

——. 1992a. A mean-variance analysis of tracking error. *Journal of Portfolio Management* 18(4):13–22.

——. 1992b. Industrial structure and the comparative behavior of international stock markets. *Journal of Finance* 47:3–41.

Roll, R., and S. A. Ross. 1980. An empirical investigation of the arbitrage pricing theory. *Journal of Finance* 35:1073–103.

Rosenberg, B. 1974. Extra-market components of covariance in security returns. *Journal of Financial and Quantitative Analysis* 9:263–74.

Rosenblatt, M. 1952. Remarks on a multivariate transformation. *Annals of Mathematical Statistics* 23:470–72.

Ross, S. A. 1976. The arbitrage theory of capital asset pricing. *Journal of Economic Theory* 13:341–60.

Rouwenhorst, K. G. 1999. European equity markets and EMU. *Financial Analysts Journal* 55(3):57–64.

Ruud, P. A. 1991. Extensions of estimation methods using the EM algorithm. *Journal of Econometrics* 49:305–41.

Sadka, R. 2006. Momentum and post-earnings announcement drift anomalies: the role of liquidity risk. *Journal of Financial Economics* 80:309–49.

Samuelson, P. A. 1965. Proof that properly anticipated prices fluctuate randomly. *Industrial Management Review* 6:41–49.

——. 1969. Lifetime portfolio selection by dynamic stochastic programming. *Review of Economics and Statistics* 51:239–46.

Sanning, L. W., S. Shaffer, and J. M. Sharratt. 2006. Alternative investments: the case of wine. Working Paper, University of Wyoming.

Scherer, B. 2002. Portfolio resampling: review and critique. *Financial Analysts Journal* 58(6):98–109.

Scholes, M. 2000. Crisis and risk management. In *Risk Budgeting: A New Approach to Investing* (ed. L. Rahl). London: Risk Books.

Scholes, M., and J. Williams. 1977. Estimating betas from nonsynchronous data. *Journal of Financial Economics* 5:309–27.

Schultz, P. 1983. Transactions costs and the small firm effect: a comment. *Journal of Financial Economics* 12:81–88.

——. 2000. Stock splits, tick size, and sponsorship. *Journal of Finance* 55:429–50.

——. 2001. Corporate bond trading costs: a peak behind the curtain. *Journal of Finance* 56:677–98.

Shanken, J. 1987. Nonsynchronous data and the covariance-factor structure of returns. *Journal of Finance* 42:221–31.

Sharpe, W. F. 2002. Budgeting and monitoring pension fund risk. *Financial Analysts Journal* 58(5):74–86.

Shepard, P. G. 2008. Integrating multi-market risk models. *Journal of Risk* 10(2): 25–45.

Shephard, N. 2005. *Stochastic Volatility: Selected Readings.* Oxford University Press.

Shiller, R. J. 1981. Do stock prices move too much to be justified by subsequent changes in dividends. *American Economic Review* 71:421–36.

Shleifer, A., and R. Vishny. 1997. The limits to arbitrage. *Journal of Finance* 52: 33–55.

Shumway, T. 1997. The delisting bias in CRSP data. *Journal of Finance* 52:327–40.

Sidenius, J., V. Piterbarg, and L. Anderson. 2005. A new framework for dynamic credit portfolio loss modelling. Working Paper, Royal Bank of Scotland.

Sinquefield, R. A. 1996. Where are the gains from international diversification? *Financial Analysts Journal* 52(1):8–14.

Solnik, B. 1971. Structure et évolution d'un oligopole. *Revue Economique* 22: 118–39.

——. 1991. Finance theory and investment management. *Swiss Journal of Economics and Statistics* 127:303–24.

Solnik, B., C. Boucrelle, and Y. L. Fur. 1996. International market correlation and volatility. *Financial Analysts Journal* 52(5):17–34.

Stambaugh, R. F. 1997. Analyzing investments whose histories differ in length. *Journal of Financial Economics* 45:285–331.

Stock, J. H., and M. W. Watson. 1989. New indexes of coincident and leading economic indicators. *Macroeconomics Annual* 4:351–94.

——. 1998. Diffusion indices. NBER Working Paper 6702.

——. 2002a. Forecasting using principal components from a large number of predictors. *Journal of the American Statistical Association* 97:1–13.

Stock, J. H., and M. W. Watson. 2002b. Macroeconomic forecasting using diffusion indexes. *Journal of Business and Economic Statistics* 20:147–62.

Stoll, H. R., and R. E. Whaley. 1983. Transactions costs and the small firm effect. *Journal of Financial Economics* 12:57–80.

Stroyny, A. L. 2005. Estimating a combined linear factor model. In *Linear Factor Models in Finance* (ed. J. Knight and S. Satchell). Oxford: Elsevier/Butterworth-Heinemann.

Sullivan, R., A. Timmermann, and H. White. 1999. Data-snooping, technical trading rule performance, and the bootstrap. *Journal of Finance* 54:1647–91.

Taylor, J. B. 1993. Discretion versus policy rules in practice. *Carnegie-Rochester Conference Series on Public Policy* 39:195–214.

Taylor, S. 2005. *Asset Price Dynamics, Volatility and Prediction.* Princeton University Press.

Taylor, W. M. 1983. The estimation of quality-adjusted rates of return in stamp auctions. *Journal of Finance* 38:1095–110.

——. 1992. The estimation of quality-adjusted auction returns with varying transaction intervals. *Journal of Financial and Quantitative Analysis* 27: 131–42.

Till, H. 2006. EDHEC comments on the Amaranth case: early lessons from the debacle. Working Paper, EDHEC Risk and Asset Management Research Centre.

Treynor, J. L., and K. K. Mazuy. 1966. Can mutual funds outguess the market? *Harvard Business Review* 44(4):131–36.

Venkatesh, P. C., and R. Chiang. 1986. Information asymmetry and the dealer's bid–ask spread: a case study of earnings and dividend announcements. *Journal of Finance* 41:1089–102.

Weil, P. 1990. Nonexpected utility in macroeconomics. *Quarterly Journal of Economics* 105:29–42.

Weisman, A. B., and J. D. Abernathy. 2000. The dangers of historical hedge fund data. In *Risk Budgeting: A New Approach to Investing* (ed. L. Rahl). London: Risk Books.

White, H., and I. Domowitz. 1984. Nonlinear regression with dependent observations. *Econometrica* 52:143–62.

Woodward, S. E. 2005. Measuring and managing alternative assets risk. *Global Association of Risk Professionals* 24:21–24.

Woodward, S. E., and R. E. Hall. 2003. Bechmarking the returns to venture. Working Paper, Sand Hill Econometrics (available at http://ssrn.com/abstract=474181).

Wu, X. 2002. A conditional multifactor analysis of return momentum. *Journal of Banking & Finance* 26(8):1675–96.

Index